Marriage, Sex, and Civic Culture
in Late Medieval London

THE MIDDLE AGES SERIES

Ruth Mazo Karras, Series Editor
Edward Peters, Founding Editor

A complete list of books in the series is available from the publisher.

Marriage, Sex, and Civic Culture in Late Medieval London

Shannon McSheffrey

PENN

UNIVERSITY OF PENNSYLVANIA PRESS

PHILADELPHIA

10   9   8   7   6   5   4   3   2   1

Published by
University of Pennsylvania Press
Philadelphia, Pennsylvania 19104–4112

Library of Congress Cataloging-in Publication Data

McSheffrey, Shannon.
   Marriage, sex, and civic culture in late medieval London / Shannon McSheffrey.
     p. cm. — (The Middle Ages series)
   Includes bibliographical references and index.
   ISBN-13: 978-0-8122-3938-6
   ISBN-10: 0-8122-3938-5 (cloth : alk. paper)
   1. Marriage—England—London—History—To 1500.   2. Marriage law—England—
London—History—To 1500.   3. Sex and law—England—London—History—To 1500.
4. London (England)—Social life and customs.   I. Title.   II. Series.

HQ616.15.L66M37 2006
306.8109421'20902—dc22   2005058498

For Alice K. McSheffrey Reiter
and Anna B. McSheffrey Reiter

Contents

Introduction

IN MARCH 1475 A YOUNG LONDONER named William Rote appeared in the Consistory court of the diocese of London to be examined by an ecclesiastical judge. His appearance was prompted by a lawsuit that had been launched against him by Agnes Wellys, who alleged that he had refused to honor the marriage vows they had made together. In answer to Agnes's charges, William told a story, which the court's registrar translated into Latin and recorded in a deposition (or testimony) book. This is how the story goes. One afternoon the previous summer, on the day before the feast of the Assumption, William had gone for a social visit to the house of his older friend, John Wellys, bringing a jug of wine that William thought they would drink together. Instead of the friendly reception he had expected, William found John Wellys very angry. Wellys accused Rote of having "violated" Wellys's daughter Agnes—whether he meant that William had raped or seduced her is not clear. Before a number of other people present at the time, including Agnes, Wellys threatened Rote: "You will marry her, even if I have to force you." William responded to Wellys's accusation by saying that he certainly had never had sexual relations with Agnes and that he had no wish to marry her. John Wellys became even angrier and pulled out a knife. He would have stabbed William, as William testified, had not another man stepped between them and held Wellys's arm back. In the ensuing scuffle William escaped from the house, running out into the street. Agnes and her mother gave chase, shouting after him, "Hold the thief!" They caught William and brought him back to the house, where John Wellys was waiting, still very angry. After that more threats followed, as William's testimony detailed:

Wellys said to him that unless this witness [William Rote] would contract marriage with his daughter Agnes, he or someone else in his name would give this witness a sign that he would take with him to his grave. Wellys also said that he would bring this witness before the mayor and alderman where he would be

confounded by such embarrassment that the shame would compell him to contract marriage with Agnes. So, as much from fear of his body as from shame at appearing before the mayor and aldermen, this witness contracted marriage there
with Agnes.[1]

By late medieval church law, a contract of marriage was the speaking, by
the prospective husband and wife, of the words of consent to the union
("I William take you Agnes as my wife"; "I Agnes take you William as my
husband"), words that in themselves made the sacrament of marriage, regardless of where they were spoken or whether or not a priest was present. William's contract was not a promise or a betrothal, but a binding,
indissoluble union—or at least, it would have been, had William spoken
the words freely and without coercion. In order to make certain that
William could not repudiate the vows he had made, John Wellys ensured
that they were spoken in the presence of a number of important men
whom he had summoned expressly for that purpose.[2]

    William Rote's story about his shotgun (dagger?) wedding is illustra-
tive of a number of themes I explore in this book. Some elements of
William's story seem familiar to the average twenty-first-century Western
reader: even if we no longer expect fathers to try to force the seducers of
their daughters to marry them, we recognize the basic plot elements of
damaged honor and redemption through married respectability. Other
elements are more unexpected: we might anticipate that marriage vows in
the Middle Ages would be exchanged in a church rather than a house, and
we might expect a priest to be present. As we will see, however, although
William's situation—being forced at dagger-point—was unusual, the location where he and Agnes made their vows of marriage, the bride's father's
house, was not. Nonetheless, despite the domestic setting and the absence
of a priest, the influence of the medieval Catholic Church is nonetheless
unmistakable in this case: Agnes, probably with the help of her father, took
her case to a church court when William refused to recognize the marriage
they had made in her father's house that August afternoon. Marriage, as a
sacrament, was under the jurisdiction of canon (or church) law and the ecclesiastical courts. Likewise, William's defense was drawn from one of the
main pillars of the late medieval Catholic theology of marriage, that the
sacramental bond of marriage could be made only through the freely given
consent of both parties. William may have said the words, but he did so
only out of fear for his life and his reputation, or so he claimed; thus,
William argued, no bond was created, and there was no marriage.

Yet while each of the parties could use theology, canon law, and the church courts and neither of the parties could easily disregard them, other forces were also at work. Paternal authority, most forcefully represented in the person of John Wellys, could and often did over-ride ecclesiastical theories of individual consent. The collective authority of older men of substantial position was also hard to resist: the men whom John Wellys summoned to witness the marriage were a draper and two grocers, both high-status merchant occupations. Their word, both in the parish and neighborhood during that summer and the following spring in the ecclesiastical court, was likely to carry a good deal of weight. More explicitly, William told the Consistory court judge that he had been coerced into marrying Agnes because he wanted to avoid the shame of being summoned before the mayor and aldermen. This threat was vague, yet obviously powerful—for William it ranked high enough to be mentioned in the same breath as the danger to his life. It is not clear if John Wellys implied that he would accuse William there of rape, fornication, or some other offense, perhaps even one he would simply invent as leverage. Nonetheless, John Wellys saw the highest officials of his city as extensions of his paternal authority: if William would not do what John said, the mayor and aldermen would make him do it. William's response is no less revealing: he needed to take care to avoid public embarrassment, anything that would detract from his reputation. His name as a man of honor and credibility, essential to his success in whatever career path he was pursuing, depended not only on his honesty and reliability in business dealings but also on his ability to keep his sexual urges in check. A man who seduced another man's daughter offended at least as much against the father as he did against the woman; he lacked respect for the integrity of another man's household and would probably be perceived as deceptive, disorderly, and dishonest in other ways as well. William was right to fear being hauled before the mayor and aldermen, whether or not he had seduced Agnes.

Apart from the various witness statements offered in this case—some of which largely corroborated William's version of events, some of which denied it—we know nothing more about what happened on that summer day in 1474. Nor do we know how the judge in the Consistory court decided the case: he may have chosen to uphold the marriage, forcing William to recognize Agnes as his wife and to take her into his home and share "bed and board" with her, as the medieval formulation put it. Or he may have agreed with William and two of his witnesses that the marriage had been coerced and declared the marriage annulled, leaving each of them free to marry again. I have not been able to trace William Rote, John Wellys, or Agnes Wellys in any further records, so we do not know what happened to them. Yet this brief story about a dramatic afternoon—which may have been completely invented by William to escape a marriage he did not desire—tells us a good deal about marriage, sex, and civic culture in late medieval London.

Sex and marriage were tightly woven into the fabric of medieval English society. Marriage was one of the seven sacraments of the Catholic Church, imbued with deep spiritual significance; while sexual congress within marriage was (at least sometimes) seen as pleasing to God, outside marriage it carried the weight of deadly sin. The marital unit of the husband and wife was also the central core of the household, the fundamental social, political, and economic unit. Marriages created political alliances at all levels, from the arena of international politics to the local neighborhood; allowed the transfer of property, goods, and labor from one family to another; initiated or deepened ties of friendship and love not only between the couple but also among the couple's family and friends; and helped forge gender identities, the husband's and wife's roles forming two of the main constituents of conceptualizations of masculinity and femininity. Sexual relationships outside marriage were, if anything, more complicated: medieval Londoners variously saw them as irrelevant, as deeply damaging to society and to the body politic, as economically productive or as wasteful of resources, as mainly due to female seduction or to male lustfulness. This book studies both how people went about forming marital and sexual relationships and how other people—parents, relatives, friends, neighbors, civic officials, parish priests, ecclesiastical judges—sought to influence, control, or prevent them. My fundamental argument is that bonds of marriage and sex were simultaneously intimate, deeply personal ties and matters of public concern, subject to intervention by everyone from a woman's or man's family, friends, and employers to the mayor of London himself.

This is a book about a particular place and time—London in the second half of the fifteenth century. It is conventional for historians to point out the limitations of their local studies, and conventionally I make no claim here that the conclusions I reach apply to other parts of Europe or even England, although in many cases they do. But equally I also make the claim that the local study presents a better picture of the lived experience of medieval people than the broader study that skims over the surface of many cultures and times. I have tried here, as far as possible, to examine issues through contemporary, London-based sources rather than through received scholarship or from sources that originate outside the time and place I have chosen. I contend here that the making of marriage and entering into both legitimate and illegitimate sexual relationships were social acts that were framed both through tradition and custom and through local particularities of time and place, of the late medieval urban situation, and the social and political contests of London in the late fifteenth century. Thus, for instance, canon law written in the thirteenth century cannot be assumed to apply in the late fifteenth-century ecclesiastical courts of London in the same way as it had in the thirteenth or the fourteenth century, or in the same way as it applied in the province of York, or indeed in the diocese of Canterbury. Economic factors that arguably allowed Yorkshire women in the earlier decades of the fifteenth century considerable freedom of choice in marriage—or the freedom not to marry at all[3]—similarly did not necessarily apply to a time and place when power and wealth were being concentrated in fewer hands and women's economic options were severely curtailed. Even given the focus on time and place, there was no one single attitude or experience among Londoners—sex, age, status, occupation, and personality were just some of the factors that shaped their marital and sexual lives—but a more closely focused lens helps to draw out those individual experiences.

It is nonetheless important to consider where the detailed picture I will draw fits into the larger landscape of European and even world history. This task of contextualization is made easier by Mary S. Hartman's recent book, *The Household and the Making of History*,[4] which takes a bird's-eye view of the historical development of marriage and household patterns in European and world history. Hartman takes as her starting point the insights of demographer John Hajnal, who first pointed out forty years ago[5] that sometime in the Middle Ages—it is unclear when, but certainly before the fifteenth century—northwestern Europeans below the socio-economic elite began to develop a pattern of marriage and household formation that is anomalous in global terms. In this demographic regime, dubbed by Hajnal the "northwestern European" pattern, both men and women first marry in their mid twenties to a partner roughly the same age. The bride and groom go on to establish their own household, and households rarely contain more than two generations (i.e., they are nuclear households). A significant proportion of the population, as much as a quarter, never marries. While modern Westerners will recognize this pattern because it conforms to our own demographic regime, as Hartman points out, it is remarkably different from the ways marriages and households were and are formed in other agricultural societies. This is particularly true of the late age at first marriage for women. In other agricultural societies, including the medieval Mediterranean and Slavic worlds, women marry around the age of puberty, in most cases to a husband who is significantly older, in his late twenties or thirties. They usually join multifamily households headed by their husbands' father or another older male relative. Only a very small proportion of the population never marries. For reasons that remain obscure—Hartman posits that the usefulness of adolescent daughters' labor on the family farm may have been the regime's origin[6]—ordinary northwestern Europeans began sometime during the Middle Ages to diverge from this pattern and to marry their daughters about a decade after puberty rather than in their early to mid-teens. By the late medieval period, when we first begin to see the system at work in some detail, other social and cultural elements had developed around this late age of marriage for women, including, as we will see in more detail, relative independence of choice of marriage partners for both men and women. The implications of this seemingly small change of marrying daughters late, Hartman compellingly argues, were immense; indeed, she contends that the northwestern European marriage pattern, with its concomitant unstable households and greater parity (although by no means complete equality) between husbands and wives, is the underlying precondition for the West's assumption of global dominance in the early modern and modern periods.

This book discusses an early, although clearly not originary, point in the evolution of the northwestern European marriage pattern. As I will discuss, many, although not all, Londoners married and formed households according to this pattern: they married first in their mid twenties to partners roughly of the same age and more or less of their own choice. In many ways my approach accords with Hartman's, even though I use a close focus rather than the wide-angle view she employs. Like Hartman, I see the household—and the marital and sexual relationships that served as major, although by no means sole, bonds in its structure—as one of the fundamental motors of late medieval political life. This is a view that sees aspects we often label "private" life as holding public significance—in other words, fundamentally influencing the course of political, economic, social, intellectual, and religious developments. The details of medieval people's marital and sexual lives hold more than prurient interest. As I will show in this book, they formed a crucial foundation for the governance of the social, religious, economic, and political order. If Hartman is right that the peculiar northwestern European pattern of marrying and forming households served as the foundation for Western expansion and dominance in the five centuries that followed the year 1500, then the ways fifteenth-century Londoners courted, married, and had sex assume far more importance than might appear at first glance.

Narrowing the focus a bit, we can also make some medium-range comparisons between the findings I present here and other work on marriage in late medieval and early modern England. Because of the spotty survival of medieval records, most of the work on late medieval English marriage below elite levels has centered on Yorkshire and the city of York, the chief city of northern England, in the later fourteenth and fifteenth centuries. P. J. P. Goldberg's influential book *Women, Work, and Life Cycle in a Medieval Economy* used the records of marital litigation in York and Yorkshire to argue that women's relatively broad economic opportunities in the post–Black Death economy, especially in the urban setting, allowed them to make quite independent marriage choices—that is, they could choose whom to marry, or not to marry at all.[7] Goldberg's findings echo those of Michael Sheehan, who argued in the early 1970s for an "astonishingly individualistic" approach to marriage formation in the diocese of Ely in the late fourteenth century.[8] I see a somewhat different picture for later fifteenth-century London: marriage options were more constrained than in Sheehan's fourteenth-century Ely and Goldberg's early fifteenth-century York. Parents and employers played a more significant role, although again it must be said that below elite levels both partners still had much more freedom than, for example, their contemporaries in Italy or Spain.

Possibly the subtle differences between my arguments and those of Sheehan and Goldberg derive from divergences in the way we see the sources, but it seems more likely to me that the differences derive from real historical change from the early to later fifteenth century and (to a lesser extent) the peculiarities of London civic culture in this period. This remains difficult, if not impossible, to prove conclusively due to the problem of available sources. Various pieces of evidence, however, indicate that there was a tightening of the supervision of marriage formation and of household governance generally in England in the latter half of the fifteenth century, perhaps most precociously in the metropolis. Economic contraction, and in particular a shrinkage in work opportunities for women, resulted in greater socioeconomic stratification and less independence for female workers.[9] The concentration of wealth in fewer hands fed the development of greater oligarchy in civic politics and in the governance of the city's guilds and crafts: the divisions between rich and poor, elite and ordinary were becoming wider and less permeable.[10] Greater concern for disorder and misbehavior, paired with the development of a confident civic Christianity, gave to leading men of the parish and city the duty to ensure proper conduct in neighbors.[11] All this arguably increased the power of householders or, in other words, patriarchal authority (understood here as the power ordinarily exercised by fathers as heads of the family and the household, and extending outward from the household into other kinds of governance in neighborhood, parish, ward, guild, city, and ultimately, kingdom). I argue that it resulted in a more conservative approach to marital strategies for daughters (and, to a much lesser degree, sons) and thus relatively more parental involvement in the making of marriage than Sheehan saw in fourteenth-century Ely or Goldberg saw in earlier fifteenth-century York.[12] This is a valuable reminder that the pendulum of historical change—in this case, the development of Western companionate marriage—does not always move inexorably or smoothly in a single direction.

While I argue that marriages formed in subtly different ways in later fifteenth-century London from those in earlier fifteenth-century York, it is also possible to draw some comparisons with a much more substantial literature on marriage and gender in the second half of the sixteenth century.[13] Many of the themes discussed earlier and on which I will elaborate remain consistent through the subsequent century, but again it seems that courtships and marriages were somewhat more tightly supervised in the later fifteenth century than they were a century or so later, although this is a difference again of degree rather than kind. Intense population growth, economic change, and religious transformations make the Elizabethan world a very different one from the late medieval one, but many aspects of courtship, sexuality, and the formation of marriage remain similar. I do not, however, see in the later part of the fifteenth century the intense gender conflicts that some historians have seen in Elizabethan London.[14] This is not to say that all was quiet and peaceful, as we shall see. In the ebb and flow of historical developments, fifteenth-century London may have seen the flow and possibly the cresting of a wave of patriarchal control of the household.

London c. 1450–1500

Let us move our gaze back to London in the second half of the fifteenth century. By this point London had long been the metropolitan hub of England. Situated north of the Thames River, at the point where that great waterway first becomes bridgeable, London had been a site of major importance since the Roman occupation of Britain. In modern terms, London's great size—it was perhaps four times the size of its nearest English rival—was only relative; the city's population of forty to fifty thousand souls crowded into a space of slightly more than a square mile, while an additional population, relatively small as yet, spilled out into the suburbs outside the City boundaries and across the Thames in Southwark.[15] Its sheer size as well as its location made London the economic center of the realm, playing a pivotal role in international trade and featuring the most diversified and specialized workforce. The population of London ranged from the poorest of the poor to the wealthiest merchants and the mightiest aristocrats of the realm, the latter often keeping London houses. As in most other urban centers in this period, London's population could not reproduce itself: the swift spread of disease in the close living conditions of the city meant that mortality rates outstripped fertility. It was through immigration that London kept its population roughly stable throughout the fifteenth century, and probably even increasing it somewhat in the decades around 1500. Many Londoners were newcomers who had their origins elsewhere in England: they frequently came to the city as adolescents to apprentice to a trade, enter into domestic service, or simply find wage labor of any kind. Others came from elsewhere in Europe: Flemings, Germans, Scots, Irish, Italians, Spaniards, French, and other "aliens" came to London, sometimes as international merchants, sometimes as manual laborers, beer brewers, or workers in other trades, sometimes falling into crime and prostitution.

This diverse population was governed by the merchant elite of the city. From their number were chosen a mayor, twenty-five aldermen, two sheriffs, and a common council that varied in size from about sixty to two hundred men. The mayor served for one year, elected from among the aldermen at an annual meeting of the *probi homines* (the good men) of the city, defined as members of the common council and leading members of the livery companies (London's main merchant organizations). The two sheriffs, also elected annually in the same way as the mayor, had the complicated task of acting both as the king's local agent and as the strong arm of the mayor; they were responsible for administering the city's prisons, for executing convicted criminals or exacting fines, for carrying out royal writs, and for gathering a certain part of the city's tax revenue. While the offices of mayor and sheriff were temporary, the twenty-five aldermen, each of whom represented a particular neighborhood of the city, called a ward, held their positions for life (although they could, and did, transfer from one ward to another in the case of a vacancy). By the fifteenth century, aldermen were chosen by the mayor and other aldermen from a list of two to four nominations submitted by the leading men of a vacant ward; the mayor and aldermen thereby ensured that only the "right" kind of men—men of sufficient substance, to put it in fifteenth-century terms—entered into aldermanic office. Fifteenth-century aldermen were invariably drawn from the wealthiest merchants of the city. Thus the office of alderman became a sign of success and status in trade.

Closely intertwined with the civic offices was the governance of the livery companies–mercers, grocers, drapers, goldsmiths, fishmongers, salters, and so on—each of which supervised both the trade and manufacture of goods in the city and the general conduct of the company's members. Within each company there were significant hierarchies, symbolized by the granting of livery—a gown made from particular fabric and colors signifying membership in the company—to the wealthier and more established members. There were also rivalries between the different companies. Although no written rule confined the office of alderman to particular occupations, in practice in the fifteenth century almost all aldermen belonged to one of the more important companies, the mercers, grocers, and drapers predominating. London government and the control of the livery companies were becoming concentrated in fewer and fewer hands by the second half of the fifteenth century, probably both reflection and cause of significant concentrations of wealth among a relatively small number in the merchant elite.[16]

Formal participation in the politics of the city above the ward level was confined to those who held citizenship or, as it was sometimes known, freedom of the city. Apart from political rights, citizenship also brought with it economic benefits: the right to buy and sell at wholesale in the city was restricted to those who were of the freedom. The number of citizens was small, somewhere in the range of about 3,000 to 3,500 out of the total population of 40,000 to 50,000.[17] Although some women gained the economic rights associated with citizenship (almost always as widows of citizens), full citizenship, including the right to participate in government, was confined entirely to men: politics in the medieval period, and of course long after, were a male privilege and responsibility. Most men, however, never became citizens; between one-fourth and one-third of the city's adult male inhabitants entered the freedom. Men who became citizens had to do so through their guilds or livery companies, who sponsored their admission. Men who did not belong to guilds—a broad spectrum ranging from aristocrats, clerics, independent shopkeepers, waged laborers, to the abject poor—could not become citizens.[18] While lack of citizenship was not always a significant handicap—some noncitizens were very wealthy—it was clearly an important marker of status and privilege in late medieval London.

*   *   *

In the course of the next seven chapters, I will look at how Londoners married one another, how they negotiated their sexual relationships, how other Londoners viewed and participated in those processes, and what place the supervision of sex and marriage had in the creation of a civic political culture. In doing so, I will draw my evidence from a number of kinds of contemporary sources. Most are archival documents from both the ecclesiastical court system and the records of city and royal government, originally written in London during the fifteenth century and now residing in libraries and record offices in and around London. I have also used books—advice manuals, chronicles, moral tales, liturgical texts—that came off the presses at the dawn of the age of print in London and nearby Westminster (where William Caxton, a London mercer, set up England's first printing press in 1478), as well as documents and texts that other scholars have published in modern editions from the eighteenth century forward. While I have not made an absolutely comprehensive study of all available evidence—one lifetime would not suffice for that—in focusing on London in particular and on one half-century of its history (1450–1500), I can make the claim that I have looked at most of the sources that bear on my chosen topic.[19]

Most of my research has involved grubbing around in the archives of medieval England's various legal tribunals, now housed in a number of pleasant record offices in London and Kew. Following Joel Rosenthal's example, I have taken "scraps of information, the scores or hundreds of throwaway vignettes"[20] in order to build a kind of narrative of the social context of late medieval London life. The kinds of sources that I have favored here, often related to lawsuits directly or indirectly involving marriage,[21] are those in which medieval people themselves told a story—not an overtly fictional one (although I have sometimes used those too) but one that purported to relate "what happened" to themselves or to people they knew. Some historians have challenged the usefulness of this kind of source: obviously sometimes people lied when they gave testimony in court, or they misremembered. The relationships from which legal action arose, whether marriages or illicit sexual unions, were by definition troubled in some way, and thus some scholars have argued that testimony from those cases gives us only questionable evidence for the normal process of marriage.[22]

These objections have some merit, but they need not cripple us or cause us to reject these sources altogether: careful analysis of the evidence can yield considerable fruit if we keep in mind the sources' limitations. In some ways, the limitations scholars have identified are actually benefits if we use the evidence in a different way. In marriage litigation, for instance—where one person sued another either to dissolve or, more frequently, to uphold a marriage—many witnesses were trying to convince the judge that the marriage *did* happen. They thus tended to emphasize the ways in which the process was normal rather than atypical. Naturally, some witnesses lied or stretched the truth, but this does not necessarily diminish the value of the evidence their testimony provides; in many ways the plausible lie—that is, a story calculated to strike its medieval audience as credible, even if it had little relationship to what "really" happened—is one of the most revealing kinds of sources we have about the expectations and practices of the past.[23] The analysis of these stories takes considerable care, however; narratives told in legal records (whether in ecclesiastical courts, in petitions to the chancellor, or in civic tribunals) were framed according to the legal requirements of the court and by the structure of the legal process the particular court used. To be successful, such narratives needed both to be socially believable and to stress the points of law necessary to prove the case. In theory—although evidently not always in practice—the narratives also had to have a relationship to what "really" happened." The influence between actions and processes outside the court and the structure of litigation and the law was not unidirectional, however: while in some cases legal counsel may have prompted witnesses' reports that people used legally precise formulae in their lives outside the courtroom, it is also more than possible that such formulae became well known among ordinary laypeople. Legal ways of thinking permeated late medieval English culture,[24] and what happened in courtrooms was not separate from "real life" but part of its texture.

This book is divided into two parts. Part I examines how church law and social practice affected the formation of marriage in late medieval London. Although by medieval canon law a marriage was irrevocably made in the moment in which a man and a woman exchanged vows of consent in the present tense before two witnesses, any time, anywhere, in practice marriage was usually a socially complicated process involving many people: family, friends, employers, neighbors, matchmakers, and civic officials. The practical interpretation of the Catholic canon law of marriage in the fifteenth century did not always follow the letter of the law. It accommodated social necessities at the same time that marital and family power relationships had to take the canon law of marriage, and the possibility of abrogations being litigated, very seriously. Marriage formation and marital litigation reveal some of the ironies and complications of medieval social relationships; gender and social hierarchies show themselves to be less than straightforward in the labyrinthine world of legal logistics and social patronage. Material manifestations of marital relationships—the gifts exchanged, the actual locations in which marriages were discussed and contracted—shed further light on the ways in which the marriage fit into late medieval London life. Part II extends these discussions to look more broadly at sex, governance, and civic morality. Medieval patriarchy (literally "father-rule") was wider than a father's governance of his biological offspring. Fathers had special hegemony over their families, recognized in law and theory, but paternal power was echoed and buttressed by the paternalistic authority exercised generally by respectable older men, the fathers of the community. Senior men had the duty and the privilege to govern and to ensure the proper working of social relationships within their sphere of action—and to prevent inappropriate social, and especially sexual, relationships from developing or flourishing. Governance in late medieval English society was practiced through many different structures, both formal and informal: the household, the neighborhood, the parish, the ward, the crafts and livery companies, and the court of the mayor and aldermen. Yet governance and its relationship to patriarchy were complicated, particularly in matters involving sex. Although self-control and the avoidance of misrule were important, at the same time sexual domination—sometimes through violence—was one dimension of men's demonstration of their ability to rule. The regulation of marital and sexual relationships reveals itself to be an important element of civic culture and political rule in the late medieval City of London.

PART I

LAW AND SOCIAL PRACTICE IN THE MAKING OF MARRIAGE IN LATE MEDIEVAL LONDON

I

Making a Marriage

MOST ENGLISH PEOPLE in the late Middle Ages married at some point in their lives, although a sizable minority of adults had not, or had not yet, married.[1] The age at which late medieval London men and women married for the first time varied substantially, both according to gender and especially according to socioeconomic status. Our best data come from the highest reaches of late medieval English society, the aristocracy, where women first married while young, between thirteen and eighteen, and men often only in their mid twenties or later (although some men, especially orphaned heirs, married very young).[2] Elite urban women, daughters of the wealthiest merchants, often followed a pattern similar to that of their gentle and aristocratic counterparts (indeed, they participated in the same marriage market), marrying young to men much older than they. Below these rarefied socioeconomic levels, our evidence is, at best, impressionistic,[3] but most scholars agree that marriage patterns among the nonelite in late medieval England conformed to the northwestern European marriage and household system, with both men and women marrying first in their early to mid twenties to partners of a similar age.[4] At the same time that the age of first marriage was important, it must be remembered that many marriages—perhaps as many as half—were between those who had been married before. In an age of high mortality, marriages were often of short duration, perhaps as short as a decade on average, and both widows and widowers chose to, or needed to, remarry. Thus those seeking marriage could be fifteen—or they could be seventy.

These demographic patterns, especially those for first marriages, had important implications for the ways in which marriage was made. In turn, the demography of marriage affected, and was affected by, wider social, economic, and political factors. Most importantly, the later age of first marriages for men and women below elite levels both allowed for and necessitated a long period of adolescence, from the early teens until the early to mid twenties. This time was spent in apprenticeship by some young men and a very few young women destined for life in a craft or trade, and in domestic or agricultural service by young women and by men not lucky enough to be enrolled as apprentices. Apprentices and most servants "lived in": young men and women moved away from their parents' homes, indeed often to a different part of the country, and into the household of their employers. This has been termed "life-cycle servanthood": for many, both rural and urban, the period between puberty and marriage was spent as a servant or apprentice, in a position of dependence on employers, but relative independence from family.[5] Both men and women often ended this period of service or apprenticeship with marriage.

While employers were responsible for their young charges, and as we will see in many ways acted as substitute parents, it is significant that many people found their first marriage partners while living away from their families. They did not always make their marriage choices entirely independently, but they exercised more choice than those who married much younger and more closely under their parents' supervision. Elite marriages—which carried with them the transfer of significant amounts of land, social prestige, and political connections—were, not surprisingly, much more closely controlled by the heads of families, especially in the case of the woman. An aristocratic woman's husband was chosen for her by her family; at best she could exercise her right to refuse consent. For many men and women in late medieval England, marriage choices lay somewhere between arranged and completely free: balancing their own desires with the expectations of family, friends, and society was complicated, as I will discuss in more detail.

Did medieval people marry for love or for money? Moral treatises aimed at the fifteenth-century urban elite urged that marriage "ought to be had in great love," but feared that instead "marriages be not duly made, but for money or other evil causes," which in turn caused the "great abomination" of faithlessness and disloyalty.[6] For modern commentators, the perceived materialism of medieval marriages has tended to induce derision rather than lamentation. It is sometimes hard not to be cynical when reading again and again of the "sale" of marriages in Chancery proceedings: Eileen Power's quip "Let me not to the marriage of true fiefs admit impediments" comes seductively to mind.[7] More recently other scholars have turned away from blaming money-grubbing parents and have given agency to the "material girls" themselves: Diana

O'Hara has argued for the sixteenth century, for instance, that even if nonelite men and women exercised free choice in their marital partners, they nonetheless chose their mates according to economic rather than personal factors.[8] Yet characterizing marriage one-dimensionally, as an economic partnership, is too limiting: below the levels of the aristocracy,[9] at least, men and women made marriage decisions based on many criteria. Marriage certainly was an economic, political, and social alliance—at all social levels, as O'Hara argues, not just the aristocracy—but added to those factors were other potent human motivations, especially sexual attraction and emotional attachment. In a society where sexual relationships were to be confined to marriage, a sexual ethic that was taken seriously by many, erotic desire became an important aspect of marriage decisions, one that often ran counter to more rational economic or political calculations. Even marriages at the highest levels illustrated this: the young king Edward IV, against all protocol and to his distinct political disadvantage, took as his wife the beautiful widow Elizabeth Woodville, an aristocrat by birth and marriage but no match for a king, apparently precisely because she had denied him her bed unless he contracted marriage with her.[10]

This is not to say that people of middling or lower status in late medieval England entered into marriage in the same way that modern Westerners do: one obvious difference is that even lower-status people often had known one another only a short time before marrying, sometimes meeting only once or twice before beginning serious discussions about matrimony.[11] Decisions made on short acquaintance accentuated economic and socioeconomic factors, but they also accentuated initial sexual attraction. They could not, however, emphasize the kind of deep attachment of "soul mates" that has come to be seen in the contemporary West as foundational to a good marriage. It remains hard for us, given the kinds of sources to which we have access, to grasp the emotional nature of late medieval marriage, especially among those below the highest social levels. It would be anachronistic for us to impute modern expectations of marriage to medieval people, but at the same time it is also clear in the language of courtship that there were strong associations between marriage and something they called "love." Its full flowering would take place within marriage, though, rather than preceding it. One common formula for making a contract of marriage—"May you find it in your heart to have me as your husband"—suggests that those making marriages hoped to choose marital partners in whom they could realize the *potential* for love.

At the same time, the formula also suggested that the place in the marital partner's heart had not yet been fully established.

The means by which possible marriage partners came to be acquainted with one another varied considerably by social class and depended particularly on the extent to which a marriage was arranged by family and friends or was freely chosen by the principals themselves. As I discuss in Chapter 3, the close supervision of young women of the civic and landed elite demanded the employment of networks of acquaintances and marriage brokers in order for marriageable men to become acquainted with suitable women and, at least as importantly, the women's fathers or guardians. At less elevated social levels, introductions made by friends, family, and employers were also vitally important, but men and women identified potential wives and husbands in other ways as well. Where women's everyday lives were far less subject to supervision, mates could be found through everyday interaction: as men and women went about their daily business, running errands and doing their work, they naturally came to know one another. Popular songs of the fifteenth century tell us that festivals—parish celebrations, fraternity feasts, Midsummer revels—could also serve as occasions for courting,[12] although they do not feature in narratives of courtship in witness testimony in marital litigation. If such depositions can be taken as representative, men and women were more apt to find marital partners through the more prosaic means of mutual acquaintance than through picturesque May dances.

Husbands were the heads of their households, and the economic functions of the household generally revolved around their work. Because men, especially household heads, controlled most economic resources, and other household members, including their wives, depended on the husband's work, some historians have tended to assume that women had a greater economic stake in marriage than did men and that in general marriage was more attractive and important for women than for men.[13] The economic relationship between husband and wife, especially in an artisanal household, was not as simple a matter as who could earn more, but a broader understanding that economic contribution to the household went beyond income or production of goods to include the maintenance of a household that allowed that income or those goods to be produced. Although the household head carried the title of carpenter or tallowchandler, without the labor of all those in the household, especially the wife, he could not function.[14] The difficulties of running a household without a mistress may account for the quick rates of remarriage for widowers as well as for widows. At the same time, we must not inflate the parity of late medieval husbands and wives: although the wife's labor was essential to the household, there was no question that her husband's work was deemed more valuable and that his authority over the others who lived in his household, including his wife, was (at least theoretically) clear.

Marriage and Church Law in Late Medieval England

By the late Middle Ages, marriage was firmly entrenched as one of the seven sacraments of the Catholic Church. As such, it came under the jurisdiction of the ecclesiastical courts, which administered their jurisdiction through canon law.[15] To think of the late medieval church as controlling marriage, however, would be fundamentally to misunderstand both the church's ability to direct and police the laity's actions and the somewhat peculiar nature of the medieval Catholic theology and canon law of marriage. Because of the particular contingent circumstances of twelfth- and thirteenth-century developments in theology and canon law, by the end of the thirteenth century the sacrament of marriage had come to be defined in such a way that it was the two principals, the man and woman marrying, who made the marriage bond rather than a priest. The sacramental bond was created by the mutual consent of the two parties alone. Marriage vows did not have to be exchanged in a church, nor was a priest's presence required. A couple could exchange consent anywhere, anytime; all that was needed to prove the marriage in a church court were two witnesses. Neither partner could be married against his or her will, and at the same time, no one else's agreement—priest, parent, guardian, or lord— was required to create a canonically valid marriage as long as both parties were of age (usually defined as twelve for girls, fourteen for boys). As Michael Sheehan remarked, this was an "astonishingly individualistic" marriage system,[16] indeed one that in many ways ran counter to the prevailing currents of medieval society that emphasized the importance of the participation of parents, guardians, and (to a lesser extent) priests in the making of a marriage. Much of this book is concerned with exploring the inherent tensions between the individualism of the consent theory and the societal pressures to marry for family advantage and according to community norms.

The exchange of consent that created a marriage was known as a contract. Although to many modern people the word "contract" calls to mind a written agreement, validated by signatures of the parties, this use of the term goes back to the more basic meaning of the word as derived from Roman law: a binding pact made through the expression of consent or agreement, at least as often oral as written.[17] While it was not necessary for words to be spoken to create the bond of marriage (making it possible for the mute to marry, for instance), in practice almost all marriages were created through the speaking of the words of consent, a performative utterance[18] that constituted the contract. The uttering of these words need not have taken place in a church nor in the presence of a priest: they could be, and were, spoken in houses, fields, and taverns. As long as both parties expressed consent, the marriage was valid before God, and as long as there were two admissible witnesses, the marriage was also valid before the church court.

While in theory any number of words could convey this consent, in practice in late medieval England the words that constituted consent took on a formulaic pattern, reflecting (or possibly even influencing) the words laid out in the marriage rite in the church liturgy. Consent could be expressed in the present tense, immediately constituting a valid and indissoluble marriage: "I John take you Joan to be my wedded wife"; "I Joan take you John to be my wedded husband." Or it could be expressed in the future tense, indicating an intention to make the marriage at a future time: "I *will* take you. . . ." In late medieval London, another formula was often used for future contracts: "I may find in my heart to have you as my husband/wife."[19] Although consummation was irrelevant in the case of a present-tense contract, making the marriage of Mary and Joseph canonical, in the case of a marriage undertaken with words of future consent, subsequent sexual intercourse rendered the contract automatically binding. Unconsummated future contracts (what we might call betrothals) could be broken up, but not easily: they could be dissolved only by mutual consent or if one of the partners subsequently made a present-tense contract with someone else. Whether a contract of marriage was made in the present or future tense, it was properly followed by the calling of banns (announcement in the parish church that the two would marry) and a church solemnization, a nuptial mass where the pair, perhaps for the second, third, or fourth time, exchanged consent in the present tense and received the priest's blessing. A couple that did not proceed to a solemnization committed a sin, but if they had exchanged consent in the present tense they were still indissolubly married. Somewhat ironically, the church's own theology of consent rendered ecclesiastical participation in the making of marriage unnecessary.

A marriage, once entered into in a canonical fashion, was indissoluble except through the death of one of the spouses, after which the surviving widow or widower could, and often did, remarry. Under specific circumstances, two other kinds of marriage termination, both called divorce (*divorcium*), could be declared by the ecclesiastical courts of late medieval England: divorce *a mensa et thoro* ("from table and bed") and divorce *a vinculo* ("from the bond"). Despite the similarity of terminology, however, we should be careful not to confuse medieval divorce with its modern counterpart: a medieval divorce did not dissolve a valid marriage, leaving both parties free to remarry. Divorce in that sense simply did not exist in the later Middle Ages, and indeed it did not become available in some European countries until well into the twentieth century.

Divorce *a mensa et thoro* resulted in what we would term separation. The marriage bond still existed and thus neither party could enter into another marriage, but the couple no longer had to share a table and a bed, suspending what was known as the "marital debt." By the tenets of medieval canon law and marriage theology, spouses owed to one another both cohabitation and the conjugal or marital debt, that is, the duty of each to agree to sexual intercourse with the other when asked. A divorce *a mensa et thoro* ended these obligations. These suits were relatively rare in medieval English ecclesiastical courts; the usual basis was cruelty on the part of the husband, although there are also some suits for divorce *a mensa et thoro* on the grounds of adultery.[20]

Divorce *a vinculo* corresponds to what we would call annulment: it was a legal ruling that the contract of marriage in question had never been valid and that the couple had thus never really been married. While consent made a marriage, not all couples were free to render consent because of a barrier between them, known as an impediment. The most common impediment was a previous marriage of one (or sometimes both) of the partners. As a marriage, once properly entered into, could not be dissolved as long as both partners lived, neither was at liberty to take another husband or wife. This did not, as we will see, prevent unhappily married people from leaving their spouses and trying again elsewhere, but any subsequent marriage contracts they made with other people were invalid and liable either to prosecution or to litigation. Prior contract or bigamy was by far the most important grounds for decrees of annulment of marriages in later fifteenth-century England. Other impediments were, by contrast, much more rarely cited in litigation. Occasionally a party to a marriage case, such as William Rote in the story with which I began this book, alleged that a contract was invalid owing to the impediment of coercion or force and fear, the claim that consent had not been freely given and thus the sacramental bond not formed. Even less frequently used as grounds to render a contract null were consanguinity and affinity—too close a relationship between the pair by blood and by sexual union respectively. In the late Middle Ages, blood relationships were considered too close if the pair were related to one another within four degrees, that is, if they had a common great-great-grandparent. Affinity, a relationship created by a sexual union including but not limited to marriage, was also deemed an impediment to marriages between those related within the fourth degree. Although some influential legal scholars such as F. W. Maitland viewed the complex and abstruse rules of consanguinity and affinity as the most important legal impediments in the contracting of medieval marriage,[21] few cases were brought on these grounds in the late medieval church courts, and only one was the basis of litigation in the diocese of London.[22] Similarly rarely called upon in late medieval litigation (with two cases found from the diocese of London) was the impediment of impotence, usually defined as the man's inability to have sexual relations.[23] One of these cases was Elizabeth Shore's 1476 divorce of her husband, London mercer William Shore, on the grounds that he was "so frigid and impotent" that she would not be able to have children. She had to appeal to the papal court, however, as, according to her petition to Rome, the official of the bishop of London's court had refused to hear her case.[24] Elizabeth Shore later became famous as the mistress of Edward IV[25] and may already at this point have become involved with the king, suggesting that Edward may have helped engineer this unusual divorce.

Impediments, apart from prior contract, rarely entered the world of marital litigation in late medieval England because the inherent structure of the church court system militated toward enforcing rather than dissolving contracts of marriage. Indeed, the best legal strategy to end an undesirable marriage was to produce—or if necessary invent—evidence of a previous contract of marriage, thereby proving that the second undesirable marriage had been invalid from the beginning and thus could be declared dissolved. Unlike modern marital litigation, which deals overwhelmingly with the dissolution of marriages, most medieval marital litigation concerned the enforcement, rather than the termination, of a contract of marriage.

"Marriage before God"

In theological terms, a marriage could be created simply by the exchange of words of consent: the sacramental marital bond was made, indissolubly, by the speaking of the words, whether or not there were witnesses present. Proving such a bond, however, was another matter: without two admissible witnesses, the church courts could not enforce any contract of marriage. The distinction between the contract made privately between the two parties and a properly witnessed one was well recognized by late medieval Londoners. The former, enforceable only in the internal forum of the conscience, was called "marriage before God," emphasizing both its sacramental and its unprovable nature.

Beatrice Stoughton, a widow of the parish of St. Nicholas Cole Abbey, testified in January 1488 that for a number of months between April and October 1486 Piers Curtes had visited her house, discussing the making of a marriage between himself and Beatrice's widowed daughter Agnes Skern. Finally the discussions came to a point, and Agnes and Piers exchanged vows of future consent, with Beatrice as their only witness. After they exchanged rings, Piers kissed Agnes twenty times and said, "You be my wife before God," Agnes responding, "You be my husband before God." Although they had contracted before God, in human eyes their promise was unprovable, as there was only one witness. Moreover, even Beatrice, who witnessed the contract, did not consider them to be fully married: they had only begun the journey to marriage, and as far as Beatrice was concerned, Piers was by no means entitled to his full matrimonial rights. That night, Piers stayed at Beatrice's house and wanted to share a bed with Agnes, reminding his mother-in-law that Agnes was his wife before God, but Beatrice would have nothing to do with this and kept them apart from one another throughout the night.[26]

Rumors of such unwitnessed contracts often resulted in questions from parents, friends, neighbors, and employers, who looked to some kind of clarification of the situation. A chaplain of the cathedral church of St. Paul, Sir Martin Jelyf (the title "sir" indicating that he was a priest, equivalent to the later title "Father," rather than that he was a knight), was visiting the home of his son,[27] Richard Jelyf, one evening, when he was called upon to use his priestly authority to clear up an ambiguous relationship between a young woman and one of his son's apprentices. He questioned the young woman, Elizabeth Willy, about a rumor that she had made a contract with the apprentice John Kendall. Elizabeth affirmed that she had indeed contracted with John: "I have made a contract with him and he is my husband before God." John, too, admitted the contract: "and she is my wife before God."[28] Such questions were not necessarily hostile or probing (although they probably were in the case of John Kendall and Elizabeth Willy, where Kendall's master was clearly displeased by the relationship)[29] but were often simply part of the process. When John Crosby was courting Agnes Eston, he visited her many times and requested of her employer that she should "want no manner of thing," for he would reimburse any expenses made on her behalf. After they had been keeping company for some time, one evening Agnes called her employer, Thomas Spencer, and his wife to come and drink with them, a cue that an announcement was to be made. When they entered the chamber where Agnes and John were sitting, John said to them, "Ye be welcome," to which Thomas Spencer said, "Master Crosby, ye be the more welcome, if it be as my cousin sayeth." John responded, "Why, what sayeth she?" and Spencer replied, "She sayeth that ye and she be man and wife before God." John Crosby said, "I say the same, and what she sayeth, I will perform it."[30]

But acknowledgment of a "marriage before God" was not the same as an actual contract: it was corroborative, but not prima facie, evidence. Agnes Eston was not able to muster witnesses to an actual contract and, indeed, perhaps John Crosby was careful enough not to make a contract witnessed by anyone but God.[31] Whereas Agnes Eston had a number of substantial supporters for her legally hopeless suit, another plaintiff, William Andrew, had an even weaker case. He sued Agnes Mason in 1473 to enforce a contract of marriage he claimed they had made together, although even he had to admit that there had been no witnesses to the exchange of consent. Agnes, when examined, said that although they had courted, she had refused to make any contract with him until he could clear his debts, a condition that was evidently not fulfilled, as William's deposition was taken on the steps of Ludgate Prison, where he was incarcerated for debt.[32] Even if they had in fact exchanged words of consent, as William alleged, without witnesses there was no chance that his claim could be legally proved. The ecclesiastical courts routinely recognized that they had no jurisdiction over what only God himself could know: in such cases, the parties could only be "released to their consciences."[33]

Clandestinity and Openness: Contracting Marriage outside Church

Because marriages could so easily be contracted—if both partners were free to marry only the clear indication of consent was required, anytime, any place—the importance of exchanging words of agreement to marry before people who could later bear witness, both in the narrow legal meaning of the word and in the larger social sense, was immense. For instance, in 1469 William Multon, a haberdasher, testified that on a Sunday afternoon in August twenty-four years before, he and Thomas Gryffyn had been crossing St. Lawrence's Lane in the Jewry on their way to Clerkenwell to watch some wrestling. In the lane they ran into John Colyn, standing in John Stocton's doorway. John Colyn asked Multon and Gryffyn to come with him up into the house's gallery (a covered balcony) to hear what would be said there between him and Joan Stocton, John Stocton's daughter. Multon and Gryffyn agreed to act as witnesses, and the three men climbed the stairs to join Joan in the gallery. Before the gathered witnesses, John took Joan by the hand and said to her, "I John Colyn take you Joan Stocton as my wife, and thereto I give you my faith," after which he released her hand. Joan then took John by his hand and said to him, "And I Joan Stocton take you John Colyn as my husband, and thereto I give you my faith." Immediately following this exchange of consent, John Colyn took from his pocket a napkin or handkerchief in which was wrapped a purse made of red velvet, which he gave to Joan, saying, "This purse I give to you as my wife." Joan accepted it, saying, "And I accept this purse from you as from my husband." Joan wrapped the purse in her own napkin and put it in her sleeve, and they kissed one another.[34]

While many contracts reported in marital litigation were made in this relatively informal, although nonetheless properly formulated and witnessed fashion, many others were carefully arranged, planned in advance, and highly ritualized. John Bramanger, a draper and citizen of London,[35] testified in May 1469 that the previous month he had been present, along with John Randolf, Lucy Braggis, William Gregory, and George Seman, in a "summer parlor" in the home of Lady Combes, Lucy's employer and the widow of a prominent alderman and M.P.[36] John Randolf asked Bramanger, Gregory, and Seman to bear witness to what he and Lucy would say and do together that day. Then Randolf asked Lucy if she was free from all bonds of marriage, and whether she had previously contracted marriage, and she responded that she had not previously contracted with any man. John Randolf said that he likewise was free and clear from any commitment of marriage. The couple, having established their eligibility, were ready to proceed to the exchange of consent. John Randolf took Lucy Braggis by the hand and said to her, "I John take you Lucy to be my wife, and thereto I give you my faith," and he released her hand. She then took him by the hand and likewise contracted by words of present consent, and they kissed one another.[37]

In both cases, and indeed in virtually every extraecclesiastical marriage contract reported by witnesses in fifteenth-century London marriage cases, couples followed a set ritual: right hands were clasped and words were spoken, in either present or future tense, that closely resembled the exchange of consent as outlined in the marriage liturgy.[38] Both John and Joan in the first case and John and Lucy in the second made present-tense, binding, sacramental contracts of marriage; the fact that in both cases the vows were made outside of a church and without the presence of a priest made the cases quite typical. The London marital litigation records yield descriptions of about two hundred separate alleged contracts of marriage and three-fourths of them were made in extraecclesiastical settings. These contracts were not inherently secret or illicit, however, and they were not ordinarily undertaken outside churches in order to escape ecclesiastical involvement; present-tense contracts made outside churches were often an integral, respectable, and sacramental part of the making of marriage, and they were frequently followed by the saying of banns between the couple and a church solemnization. A present-tense contract made in a home or a tavern was but one step in the creation of the union: although the bond of marriage was canonically created in the brief moment when the man and the woman spoke the words of consent, both in the ideal ecclesiastical scenario and in social practice marriage was a *process* rather than a discrete event.[39] The fact that the words were said in the present tense did not alter this.

As set out in thirteenth-century English synodal statutes, an ecclesiastically approved model path to marriage was laid out in several stages. The first step was the betrothal, a contract undertaken in the future tense, where the partners exchanged promises to marry before trustworthy witnesses, often in the home of one of the parties. From there the promise of marriage was publicized further through the calling of banns in the parish church of each, so as to ensure that no impediments between the two existed, especially prior contracts. After the third calling of the banns, the couple could proceed to the present-tense contract undertaken before the parish priest, just prior to a nuptial mass solemnizing the marriage between them. The omission of any of these steps in the thirteenth and fourteenth centuries rendered a marriage "clandestine";[40] in the sixteenth century and later, the term came to be applied more specifically to extraecclesiastical present-tense contracts, and from the late sixteenth to the eighteenth century both church and state officials were evidently concerned about the propriety of such clandestine marriages.[41]

The evidence of marital litigation in the fifteenth century suggests that practice in fifteenth-century London differed in a few small but vital respects from the thirteenth-century ideal. Most importantly, the first step—the contract undertaken in a domestic setting before reliable witnesses—was often undertaken in the present rather than the future tense: in other words, in many cases this initial exchange of consent was no longer a betrothal, a promise of marriage, but in canonical terms the creation of the marriage itself. Yet there is no sign that ecclesiastical officials were particularly concerned about the making of present-tense contracts in nonecclesiastical settings; they did not label such exchanges clandestine or express unease that contracts made in homes, taverns, and other locations were secretive or improper by reason of their location.[42] This is probably because extraecclesiastical contracts in no way ruled out later ecclesiastical involvement; in the normal course of things, banns and a church solemnization of marriage would follow the contract, ratifying the marriage. Such exchanges of consent could be respectable, honorable, and indeed public and were depicted by witnesses to marital litigation as unremarkable and unexceptionable. As William Bote testified in 1494:

Thomas and Margaret [Dicons] contracted marriage together in the town of Stratford by words of present consent, as he heard, and this marriage was solemnized between them in the chapel in the said town by the curate there. He knows this because on three solemn days he heard banns being issued between them by the curate, and he was also present at the solemnization of the marriage. After the solemnization, on the same day, this witness breakfasted with them. And thus for two years following they lived together as man and wife, and they had several children, and as [man and wife] they were commonly declared, held, and reputed.[43]

Thomas and Margaret Dicons were surely married to one another, Bote alleged, because they had followed all the required steps of the process: a present-tense contract followed by banns and a solemnization.[44]

The main change between the fourteenth and fifteenth centuries, then, lay in the tense of the verb used in the initial contract undertaken in a home or tavern before family and friends. One can only speculate as to why late medieval practice differed in this small but important way from the ideal set out in thirteenth-century statutes. Possibly the thirteenth-century statutes had never matched social reality. Or perhaps the lack of certainty in future contracts, the possibility of their being trumped by a later present contract with someone else, led to the frequent practice of making the contracts more secure early in the process by undertaking them in the present tense. This greater security may have compensated, in a social sense, for some of the defects of the fifteenth-century practice. One of these defects was that making the initial contract in the present tense stripped some of the original purpose of the intervening period between promise and solemnization: the general publication of the promise, especially through the calling of banns, was to bring to light any impediments to the marriage before it was solemnized. For whatever reason, fifteenth-century Londoners were willing to trade away the social usefulness of the waiting period between future and present consent for another kind of security, a more tightly binding contract of marriage.

When a couple said the words of the contract in the present tense, they stepped onto a train they could neither stop nor step off—except by the external force of an impediment such as a previous marriage. At the same time, it was a train that had to make a considerable journey before it came to its final destination, the full social recognition of marriage, for present-tense contracts outside churches were something less, in a social sense, than the fully valid marital bonds that canon law made them. Regardless of whether the marriage was contracted by present or by future words, witnesses and participants tended to regard an unsolemnized marriage as having a kind of liminal status: those who had contracted were both already married and yet not entirely married. Thus, according to witness John Maynard, Robert Allerton declared before a host of witnesses: "Katherine, standing here before you, is my wife before God and man, and as soon as she gives birth, I will marry her."[45] Robert's formulation, that Katherine *is* his wife and that he *will* marry her, was possible only because marriage was seen as a process.

The pressure to solemnize the marriage, to finish or "accomplish" it, as some of the contemporary records say,[46] according to the rites of the church, was not solely an ecclesiastical concern: it was also of keen interest to the participants and to their neighbors, who were just as anxious to have relationships clearly defined. Ann Horton reported that when the re-lationship between Ann Boteler and Robert Elyson remained unclear—they were rumored to have contracted, the couple spoke repeatedly about preparing for a solemnization, and they were well known to sleep together—there was "voice and fame" in the parish of St. Leonard that the marriage should be solemnized (*deberet solemnisari*).[47] In some cases at least, it is clear that couples did not cohabit until after the solemniza-tion, even when the contract was in the present tense.[48] When they did consummate the union before the nuptials in the church, they could be summoned before the Commissary court (a lower-level ecclesiastical court that dealt primarily with sexual offences)—probably through a pro-cess of presentment by neighbors and lay parish officials[49]—for having sex after a contract of marriage but before solemnization. This was one of the ways in which couples were pressured to finish the process.[50] Leaving off halfway through, before the train had reached the station, was not appro-priate, and apart from the social and legal ambiguities this entailed for both partners, it made one liable to be summoned before the Commis-sary court, where many such stalled proceedings were investigated.[51]

While fifteenth-century church authorities did not characterize ex-traecclesiastical contracts as clandestine, they did employ the term, but in a different way from their earlier (and later) counterparts: they most often used the term to indicate contracts made *inside* churches but solemnized improperly. In 1460, for instance, the clergy of the province of Canter-bury petitioned their archbishop regarding the scandalous problems asso-ciated with clandestine marriages, by which they meant those that were solemnized in churches without the proper calling of banns.[52] William Lyndwood's *Provinciale*, the noteworthy fifteenth-century commentary on the decrees of the English councils,[53] defined clandestine marriage in various ways—a contract that takes place with no witnesses at all, a con-tract not subsequently solemnized, a contract in some way improperly solemnized—but did not define witnessed contracts that took place out-side church as clandestine.[54] Moreover, Lyndwood, in his commentary on clandestinity, focused on the importance of the correct calling of banns before solemnization in the parish church.[55]

In fifteenth-century English ecclesiastical records, the term "clandes-tine" was rarely employed, and when it was used, it designated a marriage

improperly solemnized in a church rather than a marriage contracted outside a church.[56] The clandestinity of the cases inhered in the secretive and
underhanded way in which an improper marriage was fraudulently solemnized. In a complicated, three-cornered suit heard in the Consistory
court in 1471, for example, John Cornewell admitted that he had both
been present at and had arranged for the "clandestine solemnization
(*clandestine solempnisacioni*)" of a marriage between two parties to the suit,
Robert Hilton and Agnes Twytynge, at the parish church of Paddington. Cornewell had illicitly acquired a special license from the archdeacon
of Westminster[57] to expedite the solemnization of the marriage outside
Robert's and Agnes's parish churches and without banns, even though
all parties to the case were prohibited from marrying pending the suit.
Two different marriage contracts preceding this solemnization were alleged in the depositions in the case, both of them having been made
in Agnes's home, but only this solemnization was characterized in the
record as clandestine.[58] The fifteenth-century clandestine marriage was
one undertaken in secret but *inside* a church, either away from the parties'
parish churches or in their own parish church but in haste, without banns
having been thrice called. As in the case *Robert Hilton c. Agnes Twytynge*
(in the medieval ecclesiastical courts "c." for "contra" or "against" was
used instead of the now familiar "v." for "versus" of the royal courts),
a couple's purpose was usually to subvert or preempt a rival claim to one
of the spouses, either in litigation already underway or in possible future
legal action. In Robert Hilton's case, it was not a successful strategy, as
his marriage to Agnes Twytynge was declared invalid, despite the solemnization.[59]

It is impossible to say what proportion of marriages in late medieval
London began as extraecclesiastical present-tense contracts. They pre-
dominate in litigation, but that may be (as Richard Helmholz suggests)
because they were inherently inclined to cause difficulties and thus end up
in court.[60] Another reading, which I argue is the more probable, is that
present-tense contracts undertaken in the first instance outside churches
are common in the ecclesiastical court records simply because they were
common in general: they were (as deponents imply) a generally accepted
way of entering the marriage process. The contracts that became the subject of litigation were problematic not because of where they were contracted but because one of the parties tried to jump off the marriage train,
refusing to follow through with the solemnization.

Forms of Contract

The medieval canon law of marriage made the marital bond strikingly easy to create but very difficult to break. Canonically a man and woman were indissolubly husband and wife if they had properly exchanged vows of present consent, and contracts made by future consent were not much easier to escape. The exact words spoken were thus very important. Because of this, most exchanges of consent followed a standard pattern, the couple using, or being directed to use, words that were known to be efficacious and unambiguous. Often the formal exchange of consent in a private home was arranged and directed by a senior man who knew the rituals and the correct words to ensure a proper, canonically correct marriage.[61]

A case from London's Essex hinterland illustrates the ritual particularly well. Joan Cardif, a widow living in Enfield, was being courted by John Brocher. Once they had established through various messages and signals that each was ready to make a contract of marriage, John Brocher came to eat a meal at Joan's house, along with a number of his friends, including a yeoman (a landholder above the common farmer, but not quite a gentleman) named John Monk. Monk later testified that after they had dined and were all sitting together in the hall of Joan's house, Monk questioned Joan before all the witnesses (there were five there, all men except for Joan), asking her if she was free from all contracts of marriage and whether she could find it in her heart to love John Brocher as her husband. She responded that she was indeed free and that she wished to take Brocher as her husband, because since the death of her first husband she had not seen any other man she so loved. Monk then asked Brocher whether he wished to have Joan as his wife, and he also answered yes. At this point they were ready to exchange formal consent: John Brocher, following John Monk's instructions, took Cardif by her right hand and said to her, "I John take thee Joan to my wedded wife, thee to love and keep and as a man ought to love his wife, and thereto I plight thee my troth." And then Cardif, again at Monk's instruction, took Brocher's right hand and said to him, "I Joan take thee John to my wedded husband, thee to love and to keep as a woman ought to do her husband, and thereto I plight thee my faith." But, as Monk interjected, she had not used the proper matrimonial words (*verba matrimonialia*)—she should say "thereto I plight thee my faith *and troth*." Joan, presumably making a distinction between present and future consent,[62] refused to plight her troth without consulting her mother first. A week later, the couple repeated their vows before Joan Cardif's mother, who gave her consent.[63]

John Monk acted as a presider in the exchange of consent, which followed a ritualized pattern that most other such contracts in the depositions also observed.[64] The clasping of right hands—almost invariably reported—was evidently a key aspect of the ritual. But it was the words that were most important; concern for their exact form was evinced not only by the court, which might be expected to interest itself in canonical procedure, but also by the laypeople conducting the marriages. It was part of Monk's duty to lead the couple to speak the right words, the *verba matrimonialia*, that would make a marriage lawful.[65] The presider, almost invariably male[66] and usually apparently senior to the others present, took the place of and almost certainly imitated the priest, who solemnized the church wedding in much the same way. Indeed, one couple exchanging vows in a private home were in fact directed by a priest, the rector of St. John Zachary, London.[67] The presider was frequently unrelated to either of the principals and sometimes was of higher social position; John Monk, for example, was a yeoman. There may have been some concern that the man who directed the couple to exchange vows be an objective party, in order to prevent accusations that one or the other of the principals was suborned. In one case where the fathers of both parties were present, each father asked the ritual questions ("Will you, Lawrence, take Maude . . ."; "Will you, Maude, take Lawrence . . .") in turn, so that the vows were taken twice, once under the direction of each father, perhaps to provide a balance of interests.[68]

Not all contracts followed precisely in the same pattern. In about one in eight cases that were brought to the Consistory, the contract was made conditionally. Most commonly, the condition was the consent of parents, guardians, or employers, especially those of the woman. As will be discussed further later, these patterns indicate important aspects of the gendered nature of the entry into marriage. In addition, other conditions were sometimes imposed. James Wolmar, a party to a Consistory court suit, contracted marriage while the case was pending by adding the condition "if the laws of the church will give me license."[69] Gundrida Cornelys Lewys was summoned before the Commissary because of a claim that she had made a contract with a certain Reginald; she admitted making a future contract with him, but said that she had added this condition: "if you will in the future be a free man of the city." Gundrida, apparently herself a free woman by right of her dead husband, did not wish to lose this privilege by marrying a man who was not of the freedom.[70]

Others used words that were ambiguous, sometimes evidently on purpose. John Barker apparently thought that a contract he made with Alice Wylson should be binding only on her. On being examined before the Consistory when Alice sued him in 1475, John reported that after many discussions of marriage between them, Alice had said, "I will have you as my husband," but that he had answered, "you must not choose to have me as your husband without my consent and will, but nor will you have any other man in England as your husband unless I consent to it." After this, he had sex with her once, he said, but he did not speak any further words of marriage to her.[71] When there were discussions between William Grene and Julian Culere about contracting marriage, William, according to one witness, asked Julian if she could find it in her heart to love him, and she said yes, while he said that he "loved her by his faith." Another witness reported that William said to Julian, "will you have me?" and that she had replied, "I will have you." Julian subsequently denied any contract, while William claimed that they had indeed made a marriage, but his witnesses could bring forth only these vague expressions of loving and having.[72] What one party might regard as an understanding, another might regard as an intention unfulfilled. When "Cecily living at the Pewterpot" was cited before the Commissary in 1491 for having fornicated with John Bencham, she purged herself of the accusation with four neighbors. But when Bencham appeared before the court to answer the same allegation, he maintained that he and Cecily had in fact contracted marriage together. Cecily, examined concerning this contract, told the Commissary that two years before she had indeed dearly loved Bencham and in her mind she had been determined to have him as her husband. But more recently she no longer loved him so well, she told the Commissary, because he spent all his money on "the dice and the cards."[73] While Cecily admitted that she had once intended to marry Bencham, there was no evidence that she actually did.

Banns

William Oldale was in the hall of widow Agnes Rogers's house in the parish of St. Mary Axe on the feast day of St. Blaise, 3 February 1474, around two o'clock in the afternoon, as he later testified, together with

James Whytyngdon, John Fuller, Agnes herself, and a girl of about fourteen. Oldale claimed that James and Agnes talked together for some time
about contracting marriage together, and finally Agnes stood up, took
James by his right hand, and they exchanged words of present consent.[74]
Some two months later, on Easter Sunday, that year falling on 10 April—the
delay probably because of Lenten observances—the couple arranged to
have banns read in their respective parish churches, as each were bound
to do. The parish chaplain in Agnes's parish of St. Mary Axe, Sir Robert
Hoper, later testified that on Easter Sunday after vespers he went to
Agnes's house, presumably at her request, where he found James and
Agnes sitting in the hall. Together they asked him to issue banns between
them in St. Mary Axe the next day. James lived in the parish of St. Ethelburga, and according to the deposition of Sir Robert White, rector of that
parish, James went to him and likewise asked him to proclaim banns of
marriage between him and Agnes Rogers, also on the following day. Sir
Robert White did as he was asked, and immediately after vespers he went
to Agnes Rogers's house and told her that he had on that day issued
banns between her and James. Agnes thanked Sir Robert and seemed well
contented with it. While the rector of St. Ethelburga was at Agnes's
house, Sir Robert Hoper of St. Mary Axe came to report that he had for-
gotten to say the banns, and because of his negligence both Agnes and
James scolded him. They all agreed he could say the banns on the following Wednesday, and both Sir Robert White and Sir Robert Hoper agreed
to issue them again the following Sunday, and the Sunday after that. After
each occasion, Sir Robert White and Sir Robert Hoper came to Agnes's
house to report that the banns had been read, and each time she thanked
the priests profusely and offered a celebratory drink.[75]

After a couple agreed to marry—whether by a present or a future
contract—they were to ask their parish priests to announce before the
congregation, on a Sunday or a holy day, that the two in question intended to enter into marriage. The purpose of this announcement or
bann was to flush out any impediments to the marriage, especially any
prior contracts. After banns had been proclaimed three times, and if no
one had come forth in the parish or parishes of the couple to declare an
impediment, solemnization of the marriage could proceed, normally in
the parish church of the woman.

The calling of banns in some cases was a happy formality, even a re-
newed occasion to rejoice in the impending union, as suggested by Agnes
Rogers's alleged celebratory drinks after each announcement of impending

marriage between her and James Whytyngdon. But in other cases, the banns resulted in an objection raised by another party, known as a reclamation. In such cases, normal procedure was probably for the person who protested to explain to the parish priest his or her objection; should he or she not do so, the parish priest could refer the matter to the Commissary court.[76] A priest who went ahead and solemnized a marriage after someone had objected to it was liable to be summoned to explain himself before the Commissary: Sir James, curate of St. Nicholas Shambles, was accused in 1494 of celebrating a clandestine marriage when he married a couple even though at the proclamation of the banns a certain Master Fowler had publicly cried out, "I know this man hath made a precontract."[77] A reclamation could be the foundation for litigation: some reclamation cases deemed too complicated were referred from the Commissary to the Consistory court,[78] while in other cases the parties may have proceeded directly to litigation. When Margaret Leicester reclaimed against banns between Richard Darard and Alice Newman, she appeared before the official in the Consistory and alleged a marriage with Richard Darard herself. She requested that the official inhibit the vicar of St. Sepulchre from solemnizing a marriage between Richard and Alice pending the suit between Margaret and Richard, which he did, and he also inhibited Richard from procuring marriage with Alice elsewhere as long as the suit pended, under pain of excommunication.[79] The complicated 1471–72 suit involving Agnes Twytynge and Robert Hilton, Richard Smalwode, and Robert Tryse, which eventually made its way to the papal court, may have had its origins when Richard Smalwode cried out at the second reading of the banns between Robert Hilton and Agnes Twytynge in the parish churches of St. Clement Danes and St. Nicholas Shambles.[80]

Reclamations were not always made for canonical reasons: Hugh Ford of Enfield objected to a marriage between his daughter, Margery, and Richard Cordell, and when summoned to answer for his reclamation against their banns, he explained how and why he made his protest: "He went to the vicar of Enfield who was in his church on Sunday at the time of the high mass, and said to him that by no means should he issue banns between Richard and Margery his daughter until Richard and Margery are better agreed. . . . And he said that he did this by his own authority and not by the authority or command of anyone else."[81] Canonically, neither fathers, mothers, nor anyone else had any authority to stop a marriage (socially it was a different situation, as I will discuss later). Nonetheless, other parents, guardians, and employers were accused of impeding solemnization of properly contracted marriages.[82] In one case, a father may have used his position as parish clerk in addition to his paternal power to prevent the solemnization of his daughter's marriage: William Kyngrate, parish clerk of St. John Zachary, was accused both of impeding the solemnization of a present-tense marriage contract made between his daughter and John Wellis and of refusing to hand over his daughter's belongings to her and her husband. The Commissary did not chastise his daughter for contracting outside a church but rather Kyngrate himself for impeding the contract's solemnization: he was required to give reason why he should not be excommunicated for his interference.[83] Kyngrate himself should have known that the law was not on his side, but nonetheless he and many other parents felt they had the social right to intervene.[84]

If ecclesiastical officials were not particularly concerned about the prevailing practice of contracting by present words outside churches, they certainly were worried about the proper calling of banns, due no doubt to the problem of bigamy: the main purpose of banns was to make sure neither potential spouse had an abandoned husband or wife. Yet sometimes the improper reading of the banns even took precedence over bigamy in the bureaucratic minds of some ecclesiastical officials: Master Thomas Johnson, rector of St. Mary Somerset, was chastised for having solemnized marriage between John White and Elizabeth Laurence, both of his parish, "notwithstanding that banns had only been solemnly proclaimed twice, and also because John had another wife living in Ireland."[85] If the man and the woman were of different parishes, notice had to be given in the parish churches of both the prospective bride and the prospective groom, and the rector or curate of the groom's parish or the layman who assisted in parish administration, known as the parish clerk, was expected to certify this to the celebrant before he solemnized the marriage in the bride's parish.[86] In 1481, the chaplain of the parish of St. Bride was cited before the Commissary for having solemnized marriage between Thomas Thorne of the parish of St. Martin Ludgate and his own parishioner Joan Here, without having issued banns in St. Bride's and without having received certification from the rector of the parish of St. Martin that banns had been read there. When he appeared, the chaplain said that he had issued the banns properly in his own parish, but admitted that he neglected to ensure that they had also been announced in St. Martin's.[87] Even twice was not good enough. The parish clerk of St. Mildred Poultry informed the curate of St. Mary le Bow that banns had been thrice proclaimed in

St. Mildred's regarding parishioner Ralph Westwode and a woman of St. Mary le Bow, indicating that their solemnization could proceed. Perhaps he was forgetful and tried to cover up his negligence by stretching the truth, because as he admitted later before the Commissary, banns had only been proclaimed twice, thus rendering improper the solemnization of the marriage in St. Mary le Bow.[88]

Celebrants could be under considerable pressure, however, to go forward with a solemnization even when the forms had not been followed: William Weston apparently called the vicar of the parish of Islington a "false priest" and an "extortioner" because the vicar did not want to solemnize marriage without proper certification.[89] And some parish priests did take their responsibilities seriously: Sir Thomas Gilderson, chaplain in the parish of Laindon, Essex, issued banns in 1490 between Margery Philippis and Richard Chevircourt, but apparently expected Robert Dow to cry out against them as Sir Thomas had heard that he had previously contracted with Margery. Robert, however, stayed mum even though he was present in the church when the announcement was made. When Sir Thomas later heard that Robert had recently received a cow from Margery's mother, he guessed that this had been the price of his keeping quiet. He summoned Robert to speak to him and asked him pointblank whether he had previously contracted with Margery. Robert admitted that indeed he had, so Sir Thomas cited all the parties to appear before the ecclesiastical ordinary in St. Paul's.[90]

Any solemnization of marriage without banns having been properly proclaimed in both parishes was to proceed only with special dispensations. There was, however, concern that such dispensations were being given out too easily, resulting in too many improper solemnizations. Such negligent issuing of dispensations was certainly the case in the competing suits of *Hilton c. Twytynge* and *Smalwode c. Twytynge*. Robert Hilton's friend John Cornewell was able to convince the archdeacon of Westminster to issue a special license for the solemnization of marriage between Hilton and Agnes Twytynge in the parish of Paddington, in which parish neither lived, without any proclamation of banns, and even though all parties to the case were inhibited from marrying pending the suit.[91] The archdeacon of Westminster may have made a business of using his jurisdiction in profitable ways for those who sought easy solutions to marital problems: in 1460, the clergy of Canterbury province petitioned the archbishop that the archdeacon of Westminster be warned to proceed only in hearing marriage cases among those subject to his jurisdiction; various pretended causes being heard before him were causing scandal for the whole church.[92] Although in Robert Hilton's case the strategy may have backfired, in another case it seems to have been successful: in 1497, Richard Clerk, who had (according to a citation in the Commissary court) contracted with Alice Ellesdale, procured a dispensation from "Master Cutford," official of the archbishop of Canterbury, to marry Cecily Hogdon in St. Mary Fenchurch after banns were said twice in the chapel in Stratford and only once in Fenchurch. To obtain the dispensation, Richard Clerk paid Master Cutford 2s. and his clerk 8d. After Master Cutford himself appeared in the Commissary court to verify that he had given such authority, apparently the marriage was allowed to proceed.[93] Certainly the diffuse nature of ecclesiastical jurisdictions in the late Middle Ages allowed those with connections and know-how to shop around until they found someone willing to ignore the rules or issue licenses without asking too many hard questions.

Preparations for the Nuptials and Growing Rings of Publicity

The preparations for the day of the nuptials, according to the evidence of the London records, consisted mostly in the preparation of clothes for the couple, especially for the bride. Frequently deponents made reference to the preparation of nuptial clothes and ornaments for the woman as evidence that the couple had made a contract of marriage.[94] In some cases, the nuptial clothes—or cloth out of which to fashion them—were among the gifts exchanged at the time of the contract. When Laurence Wyberd and Maude Gyll exchanged words of future consent, Laurence's father gave Maude four yards of white cloth to make Maude a new kirtle, or gown, for the wedding.[95] Sometimes a woman who married a widower was given the finest gowns of the husband's previous wife: as Diana O'Hara has suggested, this "betokened the transfer of sentiment" from a previous spouse to the next.[96] Christopher Moyne, for instance, gave Margaret Broke a gown of violet cloth woven through with grey after they contracted, saying that it was the wedding gown of his dead wife.[97] John Ely showed Agnes Whitingdon, with whom he had just contracted marriage, his previous wife's clothes: he told Agnes that she could wear a blue kirtle on the day of the nuptials, along with a particular girdle or belt, and the same gown with another girdle the second day.

On another occasion, John Ely promised new nuptial clothes to be made instead: he asked Agnes's employer to arrange for a wedding gown to be made for her, and the employer agreed to contribute 6s. 8d. for this new kirtle. John told another man that he wanted Agnes's wedding gown to be of violet cloth, while he himself would have a fur-trimmed gown for the occasion.[98]

In some cases, the money spent on the preparations for the marriage was considerable, and indeed those who paid the bills sometimes put pressure on the couple to complete the marriage so that the investment would not be wasted. Robert Rokewode, for instance, admitted that he had tried to force Peter Hanham to solemnize marriage with his daughter Alice because Peter had spent £9 of Rokewode's money on ornaments for the nuptials.[99] Similarly, Margaret Heed's father beat her when she refused to go through with a marriage to William Hawkyns, complaining not only that banns had been twice issued between the couple, but also that "many ornaments suitable and prepared for Margaret's body for the nuptials" had been purchased.[100] Richard Cawdrey, rector of the church of St. Botolph without Aldersgate and dean of the free chapel of St. Martin Le Grand, complained to the chancellor that he had "spended about the marriage" of his nephew and Katherine Bron "to their worship" (i.e., in keeping with their social station), 10 marks, along with a silver cup worth £4, not to mention having settled a tenement in Smithfield on the couple, before he learned that Katherine had made a precontract with someone else.[101] The "ornaments" could include hair adornments (such as the "circlet of maidens when they be married" bequeathed to the parish church of St. Margaret Westminster by a goldsmith's wife in the early sixteenth century)[102] and possibly other kinds of jewelry.

As the banns were read and preparations for the nuptials went ahead, word would spread through the parish and neighborhood that the couple's marriage was to be celebrated. As the ecclesiastical formula had it, "public fame" kept a close eye on the relationships of men and women, both from prurient curiosity (marriage, involving both money and sex, was the classic interesting subject) and—as I argue in the following chapters—because many others, from family members to employers, friends, and neighbors, felt that they had a stake in marital relationships. The spreading of the word allowed interested parties to gather for the wedding. Thomas Thomson, for instance, testified that he was drinking one day with his sister-in-law Beatrice Thomson, her servant Alice Billingham, and a young man whom he did not know at the sign of the Bells in

Warwick Lane. After some time, the young man left, and Thomas asked Beatrice who he was, and she responded, "He is a skinner's son and a skinner himself. I trust he shall have Alice here to his wife. Will ye offer with them?" The witness said that he would do so willingly.[103] At the appointed time, kinfolk, friends, and neighbors would gather and "offer with the couple" at the Mass, an act of encouragement and fellowship with the man and the woman as they embarked on their new life.[104]

The Solemnization of Marriage

Solemnization was to take place, according to thirteenth-century statutes, in the morning, and indeed all the solemnizations described in the London records took place before noon. At least two were, by modern standards, very early in the morning indeed, at five o'clock,[105] but most were between eight and eleven o'clock. Although only a few sources mention this, it may have been customary for the bride to be led to the church by her father or guardian. Geoffrey Leke, the employer of Rose Ryvers, "led the said woman to the church and there he gave her to the friar, as is the custom in the solemnization of marriage."[106] When Alice Raby married John Bolton, a witness to the case noted that Alice had been led to the church by John Burton and Thomas Lopworth, whose relationship to Alice is not clear.[107] Her own father, Robert Raby, testified that "as the father of the said Alice he gave her to the priest [presumably in the part of the liturgy immediately preceding the present-consent contract], and after the mass was finished he led her to his house,"[108] where he probably hosted a wedding breakfast.

The first part of the solemnization, the exchange of consent, was to take place *in facie ecclesie* according to thirteenth- and fourteenth-century synodal statutes and prevailing marriage liturgy, and the same formula was frequently cited by deponents in London litigation.[109] This Latin phrase is somewhat ambiguous and apparently had two different meanings in the late medieval context. *Facies* could mean the front or entrance of a building, and both medieval and modern commentators have often translated *in facie ecclesie* as "at the church door."[110] Probably the more common medieval meaning of the phrase, however, was "in the presence of the people of the church gathered in the church," as the canonist William Lyndwood glossed the phrase in his fifteenth-century canon law commentary on marriage.[111] Although evidently church door weddings were

common at various times and places in England in the Middle Ages, London records indicate that by no means was a church door contract the
rule in London, and perhaps it was not even usual. Most witnesses to
London cases who described solemnizations either noted vaguely that the
couple were married in the parish church or that they were married *in facie ecclesie*, but on a number of occasions the witnesses were quite explicit
that the exchange of consent took place in the nave, "as is the custom in
the English church," not in the porch or at the church door.[112] William
Geffrey, for instance, testified that "on the Sunday after the feast of the
Assumption a year ago [16 August 1489], he was present in the nave of the
parish church of All Saints at Maldon, and there he heard when Alice and
John Grose contracted marriage together *in facie ecclesie*."[113] Only once
in the London records did a deponent describe a marriage at the church
door, which she had seen at Cambridge.[114] The location of the first part
of the solemnization ceremony was probably contingent on many
factors—the particular church's architecture, the weather, the size of the
crowd.

Similarly, evidence regarding the form of the marriage liturgy used in
London solemnizations suggests that there was more variation in practice
than a straightforward reading of the written rite would suggest. It is
worthwhile to compare the service as laid out in late medieval English
mass books with the accounts of solemnizations that witnesses described
in their testimony.

The approved liturgy used during the solemnization of marriage and
other church services in the province of Canterbury during the later Middle Ages was known as the Sarum rite (named after the diocese of Salis-
bury from which it spread).[115] The Sarum rite of marriage became the
basis of the wedding ceremony in the Church of England's Book of Common Prayer, as well as remaining the standard form of the Catholic marriage liturgy, and thus much of what is described in the following
paragraphs will seem familiar to many readers.

As a mass book printed in 1497 directed, the couple gathered at the
church with the celebrating priest, along with any relatives and friends
who wanted to participate in the service. The man and the woman were
to stand either at the door or inside the church, the man on the right and
the woman on the left, because Eve was fashioned from a rib on the left
side of Adam. The priest then proclaimed the banns one more time and
then said in English to those assembled: "Behold, brothers, we are gathered before God and his angels, and all the saints, in the presence of the

church (*in facie ecclesie*), to join together two bodies, that is this man and this woman, so that from henceforth they will be one body, and that they may be two souls in the faith and the law of God, so that together they may earn eternal life whatever they may have done before this."[116] Then, in the scene beloved of Hollywood scriptwriters, the priest charged that if anyone present knew of any cause why the two should not be lawfully joined together in matrimony, he or she should then speak, and the man and the woman were similarly charged to reveal any previous vow or any other impediment. As the missal emphasized, if anyone should raise any impediment, the marriage was to be deferred until such time as the matter was fully investigated.

After this, the priest was to say to the man, again in English (although the missal itself retained this passage in Latin), "N., will you have this woman to your wedded wife, and love her and honor her, hold her and keep her, in health and in sickness, as a husband ought his wife, forsaking all others for her, so long as you both shall live?"[117] The man was to answer, "I will." Similarly, the priest asked the woman, "N., will you have this man to your wedded husband, and obey him and serve him, love, honor and keep him, in health and in sickness, as a wife ought her husband, forsaking all others for him, so long as you both shall live?"[118] The woman was, of course, also to answer, "I will." This was a future-consent contract, but spoken by the priest instead of the principals (the principals simply assenting to it); it functioned in the service as a point of departure.

After the consent of both parties to the union had been established, the consent of the woman's family or friends—not canonically necessary, but socially essential—was also demonstrated. The woman was given to her husband by her father or a friend, literally handed over as her hand was placed into that of her new spouse. If she had never before been married, she was to have her hand uncovered; if she was a widow, it was to be covered. As the man took her right hand in his right hand and followed the instruction of the priest, he said the following words, the missal here recording the passage in English—perhaps to ensure that these words, the words that in themselves created the sacramental marriage bond, were said correctly: "I, N., take thee, N., to my wedded wife, to have and to hold from this day forward, for better, worse, for richer, for poorer, in sickness and in health, till death us depart, if holy church will it ordain; and thereto I plight thee my troth."[119] He then withdrew his hand. Then the woman, likewise taking the man's right hand and following the priest's instructions, said, "I, N., take thee, N., to my wedded husband, to have and to hold from this day forward, for better, for worse, for richer, for poorer, in sickness and in health, to be bonour and buxom in bed and at board, till death us depart, if holy church it will ordain; and thereto I plight thee my troth." The bride's promise to be "bonour [a word having no precise modern English equivalent, but connoting *good* and *obliging*] and buxom in bed and at board" suggests that her wifely duties centered on her cheerful willingness in sexual relations with her husband and her equally cheerful provision of food for his table and other domestic services.

After these vows had been exchanged, the man was to put a coin and a ring on a dish or a book, and if the ring had not been previously blessed, the priest was to say a blessing over the ring, and holy water was sprinkled over it. The priest then gave the ring to the man, who put the ring on the thumb of the bride's hand, saying, "In the name of the Father"; then on her index finger, saying, "and the Son"; then on her middle finger, saying, "and of the Holy Ghost"; then upon the ring finger, saying, "Amen," and leaving it there. As the missal explains, in that finger is a vein that leads to the heart. Then he was to say, again following the priest's instructions: "With this ring I thee wed, and with my body I thee honor, and with all my gold I thee endow. In nomine patris, et filii, et spiritus sancti [in the name of the father, the son, and the holy spirit]. Amen."[120] Following the ritual of the ring, the priest said a number of blessings and prayers over the couple, after which they proceeded to the stairs leading to the altar, where the newly married couple knelt. The priest then proceeded to say a nuptial mass, during which various special prayers were dedicated to the happiness, peace, and fruitfulness of the couple.

This was the liturgy as laid out in the Sarum missal. As one might expect, descriptions of solemnizations in depositions from marital litigation are much less detailed. Somewhat more surprising, however, are the emphases of the witnesses' descriptions. Some elements of the marriage liturgy are never mentioned by witnesses, suggesting either that they were not universally practiced (perhaps being subject to local variation) or that some elements of the solemnization were more likely to be remembered than others.

Sir Robert Tellerton, for example, a canon of the priory of St. Bartholomew in West Smithfield, described in 1470 his own solemnization of a marriage between Katherine Stevyns and Robert Mortymer alias Dorward four years previously. After having issued banns between the couple,

On a certain Wednesday in the month of June, in the chapel of St. Mary in the priory of St. Bartholomew, this witness publicly celebrated marriage between the said Robert and Katherine according to the customs of the realm of England. That is, the said Robert took Katherine by the hand and said to her, following the instructions of this witness, "I Robert Dorward here take you Katherine as my wife, and thereto I give you my faith," then withdrawing his hand. And then Katherine took Robert by the hand and said to him, "And I Katherine here take you Robert as my husband, and thereto I give you my faith," with other words and solemnities used and observed in such marriages in the realm of England.[121]

For obvious reasons, most descriptions of solemnizations of marriage in marital litigation focus on this central canonical moment, the actual contract of marriage itself, rather than the "words and solemnities" of the rest of the rite. It is worthy of note, however, that none of the descriptions of the exchange of consent in church, including those reported by the celebrants themselves, used the longer form ("for richer, for poorer . . .") outlined in the missal. None of the descriptions mentioned the blessing of a ring for the woman, although, as I will discuss later, the giving of rings at other parts of the marriage process was commonly cited. Nor did any of the deponents ever refer to a ceremony described in the missal where, after the *Sanctus*, the man and woman (if neither had previously been married) were to prostrate themselves in prayer at the step of the altar while a *pallium* or linen cloth was extended over them, being held at the four corners by four clerks in surplices, while a prayer was said over them.[122] It seems improbable that many of the solemnizations described in the deposition books would have had four clerks in attendance, although perhaps one clerk could hold down the cloth in a pinch. In a number of cases, the parish clerk, one of whose jobs was to hold the mass book for the celebrating priest while he said the prayers, testified as a witness, as it was a normal part of the duties of the parish clerk to assist at the solemnization of marriages.[123] Some witnesses mentioned what was apparently a clear marker of a nuptial mass—the kneeling of the couple before the altar[124]—notable, no doubt, as this was the only time a layperson so closely approached the altar during a service. Altogether, it seems possible that many solemnizations were considerably less elaborate than the rite described in the Sarum missal.

Following the solemnization, the couple and their family, friends, and neighbors proceeded to a wedding breakfast. In a number of cases, this meal was said to take place at the couple's new home,[125] although in one case, the father of the groom was the host for the wedding breakfast.[126]

Sitting down with the couple at the wedding feast was a memorable enough social occasion to be mentioned frequently as evidence that the couple were publicly married.[127] Although the depositions unfortunately offer no details about the wedding meal, we know at least that sometimes minstrels were hired to provide music: in 1500, the wardens and fellowship of minstrels in London complained that "foreign" minstrels from other parts of England were taking away their business, and besides which they were grievously annoying the citizens of the City by "pressing to their tables upon the church holidays, dedications, churchings, weddings, and other feasts."[128]

The solemnization of the marriage functioned as sanctification, celebration, and (in many cases) a ratification of the couple's marriage bond. It was, at least ideally, an occasion both serious and joyful. During the period between the initial contract and the solemnization, while publicity of the marriage was growing through the saying of banns and common talk in the parish and neighborhood, preparations for the nuptials were made. On the day of the solemnization, the couple gathered with their kinsfolk and friends at the church and exchanged words of present consent under instruction from the presiding priest, followed by a nuptial mass. After the solemnization, the couple and their guests celebrated their union in a wedding breakfast. The couple's marriage was now complete. In the following chapters, I examine more closely the social interactions between the couple and among their friends, neighbors, and relatives that brought them to this moment.

2

Courtship and Gender

PERHAPS MORE THAN ANY OTHER TIME IN A medieval person's life, the preliminaries to marriage demanded particular behavior on the parts of both the prospective husband and the prospective wife. Medieval and modern commentators have often used the potent metaphor of the dance to describe these rituals and negotiations of courtship. Among late medieval Londoners, the courtship dance was relatively free-form, with only a few required elements. But a virtually inviolable rule was that the man should take the lead while the woman followed. Transgressions of this choreography were rare; to do differently was to act improperly and disreputably, and specifically to project an inappropriate image to a prospective spouse and family. The roles of leader and follower prefigured the relative roles of husband and wife in the ideal medieval marriage, where the husband was to command his wife lovingly, taking responsibility for the direction of his household, while his wife cheerfully obeyed her husband and depended on him.

The proposal of marriage itself is perhaps the clearest example of a ritualization of the expectation that men acted and women reacted: normally, men proposed while women accepted or rejected. The exchange typically took one of two forms: in the first, the prospective husband directly asked the woman if she would have him as her husband, and she replied yea or nay; if she was agreeable, she might then respond with a similar question of her own.[1] In some cases the proposal and the answer, the action and the reaction, were a long drawn-out process of subtle negotiation. One witness, for instance, reported that Thomas Torald came to her and her husband one afternoon and told them that he had spoken with Maude Knyff a number of times about contracting marriage between them. The last time they spoke, he reported, he had found her well disposed toward him, and he felt sure that with a final proposal she would at last acquiesce.[2] Maude Knyff was able to use noncommittal and yet increasingly encouraging responses as a strategic ploy; because she was a wealthy widow with a number of suitors, the expectation that she play a reactive role was probably not a great handicap to her.

As we have seen,[3] in the second form of exchange of consent, a third party, usually a layman of substantial status, directed the couple to exchange the proper words, in effect playing the role of the officiating cleric. He would ask each in turn if they were willing to take the other as a spouse and then instructed them about the exact words to say.

Thus in the actual exchange of consent, courting men sometimes took an active role and sometimes a responsive one. By contrast, women almost always responded to questions about marriage rather than initiating them. In the exceptional cases where women directly played the active role in a proposal of marriage, they were unsuccessful. Indeed the circumstances of the cases indicate that these active women breached the pattern because they were in desperate straits and were left with few alternatives. William Knollys, for instance, when examined before the court, said that Agnes Lanther "very often and on diverse occasions wished to have him as her husband," but while he admitted that he had often known her carnally and had indeed had a child by her, he denied that he had ever consented to marry her.[4] He implied in his examination that her requests were somehow pathetic and foolish and destined to failure. In a similar case, Alice Skevyngton deposed that she had seen a pregnant Katherine Aber kneeling before Robert Allerton and weeping, begging him to make her his wife and not to defer the marriage any longer; he, however, continued to put her off and when brought before the court denied that he ever intended to marry her.[5] Such direct action on a woman's part was clearly not a very fruitful strategy. As William Caxton put it in his translation of the book of the Knight of La Tour Landry, a conduct manual aimed at young aristocratic women (and in Caxton's printed translation, probably read by London's civic elite as well), a man rejected a young woman as a possible wife because of her "over-great malapertness," her too-familiar manner and light tongue. The prospective husband sensed that the woman's loose tongue was the outward sign of her potential for sexual laxity, a suspicion that was vindicated when she was embroiled in scandal within half a year after his decision not to pursue her, and then died (the wages of sin in such stories almost always being death). The Knight's lesson: "many have lost their marriage" by talking too much and being indiscreet.[6]

A more effective tactic for women was an approach through which they could take initiative yet retain the appearance of passivity, meekness, and reaction.[7] A woman, for instance, might coyly prod a suitor to make a proposal of marriage through seemingly ingenuous requests. Thomas Berford testified that he was present on a summer Sunday afternoon in John Saunder's shop and saw John Barnet and Agnes Saunder sitting together and talking. Agnes saw John wearing two gold rings on his finger and said to him, "John, would you give me one of those rings that you're wearing?" He responded that he would be happy to, but on one condition; when she asked him what that condition was, he said, "that you will be my wife." He then gave her the ring and they exchanged vows of consent.[8] No doubt both had come to the shop that day with the understanding that marriage vows would be exchanged—presumably that is why John had brought the second ring—but if Agnes wished to hurry the process along, her best tactic was a coyly teasing one.

One interesting case, *John Holder c. Agnes Chambyrleyn*,[9] offers three divergent perspectives on an alleged exchange of consent; the differences between the three accounts illustrate aspects of the gendered nature of courtship and the ways in which people chose to present themselves to suitors and to the ecclesiastical court. Two of the three accounts were offered to the court in support of John Holder's suit to enforce a contract of marriage he claimed he had made with Agnes Chambyrleyn. These two narratives differ only subtly from one another, but in revealing ways. In the first scenario, John Holder himself, appearing before the court, offered this story in his examination: he said that he was standing in the doorway of Agnes's mother's house in the parish of St. Mary Colchurch, talking to Agnes in the presence of three witnesses, William and Marion Phyppis and John Jonson. John said to Agnes, "Agnes, you sent for me; I would like to know why." She replied, "I sent for you so that we could complete the business about which you know very well." He responded, "So, finish it." Then she took him by the hand and asked, "What should I say to you?" He answered, "Say, 'I will have you as my husband, and thereto I give you my faith.'" Immediately Agnes, following John's instructions, said to him those exact words, and he replied likewise, and they kissed.[10] In John's version, Agnes takes the initiative, asking him to meet her; once they meet, however, she is reluctant to take the active role and attempts to prod him into taking the first step.

John's witness William Phyppis presents a slightly different version of the same scene. In his account, it is John who calls Agnes to meet him. She asks him why he has called her there, and it is he who answers that he wants to finish the matter between them about which she knows well. Then she replies, "What should I say?" and the scene plays out in much the same way as John Holder had reported.[11] In other words, in William Phyppis's account, the speaking roles at the beginning of the scene are reversed, with John taking the initiative and prodding Agnes to bring the matter to a conclusion. The stories do not quite match up, as frequently happens with courtroom testimony: in this case the third version of the story may explain why. Agnes and a host of witnesses called on her behalf claimed that she had never made such a contract and that John Holder, William Phyppis, and John's other witnesses had all perjured themselves.[12]

But whether or not they lied, John Holder's and William Phyppis's testimony differ from one another in ways that illuminate their underlying assumptions about gender and agency. On the one hand, perhaps both John and William told the truth as they saw it, implying interactions between memory, perception, and gender expectations—William may have, for instance, unconsciously rewritten Agnes's unconventionally active role by ascribing her actions to John in his memory of the episode. Or on the other hand, as their opponents charged, perhaps both colluded to give doctored testimony, an all too frequent occurrence in ecclesiastical courts. If so, John Holder, who brought the suit against Agnes and thus presumably desired the marriage, nonetheless constructed the scene so that Agnes was pursuing him: it was she who wanted him, he implies, and thus her refusal to honor the contract is all the more unreasonable. Yet even though she summoned him to meet with her, he soon takes control of the proceedings and thus does not refuse his appropriately dominant role as the male partner.

The prevailing supposition of male agency and female reaction, as well as the assumption that women were both easily influenced and vulnerable to coercion, lay behind the frequent practice of sequestering women involved in marriage suits. The sequestration of the female party, designed to prevent parties to marital litigation from attempting to circumvent the proceedings by making or solemnizing new contracts, became common in the province of Canterbury by the later fifteenth century. An order of sequestration was probably not automatic but undertaken at the request of one or another of the parties because of a perception that a woman was vulnerable to influence or pressure.[13] In some cases, at least, the perception was apparently justified, as a number of sequestrations were violated.[14] The most dramatic was the consensual abduction of Margery Shepard. She had been sequestered in the home of

Richard Spencer, the married notary who acted as the Consistory's court clerk,[15] for the duration of the suit that had been launched against her by Richard Tymond. After she had stayed there about two weeks, she saw an acquaintance, Richard Scimon, on the street outside Spencer's house who offered to accompany her upon hearing that she needed an escort to walk to her father's house. On the way, they happened to encounter Richard Tymond's rival for her hand, John Sem. Sem told her that he was spending a lot of money (presumably contesting the suit), and he wanted some reassurance and indeed more than reassurance: "if ye love him [Tymond] better than ye do me, go home again, and if [ye] love me better than ye do him, I desire that ye come with me." Sem persuaded Margery Shepard not to return to her sequestration in Spencer's residence, and they both spent the night at Scimon's house. At four o'clock the following morning, accompanied by Richard Scimon and with the advice of the butler of the mayor of London, the pair fled to Winchelsea, outside the bishop of London's jurisdiction. There Sem left Margery in the safekeeping of a former mayor of Winchelsea, where she stayed for seven weeks.[16] While Margery herself was a willing participant in the abduction, the terms in which the episode was described both by her and by Sem emphasize that she was always in a man's custody, proper or improper. Even a woman challenging paternal and ecclesiastical authority in order to marry a man she preferred did so in a way that conformed with cultural expectations that respectable young women were dependent on male supervision and protection.

While young women were expected to be passive and reactive in courtship, widows looking to remarry were in a somewhat different situation, although the expectations that they would consult with friends and even parents did not necessarily disappear. In a number of cases, widows contracted marriage in the presence of their parents and sometimes even required their mother's or father's consent.[17] In the mid-1480s, for example, Piers Curtes[18] allegedly made contracts with two different women, both widows. From Easter to October 1486, Curtes frequently visited the house of Beatrice Stoughton in the parish of St. Nicholas Cole Abbey in order to court Stoughton's daughter, Agnes Skern, a widow probably in her thirties.[19] After months of their keeping company, Beatrice Stoughton apparently pushed the two to declare themselves. According to her testimony in the case, Beatrice said to Piers, "Ye have made labor many days to have my daughter. She hath put her will to mine," and then asked him, "Be ye the man that intend to have my daughter to your wife?" When

Piers confirmed that he did, the couple made a future-tense contract in Beatrice's presence.[20] Although according to Beatrice Stoughton, Piers Curtes subsequently labored diligently to recover certain lands and tenements that had belonged to Agnes's late husband, and according to his own deposition there was another exchange of consent in front of other witnesses, the marriage did not progress beyond the future-tense contract (to the surprise of some of Agnes's neighbors).[21] The following autumn, Curtes was apparently looking elsewhere for a wife and again settled on a widow. In September 1487 he went to the house of a grocer, Thomas Clarel, and told Clarel that he had come there for the sake of taking Clarel's daughter Margaret Niter as his wife. Clarel thanked Curtes, and Piers Curtes and Margaret Niter proceeded to exchange present consent before Clarel and another witness.[22] Both widows exchanged consent with Curtes under parental supervision, just as they might have had they been marrying for the first time. Both also had particular reason to resort to parental aid. Margaret Niter's father indicated in his testimony that he wished to give the couple further property worth £40, apart from what her first husband, a gentleman, had left her.[23] His presence and implied consent to Margaret Niter's marriage to Piers Curtes reflected this.[24] Agnes Skern's situation was more difficult. She had had four children from her previous marriage,[25] and she was having problems gaining access to her husband's estate. She may have desperately needed the help of a husband to assert her legal rights, and her mother was trying to help her in this. Agnes won her case against Piers and became his wife.[26]

Other widows were probably more independent, although the extent of their ability to exercise free choice and agency was constrained by their financial situation and their personalities. The desperate might resort to magical means to gain a husband: about 1480 Richard Lankiston of London offered to help a widow named Margaret Geffrey to find a husband, saying to her, "Thou art a poor widow and it were alms [it would be merciful] to help thee to a marriage, and if thou will do any cost in spending any money, thou shalt have a man with goods worth a £1000." When Margaret responded, "How may that be?" Richard replied, "my wife knoweth a cunning man that by his cunning can cause a woman to have any man that she hath favor to, and that shall be upon warranty, for she hath put it in execution before [this] time, and this shall cost money." Margaret remained cautious: "I have no goods, save two mazers [drinking bowls] for to support me, my mother, and my children, and if they were sold and I fail of my purpose, I, my mother, and my children were undone." But

Richard reassured her: "deliver me the mazers and I will warrant thine intent shall be fulfilled." Margaret then gave him the two mazers, together worth 5 marks, 10s. Both Richard and Margaret were summoned before the Commissary court, where Richard was ordered to return the mazers to Margaret, and Margaret was assigned the penance of walking in the Sunday church procession for three successive Sundays, with feet and head bared, bearing a penny candle.[27]

Widows, Widowers, and Remarriage

Others had more freedom of choice than poor Margaret Geffrey. Widows of substance were sometimes the object of considerable competition and could play suitors against one another. Many of those marrying, and many of those who had marital disputes that ended up in the ecclesiastical courts, were marrying for the second, third, or fourth time and were well past the first flush of youth. Alice Cademan and Nicholas Vavecer, for instance, who engaged in courting activity in the spring of 1474, each had adult children.[28] Although there were many similarities in courtship rituals for those who were contemplating remarriage, there were naturally some differences as well: often more money was at stake, and fecundity is less likely to have been an important consideration, especially if previous marriages had produced children.[29]

The relative gender roles may have been somewhat different as well: greater life experience and wealth may have given both partners a more active role in the courtship process and in decision making, although this was probably more marked for women than for men. This is not to say that widows openly initiated courtships or took the leading role in the courtship; indeed in some cases, as we have seen, widows not only sought advice and help from family and friends but even sought parental consent, acting as dependently as young, previously unmarried daughters.[30] Nonetheless widows were more likely to receive suitors and consider offers of marriage without explicit recourse to the advice of family or friends. And while they may not have actively pursued men, this was not necessarily a handicap for them: in some cases it is clear that they could exercise considerable power in receiving a number of suitors and choosing from among them. A rich and attractive widow was a valuable commodity, and her wealth and her body were hers to bestow on whom she liked. The most vivid depictions in court records of women demonstrating and exercising considerable agency, setting suitors against one another or dangling them on a string for a considerable period of time, come from widows: this was probably owing to wealth inherited from previous marriages and a combination of age, experience, confidence, and possibly sexual attractiveness. Elizabeth Kirkeby, who was certainly wealthy, kept George Bulstrode dancing attendance and offering sumptuous gifts for three years before she finally died, without having made good on the promise of marriage he claimed she made with him.[31] Fierce competition for the hands of certain widows, involving two, three, or more men, sometimes eventuated in complicated marital litigation. Agnes Twytynge, for example, a widow of the parish of St. Clement Danes on the west end of London, spoke seriously of marriage with three different men, Robert Hilton, Richard Smalwode, and Robert Tryse, in a period of six weeks in the spring of 1471, culminating in her allegedly making present contracts with Robert Hilton and Richard Smalwode on 1 May and 3 May, respectively.[32] Why there was so much frenetic courtship activity around the widow Twytynge in such a short period of time is unclear, but the flurry may in fact have been prompted by the event that put her on the remarriage market: her previous husband's death.

The length of time that widows and widowers should wait after the death of one spouse before taking another was a matter of some delicacy. Some women explicitly refused to entertain new offers until a year after the death of a husband; John Tailour, for instance, repeatedly spoke to the newly widowed Agnes Fry about marriage, but she claimed that she told him each time that she would not consider remarrying until after the anniversary of her husband's death.[33] Agnes Rogers observed the anniversary of her husband's death by wearing a black gown and inviting a number of guests to dine with her; according to some witnesses, she also made a present-tense contract with James Whytyngdon that same day. Whether or not she made the contract with Whytyngdon (she denied that she did), the anniversary evidently marked her reentry onto the marriage market, as she admitted seriously discussing marriage with Whytyngdon in the weeks that followed and apparently made a contract with another man soon after.[34] Joan Broun agreed to marry William Case in 1490 sometime soon after the death of her husband John Broun, but when Case asked her to call in neighbors to witness the contract, she demurred, "because she did not want them to know that she had made a new vow so close to the death of her previous husband."[35] Other women were more open in remarrying within months of their previous husband's death. Joan Qualley, whose husband William died sometime in the second half of September 1491,[36] allegedly contracted with one man in October and another in the first week of November.[37] Maude Knyff received suitors and made one or more contracts of marriage three weeks before her late husband's will had even been probated, suggesting that this was soon after her husband's death.[38]

Although evidently some thought it important to observe a mourning period after a husband's death, it was not necessarily disrespectful to remarry quickly; indeed Maude Knyff, according to some witnesses, mentioned the love she had borne her late husband while making her new marriage. In the contract witnesses claimed she made with Robert Grene, Maude explicitly linked her new marriage to her old: just before they exchanged words of present consent, Robert took a ring from Maude's finger and Maude asked him "to keep that ring safe, for her love and for love of her late husband."[39] Men, too, remarried in some cases very quickly after the death of a wife: one witness said that William Baynard made a future-tense contract with Elizabeth Slee a remarkable four days after the death of his previous wife.[40]

A widow had to balance a number of factors in making a decision to take a new husband. Maude Knyff, for instance, may have needed to remarry quickly: her husband had been a corser or horse dealer, a business that was probably difficult for a woman to conduct on her own, and she had an underage son.[41] Widows with young children may have found it highly desirable to remarry: Agnes Skern, who had four children by her late husband, needed a husband to help her negotiate the maze of legal problems the administration of her late husband's estate had left.[42] For other widows, however, remarriage meant loss of status: widows of London freemen could become free women, but only as long as they remained unmarried. Similarly, widows controlled the property they inherited from their husbands, but often only until they married again. For some widows, the loss of independence and control of their property may have been an important factor in choosing not to remarry: Agnes Fry, for instance, turned down an offer of marriage from John Tailour in 1487, and she remained unmarried until her death in 1501 or 1502. Her will suggests she was a woman of some property, and she may have preferred to remain under her own governance rather than submitting to the rule of a new husband.[43] Women may also have wanted to remarry for some of the same reasons women married in the first place: companionship and sex.

Just as with any marriage, though, there were risks, and these may even have been magnified when inheritances and children were involved. When Ann, the widow of Richard Alp and mother of four underage children, married Richard Styward, something resembling a nightmare resulted. By Styward's own admission, after their marriage was solemnized, he "violently and seriously beat" her, he spent much of Richard Alp's estate (as he noted, this was his right as her husband), and after they separated he refused to pay the alimony the court ordered him to render to her, leaving her and her children little to live on as he had custody of the property from her previous marriage except for her clothes.[44]

If women sometimes married men because men could represent them more effectively legally and politically, so also did men remarry because households needed mistresses. William Baynard, although he denied he had made a contract with Elizabeth Slee, said that he had "hired Elizabeth to keep his house, because he was alone, and later he told Elizabeth that if she kept his house well that she could have it as her own house."[45] Although he gave her a pair of beads (probably for a rosary) and a groat (a coin worth 4d.) as marriage tokens, he changed his mind, and within two months he had contracted with and solemnized a marriage with another woman.[46] Perhaps she was not a good housekeeper.

The remarriage of a prominent widow or widower occasioned conjecture, gossip, and even wagers. In one peculiar Chancery case, London mercer John Osbern complained to the chancellor that he had wagered £4 with Ambrose Grysaker, gentleman, and John Lambard, mercer, that John Yonge, a prominent alderman, mayor, and M.P.,[47] would remain unmarried through May of that year. Although Yonge did not remarry until long after (and the priest who later presided over the marriage's solemnization was brought forward to testify to this), Grysaker and Lambard nonetheless sued Osbern for debt.[48] The death of Yonge's first wife, Agnes, occurred while Yonge was serving as Lord Mayor, and was well known enough to have been recorded in a London chronicle;[49] his possible remarriage obviously sparked speculation. Another Chancery case involved the remarriage of a widower: plaintiff Robert Duplage of London, tailor, said that he and Sir William Capell, knight, citizen, and alderman of London, were in company together, and among "other idle and merry communication" Sir William gave Duplage a gold ring, worth no more than 13s. 4d., saying that if Duplage should remain unmarried after the decease of Duplage's then wife, Joan, he would never demand back his ring. But Sir William had an obligation drawn up in which he claimed that the ring was worth £20, to which Duplage agreed without knowing the contents because he trusted Sir William. Later, presumably because Duplage had remarried, Sir William sued him for £22 pounds before the sheriffs of London. Duplage asked the chancellor to intervene, because the whole thing had been a joke; and in any case he had offered back the ring, which was not worth anywhere near £22.[50]

The Exchange of Tokens

The giving and receiving of tokens or gifts was an important part of the ritual of courtship, an exchange that carried with it meanings that went well beyond the literal value of the items that were offered and accepted. As in other parts of courtship, the giving of gifts was also significantly gendered, although not in a straightforward way. It was also a ritual that involved others, as frequently tokens were offered through intermediaries.

The exchange of gifts in medieval society was a complicated matter, ripe with meaning.[51] Both during a courtship and at the time of the actual contract of marriage itself, couples exchanged gifts, or tokens as they were termed. This practice mirrored the exchange of a coin or a drink at the time of a commercial contract at the same time that it represented the emotional bond that had formed (or would form) between the partners.[52] The offer, and acceptance, of a gift, often made through an intermediary, could be an important stage along the way to making a marriage contract: it could act as a sensitive test of whether a prospective mate would welcome further courtship activity, or indeed whether the courtship had progressed to such a point that the question was ready to be asked. John Miller, for example, a seventy-year-old weaver, went one morning to visit his widowed stepdaughter, Joan Cardif of Walthamstow, Essex, at the request of an admirer, John Brocher. Miller brought with him a gift of fish from Brocher and the message that Joan was to cook the fish for dinner, because Brocher was bringing some people to her house to dine. Fish, as Christopher Dyer has pointed out, were frequently used as presents; they were luxury items and a particularly suitable gift on a fish day (Brocher gave his fish to Cardif on the Tuesday before Easter).[53] Cardif received the fish happily and then asked Miller if this gift indicated that John Brocher wanted to marry her. Miller replied "that if she could find it in her heart to love him as her husband, John would be hers forever."[54]

Miller and Cardif then discussed how much money Brocher had and what his debts were, and Cardif offered her stepfather 40s. to give to Brocher to pay off his debts.[55] This exchange must have been prearranged, at least to some extent; Joan Cardif and John Brocher obviously knew one another and had probably engaged in some courting, although apparently they had not directly discussed marriage. But Brocher's conveyance through Miller of food for Cardif to prepare (a customary duty of a wife) served as a signal that he was ready to ask the question. Cardif picked up on the signal and asked her stepfather what Brocher's intentions were, expecting Miller to know the answer. Indeed he did: he was not only aware that John Brocher wished to "be hers forever" but also knew all about his goods and debts. For the gift to do its work, it had to be given, and received, as a token of marriage, both parties recognizing it as such. In depositions, the response of the recipient, whether he or she received the gift willingly and happily, was often recorded, as without that information the meaning of the gift remained ambiguous.

In some cases, especially when the prospective mates were of high social station, courtship gifts could be elaborate. George Bulstrode, a London mercer, complained to the chancellor about 1490 that he had made a contract of marriage with Elizabeth Kirkeby, a wealthy woman who had been widowed three times, and because of that contract he had given her many gifts, including precious jewels, and had "delivered her and paid for her in ready money at diverse times" a sum of £140; moreover he had paid out a good deal of money toward "the furnishing of the same marriage," and "by the space of three years and more applied himself about the occupation of merchandise and other business" on her behalf, including trips overseas, knowing that it would ultimately be to his profit because of the forthcoming marriage. But when he was overseas in Seville certain evil-disposed persons—namely her brother John Heron—influenced her to renounce the marriage. Bulstrode sued Kirkeby in the Court of Arches to uphold the contract, and it would have been sufficiently proved, he wrote in his petition, as there were many witnesses to it, but Elizabeth herself became too ill for the case to proceed. On her deathbed she at last relented, agreeing at least that the goods and jewels, plus £40 for his trouble, should be returned to him. At the time, John Heron, her brother and executor, agreed to fulfill her wishes, but after Elizabeth died Heron utterly refused to give Bulstrode his due, occasioning Bulstrode's petition to the chancellor to issue a writ of subpoena so that the chancellor could hear the case.[56]

Annexed to the Chancery bill was an inventory of the gifts Bulstrode gave Elizabeth Kirkeby, detailing the kind of luxury goods that pleased the civic elite of London and that might function as courtship gifts: jewels, including "a great ring of fine gold with a great pointed diamond," a small chain of gold with a little agnus dei (lamb of God) figure, a signet of gold with her arms engraved on it and a ruby and an emerald set into it, and a large ring of fine gold set with a turquoise that he had had made for her in Seville; other luxury items such as a popinjay or parrot "which I might have sold to my lady Hungerford for five marks"; fine cloth, furs, ribbons, and laces; and "diverse dainties, as figs and raisins, dates, almonds, prunes, capers, sugar, and other spices, tunny lampreys conserve, pomegranates, and oranges"; and 38s. 8d. for New Year's gifts to her servants, friends, and kinsfolk. In addition to these gifts, he had also loaned cash to Kirkeby's son and to her friends and bought a good deal of merchandise on her behalf—all itemized in his inventory (for instance, "Item, twenty-nine tuns and a pipe of bastard [a sweet Spanish wine]; item, forty-four butts of rumney [a sweet Greek wine]; item, a tun and thirteen butts of wine sack [Spanish white wine]; . . . item, two butts of capers; item, one butt and a hogshead of prunes").[57]

Bulstrode's accounting of the gifts he gave to Elizabeth Kirkeby during the period of their courtship provides us with some insight into the process of making a marriage among the London elite. Although George Bulstrode as international merchant and Elizabeth Kirkeby as thrice-widowed woman of considerable wealth were by no means garden-variety wooers, the patterns of money and gifts paid out by Bulstrode in trying to win her hand give us a good idea of the wider expectations of courtship and marriage. Bulstrode courted Elizabeth Kirkeby for an unusually long period, at least three years, over which he spent time and money to promote her business as well as his. His deliveries of "ready money" to her stepson, Richard Kirkeby, and to others, along with the delivery of merchandise worth more than £400, indicate the extent to which their marriage would be as much, and indeed probably more, a joining of their businesses as a union of their hearts. Yet George's courtship of Elizabeth was more than a hard-headed business merger: George also gave to Elizabeth a number of "jewels and tokens," obviously material things of some value, but then as now heavily imbued with symbolic significance: rings set with fine gems, parrots, fine cloths, furs, ribbons, laces, luxury foods, and wines. Elizabeth was a woman who enjoyed luxury judging by her will, which describes in loving detail the fine clothing, linen, and jewelry that she bequeathed to her friends and relatives.[58] George clearly catered to her predilections. Most interesting, perhaps, are the sums that George spent not only on Elizabeth but also on her friends; she "caused" him to make for her and her friends hippocras, a spiced wine, and he said that he gave New Year's gifts, a common custom especially among the gentry and aristocracy,[59] over several years to her servants, friends, and kinsfolk. Winning a woman's hand meant, in many cases, a wooing of her friends and relatives as well; indeed, as George Bulstrode discovered, opposition from an important family member or friend could spell the end of a long courtship.

As with George Bulstrode and Elizabeth Kirkeby, other cases involved people of some substance exchanging gifts of considerable variety both before and after the contract. Immediately after Christopher Kechyn made a contract with Margaret Broke in 1497, "in sign of the marriage" he gave her a ruby and sapphire ring and an emerald ring, after which Margaret's employer (acting in loco parentis) gave Christopher 20 marks in gold as her dowry (a moderate amount, suggesting that the principals were substantial but not among the higher reaches of London society).[60] Later Christopher gave Margaret a number of other gifts befitting a wife: a gown of violet ingrained with gray (the wedding gown of his dead wife), more jewelry, measures of cloth to make other gowns, and miniver and lettice fur for trimming, a silver gilt cup, and a belt made of gold with a silver gilt buckle and pendant. In return Margaret gave Christopher a claw of a bittern (a bird similar to a heron) mounted with silver and gilt, a stomacher (waistcoat) of fine woolen cloth furred with white lamb, and a silk lace. As the witness, Margaret's employer Lancelot Holme, testified, Margaret gave these gifts to him "as to her husband [*tanquam marito suo dedit*]," and Christopher "received them as from his wife [*tanquam a sua uxore recepit*]."[61]

Most couples exchanged tokens that had obviously become conventional and that were much less valuable (although in relative terms, if the couple was of lower socioeconomic station, the gifts may have been worth a considerable amount). Rings, made of gold or silver gilt, were commonly, but not invariably, exchanged at the time of the contract as well as at other stages of the marriage process, although rings did not have the preeminent status they have now in Western culture as a sign of marriage. Although more often rings were given by the man to the woman, in many cases rings were exchanged, and in several cases a ring was given by the woman to the man.[62] On one occasion, in a ritual for which there are no other examples in the London records, a man broke a silver ring in the middle, keeping one piece and giving the other to the woman "as a sign of the contract."[63] The giving of a coin—often one of fairly low value—and its willing reception could also act as a kind of surety for a contract. Robert Smyth, after he contracted marriage with Rose Langtoft, gave her a groat (a coin worth 4 or 5d.), which she received happily.[64] Similarly, when Robert Walsh and Margaret Flemmyng contracted, he gave to her a groat and a ring, and she gave him 2s.[65] The value of the coin was more symbolic than actual: on another occasion, Richard Stacy gave Joan Say half a penny on the occasion of their contract.[66] Kerchiefs, gloves, beads, and ribbons or belts were also frequently offered as tokens,[67] as were small religious objects—especially crosses, crucifixes, and agnus dei figures.[68] Pairs of beads—most often fashioned from coral which, according to fifteenth-century lapidaries, was thought to bring love and aid fertility[69]—were a common gift, usually, but not invariably, from men to women.[70]

Indeed, in general men gave gifts to women more often than the reverse, although mutual gift giving was also common. In courtship activities involving gifts, in almost two-thirds of the cases, men gave gifts to women; gifts were mutually exchanged about one-third of the time; and in a very small minority (about one in twenty cases), women gave men gifts without evident reciprocity.[71] The prevalence of men's giving probably had several underpinnings. First, men's active and women's reactive roles are once more illustrated: men gave, women gratefully received. A somewhat different pattern that nonetheless adhered to the active/reactive pattern is seen in the reciprocal gifts: in most cases, the man first offered gifts to the woman, and she responded with gifts of her own. Eleanor Acton, for instance, testified in 1474 that she acted as an intermediary between Nicholas Vaveser and Alice Cademan: two or three days after they contracted marriage, "she gave Alice at Nicholas's request half a quarter of pippins, eight oranges, and a gold ring, which Alice received in Nicholas's name, as from her husband. And immediately after she received these things, Alice gave a golden heart to Eleanor to give to Nicholas as to her husband, which Nicholas received from her gratefully."[72] Those few cases where women were said to give gifts to men without reciprocity tended to be exceptions that prove this rule. A woman who initiated gift giving was too forward, or perhaps desperate. Thomas Sylvester admitted in 1473 that he had frequently known a certain Margaret carnally and that he believed that she was pregnant by him. He also admitted that she had given him seven groats as a gift and that she had given him the money for the sake of marriage; he, however, did not receive them "as from his wife."[73]

Men may have given gifts to women more frequently than women gave gifts to men for other reasons as well. In some cases, the gifts husbands gave to wives, especially at the time of the contract, were a symbol of the chattels with which a wife was traditionally endowed by her husband. She, in turn, brought with her a dowry. Gifts generally demand reciprocity: if the payback is not immediate and in kind—as it often was in fifteenth-century London—it came in different form.

The meaning of a gift was determined not only by the substance or symbolism of the gift itself and by the willingness of the recipient but also specifically according to whether it was offered and accepted as from a husband to a wife or a wife to a husband. The meaning of gifts exchanged between people could change as the relationship between two people changed, as is illustrated by the story Alice Scrace told in the Consistory court in her answer to a suit launched against her by Richard Cressy. The litigation between Richard Cressy and Alice Scrace was apparently not adversarial: it was not she, but her brother and employer who opposed the contract, and the suit was likely a means for the couple to have the marriage officially recognized in the face of her friends' antagonism. As Alice testified, about 1483 Richard Cressy was a law student at one of the law inns—Alice could not remember which one[74]—in the western suburbs of London (these inns of chancery and inns of court were the means by which young men, usually in their teens or early twenties, acquired legal training in late medieval England). He became friendly with Alice's brother Richard, another student studying at the inns, and Richard Scrace invited Richard Cressy to spend three weeks of summer vacation with the Scrace family in Sussex. After Cressy's visit, he sent a number of gifts to members of the household: the household servants received pin cases, Richard Scrace a "hanger" (either a belt or a short sword), and the daughter of the house, Alice Scrace, a pair of "tires," ornaments for the hair. Alice, probably a young teenager at the time, found her brother's friend obliging and kind during his stay, as she later testified, but she did not meet Richard Cressy again for almost six years. When she encountered him again in 1489, her father had died and she was living in London as a servant. Both she and Richard were older and of suitable marrying age, and, as Alice described it in her examination before the Consistory, they fell in love. They exchanged many tokens: Richard gave to her a smock, two kerchiefs, a pomander, a mirror encased in ivory, two gold rings, a silver earpick (for cleaning out earwax), a St. James's shell and a small silver staff (both probably pilgrimage souvenirs), and a silver heart, and she gave to him a small piece of wood with a figure of a crucifix.[75] The first gift Richard gave to Alice, the "tires," had been in appreciation of the hospitality he had received at her father's house and with friendly intentions, but the gift did not carry with it any particular meaning related to courtship, although the gift itself, hair ornaments, was no different in kind to many of the gifts he gave her later. But the subsequent gifts were given specifically in the context of a courtship, and both parties recognized the alteration in significance. While the first gift was sent openly and carried relatively little symbolic freight, the later tokens, heavy with meaning, were conveyed secretly, through an intermediary, as the courtship between Alice and Richard was opposed by her employer and family.

While Richard and Alice were in agreement about the meaning of the gifts they exchanged, in other cases there was ambiguity or disagreement regarding the intentions of the donor and the recipient. Joan Blacman, who admitted that she and John Yonge had said that they loved one another but not that they had made a contract, also denied that the gifts they exchanged—John sent her white kid gloves and a silver "cheppe" (possibly a figure of a shepherd[76] or a ship), she sent him black silk—were for the sake of marriage.[77] Elizabeth Willy had a number of ingenious explanations for the tokens that John Kendall submitted had been given to her for the sake of marriage. As she said when examined, she "gave no gifts to John Kendall nor did she receive any from him. But," she admitted,

on a certain day around the feast of Pentecost last past John came to her and borrowed from her 4d. with the intention that she would have another 4d. back for them. And on a Sunday after the feast of Pentecost, John gave her a pair of beads, asking her to give them to a certain stainer [that is, a man who stains wood for a living] living next to the tower of London, who at that time often visited the house of her sister, who lived next door to her parents. Moreover she says that this witness gave him two breast kerchiefs because John's shirt was very dirty and soiled, and John was often asked and urged by this witness to give back the kerchiefs but he would not do so and still will not.[78]

Although women might claim that items they received from men were given for safekeeping[79] or in friendship,[80] and both men and women could claim that the items were not gifts at all but loans or purchases,[81] men had an ace up their sleeve that women could not play. Several men sued for not upholding a contract claimed that gloves, rings, and other items they gave to the woman were not tokens of marriage but payment for sex.[82] William Knollys, for instance, recognized the ambiguity of intentionality in the giving and receiving of tokens, not to mention the varying interpretations a man and a woman might give to sex, but stubbornly insisted that his intentions were the ones that counted. He admitted that he had given Agnes Lanther "a pair of knives, 9d. to buy a purse, and a pair of gloves, but he did not give her these gifts for the sake of having her as his wife but rather to please her and continue with her in sin. And Agnes gave him a girdle [a kind of belt] and a belt of black silk, with the intention, he believes, of having the witness as her husband."[83] But just as important as Agnes's intentions was the spirit in which William received the gifts; both parties had to agree on the meaning of the token for it to function as a sign of marriage. The official of the Consistory agreed with William's reasoning, assigned him a penance for fornication, and dismissed the case.[84]

Tokens were not in themselves evidence to prove a contract, but they clearly had important significance socially and were of sufficient legal interest as corroboration that the exchange of gifts was frequently introduced as evidence in marriage cases. A woman who did not wish to receive the attentions of a particular suitor could make her wishes very clear by rejecting a gift: when William Yewle sent Katherine Garyngton, through her brother, a stomacher (a waistcoat or decorated cloth worn under the lacings of a bodice), she would not accept it and sent her brother to give it back to William.[85] Others tried the opposite tactic: if the contentions of some defendants are to be believed, some people went so far as to steal items from the unwilling object of their affections in the hope that the reluctant man or woman could be forced by that evidence to recognize a contract. Maude Knyff, sued by Robert Grene, claimed that Robert forcibly removed a gold ring with a blue gem from her finger on one occasion, and on another picked up a kerchief that she had been using to bandage a wound when it fell to the ground, refusing to give it back to her.[86] Agnes Fry accused John Tailour of having stolen out of her purse the silver ring he was claiming as a token.[87] Alice Markatell, responding to the claim that she and John Songer had exchanged rings as token of marriage, alleged that "John Songer violently, against her will, took a gold ring from her finger on the Sunday before Lent last past. Afterwards she asked for her ring back from John and he gave her a gold ring, which she received thinking that it was hers, but when afterwards she looked at it closely she understood that it was not hers."[88] John Remyngton denied in 1493 that he had made a contract with a woman named Alice; he admitted that he had had sex with her (although he said that this was more her fault than his, as she kept climbing into his bed at night), but he said that she had stolen the gloves that she was claiming as a token of a marriage contract from a chest in his bedchamber.[89]

Similarly, if even a stolen token meant something, although perhaps not as much as the thief hoped that it would, then so also according to some witnesses did returning tokens constitute an end to the relationship and the contract. Elizabeth Croft's sister objected to a contract that Elizabeth had made with Herbert Rowland, and according to one witness she said to Elizabeth, "Deliver him such tokens as he hath given you, and then he hath done with you."[90] The quest to recover courtship gifts sometimes sparked bitter tactics on both sides, reflecting the bruised feelings and resentment that a failed courtship could engender. Walter Goderch tried a number of different legal avenues to have returned to him the tokens he had bestowed on Thomasina Berkeley when she made a contract with another man: he first sued her before the sheriffs of London, then shifted to the king's court when it appeared that Thomasina and her new husband had the sheriff's jury in their pockets, and when that resulted in his arrest at the hands of Thomasina and her husband, he petitioned the chancellor for a remedy.[91] Walter had no doubt by this point expended more than enough expense and trouble than the 6 marks' value of his courtship gifts to Thomasina had warranted.

Courtship and Premarital Sex

Many factors were considered by the couple and by their family and friends when a marriage contract was made. Sexual attraction was undoubtedly important, although its power almost always lay beneath the surfaces of the courtship narratives that are recorded in the depositions of marital litigation. Would a couple have had sexual relations before a present-tense contract or a solemnization of their marriage? As in many Western societies, there was considerable variation in later fifteenth-century London: for some, premarital chastity was evidently important; for others, it may have meant little or nothing.[92] When the couple barely knew one another before they married—in some cases having met one another on only a few occasions before the contract was made—it is difficult to imagine that they might defer consummation of the relatio..ship until after the solemnization. In other relationships, men and women had evidently had a long sexual history, including children born of the relationship, before they made a contract of marriage. The range of expectations and attitudes toward sex before marriage—as with sex outside marriage, discussed in Part II—was far from straightforward, and the subtleties are mostly indiscernible at this historical remove. There may well have been class differences—it may have been more acceptable, for instance, for a woman of lower station to have some sexual experience before marriage, whether or not with her prospective husband, than for a daughter of a wealthy merchant. There certainly were gender differences, although not necessarily the stark double standard some historians have posited.

A woman's reputation for chastity was clearly a matter of some importance, although the way it played out in practice was complicated. Witnesses in several cases where women claimed defamation swore that these women lost value on the marriage market because of allegations of sexual misbehavior—although their hyperbolic testimony must be taken with a grain of salt. The witnesses who claimed that women were irredeemably wounded by sexual defamation were testifying on behalf of and in support of those same women: one of the paradoxes of defamation litigation was that a plaintiff had to bring forth witnesses who said that their opinion of the plaintiff had precipitously declined as a result of the uttering of the defamatory words. When Joan Rokker called Joan Sebar a "strong whore" and accused her of fornicating in a doorway, her reputation was allegedly deeply wounded. One witness said that "if this deponent were free to contract marriage, he would give her little faith or favor and would more quickly refuse to marry her because of the imposition of this crime on her."[93] Another witness in the same case said "that he believes in his conscience that the said Joan Sebar, who is a young woman and suitable for marriage, is so wounded by the speaking of these words that she will never or only with great difficulty overcome the wounding of her fame."[94] One unsuccessful suitor to a woman's hand tried to use the fragility of women's sexual reputations as a strategy to force her to marry him. When another man asked William Markis why he defamed Alice Brigge by saying he had fornicated with her, he replied, "Because she would not have me, therefore I said I lay by her that she should be loathsome to any other man." According to the witness, Markis's ploy succeeded in driving off other potential husbands, although she still did not agree to marry him.[95] By contrast, there are no instances where men's unchastity was said to make them unmarriageable, although (as I will argue in Part II) men's sexual conduct was far from irrelevant to their overall reputation and good name.

Yet what is also clear is that unchastity did not, in itself, necessarily make women unmarriageable, despite what Joan Sebar's witnesses said: many women who had had sexual relationships outside marriage were nonetheless sought as wives.[96] It is possible that their marriages were less to their advantage than they might have been otherwise, but it is difficult to determine this with the evidence we have. Compensation given to victims of rape suggests this: the rapist sometimes made a financial settlement with the victim or her family, which was to be applied to the victim's marriage as a dowry,[97] suggesting that it was assumed that the victim still could be married, although a larger dowry might be needed to compensate for her "defiled" state.

The evidence suggests that there was considerable ambiguity in particular about premarital sex, for example sexual intercourse between those who were not yet but some day would be married, as opposed to sexual intercourse between a man and a woman who never would or could marry. In some cases, both partners probably agreed on the nature of the sexual relationship. If a nobleman had sex with a scullery maid, it is improbable that either thought that the relationship would end in marriage. Likewise some couples undoubtedly unproblematically anticipated their marital sexual relationship, with neither having any hesitations about carrying through with the contract and solemnization when the time came.

In other cases, however, one partner might believe—or hope—that the sex was premarital, while the other partner had no such intention. The scenario wherein naïve maidens were seduced by unscrupulous knaves (often priests) who then abandoned them with their swelling bellies was a common subject of late medieval ballads, as Judith Bennett has elucidated.[98] In "Ladd Y the daunce [Led I the dance]," for instance, Jack the holy-water clerk promised a young and fair maid at the Midsummer dance a pair of gloves—a common token of marriage, as we have learned—if she will come with him to his chamber. The maid might plausibly have thought he meant marriage even though he was a clerk: in the mid-fifteenth-century, holy-water (or parish) clerks were increasingly likely to be wedded men.[99] She did not suspect a thing, she stresses

("Thought I on no guile" was the refrain), and after many pretty words they went to his chamber and into his bed. She passed "the merriest night that ever I came in," but afterwards was beaten by her mistress and her "womb wax[ed] out."[100] As Bennett points out, these songs carried mixed messages: the sex these maidens had was invariably very "merry," but the consequences for the woman were ruinous. The lesson a young woman might take from the singing of such songs at parish festivals and Midsummer celebrations was far more complicated than the one she might learn from the much more straightforward advice manuals: a young woman must save herself for the marriage bed, but if she does so she misses out on great delights. Women suffer the full consequences of original sin, but Jack and the other seducers of the ballads apparently get off scot-free.

Advice manuals aimed at young men were more prone to point out potential unpleasant consequences for the male partner who made promises he did not intend to keep. As Peter Idley, the author of a fifteenth-century moral treatise, put it:

> Some men give their troths privily
> Unto women with flattering countenance,
> And all is only for to lie by them . . .
> He speaketh of wedlock, but he thinketh it not
> But he would his sin were wrought.[101]

Idley noted that such "blind bargains" made "in dark corners" were liable "to the Consistory after to be led,"[102] and indeed a number of London Consistory cases feature scenarios similar to the ones Idley and the balladeers described. In the ballads, in Idley's poem, and most of the time in London marital litigation, it was the women who hoped that sex meant marriage, while the men denied it. This starkly gendered pattern is hardly surprising given the simple biological facts of pregnancy risk and the relatively greater emphasis on women's chastity.

But if the general pattern seems to have been that men dangled marriage to get sex, not all women who engaged in sexual activity wanted to marry their partners or perhaps wanted to marry at all. If naïve maidens seduced by knaves were a stock figure in late medieval English ballads, so also were lusty women who simply liked sex.[103] The legal records also show that women did not always have sex in the hope of marrying their partners and, indeed, in some cases actively resisted marriage when men

pressed it: when Margaret Isot and Thomas Wulley were caught fornicating and forced to marry, it was she, not he, who resisted enforcement of
the marriage contract.[104] Similarly, a woman of ill fame such as Nan Hop
might nonetheless resist a properly confected marriage, as in her citation
to appear before the Commissary court in 1493:

> Nan Hop is a violator of the faith and a perjurer because she contracted marriage
> with Thomas Robardson, shoemaker, and matrimonial banns were legitimately
> proclaimed between them for three Sundays in a row; notwithstanding that, she
> now denies and refuses this marriage. And as it is said, by the persuasion of John
> Norfolk, who held her in concubinage, she was persuaded to pass the night in
> stews several times. She is a contemptress of the court who says and said "curse
> and bliss, I set not a straw by the cursing there."[105]

The citation's form suggests that neither her status as Norfolk's concubine
nor her contempt of the court was the prime issue—they merely added to
and confirmed her generally unfaithful nature. The purpose of the citation,
whether it was made on Robardson's behalf or not, was to force her to
recognize her marriage with Robardson, which she was for some reason
unwilling to do. Some women preferred sex outside marriage.

Given the social and biological disadvantages of premarital sex for
women, however, it was more common for women to use sex as a bargaining chip, to withhold sex until marriage was promised (a tactic that
apparently worked well for Elizabeth Woodville, wife of Edward IV).[106] In
one case, Alice Parker attempted, almost certainly unsuccessfully, to sue
Richard Tenwinter in 1488 after an alleged contract of marriage was made
while they were in bed together. In Richard's own version of the story—
largely corroborated by Alice's only witness, who overheard the conversation while standing in the hall of the house—Richard and his friend
Robert Adcok went together to the house in which Alice lived. Adcok
waited downstairs while Richard and Alice went up to her bedchamber;
once he was alone with Alice in her bedchamber, Richard pleaded with
her to let him spend the night with her. She at first demurred (she was
afraid the butcher, who lived in the next room, an early riser, would see
him leave), but then she relented, saying that he could stay if he would
marry her. He responded, "I will wed you as well as I can," by which he
meant, he later told the court, that he would have sex with her, and so he
did, that night and for many nights thereafter. That was as far as his "wedding" went, however; as far as he was concerned, he had not made a contract of marriage, and given the vagueness of the words exchanged and

the lack of a second witness, it is improbable the judge would have found in Alice's favor.[107]

The similarities between premarital and concubinal relationships provided considerable room for uncertainty and competing claims—and for parties to attempt to use those ambiguities to different effect, on the one hand to claim an unusually advantageous marriage and on the other to gain sexual access. A young man named John Crosby, for instance, was sued in 1494 by a woman named Agnes Eston, who alleged that the two had contracted marriage.[108] It is likely that the John Crosby in this court case was identical with the man of the same name who was the son and heir of the late and very wealthy Sir John Crosby, alderman; if the John Crosby of this court case was indeed one and the same with the alderman's son, he was probably in his mid to late teens when the relationship with Agnes first developed in about 1491 and would come into a large fortune when he came of age (in the late fifteenth-century the age of majority for men was usually somewhere between twenty-one and twenty-six).[109] Agnes Eston's antecedents, on the other hand, are obscure; she lived, probably as a servant, with relatives named Thomas and Alice Spencer and was almost certainly of lower socioeconomic station than Crosby, although of sufficiently high estate to be described (probably flatteringly) as a gentlewoman. As witnesses in the case alleged, Crosby often came to visit Agnes at Spencer's house, and the Spencers apparently allowed the couple a considerable amount of freedom during these visits: as Thomas Spencer testified, John came frequently, going up to Agnes's chamber where "they communicated familiarly between themselves."[110] Crosby reportedly gave Spencer money for Agnes's upkeep, saying, "Brother Spencer, let this gentlewoman want no manner of thing, for whatsoever she takes, I will content it."[111] Although the money Crosby offered might well have been interpreted differently, the Spencers in their testimony presented it as the financial support of a future wife rather than payment for sex; this interpretation was bolstered by their testimony that Crosby acknowledged before them that he and Agnes had contracted marriage and were "man and wife before God."[112] Other witnesses testifying on Agnes's behalf—including Master William Dawbeney, a papal notary and proctor for marriage cases appealed to the papacy—similarly testified both that Crosby often spoke of having contracted marriage with Agnes and that he wished to sell a gold chain worth £50 sterling to support their marriage.[113] But if Agnes and John did contract marriage together, Agnes was unable to produce any witnesses who were present at the time—they may have been married before God but not before man. As usual, there is no evidence about what the court decided in this case, but it is hard to see how Agnes could have won given that she had no witnesses to a contract. The John Crosby who was son of the alderman died in 1501, unmarried.[114]

This case raises interesting issues about marital strategies pursued by young women and those who surrounded them. The Spencers—Agnes's employers and thus responsible for her conduct and reputation—were unusually complicit in (or at least unusually willing to acknowledge their complicity in) the apparent sexual relationship between Agnes and John. But allowing Crosby sexual access to their servant may have seemed to them to be a reasonable risk under the circumstances. Crosby suggested that he viewed their relationship seriously and marrying the heir of Sir John Crosby would have been a significant rise in status for virtually any woman. But it was a precarious course and at least one of Agnes Eston's witnesses seems to have seen it as naïve: John Baynard testified that when Agnes told him that John Crosby was going to marry her, he told her to make sure that she had trustworthy witnesses. Perhaps John Crosby at one point really did mean to marry Agnes: a quixotic young man of fourteen or fifteen—and John Crosby may have been that young at the time the relationship began—could have been maneuvered into making a canonical marriage that would have been very much to his social, political, and economic disadvantage. Indeed, Crosby may have hoped that he and Agnes, who would probably have been denied access to Crosby's inheritance until he came of age, could live from selling off chattels such as his valuable gold chain. But whatever his initial intentions, Crosby never actually made a contract that could be proved in court. If Agnes Eston and the Spencers were playing a high-risk game with John Crosby, he could easily have been double-dealing with them, being careful to maintain the hope that he would make the relationship legitimate but never actually making a witnessed contract. A later case supports this possibility: in 1495, William Warton accused Crosby of having seduced his daughter Lucy away from the service of her mistress and into a life of misrule and dishonest conduct.[115]

*   *   *

What does this tell us about men, women, and gender in late medieval London? My findings here generally support what might be called a pessimistic vision of gender relations in later medieval England, wherein the fundamental paradigm held women to be dependent on and subordinate to their menfolk. Women's resistance to their relatively more restricted freedom of choice in marriage took forms that tended to reinforce that paradigm through manipulation of its basic premises. The cultural expectations about behavior during courtship had considerable importance for gender and identity in late medieval English society, setting a basic pattern for male-female behavior in the central social institution of late medieval society, the family.

3

By the Father's Will
and the Friends' Counsel

IN THE SPRING of 1488, Margaret Heed and William Hawkyns discussed marriage. Both were of London's merchant elite: Margaret was the daughter of Henry Heed, ironmonger and citizen, while William Hawkyns was later described as a citizen and a salter. Sometime in early to mid-April, Margaret agreed to marry William, and banns were issued twice in Margaret's parish of St. Sepulchre over the coming weeks. The marital process apparently progressed normally—in addition to the banns, wedding clothes and ornaments were prepared—until Whit week (the week following Pentecost, seven weeks after Easter), when Margaret began to show reluctance to go ahead with the marriage. On Whit Tuesday (27 May 1488), Margaret's father, Henry, confronted her in William Hawkyns's presence, asking her point-blank whether she wished to marry William or not. He assured her that it was her decision to make, referring to the canonical doctrine of consent: "I have been with thy uncle, prior of Hertford, and it is his will and mine also that thou shalt have thy free liberty to take an husband where thou wilt, and not to take Hawkyns but it come of thine own stomach." Whatever hesitations Margaret might have previously had, on that day she affirmed her agreement to marry Hawkyns: "him will I have and none other."

Two days later, however, the storm that had obviously been threatening finally broke. On Thursday, 29 May, Margaret's maternal grandfather, William Fleet, came to Henry Heed's house to tell him what he had just heard from a man named Copwode about Margaret and his son: the elder Copwode had told Fleet that Margaret loved his son better than William Hawkyns. When Henry Heed confronted Margaret about this other relationship, she admitted that she did indeed love the young Copwode. At this her father cried, "Thou whore, why didst not thou tell me this before?" He began to beat her, frustrated (as his wife, Margaret's stepmother, later testified) because Margaret had so many times said that she wanted to marry William Hawkyns, and banns had been read and clothing and ornaments "for Margaret's body" had been prepared for the nuptials. Although just two days before Margaret had given in to her father, this time she remained adamant, crying repeatedly even as her father beat her, "I will never have Hawkyns!" Margaret fled later that day to her grandfather's house, telling him that her father had forced her to contract with William Hawkyns and that she had never wanted to have Hawkyns as her husband. Her grandfather chided her, telling her that she should have told her father that she did not want to marry William before the banns were read.

Margaret stayed at her grandfather's house until Friday, when he and Gregory Brent, an ironmonger like her father, led her back to her father's house, seemingly repentant and at last ready to acquiesce. Gregory Brent later said that he then urged her, "Cousin Margaret, establish your mind, and I pray send Hawkyns some word of comfort." Chastened, she answered, "When was he here? I have said so much against him I am ashamed to speak with him." Brent, with Margaret's consent, went to get Hawkyns and brought him back to Margaret's father's house. When William Hawkyns arrived, Margaret said to him, "I am ashamed that I have said and done to you as I have. I am sure if ye marry with me ye will love me the worse." He replied that if she would make up her mind he would not hold it against her, but would forgive her all the things that she had done. Margaret's father came in and asked her, "Thou, girl, wilt thou have Hawkyns here to thy husband?" She answered, "Yea, father." Henry Heed warned her, "Say not one tonight and another tomorrow," and she answered, "Nay, father." William Hawkyns gave her five nobles in silver as a token. The next morning, Saturday, 31 May 1488, a number of people, including her grandfather and his wife, gathered at the house of Henry Heed to hear the contract. Henry Heed again asked his daughter to be sure of her mind: "Then, girl, say now before these honest men whether thou wilt have Hawkyns in thy husband or no, for it is my brother's will, the prior of Hertford, that I shall not marry thee against thy will. Say now whether thou wilt have him or no." She affirmed that she would, and following the instructions of Henry Heed, William and Margaret exchanged vows of future consent.

Although the story of Margaret Heed and William Hawkyns as told in testimony offered in the Consistory court finishes there, the fact that the case ended up in court tells us that there was another act or two in the

drama: in mid-June William Hawkyns sued Margaret to uphold the contract made on 31 May, indicating that although Margaret had apparently
acquiesced on that Saturday, in the weeks following she once again
moved into a position of resistance. Margaret's father, stepmother, grandfather, and two other men testified on William's behalf before the Consistory.[1] No witnesses appeared for Margaret, although the testimony of
several of the witnesses was equivocal on the question of how much coercion was involved in Margaret's consent on that Saturday. There is, as
usual, no record of the judgment in the case: it would not have been implausible for the official to have found that the contract was void because
of coercion. But Margaret did marry William Hawkyns, as is clear from
her father's will,[2] and they lived together as husband and wife until 1515,
when William died. They had at least three children together, and William
left Margaret a wealthy widow.[3]

    There are various ways to read this case. Margaret's vacillations were
clearly frustrating to all who were concerned with her marriage, and one
interpretation would see Margaret as a foolish and intermittently stubborn girl who could not make up her mind and who failed to see that her
elders knew better. Her father was forced to take harsh measures—
beating her, testifying against her in the case—in what he probably saw as
Margaret's best interest. As he apparently said many times, at least twice
explicitly linking the issue with the ecclesiastical opinion of his brother,
the prior of Hertford,[4] she was to have free choice in the matter of her
marriage partner, and he did not want her to marry William Hawkyns
"but it come of [her] own stomach." Nonetheless she was not free to
keep changing her mind, especially after she had made a contract. In the
long term, she and her father were apparently not estranged: he made her
a bequest, and her husband, William Hawkyns, described as "well beloved
son," was a supervisor to Heed's will.[5]

    Another interpretation, however, could be considerably more sympa-
thetic to Margaret. She was evidently young and had less control over the
situation in a real sense than her theological right to freedom of choice
suggested. Her father may have paid lip service to the idea that she must
consent to the marriage, but his actions—beating her and calling her a
whore when she said that she wanted to marry elsewhere—said otherwise.
Henry Heed was involved in another case before the Consistory, accused
of defaming one of his apprentices in public, where the witnesses suggested that he was an intemperate man, prone to outrageous outbursts.[6]
Margaret was indeed inconstant, but arguably not out of sheer flightiness;

she was not always able to gather the strength of will to oppose her father's wish that she marry William Hawkyns. Her right to withhold consent from a contract she was unwilling to make was not untrammeled, but
was subject to pressure from all sides. She had no allies: when she tried to
appeal to her maternal grandfather, she did not find that he was willing to
support her cause. Thus she intermittently gave in to what might have
been unendurable pressure; she had suffered the banns to be read twice,
and then after the terrible episode with her father on the Thursday of
Whit week she gave in, agreeing to make a contract with William Hawkyns
despite herself. But later she once again refused to honor that contract, at
which point the final weapon was brought into play: William sued her in
the Consistory, and her father, her stepmother, and her grandfather all
testified against her. Whether she won or lost the case, the cards were
stacked against her, and she married William Hawkyns.

What "really" happened is, of course, impossible for us to re-create
and in any case was probably experienced and interpreted quite differently
by the individuals who were involved. What is clear is that to speak of
Margaret's choice of marriage partner as being "free" would be to under-
estimate the extent to which her choices were circumscribed by the pressures exerted against her by her father and other family members. Her
own possibly vacillating mind could not make a choice without being
subject not only to the forcefully expressed will of her father but also to
the expectations of a daughter of a wealthy and well-connected citizen.
She was to be obedient and respectful of her father's wishes; she was to
behave responsibly; she was to be mindful of her father's expenses already
made in preparation for the wedding. The elements of life below the surface of the documents that may well have been obvious to all involved in
the case, including the Consistory official, but which remain invisible to
us now, would help us further if we had access to them. The relative ages
of William and Margaret may have been a factor, for instance: although
Margaret was clearly young, repeatedly addressed as "girl," there is no evidence at all about William's age. The identity of Copwode, the other
man to whom Margaret had given her love, may also have been critical to
the drama. Perhaps William was a steady but unexciting fellow, physically
unattractive, while the unknown Copwode was dashing, young, and hand-
some, yet poor, or irresponsible, or even a gold digger.

While canon law gave the man and the woman making the contract
of marriage the exclusive right to make, or refuse to make, a marital bond,
in social practice the making of marriage was much more complex. There

is little evidence to support the old chestnut that all medieval marriages were arranged by fathers or lords—below elite social levels, at least, late medieval English men and women usually chose their mates themselves— but at the same time, a decision as important as the choice of spouse was not made without recourse to the advice, help, and sometimes the consent or even the coercion of the important people in a young man's or young woman's life.[7] The pressure exerted by Margaret Heed's father and other family members and friends in her marriage choice was more explicit than in most other situations and was partly a reflection of her relatively elevated social status and the high level of economic exchange that such a marriage represented, but by no means was the participation of others in the making of her marriage decisions unusual. There was probably a correlation between the amount of property that changed hands on the occasion of a marriage and the level of control or influence exerted by third parties in the making of a marital bond,[8] but it seems likely that few, if any, English people married one another completely independent of the participation of others in the process.

The sensitive and subtle negotiations surrounding a courtship— indication of interest, conveying of gifts, asking of questions—often resembled a choreographed dance featuring many performers rather than a pas de deux. A man and woman contemplating marriage did not make decisions about this all-important life step in a vacuum, but were surrounded by families, friends, employers, and neighbors who gave advice, acted as go-betweens, and witnessed the exchange of vows. As the fourteenth-century poem "How the Goodwife taught her Daughter" put it, a young woman should consult her friends if she received a proposal of marriage: "If any man . . . would wed thee, . . . show it to thy friends."[9] The poet William Langland similarly assumed the participation of intermediaries, fathers, and friends as well as the man and woman themselves in the formation of a marriage:

> And thus was wedlock wrought • with an intermediary [mene
>   persone];
> First by the father's will • and the friends' counsel
> And then by assent of themselves • as they two might accord.[10]

In fifteenth-century usage, a person's "friends" were those on whom he or she might rely for advice and advancement, especially in important matters such as marriage or career. Friends were not usually in the same age cohort, but older, and included both nonkin and kin.[11] They played roles in both helping a young man or woman find a suitable marriage partner and coaching them along the road to making a canonical marriage, but they also often held the purse strings—guardians of orphans, for instance, who controlled the disposition of the inheritance, were often known as friends.[12] Those without friends might find it difficult to marry; one London testator bequeathed £20 for the marriage of twenty "poor maidens" of London "having few friends and little sustenance or help to marry them withal."[13] Langland's "mene persone" and "friends" are evinced also in the records of marital litigation from the fifteenth century, their roles frequently proving instrumental in courtship and entry into marriage.

A typical "mene person's," or intermediary's, role was played by William Love, an embroiderer and parish clerk of the church of St. Botolph Billingsgate, London. He testified in the 1469 case of *Robert Pope c. Lucy Braggis* that he had been "a mediator between [Robert and Lucy], and he had made efforts to induce them to contract marriage between them, having been asked to do so by both parties."[14] William Love, whose status as parish clerk probably gave him a certain authority, was evidently not related to either Robert Pope or Lucy Braggis[15]—indeed intermediaries were ideally disinterested or at least equally interested in both parties. At Pope's request, Love privately asked Lucy Braggis if she was committed to any other man and if she was interested in Pope. He then relayed her reply back to Pope—she was free of commitments and she was agreeable to speak and drink with him. Soon after, according to Love, the pair formally contracted marriage following a Sunday dinner in his house, Love himself acting as witness. He testified that his young stepdaughter and servant also heard the contract, eavesdropping from a balcony overlooking the hall where Love, Lucy, and Robert were eating. Love's wife, Alice, deposed that after this contract, she also participated in the courtship, albeit in a more informal capacity, bringing gifts from one to the other.[16] This sponsorship of a marriage by an older married man, sometimes with the help of his wife, was characteristic of the path many couples followed to matrimony.

If friends could help to make a marriage, they could also break it. Beatrice Thomson, like many other mistresses of marriageable young women, took it upon herself to find a husband for Alice Billingham, a young woman recently come into service with her. Beatrice testified that around Easter 1486, she approached a former servant, a skinner named

John Wellis, and suggested that he consider her servant Alice for a wife. John replied that he wanted to see her first, and when he had seen her, he told Beatrice that "her person pleased him well [*placuit sibi bene persona eiusdem Alicie*]," and that if her friends were willing to offer a sufficient marriage portion, "it may fortune I will marry with her."[17] Soon after this conversation, Beatrice, on Alice's behalf and at her request, gave John a jemew (a two-part ring) of gilt silver or gold.[18] At least at first, Beatrice appeared to think that the relationship was progressing as it should. According to another witness, around the time of her advances to John Wellis, Beatrice came to the shop of Alice's brother, Robert Billingham,[19] where she told two of Billingham's servants, "I am glad that ever Alice Billingham came in mine house, for I trust to God she shall have a good husband." It was a done deal, she intimated: "and she is as sure as I except wed."[20] She told others, too, that Alice Billingham and John Wellis were imminently to solemnize their marriage, and invited these others to offer at the mass with them.[21] Within the neighborhood, word of the relationship spread: as Robert Wild testified, he heard many people say when they saw John Wellis crossing the street, "yonder goeth Alice Billingham's husband."[22]

For some reason, the relationship soured, and Beatrice herself no longer worked for the marriage but against it. Agnes Bullok and Constance Stileman both testified that they heard Beatrice boasting that what she had made she could unmake: "I have made a marriage between Alice Billingham and [John[23]] Wellis, and her brother would give any goods with her. And she is stubborn of heart; it is a pity that ever she should meet with him. I will bring it as backward as ever I brought it forward."[24] Beatrice Thomson's most crucial and powerful role came not in her talk among her neighbors, however, but in her role as witness in the case brought before the Consistory court. Alice Billingham's case against John Wellis was based on a contract she claimed had been made before two witnesses: Agnes Weston, who testified that the two exchanged vows of present consent, and Beatrice Thomson, who denied that any such contract had taken place.[25] Whether Beatrice was telling the truth when she said that she had witnessed no contract, or whether she was perjuring herself either as John Wellis's friend or simply out of displeasure with Alice, Beatrice indeed did have the power to make or break the marriage as she allegedly boasted. The participation of another set of Alice's friends in bringing the suit is also evident: some of the witnesses said that they testified at the request of William Maryner and his wife, whose relationship to

Alice is unclear, but who unmistakably played the role of "friends" in their aid to her in organizing and possibly financing the case.[26]

As in *Billingham c. Wellis*, the help friends gave to men and women trying to enter or escape from a marriage came in various forms: making preliminary advances to suitable candidates, arranging for the two to meet under appropriate circumstances, conveying gifts from one to the other, spreading word of the marriage, and if a problem arose in completing the marriage, organizing, financing, and testifying (possibly perjuriously) in a case before the Consistory. Henry Brond, a fifty-two-year-old citizen cordwainer, played the role of mediator and friend, indeed substitute father, in the courtship between William Halley and Agnes Wellis, at the request of Agnes's mother. Brond testified that in the late spring of 1487, Margery Butler, Agnes Wellis's mother, came to him and told him that William Halley came frequently to her house to visit Agnes. "I understand he hath pretty livelihood and me think it should be a meetly marriage between my daughter and him," she said. "I pray you wit [discover] whether there be any contract between them or none, or else make one, for it is told me he is sent for by a letter to Coventry to have another marriage." At Margery Butler's request, Brond came to her house and in a parlor he found William and Agnes talking together. He asked William, "God speed you, ye be always together; show me your mind, in what intent ye come hither? It is noised ye shall have this damsel." William replied, "by my troth, I come hither in none other intent, and that knoweth God, and she knoweth my mind as well as any man." Brond then prompted the couple to make a contract by future consent.[27]

Friends were not always as benevolent and evenhanded as Henry Brond painted himself to be; they could exert a considerable amount of pressure on men or women unwilling to make a final commitment, sometimes manipulating them into making marriages that could have been considered unsuitable. Joan Blacman, for instance, the orphaned daughter of a citizen tailor, was arguably bullied into making a contract with John Yonge. Joan had engaged in courting activity with John Yonge in January 1467: they drank together at the sign of the Ave Maria in Billingsgate, and through their mutual friend, Joan Boon, John sent Joan a number of gifts, including white gloves and a piece of black silk. In early February, about seven o'clock in the morning, Joan Blacman met Thomas Boon (Joan Boon's husband) in the street in the parish of St. Mary at Hill, and Thomas told her that he and his wife expected her at breakfast that morning. She went to the Boons' house, but while she was upstairs

in a chamber, she heard John Yonge downstairs in the hall: as Joan Blacman later implied in her testimony, she realized at that point that she had
been set up by the Boons, and she refused to come down and talk with
Yonge. At length, however, she was persuaded to come down into the
hall and breakfast with Yonge and the Boons. At the end of the meal,
John Yonge took a groat out of his purse to pay for his meal, but Thomas
and Joan Boon refused to accept the groat, and so instead John Yonge
took the groat, added two more, and put them into a silk purse and gave
them to Joan. After the meal, Joan went back upstairs to the chamber and
Thomas and Joan Boon followed her. In the chamber Thomas Boon
urged her to contract with John Yonge, as otherwise he would fall into a
rage. Thomas called John into the chamber. John came in and, holding
both her hands, said to her that Thomas Boon had told him that she
loved him, and she replied that Thomas Boon had said the same to her.
Both admitted that they loved one another in an honest way (*in modo
honesto*). This was as far as Joan Blacman was willing to admit the relationship progressed; when John Yonge later sued her in the Consistory, Joan
denied that they had done more than exchange words of love. John
Yonge, however, brought forth two witnesses, Joan Boon and Christine
Complyn, who said that on that day Joan and John had gone beyond
words of love, exchanging words of present consent in the upper chamber
of the Boons' house. In their depositions, both witnesses emphasized that
Joan Blacman had not been coerced in any way: Joan had come to the
house voluntarily, and neither witness had made any efforts on John's behalf. Christine Complyn added, revealingly, that "she believed in her conscience that even if Joan's friends had been present there, Joan would
have contracted in the same way with John Yonge."[28]

Where *were* Joan's friends? Joan was a minor in July 1466, and thus at
the time of the alleged contract six months later still very young, probably
in her later teens at most, with a moderately sizeable inheritance, chattels
worth about £25.[29] Such a young woman should have been closely supervised to keep her from falling into a situation precisely such as the one in
which she found herself, contracted to a man of whom her friends did not
approve. Although there is no record that either her widowed mother
(still alive in 1466) or the other trustees of her inheritance as an orphan of
the City became involved in the situation, her employer Simon Wryxworth, the man responsible for supervising her social life, did. Wryxworth
was apparently incensed that John Yonge had made a contract with Joan
Blacman without his consent and was even more angry when John Yonge

won his case in the Consistory. Evidently Wryxworth tried in some way to interfere with the solemnization of the marriage, for which he was later summoned to appear before the Consistory. There he admitted that he had said that he would rather spend £40 than see John Yonge have Joan Blacman "against justice."[30] Witnesses appearing on John Yonge's behalf testified that Wryxworth's words were somewhat stronger. According to Robert Thypthorpe, Wryxworth said that he would see John Yonge hanged by the neck before he would see them married. William Myddylton reported that soon after the day of the contract between John Yonge and Joan Blacman, Wryxworth sued Yonge before the sheriff's court in the Guildhall, probably on a plea of trespass for having withdrawn his servant. Myddylton tried to intervene on John Yonge's behalf, pleading with Wryxworth to dismiss his rancor against John Yonge, but Wryxworth replied that he wanted to make John Yonge sorry that he had contracted with his servant against his will; he would not let John in peace, he said, until John had spent every last penny he had. Yonge apparently also encountered some difficulties claiming Joan Blacman's inheritance from the chamberlain of the city, and Myddylton acted on his behalf there too.[31]

The marriage between Joan Blacman and John Yonge thus became a battle fought on various levels, involving a number of different kinds of friends playing various roles. The Boons acted on John Yonge's behalf, Joan Boon acting as a go-between in the giving of gifts to Joan, Thomas Boon performing the delicate work both of conveying words of love from each to the other and of using a certain amount of coercive pressure on Joan (the specter of John's fury if she did not contract) so that she should give her consent to John. Joan Blacman's own friends may have been unaware of the situation until after the day of the alleged contract, but soon after, Joan's employer, Simon Wryxworth, acted quickly and forcefully in taking out a plea against John Yonge before the sheriff's court. Wryxworth's motives appear to have been a mixture of pique and righteous indignation that John Yonge should have stolen his servant from under his nose; his ill will, and his overreaction, may have been increased by his own sense of responsibility for having allowed the situation to get out of hand (Joan's examination suggests that she and John Yonge had had plenty of opportunity for uninhibited courting). When Wryxworth began his campaign against John Yonge, however, other friends came to Yonge's assistance, helping him both in attempting to arbitrate with Wryxworth and in acting on his behalf in collecting Joan Blacman's inheritance.[32]

Employers such as Simon Wryxworth had a duty to ensure that their servants were not married improperly. A number of Chancery cases were occasioned by employers who stood in the way of a marriage contracted by one (or sometimes two) of their servants. Richard Osborn and Alice Bonyfey, for instance, were both living in the household of John Olney, a mercer and former London mayor, as servants. They decided that they wanted to marry, but feared doing so openly would displease Olney. Richard Osborn instead asked three other men, including a notary, to come to the house and witness the contract; Richard and Alice contracted marriage before them, "meaning no harm nor malice in that matter." Predictably Olney was enraged, and he sued Richard Osborn and the three witnesses to the contract for withdrawing his servant.[33] Other masters sought to ensure that relationships proceeded appropriately and respectably. John Ely was courting Agnes Whitingdon when he was confronted by her master, a man named Hawkyn, who asked him if he wanted to marry Agnes. Eventually Hawkyn pressured Ely to make a contract with her.[34] William Hylle, tailor of London, similarly testified that William Chapman had frequented his home so many times that finally he asked Chapman why he came so often. Chapman replied that he came out of love for Hylle's servant, Joan Walter. Soon after, presumably at William Hylle's arrangement, Chapman came to the house and in the presence of a number of witnesses gathered for the occasion, he and Joan exchanged vows.[35] Joan Audely testified that she had heard her father questioning John Crosby about his numerous visits to his house, and Crosby replied that he wished to marry Isabel Hamond, Audely's servant. There and then Hamond and Crosby exchanged consent.[36]

Not only did employers have the duty to prevent inappropriate marriages, but they had certain kinds of privileges in controlling their servants' relationships: by secular law, they could charge a man who married one of their servants for withdrawing that servant. Similarly, apprentices were commonly forbidden to marry during the term of their service. This clash between individualistic notions of marriage choice promoted by the church's doctrine of consent and the patriarchal rights of employers and heads of households resulted in some unhappiness; as Antony Pontisbury, apprentice to London mercer William Marlond, complained in the early sixteenth century when his master forbade his marriage, rules forbidding apprentices from marrying were "contrary to the laws of God and causeth much fornication and adultery to be within the said city."[37]

Modern sympathies tend to lie with the apprentices making their pleas for freedom to marry, but by the standards of the fifteenth century their duties toward their employers were more important. While apprentices or servants were permitted by church law to marry whom they would, their employers might have felt that in such cases their apprentices' obligations to them had been so rashly violated that suits before secular courts, whether warranted or feigned, were justified in order to prevent or damage a marriage or simply to vex those who were disobedient. Sometimes it seemed necessary to manipulate the law so that justice would be served. Certainly it was frequently necessary to manipulate the law in order to gain one's own objective. Chancery and Consistory court cases show that such maneuvers were by no means infrequent.

In some cases, employers used strong tactics to encourage rather than prevent the marriage of their servants, or at least so alleged William Gerardson in his petition to the chancellor. Gerardson, a beer brewer, told the chancellor between 1475 and 1485 that over the previous year, when he had been in and out of the house of John Evan, delivering beer, Evan had frequently "exhorted, moved, and willed" him to take one of Evan's servants as his wife. But because the servant was "of no virtuous condition, as the said John more largely knowith,"[38] Gerardson refused to marry her, for which reason Evan "grievously troubled" Gerardson. Evan took out an action of trespass against him before the sheriffs of London, alleging that he had come into Evan's house without permission and beaten the said servant, to the damage of £20. This was utterly untrue, Gerardson averred, but Evan had at his will "such persons impanelled in the inquest, which been quotidianly used to pass in juries and have right small conscience," and they would surely find against Gerardson because he was Dutch and a stranger, and he would be thrown in jail unless he wedded the said servant.[39]

It was not only male employers who had a hand in supervising, promoting, or discouraging marriages: women who were mistresses of households not infrequently took it upon themselves to see those servants, usually young women of marriageable age, properly settled in marriage. We have already seen Beatrice Thomson's efforts both for and against Alice Billingham's marriage to John Wellis. Other mistresses also undertook an active role in finding their servants husbands, especially in cases where the young woman's parents lived some distance away, when the mistress might be deputed to speak for them. Joan Ingaldesthorp, for instance, the widow of a knight and the sister of an earl, was the mistress of Isabel Merley, niece of Sir William Plumpton of Yorkshire. When a marriage was "moved" between Isabel and Thomas Batell, a London mercer, Lady Ingaldesthorp consulted Sir William about what Isabel was to have for her dowry. He gave her certain guidelines, but otherwise left the negotiations to her discretion. She and Batell came to an agreement, the marriage was contracted, and she paid 40 marks to Batell on Sir William's behalf.[40] The Consistory court case *Joan Burgh c. John Spenser* gives a more detailed account of how a mistress might go about proposing a marriage. One day in mid-August 1471 widow and silkwoman Margaret Hawkyn made advances on behalf of her servant, Joan Burgh, toward John Spenser. Margaret went to visit John at his home, where she told him that she knew of a woman suitable for him; she was able to promise, on behalf of Joan's friends, a marriage portion of £40 and fifty quarters of malt. John replied that he would like to see such a woman and talk with her; if indeed she would bring £40 with her, he would be very interested in contracting marriage with her. After these "mediations and discussions [*mediaciones et communicaciones*]," John came to Margaret Hawkyn's house a number of times, where he and Joan talked, ate, and drank together. About three weeks after her initial proposal of the match, Margaret Hawkyn again went to John Spenser's house, where she again urged him to come and speak more formally with Joan at any place he cared to name. John subsequently met with Joan at the home of a third party, Thomas Clyfford, where (according to Margaret Hawkyn) John promised to ride to Stourbridge fair, near Cambridge, to talk to Joan's parents in person.[41] The proposed match apparently came to nought: although Joan Burgh sued John Spenser in the Consistory, her sole witness, Margaret Hawkyn, could only testify that she believed there had been a contract, but she had not actually heard one herself.[42] Such forward behavior would have been unsuitable for the young woman herself, yet her mistress, twice widowed, evidently active in her own trade, and (probably) of elevated social status, could play such a role without scandal. And perhaps Margaret Hawkyn would not have been so bold on her own behalf; another wealthy and prominent widow, Maude Knyff, was more demure than Margaret Hawkyn, but she was the prospective bride, not an intermediary.[43] The reactive or passive female role was particularly important when advertising oneself as a potential wife, but less important outside that context.

Both women and men could act as intermediaries, although the scope of the mediator's activity depended somewhat on gender. Women's roles were usually informal and especially involved the conveyance of gifts from one partner to the other; in the case of mistresses of households, sometimes, as we have seen, women might go so far as to approach suitable candidates to propose matches for their female servants. Men's roles similarly included the more subtle and informal aspects of the courtship game, but extended additionally to more formal participation in the making of the marriage. As we saw in Chapter 1, senior men in a position of authority—frequently with a familial relationship with one of the principals, but often enough simply interested parties—played a particularly important role in the process of courtship and marriage. Apart from prompting couples who were keeping company to take the next step and acting as a go-between in negotiations before the agreement to marry, the senior man present at a contract of marriage often officiated in a formal sense at the exchange of consent, taking the place of the priest in instructing the couple on the precise words and gestures that would make a valid exchange of consent. There is no evidence that the men who presided over these marriages received or hoped to receive any financial compensation for their services as mediators or presiders, as might be the case for the marriage brokers sometimes used by the nobility or gentry. It seems that in relation to marriages of lower-status people, such activities were viewed as the responsibility and privilege of men of a certain age and status.

Third-Party Consent and Contracting Marriage

While many men and women were helped and influenced by family, friends, employers, and neighbors in the making of their marriages, in some cases the participation of other parties was even more marked, as when the marriage was made conditional on the consent of third parties, usually parents, guardians, or employers. While the permission of others was not required to create a valid marriage, nonetheless, late medieval women and men often consulted their parents and other "friends" when making this crucial life decision. Sometimes they even refused to make such a commitment without the consent of the important people in their lives, asserting that they would, or could, marry no one without it. Legally, only the present consent of the principals was necessary to create a binding contract of marriage; but socially, the right and wise thing to do was to marry with the advice and sometimes the consent of relatives, employers, and friends. Sometimes the wisdom of this course was bolstered by the economic control exercised by parents or guardians: in some cases, men and women who chose to marry without parents' or guardians' consent stood to lose marriage portions or inheritances, a sacrifice many were not willing to make.

According to witnesses giving testimony in the late medieval London church courts, most late fifteenth-century couples from the metropolis and its environs made no explicit reference to the consent of others when they married one another. In the majority of cases, the principals exchanged consent unconditionally ("I John take you Margaret" and "I Margaret take you John") in a domestic setting before witnesses. This corroborates what Michael Sheehan and others have argued: that young people below elite social levels routinely chose prospective mates for themselves through the normal course of social interaction and that the canonical requirement of consent was typically observed.[44] But, as I observed earlier, couples did not find and marry one another in a social vacuum; the people who lived around a couple—their relatives, friends, neighbors, and employers—assisted, prodded, and mediated in the making of a marriage. Most exchanged consent in the presence of family, employers, or significant others of some sort, indicating their tacit consent to the match. This was especially true of women and of those who were marrying young and for the first time.

Thus for many, consent of parents or others acting in their place was implicit.[45] Less common was the practice of making a contract of marriage explicitly conditional on the consent of family or friends. But by no means was this unusual; witnesses in about twenty-five cases in the late fifteenth-century London deposition books testified that such a condition was made. Typical of these was the response of Joan Kenryk of London, who testified that she answered William Heley's proposal of marriage in 1468 thus: "if she could acquire and have the will and consent of her great-grandfather, David Kenryk, she freely wished to consent to have him."[46] Such a condition was not necessary for all, but was well within the range of expected behavior for young people embarking on matrimony. As in the case of Margaret Heed, the rhetoric of free choice often coexisted with strong expectations that young people, especially young women of some fortune, should marry with the advice of their friends. In 1454 the London merchant Thomas Hawkyn bequeathed £200 each to his under-age and unmarried daughters, Elizabeth and Joan, under the twin conditions that they "be married wisely and discreetly after the counsel and advice of mine and their friends most wise and discreet, and be not married against their will nor had away by force." Hawkyn emphasized the importance of Elizabeth and Joan marrying wisely by adding "that if any of mine said daughters cast away herself contrary to this my will, or live uncleanly, that then the part of her so doing be equally divided between [her brothers]."[47]

While the twenty-five cases from the Consistory deposition books that involve contracts conditional on third-party consent were by no means atypical of general expectations in late medieval English society, they do have one striking (although again hardly surprising) element: gender difference. About four-fifths of those who made this qualification were women. The depositions as a whole show that young men often acted independently in their marriage choices, whereas young women were more reliant on and subject to the involvement of parents and others in making this pivotal decision. These roles prefigured the relative status of obedient and dependent wives and decisive and independent husbands.

The involvement of other parties besides the principals in the formation of a marriage, offering advice, mediating, or in fact making the marriage decision themselves through the giving or withholding of consent, indicates a number of things about the courtship process. Expectations that young people, especially women, would marry according to the wishes of those older and wiser sometimes indicated a real conviction on the parts of the principals and the advisors that a good marriage would result.[48] At other times, the invocation of parental approval reflected the financial or physical power some parents wielded over their young marriageable daughters or sons: he who pays the piper calls the tune. But appeal to the consent of third parties could also be used as a strategy in marital negotiations, especially by women whose reactive role in courtship left them few other ways to control the process.[49]

Both partners sometimes used the condition of parental approval pro forma, as a courtesy that established good relations in the future between parents and the newly married couple. When Maude Gyll was asked in 1491 if she would take Laurence Wyberd as her husband, she answered yes, but conditionally: "with my father's leave and my mother's." Her parents, who were there present, immediately replied, almost formulaically, "Thou shalt have good leave thereto, and God's blessing and ours."[50] When Elizabeth Isaak and John Bolde exchanged consent in 1470, Elizabeth placed the proviso that her twenty-year-old brother, witnessing the contract, would give his consent. He, like Maude Gyll's parents, immediately proffered his blessing, thereby fulfilling the condition.[51]

The bride's invitations to her family to participate, in effect, in her offer of consent to the union deflected part of the decision making onto a third party, so that a young woman not socialized to be decisive might be relieved of some of that burden. Equally important, such invocations also helped to secure the goodwill of the bride's parents. John Bolde says this explicitly when later he met Elizabeth Isaak's mother, Beatrice Isaak, and asked her approval of the match, "to this end, that Beatrice would love John better, because he had taken Elizabeth as his wife."[52] Beatrice immediately acquiesced and gave her blessing. In this case, John asked Elizabeth's mother's consent after the marriage was already a fait accompli; withholding it could not prevent or end the marriage, but the fact that he had asked her might lead her to "love John better."

For others, appeal to the advice and consent of third parties was more than a gesture of goodwill—it reflected a real expectation that women should rely on the advice of others before making a firm decision about marriage. Joan Bacster's answer to Richard Parker in 1474 exemplifies the stance of proper behavior adopted by many women: "I will have you as my husband if my uncle Thomas Roby and his wife Ann, my aunt, will consent to it; otherwise I will never have you as my husband nor any other man."[53]

The 1467 case of *Robert Forster c. Katherine Pekke*[54] shows some of the complexities involved in a young London servant's recourse to the advice and consent of her employers in the matter of her marriage. Katherine Pekke told the court when she appeared to answer Robert Forster's suit that she had agreed to marry Robert on the condition that her master and mistress would give their approval. But when she broached the subject with John Reymonde, her master, he told her that he was not inclined to the match: Katherine was still too young and Robert was not very suitable. Besides, Reymonde later told his wife, Robert had not come in person to speak to him about the marriage as he should have. So Katherine reluctantly dismissed Robert, thanking him for his kind offer.

Soon another suitor, Thomas Goolde, sought her hand and, bolder than Robert Forster had been, he solicited and gained her master's consent. Katherine told her employer Reymonde that she was ready to contract formally with Goolde, and Reymonde arranged for him to come to the house to make a properly witnessed contract. But as Reymonde made preparations for this formal ceremony, his wife came to him and advised him to put Goolde off for the time being. Katherine had confided to her that perhaps she had, after all, exchanged unconditional vows of present consent with her first suitor, Robert Forster. Katherine, when consulted about the problem, "said that she wished to be ruled by them in all things"[55] and would do whatever they thought best. Reymonde decided that Robert Forster was not such a bad match after all and invited him to come to the house. Robert and Katherine formally exchanged vows of present consent in front of Reymonde and his wife and Robert's own master and mistress.[56]

In this case, Katherine Pekke played the role of the obedient although perhaps foolish young woman who wanted to marry appropriately and with her employers' consent. Whether her actions were in fact disingenuous is an open question—in the end she contracted with the man she had apparently wanted. But certainly her testimony and that of Reymonde and his wife indicate that she very properly appeared to desire to abide by their wishes in the important matter of her marriage.

Although women's marriage choices were clearly circumscribed by the custom of acquiring the consent of family or others to their marriages, women could sometimes employ this apparent restriction to their advantage. Some used the convention of seeking the consent or advice of important people in their lives to prevaricate when faced with a proposal of marriage they were not yet sure they wanted to accept or reject. A conditional contract of marriage provided an escape clause, serving the function of both buying time and displacing rejection to another person. Lucy Braggis, for instance, told Robert Pope that before she would contract with any man she wished to have the advice of her brothers. Later, when Robert pressured her to give a final answer, she responded to his ultimatum by saying that her brothers would easily provide her with another husband: there were plenty of other fish in the sea.[57] William Knollys of Hornchurch, one of the few men who made their contracts conditional on the consent of parents, seems to have used the condition of his mother's approval quite cynically, saying that he had never in fact intended to marry Agnes Lanther but contracted conditionally with her and gave her gifts in order to "continue with her in sin."[58] In other cases the motive may have been more generous; despite the answer of Agnes Parker of Twickenham to John Pollyn's offer of marriage, "that she wished to be governed following her parents and her friends, and otherwise not," she later contracted with another man apparently without condition.[59] An answer that passed off the rejection to an amorphous group of authoritative people such as "parents and friends" could leave options open and save bruised feelings.

In some cases the displacement did not work: some children expecting their parents or employers to perform the hard task of delivering a negative answer were disappointed. Joan Cardif of Walthamstow refused to give her final consent to a marriage until her mother had offered her approval; when her mother gave her blessing, however, Joan refused to go through with the marriage. Her desire to have her mother's consent may have reflected her own ambivalence about the marriage. When she had made up her own mind, though, her mother refused to cooperate and in fact testified against Joan when the man in question sued her.[60] Similarly, when Richard Tymond asked Margery Shepard to marry him, she contracted conditionally, saying, "I will never have none against my father's will." Like Joan Cardif's mother, Margery's father later consented; but despite her protestations of filial obedience, Margery balked at honoring the contract, even when her father likewise appeared in the case as the opposition's witness.[61]

Women sometimes placed the onus to seek and obtain the consent of their families or employers on the man making the offer of marriage. This could function as a test of commitment, almost a quest, before the hand of the fair maiden could be won. Joan Corvey of Rayleigh (Essex) responded to Robert Philipson's marriage proposition by saying that she would marry him if he could procure the consent of her parents and of John Pyke, her master.[62] One London woman, Alice Cawode, contracted conditionally with two different men, Gilbert Nicolson and John Wymysbury, each under the proviso that they obtain the consent of her father. But in her case, the condition may have served only as a courtship strategy to illustrate her coy reluctance, because with both men she quickly dropped it to contract unconditionally.[63] In other cases the consent of the third party was a real necessity; when Herbert Rowland pressed Elizabeth Croft to marry him, she told him she would never marry anyone without the consent of Master Banks; "if that ye can get my Master's good will," she told him, "ye shall have mine." Later, though, when she did give in and married Herbert without her employer's knowledge, her actions caused considerable ire.[64]

Prevarications could cloak women's attempts to control their marital choices with an invocation or even a pretense of meek obedience to proper authority. Women's manipulation of these customary expectations could work both in courtship and in court. Rose Langtoft did what many other women did when faced in a suit with a contract they did not wish to fulfill: she claimed that the contract she had made with Robert Smyth had been conditional on her parent's consent. Only later did she admit that she had contracted with him freely and without condition.[65] When looking for an escape, many women seized upon a version of events that painted them as cautious, obedient, and appropriately respectful of the wishes of their parents or employers. Men's escape hatches were different but also culturally constructed: as we saw in the previous chapter, one common excuse offered by men but never by women was that they may have implied marriage in order to gain sexual favors but that they never explicitly agreed to marry nor did they ever intend to.

The prevarications of Rose Langtoft and others worked, however, only because many women did indeed wish to have the advice and consent of their family, employers, and friends and because in some cases the consequences of marrying without that advice and consent were grave. In other words, a convention can be manipulated only if it represents a normal expectation. Many depositions make clear that a couple heading for marriage and those who lived around them presumed the influence and interest of family or employers in matrimonial negotiations. John Fynk of Walthamstow assumed that Joan Munden's brother held great sway over her when he asked the brother to advise Joan to end her relationship with a certain "knave" so that John Fynk could marry her himself.[66] These interested third parties, naturally enough, often witnessed the exchange of consent. As John Gardiner said when he asked Ellen Harrison and William Gilbert of London to contract marriage again in his presence, he wanted to know for certain about the contract precisely "because she [Ellen] is my relative."[67]

As witnesses testified, some women anticipated and feared the disapproval of their parents. When Thomas Smyth met Agnes Chambyrleyn in Botulph Lane and commented, "Agnes, they tell me that you are John Holder's wife and promised to him," she answered, "I am amazed that you know about this matter between him and me. I beg you not to tell my parents, because if you do, they will be angry with me."[68] John Bryan, acting as an intermediary between William Fostar and Joan Harries, asked Joan whether she loved William and wished to marry him. She replied that she loved him as much as he loved her, but she begged John Bryan not to reveal this to anyone before she had the assent of her parents to the match.[69]

In a few cases, the ability of parents and friends to veto a marriage by withholding consent went so far as virtually to exclude the participation of one or other of the principals (usually the woman) altogether. John

Mendham, for instance, stated in his examination that he had arranged with Elizabeth Seyve's uncle that she would marry him before he ever approached Elizabeth about it. He later met Elizabeth in a London tavern and asked her there if she wished to fulfill the promise of marriage made between him and her uncle.[70] Similarly, William Chowe told the court that he went to the home of Ellen Mortymer's father in Bermondsey (a manor lying across the Thames and slightly to the west of London) and told Mortymer that he had come there with the intention of having Ellen as his wife, "if it please you and her together." Ellen's father and William proceeded to discuss the marriage. The father ended by saying, "I may find in my heart that ye shall have her to your wife"—an interesting parallel with the phrasing commonly used by the principals in an exchange of future consent. Ellen herself was literally marginalized in the deposition; while the scribe noted her presence at this discussion in the main body of the text, he squeezed her own words of consent to the marriage (without which the case had no canonical validity) into the margin.[71] In these cases the couple may have come to a decision about their marriage independent of and prior to the negotiations with the woman's male relatives, but the versions the men presented to the court foregrounded their discussions with the male relatives rather than with the women themselves.

In many cases the interests of family and the interests of the marriageable daughter or son could coincide and the path to marriage run smoothly. But a child who married contrary to the wishes of the important people in his or her life could expect repercussions ranging from displeasure to disinheritance and disownment. Parents and employers had a number of ways of realizing their wishes if the marital choice of their children did not match their own. Their most effective weapon was financial. According to his own confession, Stephen Robert, a young Kentish gentleman, desperately wanted to marry Angela Harewe, the stepdaughter of a London merchant, but he steadfastly refused to contract with her without the consent of his friends. His father's will makes clear the reason for his reluctance to follow his own whims rather than his friends' advice: the executors, no doubt the friends to whom he referred, were to deliver his inheritance to him only at their discretion if he married before the age of twenty-four.[72] Dowries that parents often provided for a woman's first marriage represented an obvious means of control of marriage choice. In some cases men made their contracts conditional on the consent of the woman's parents and their delivery of a suitable gift. James Wolmar of London made the transfer of a dowry a condition of consenting to marriage with Agnes Henley.[73] John Ely of London agreed to marry Agnes Whitingdon only if her father's delivery of 5 marks was assured by a certain date.[74] Some expressed willingness to face penury for love, such as Londoner Alice Seton, who confessed to another female servant that she would marry John Jenyn even if he received nothing from his uncle and she received nothing from her aunt. In the end, though, Alice Seton did not fulfill this high-minded wish and backed out of the marriage.[75] While parental influence over marriage choices was usually made through the wife's dowry, the prospective husband's parents' agreement might also be indispensable. According to one witness, when Alice Billingham "solicited" John Wellis to be her husband (itself an inappropriately forward action for a woman), John told her that he could not marry her without the consent of her parents, adding that "it takes more to make a household than four naked thighs."[76]

Family members and employers had other means of expressing their disapproval of an unsuitable match and of imposing their own choice. While both men and women attempted to force their will upon their children, the depositions show that fathers tended to be more successful.[77] Men had more political and legal savoir faire because of their greater participation in public life, and some fathers used their connections and skills in these arenas to make or break matches. Although canon law made no provision for parental consent, some fathers, such as Henry Heed, evidently felt it was their right to interfere, a sense that was corroborated by the father's giving of the bride in the ecclesiastical marriage rite. When Richard Cordell of Enfield arranged to have banns of forthcoming marriage issued between him and Margery Ford, Margery's father, Hugh Ford, objected vociferously. When he was asked in court on whose authority he did this, he answered that it was on his own authority, and no one else's.[78] According to a witness, Robert Bate of St. Albans objected when his daughter Christian made a contract with John Lorymer and was somehow able to impede church solemnization of that marriage. Instead he moved to promote a marriage between Christian and another man, William Twygge. When both men sued Christian in the London Consistory court, the witnesses for William Twygge's case said that they testified at the request of Christian's father, suggesting that he was orchestrating Twygge's suit.[79]

It is unclear from the testimony how Christian felt about her father's maneuvering to get her out of her contract with John Lorymer, but some other women clearly opposed their parents' interference. The father of

Margaret Flemmyng of London arranged that Robert Walsh would contract marriage with his daughter, but Margaret herself had other ideas.
According to witnesses to the case, she loved Mark Patenson and wanted
to marry him; he apparently felt the same way and had given her a gold
ring. Margaret's father, however, on discovering the ring, showed his displeasure by ripping it from her finger.[80]

Compulsion could also be exercised on men, although not in the
same way as it was imposed on women: there are no cases in the deposition books of fathers or mothers coercing their sons to marry a particular
woman. Instead, fathers of women who had been wronged financially or
sexually compelled men to marry their daughters, in medieval equivalents
of shotgun weddings. Robert Rokewode of Colchester admitted that
he had forced Peter Hanham to contract with his daughter Alice but felt
justified. Peter had sold £9 sterling worth of clothes and other ornaments
that he, Robert Rokewode, had bought for the wedding.[81] In the story at
the beginning of this book, John Wellys of London used a full artillery of
weapons against William Rote in forcing him to marry his daughter
Agnes Wellys, including physical intimidation and threats of humiliating
Rote before mayor and aldermen. Even when the daughters were fully
supportive of the coercive tactics undertaken against the men reluctant to
recognize a marriage with them, they usually had to rely on their fathers
to accomplish the intimidation.

Friends and Matchmakers in Elite Courtship

Marriages at all social levels involved participation by others in bringing
together likely partners, aiding courtship rituals, and witnessing or directing the exchange of consent. These social mechanisms became even more
complicated for the social elite. More so than among the middling sorts
who brought their marriage problems to the Consistory court, in elite
courtships others besides the principals participated in the process of
making a marriage, identifying suitable matches, helping the principals
conduct the courtship, advising the parties on the financial aspects of the
marriage, and acting as intermediaries in the negotiations. Marriage making was part of an elite sociopolitical world characterized by networks of
service and favor. John Paston III wrote to his mother in 1478 to describe
the maneuvers involved, and the favors exchanged, in arranging a possible
marriage for his brother Edmund with the daughter of a London merchant

who had recently died: "Also, mother, I heard while I was in London where was a goodly young woman to marry, which was daughter to one Seff, a mercer, and she shall have two hundred pounds in money to her marriage and twenty marks a year of land after the death of a stepmother of hers who is upon fifty years of age. And before I departed out of London I spoke with some of the maid's friends, and have gotten their good wills to have her married to my brother Edmund." But the good will of those friends, Paston went on to explain, was not going to be enough. The friends advised him in addition "to get the good will of one Sturmyn." Luckily, Sturmyn was in trouble with and anxious to please Master Pyken-ham, the dean of Arches, who in turn was friendly with the Paston family. When John "moved this matter" to Master Pykenham, the latter immedi-ately "sent for Sturmyn and desired his good will for my brother Ed-mund." Sturmyn granted it and pledged moreover to obtain the good will of the other executors of Seff's will as well. That was where the mat-ter stood at the time of writing the letter.[82] Despite these complex maneu-vers, it came to nothing; a year or two later Edmund married another woman, the widow Katherine Clippesby.[83]

Such networks and mutual back scratching facilitated the landed and wealthy merchant classes' resort to a wide geographical pool in their mar-riage choices. Patterns of patronage might allow a Norfolk gentleman to marry a woman from Calais, with London often acting as the meeting point.[84] As many fifteenth-century historians have before me, I have taken advantage of letter collections for the insights they offer into the lives of aristocrats and elite London merchants, who often intermarried in this period, making use of the London-related letters from the Pastons of Norfolk, the Stonors of Oxfordshire, and the Plumptons of Yorkshire and the correspondence of a family of merchants centered in London and Calais, the Celys.[85] The Paston, Stonor, Plumpton, and Cely letters tell us a good deal also about elite London marriages, as the men and women of these families describe their quests for suitable spouses for themselves, for their relatives, or for their friends.

Among the most important roles of the "friend" in the formation of elite marriages was to identify and effect introductions between prospec-tive partners. Simply identifying candidates was a useful service: Margaret Paston, for instance, wrote to her husband in 1463 to tell him that a gen-tleman named Wrothe had seen and been impressed by their daughter Margery (probably then about fourteen), whom he had met at a social occasion at her grandmother's home. When he praised her as a "goodly young woman," her grandmother "prayed him for to get for her some good marriage if he knew any." He replied that perhaps Sir John Cley's son, eighteen years old and well connected, worth 300 marks a year, would be suitable; Margaret then hastened to write her husband to pursue the matter.[86] Introductions, too, were essential: Edward Plumpton, a widower and lawyer working in London at the inns of court, wrote his cousin and patron Sir Robert Plumpton to tell him that "by means of my lovers and friends" Edward had been brought "to the sight and acquaintance" of Agnes Drayate, a London widow whose wealth would firmly establish his position.[87] It was no easy feat to become acquainted with respectable women of privileged families; there were few, if any, avenues of social interaction that allowed men and women at this social station to meet one another freely. The very notions of respectability and chastity (indispensable attributes in a wife) demanded that elite women have access to men only under familial supervision and through proper introductions. While the fifteenth-century gentry sometimes found their spouses among other gentle families of the same county,[88] at other times the gentry and the wealthy merchant families with whom they frequently intermarried were forced by the small pool of appropriate partners to search more widely, beyond their immediate acquaintance. The social mechanism that allowed wide marriage choices despite these restrictions was the role played by the family "friend," a role that sometimes doubled as marriage broker among the elite.

Some older men and women made it their business to act as a kind of introduction service, matching up men seeking wives with marriageable women with large dowries and good families. Some clearly had their ear to the ground: in 1449 Elizabeth Clere, a cousin of the Paston family, wrote to the young John Paston, at that time staying at the Inner Temple (one of the inns of court) in the western suburbs of London, that she had heard that there was a "goodly man in your Inn whose father has lately died." If John considered that this man would make a good match for John's sister Elizabeth, he should "labor" to him.[89] Several years later, Elizabeth was still unmarried, and John Paston's wife, Margaret, similarly urged him to follow up rumors about a man whose wife had just died and who thus might be a good match for Elizabeth.[90] Young London and Calais Staple merchants Richard Cely the Younger and his brother George Cely similarly availed themselves of older male "friends" who were on the lookout for nubile women. In 1482, Richard was a hot marital prospect: he was probably in his mid to late twenties, and with their

father's death in January 1482, Richard and George had become full pro-
prietors of the family business. Two months after their father died,
Richard wrote to George that lately he had "been spoken to for a wife in
two places."[91] Richard's search for a wife in the months that followed,
vividly described in his letters to his brother, illustrates the importance of
friends in spreading the word that he was available and interested, in identifying suitable matches for him, and in effecting introductions to the
families of marriageable women.

Richard reported to his brother in May 1482 that while travelling in
Gloucestershire on business, he met up with a fellow merchant named
William Mydwyntter. Mydwyntter, having heard that Richard was not "in
any way of marriage," told him that he knew of a likely candidate. According to rumor, Mydwyntter told Richard, the daughter of a local gentleman named Limrick, who was "the greatest ruler and richest man in
that country," had £40 a year from her deceased mother in addition to
whatever her father might give with her. Richard indicated his interest in
this young woman with wealth and political connections, and so Mydwyntter in turn told one of Limrick's friends to suggest Richard as a potential husband. Limrick's friend came to tell Richard that Limrick was
"right well pleased" with Richard and asked him to stay in Gloucestershire until after May Day so that Richard would be able to see the young
woman (whose first name we never learn) and make her acquaintance in a
suitable setting and with supervision. Richard learned that she would be
attending matins with her stepmother on May Day and he, too, went to
the service to have a look at her. Between matins and High Mass, he sent
the young woman and her stepmother a jug of "white rumney" (sweet
wine) for their refreshment. After Mass he went and made their acquaintance in person, and after dinner he went to have a drink with them.
Richard and the young woman had "right good communication," and,
as he reported to George in his letter, her person pleased him well: "she is
young, little, and very well-favored and witty, and the country speaks
much good by her." Richard concluded his letter to his brother by saying
that all depended on subsequent negotiations with her father.[92] Richard's
account of his wooing gives us a sense of the subtle nature of courtship
and the importance of intermediaries in making connections between
sheltered young gentlewomen and young merchants vying for their
hands.

The project never came to fruition, however, and we hear no more
about the Limricks of Gloucestershire. Soon after, Richard wrote his

brother again, saying that another friend, fellow merchant Harry Bryan, "labors me sore to go and see Rawson's daughter."[93] Richard Rawson was a wealthy mercer from Yorkshire who became alderman and sheriff of London, and Harry Bryan was a close friend of the Rawson family.[94] Bryan had also conducted business with the Cely brothers over the previous year.[95] In acting as an intermediary between young business acquaintances and the daughters of his friends, Bryan performed a valuable service to both parties. As Richard wrote to George, "I am beholden to him for his labor, for I know well that he would I did well." And Bryan's urging to Richard "to go and see Rawson's daughter" was successful, for Richard married Anne Rawson not long after.[96]

Part of the job of the "friend" was to convey financial expectations to the other parties, perhaps as a way of distancing the principals from the mercenary details. Such negotiations and discussions might be held over dinner: Elizabeth Stonor, wife of Sir William Stonor, daughter of a prominent London family and widow of a London mercer, was looking in 1476 to marry off one of her daughters from her previous marriage. She went to London to stay with her parents, and while she was there they held a dinner party to which they invited "the friends of the child" who had been proposed as a husband for one of Elizabeth's daughters the last time Sir William had been in London.[97] These friends were apparently entrusted with the power of bargaining the financial aspects of the mooted match. The terms were not as favorable as Elizabeth had hoped ("truly it was nothing as it was spoken of at the beginning," as Elizabeth wrote to Sir William), and so she put them off by saying she would have to discuss the matter with William before making any firm commitments. The delicate negotiations, undertaken in the context of a social engagement, were made between the "friends" and the mother of the two principals. The identities of the prospective spouses were relatively immaterial: Elizabeth Stonor refers only to "one of my daughters" and the prospective mate was only a "child." The principals involved in marriages made at the elite level, especially the young woman, were often bystanders in the process; whether parents or other negotiators considered their wishes or the likelihood of compatibility seems to have depended on the parent. Henry Heed paid lip service to the notion that his daughter must consent, that her consent must come from "[her] own stomach"; if Heed's real commitment to this principle is dubious, some must have truly taken their children's personal happiness seriously. For others, though, a child's marriage was too important a means of alliance to be held hostage to adolescent (or indeed preadolescent) whims; as Sir John Fastolf put it in a letter to John Paston I, he was "right glad to hear of" the possibility of a marriage between Fastolf's ward and "a daughter" of John Paston, as it was a means whereby "your blood and mine might increase in alliance."[98] Paston's daughters were under ten years old at the time,[99] and thus played no role at all in such proposals, although neither this nor any other early negotiations for John Paston's daughters was realized.[100]

Friends also advised on the suitability of a proposed marriage. Women, especially, often repeated the sentiments of the widow Agnes Drayate; although she apparently desired Edward Plumpton as her husband, she could make no decisions without paying attention to "her friends that she is ruled by."[101] At the same time that this aspiration to abide by the advice of those older and wiser fit into expected behavior, especially for women who were to be always deferential, humble, and pliable, it could be used as a negotiating ploy when considering a number of offers. And it could reflect the practical financial control a "friend" could exert. Edward Plumpton's letters to his cousin and patron Sir Robert Plumpton in 1497 telling him about the "goodly and beautiful, womanly and wise" Agnes were occasioned by Edward's reliance on Sir Robert's financial generosity in order to make this advantageous marriage. Edward begged Sir Robert to provide a jointure (property that would be guaranteed to Agnes in widowhood) as part of a marriage settlement, for this widow would bring with her lands and goods "of great value," and Edward had nothing himself. This match would be his "making in the world," Edward stressed to his cousin; upon the jointure Edward hoped Sir Robert would provide "lieth my great wellbeing, and if it were otherwise, my utter undoing forever."[102] Edward Plumpton's three letters to his cousin persuading him of the importance of this match reveal the complex mixture of motives behind marriage decisions among the English elite in the late Middle Ages.[103] The woman's appearance, youth, character, breeding, and wealth were all important factors, even if the latter appears to have been uppermost in Edward Plumpton's mind. A good marriage in the material or political sense was immensely important for a man's or woman's future, as his pleas make clear.

While financial and political advice made up a substantial aspect of the roles played by friends, the rhetoric employed by the letter writers shows that they also expected personal compatibility and attraction to be considered. Those who described potential mates often alluded to their affection or love for the man or woman, even as they mentioned their wealth.[104] John Paston II's recitation of the virtues of his prospective sister-in-law Margery Brews (calculated to convince his mother that she had done the right thing in settling land on the couple) is classic: what a "wealthy and convenient marriage" it will be, considering

her person, her youth, and the stock that she comes of, the love on both sides, the tender favor that she is in with her father and mother, the kindness of her mother and father to her in departing with her [i.e. the amount of property they have given to her marriage], the favor also and good conceit [regard] that they have in my brother, the worshipful and virutuous disposition of her mother and mother, which prognosticateth that of likelihood the maid should be virtuous and good.[105]

Edward Plumpton, who dearly wanted to marry his wealthy London widow because it would materially set him up for life, also noted that it was his "heart's desire" to marry this "wise and goodly" woman.[106] He emphasized that because of her attachment to him, she had "refused for my sake many worshipful men and of great lands," some offering her twice the jointure that he had.[107]

The personal attractions of the principals were often also an integral part of the negotiating strategies leading to a marriage. A pleasing appearance might allow a young woman to make a better marriage than her father's means alone might gain her. This was probably what Margaret Paston meant when she reported her mother-in-law's wisdom to her husband John: he should make serious efforts to marry off his daughter Margery, at that point in her mid teens and attracting admiring male attention, for a good marriage "should be got for less money now . . . than it should be hereafter."[108] But it was not only women whose physical appeal made them attractive mates. As Barbara Harris has noted, by no means was it unusual for landed widows to make love matches to men of lower social station and wealth:[109] a young man of the lower to middling gentry (or, as we shall see, of the middle echelons of the civic world) could use his sexual capital as a means to significant social advancement. Those who acted as friends of a particular man and woman contemplating marriage clearly thought that the tenderer sentiments might sway the principals and their parents or guardians to make matches that were less advantageous materially. Such a possibility lay behind the young Oxfordshire gentleman William Stonor's 1472 courtship of the wealthy and socially prominent Margery Blount, daughter of Sir Thomas Etchingham and widow of William Blount.[110] William Stonor was, however, not a natural wooer, and he was extensively coached by Thomas Mull, probably

William's uncle by marriage.[111] Mull was mandated by William's father, Thomas Stonor II, to act as William's friend in the courtship. Mull not only effected introductions but also orchestrated and encouraged the inexperienced suitor's courtship of Mistress Blount, down to giving William pep talks to bolster his sagging confidence and arranging through whom the secret love letters would be passed (Mistress Blount's confessor). Mull, William, and William's father, Thomas, hoped that William's use of the fine arts of wooing would convince the wealthy Margery Blount to stoop to take William as her second husband despite a considerable gap in their fortunes. While Mistress Blount rejected William's fumbling advances, apparently with some disdain, William may have found Mull's coaching useful in his subsequent marriage to the widow of a London merchant, Elizabeth Ryche. Similarly, Sir John Paston (II) gave his brother, John III, useful advice on how to approach the daughter of the late Sir Geoffrey Boleyn (a London mercer and alderman who had moved into the gentry).[112] Lady Boleyn, Sir Geoffrey's widow, was unfavorably disposed toward a match, but she had not positively declined. John III was to take advantage of the attractions of his person, "getting once in the sight of the maid, and a little discovering of your good will to her, binding her to keep it secret." He should tell her "that you can find in your heart, with some comfort of her, to find the means to bring such a matter about as shall be her pleasure and yours." Beyond that, Sir John told his brother, "Bear yourself as lowly to the mother as ye list, but to the maid, not too lowly."[113] For some young men, the ability to translate their attractiveness into a match beyond the normal expectations of their station brought them other professional rewards as well as great wealth: Edward Grene, a young mercer not of the livery (meaning that he was as yet a junior member of the company), greatly impressed the leading men of his craft in 1487 when they heard he was to marry a wealthy vintner's widow: for "a young man out of the livery to be preferred to such a rich marriage," they recorded, "is a worship to the fellowship," and so they admitted him to the livery on the strength of it.[114]

It is uncertain whether the friends named in the Stonor and Cely letters were paid for their services in effecting introductions to suitable mates. Introductions and other mediations in the making of marriage were often part of the complex interchange of favors characteristic of late medieval English political and social life: a service rendered here would be repaid by a favor returned at a later date.[115] A number of Chancery suits, however, make it clear that, in some circumstances at least, paid brokers were

involved in arranging elite marriages. In all the Chancery cases involving
brokers, the brokers worked on behalf of the men, suggesting that at elite
levels the marriage market tended to favor women and underscoring the
active male role (seeking a wife) and the passive female role (waiting to
be sought). Richard Bruyn petitioned the chancellor about 1458, saying
that William Whetenale, a London grocer and alderman, had retained
his services to arrange a marriage between Whetenale's son, also named
William, and Margaret Hexstall. Whetenale promised to pay Bruyn £20
after the marriage had taken place.[116] Promises of financial reward for
bringing off a match added urgency to attempts to persuade men and
women to contract marriage: Margaret Wodevyle, a widow, complained to
the chancellor between 1475 and 1485 that her brother-in-law Richard
Wright pressured her to marry a man whom she did not know. She was
credibly informed that Wright's interest in the matter was a sizeable fee if
the marriage was accomplished, but she refused to go through with it. As
a result, her brother-in-law caused her to be arrested and imprisoned for
debt, even though (as she claimed) she owed him nothing; unless she
agreed to the marriage she was destined to languish in prison without the
chancellor's aid.[117] Others who could be supposed to have influence over
a woman of fortune also sought, like Richard Wright, to cash in. Alexander Brownyng of London claimed in the early 1450s that John Lawley had
promised him £40 if he could arrange a marriage between Lawley and
Brownyng's aunt, Elizabeth Rothewell.[118] Nicholas Boylle alleged to the
chancellor that John Walsale approached him, suggesting that he knew a
widow worth 2,000 marks, who "would be greatly advised by him [Wal-
sale]"; for a fee, Walsale could fix a marriage between them.[119] In other
cases a high proportion of the woman's fortune was expected as payment:
John Lyonhyll of London, goldsmith, had been approached three years
before his petition to the chancellor by a clerk named John Alcok, who
"moved and showed to your beseecher [Lyonhyll] that he could find and
labor the means that he should marry a daughter of one William Phelyp-
pys, goldsmith and chamberlain of London." Lyonhyll was interested.
The deal was that Lyonhyll might expect £80 as the daughter's dowry;
Alcok was to receive in recompense some £24. Although the marriage
came off, the young wife died soon after, and her father refused to pay the
whole marriage portion; Alcok nonetheless expected his full fee.[120]

Sometimes the line between marriage brokering and benevolent
matchmaking was not entirely clear; while in some cases precise sums
were named as fees for bringing about a marriage, in others, there may

have been an expectation of a gift given in gratitude, a more amorphous arrangement that was open to interpretation or abuse. About 1450, plaintiffs Henry and Isabel Yole petitioned the chancellor because of what they claimed was an extorted brokerage fee. After Isabel had been three months in the service of Thomas and Agnes Haseley of Chelsea, Isabel and Henry Yole, "by means of diverse friends," became betrothed. Margery Terry, also a servant of the Haseleys, "of a subtle and an untrue imagined deceit," called Isabel to her in the "chapel chamber" and "by many subtle words and gay language" she told Isabel that Isabel's furtherance was owing to her (Margery's) and the Haseleys' "labor and means [assistance]" and that therefore they all deserved some reward. Isabel denied this, saying that the betrothal had come "by entreaty and labor of such friends as she had and especially the entire love that the said Henry had to her," rather than anything that Margery or the Haseleys had done. Margery then turned and left the chapel, locking Isabel inside, telling Isabel that she would be put out of the house in shame. Isabel eventually conceded to Margery's request out of a desire to keep her "good name and her worship as a woman," swearing to pay for presents of gowns, furs, and other goods for the Haseleys and Margery.[121] The framing of Isabel's petition highlights not only Margery's blackmail and extortion but also Isabel's alternative narrative of the match she made with Henry: it was *her* friends and especially Henry's love for her that had brought about what was presumably an advantageous marriage.

Friends such as William Mydwyntter and Harry Bryan played an indispensable part in the marital culture of the late medieval English elite, functioning as links between wealthy families with nubile daughters and men in the market for wives. As agents for the families of marriageable women, they screened the candidates, presumably acting as something of a guarantor for the suitability of the prospective suitors. For their young male friends, they utilized the contacts built up over a long career, investigating the possibilities among the daughters of the families with whom they were acquainted, exercising their patronage networks. The place of "friends" in negotiations was strengthened by their relative disinterest in the outcome: their urgings, as impartial mutual friends, may have carried more weight than those of the immediate family. Ideally, the system worked to the advantage of both the men and the families of the women; through these friends both parties were able to widen their circle of possible marriage partners considerably. In a wider sense, "friends"—almost invariably the same older men who controlled the political and economic basis of late medieval English society—also ensured that marriage choices were in accordance with the interests of those who governed.

In Loco Parentis: Orphans of the City

When a citizen of London died in the late Middle Ages, any surviving underage children became orphans of the City. Many such children were not motherless, but in medieval English practice the father was the guardian of the children of a marriage, and fatherless children were orphans. After a citizen father's death, paternal duties, along with custody of the children's inheritance,[122] passed to the City in the persons of the mayor and aldermen; in turn, the mayor and aldermen delegated responsibility for the orphaned children to guardians designated in the citizen's will (who frequently included the mother) or to other suitable persons.[123] While the guardians themselves often played a significant role in the formation of orphans' marriages, the mayor and aldermen did not entirely relinquish their paternal role: the civic records reveal a number of occasions when the part normally played by fathers and friends in supervising courtship and marriage was handled by the mayor and aldermen in their court. The journals of the Court of Common Council of the City of London throughout the fifteenth century record licenses for men to marry female orphans: in 1463, for instance, the journal recorded, "On this day, license is given to Thomas Kelet, grocer, to marry Petronill, daughter of Robert Stokker, draper, orphan of the City."[124] By doing so the mayor and aldermen effectively granted parental consent for the hand of the deceased citizen's daughter.

The mayor and aldermen exercised their paternal role with zeal in some cases. In August 1448, the mayor and aldermen heard a number of depositions involving the marriage several days previously of the orphan Elizabeth Pouter, who contracted by words of present consent with John Goldwell, mercer, in Goldwell's master's shop, in the presence of several apprentices but, notably, in the absence of anyone likely to be acting as her guardian. After hearing the depositions and perhaps in the meantime investigating Goldwell's prospects, the mayor and aldermen decreed about a month later that John Goldwell could in fact have Elizabeth Pouter as his wife.[125] If the marriage had indeed been contracted by present words, the mayor and aldermen had no more power canonically than Elizabeth's parents would have had in refusing to grant their permission to the marriage, but just as Elizabeth's parents could have withheld her marriage portion, so also could the mayor and aldermen. In 1500, Elizabeth Arnold, an orphan, was sequestered in the house of the City's chamberlain while the Court of Aldermen investigated whether or not she had contracted marriage without their consent.[126] In many other cases, such enquiries were probably less formal, thus rarely recorded, but occasionally their traces come into the civic archives. In 1455, for instance, John Porter, a draper, appeared before the mayor and aldermen to report that he had examined his apprentice, Robert Hanson, concerning whether he had made any contract with a city orphan named Margaret Goodson and that Hanson had denied any contract. The next day, Robert Hanson was called before the alderman of his ward and together the alderman and his master "diligently examined" him again, making him swear an oath that he had neither contracted with Margaret nor gone to the bishop's court at St. Paul's to get a copy of Margaret's father's will. Both Porter's report to the mayor and aldermen and another entry suggesting that there was some defamation concerning Margaret Goodson indicate that rumors about Margaret Goodson and Robert Hanson were flying about. While a father might confront a young man rumored to be dallying, with good or ill intentions, with his daughter, in the case of an orphan the paternal role was taken by civic officials.

In other cases men were fined for marrying orphans without the permission of the mayor and aldermen. In 1481, an apprentice named Robert Deynes was fined £20 for marrying Elizabeth, the orphan of Robert Gregory, without license from the mayor and aldermen. Robert Gregory, who had died in 1466, was a mercer of considerable wealth and his daughter thus a substantial heiress.[127] This case was notorious enough to have been recorded in London chronicles.[128] John Smyth, mercer, was likewise fined £10 in 1483 for marrying the unnamed daughter of William Whitwey.[129] Another man, suspected of intending to marry another Elizabeth Gregory, was bound over in 1495 to prevent him from inciting or provoking the said Elizabeth to marry him without permission of the mayor and aldermen, and he was also forbidden to frequent the house in which she lived.[130] Although in almost all cases in the civic records the orphans who encountered marital difficulties were female, in one case the mayor and aldermen worried that an underage male orphan—underage in this case meaning in his early twenties—was being forced into a marriage. In 1454, George Combes, the son of the late William Combes, had to appear before the mayor and aldermen to assure them that his desire to marry Margaret, the daughter of Hugh Dene, was entirely his idea and not due to the incitement of his mother or any of his other friends. George was heir to considerable property as his wealthy and prominent father's only child; Margaret Dene, on the other hand, was the daughter of a citizen, but probably not in the same league as Combes. The mayor and aldermen obviously felt some concern about the disparity between them, but upon hearing George's assurances they granted him permission to marry Margaret.[131]

The mayor and aldermen evidently feared that orphans' marriages could become the object of manipulation, both from those seeking their inheritances and from even more unsavory motives. In 1467, John William, brewer, was committed to Newgate prison because he made Alice, the daughter of the late William Luke and orphan of the City, not yet aged eleven, contract marriage with a certain unnamed gentleman. William confessed that Alice had indeed contracted marriage, but only under the condition[132] of her uncle Edward Luke's consent.[133] Given that Alice Luke's inheritance was not particularly large (under £30),[134] and the marriage of ten-year-olds was far from common in London, it is possible that the gentleman in question was a pedophile rather than a fortune hunter. In another case, the mayor and aldermen became concerned that a man who wished to marry an orphan might already be married. A month after they had granted license in September 1462 to Hayman Voet, a physician, to marry the orphan Agnes Heydon, before they would deliver her inheritance they forced him to provide surety that should his marriage to the orphan be declared void in the ecclesiastical court by reason of a precontract on his part he would return the orphan's legacy to the chamberlain. It is unclear whether during the intervening month specific information had reached the mayor and aldermen that Voet would be (or even already had been) sued in the church court, or whether they were simply being cautious because Voet was older and probably a foreigner, thus with an unclear marital history.[135] The mayor and aldermen exercised vigilance on behalf of the orphans, making efforts to exercise paternal supervision over the marital lives of the city's wards.

*   *   *

The involvement of families and interested others in the marriages of English people in the later fifteenth century ranged from the coercion of the dagger to supportive assent to an independently made contract. As we have seen, women in particular called upon the advice of others and were sometimes expected to await their consent before committing to a contract of marriage. Women could turn these conventions to their advantage. Margery Shepard's assertion of daughterly obedience, "I will never have none against my father's will," was in her case ironically a statement of independence and refusal to be pressured, but as medieval English social conventions required, it displaced the refusal onto an older man, perhaps remote and authoritarian. Similarly, Elizabeth Stonor, in her marriage negotiations for one of her daughters from a previous marriage, was able to use her subordinate status as wife to prevaricate when she wanted more time to think about an offer: she told the prospective husband's family "that though she were my child . . . I could not answer that matter without [my husband] nor nought would do."[136] While women could use the approval of others as a bargaining chip in the emotional and economic negotiations preceding an agreement to marry, men, on the other hand, could not use this particular ploy with much success—appearing to be dependent on the advice and consent of others was not an attractive image to present to a prospective wife or her family. But the reason that women were able to use this ploy was precisely because the stance of obedient daughter willing to be governed in all things by a wise and all-knowing father was a real expectation of female behavior. While some couples in late medieval England made their marriages taking full advantage of the freedom of choice offered to them by the consent theory of canon law, most took their marriage vows only after consulting and sometimes obtaining the permission of their families, employers, and friends.

4

Gender, Power, and the Logistics
of Marital Litigation

THE HELP, influence, and force that those surrounding a courting couple offered and imposed on them extended beyond the process of identifying a prospective mate and making a contract. Integrally related to the process of making a marriage contract in late medieval England was the possibility of enforcing, or challenging, that contract through the ecclesiastical courts and through associated legal processes such as arbitration. Legal proceedings were—alongside emotional appeals, the withholding of financial settlements, and threats of physical force—powerful tools for the enforcement of marital norms. Spurned partners, neighbors, and parents and guardians could use court action to achieve a desirable marriage or break up an undesirable one, as Margaret Heed, whose father and stepmother testified against her in William Hawkyns's suit, found. At the same time, the peculiarities of the late medieval canon law of marriage, with its emphasis on consent of the principals, also provided the possibility of resisting those norms. As with any legal system, however, access to the possibilities of justice in the ecclesiastical court system of late medieval England was fettered by wider societal distinctions of gender, social station, and access to influence.

Negotiating the maze of legal jurisdictions in late medieval England, in both ecclesiastical and secular courts, required a good deal of money, knowledge, and legal proficiency as well as significant political connections. It was not for nothing that the English gentry of the fifteenth century favored a legal education for their male offspring, preparing them for their careers as gentlemen in that notoriously litigious age. Because ecclesiastical courts primarily served suitors of lower socioeconomic status, they probably had a more diverse clientele than, for instance, those higher secular courts that dealt mostly with land disputes, but they were nonetheless hardly open to all equally. Bringing a suit of any kind to any court was an expensive undertaking, and the ecclesiastical courts were no exception. When John Yotton, the dean of Lichfield Cathedral, died in 1512, he left land to Lichfield Cathedral both to maintain a priest to preach the gospel in parishes in Lichfield and surrounding areas and to help poor litigants plead in the bishop's Consistory court without fee.[1] In addition to money, one needed also to have access to the right kinds of advice, connections, and understanding of the legal systems if one wanted to launch a suit.

A consideration of the logistics of launching a marriage case in a fifteenth-century English ecclesiastical court suggests that men, by and large, may have found it easier to sue than did women. Suing was expensive, and men generally had greater access to material resources than did women. Suing in a church court also required some legal know-how, knowledge to which men had more direct access than did women because of their greater participation generally in legal and political life. And when we look at the sex ratios of the plaintiffs in the London Consistory court cases, this notion is borne out to some extent: more cases were sued by men than by women (about a 55/45 split).[2] Sixteenth-century evidence from various dioceses indicates that the ratio of male to female plaintiffs ran as high as 3:1 in some places.[3] Yet in medieval York, according to Charles Donahue's investigation of the Cause Paper evidence, the ratios were almost exactly the opposite, with women suing more frequently than men,[4] and even in fifteenth-century London, women sued at least 40 percent of the cases. The hypothesis that male suitors were favored over female suitors is thus too simplistic. In particular, it ignores a crucial factor: in most cases plaintiffs, both male and female, did not launch their suits on their own but rather were aided by their friends.

It is important not to confuse the legal forms—where the plaintiff and the respondent must be the parties directly concerned with a case—with the reality of who directed or even desired the litigation. While a Chancery petition, for instance, was written in a first-person voice, in many cases—such as when the plaintiff was a seven-year-old girl[5]—the notion that the bill was written by or even at the instance of the plaintiff was clearly a fiction. The active role of fathers, mothers, employers, neighbors, and others behind the scenes in matrimonial causes brought before the Consistory court makes sense, given that the parties themselves were frequently young and inexperienced. This involvement was part and parcel of the participation by a host of people in the marriage process as a whole.

Arbitration and Other Informal
Means of Dispute Resolution

We know most about disputes that were taken to court, as surviving documents are mostly records of those more formal and official proceedings. Many legal quarrels in late medieval England, however, were evidently taken first through more informal (and mostly unrecorded) channels of arbitration or mediation,[6] and marital disputes were no different. Here perhaps even more than in formal legal proceedings were the influence and power of local men of power, both lay and clerical, in evidence. In 1487, for instance, before testimony in the suit *John Pollyn c. Agnes Parker* was heard, a witness was questioned twice by committees of local men. In the first instance, several men from the parish of Twickenham gathered in the cemetery of the parish church (a common meeting place for men to transact affairs of various kinds, including arbitration)[7] one Sunday, after matins and before mass, to interrogate Thomas Cordrey about what he intended to testify in the suit.[8] Soon after, Cordrey was again questioned, this time in the hall of a local gentleman's house, by local notables of the parish and neighborhood, including the vicar of the parish and other gentlemen. The vicar and a gentleman "questioned and examined" him about what he knew of any contract between the parties.[9] The case *Alice Cademan c. Nicholas Vavecer* may also have undergone a mediation phase before it reached the Consistory: several witnesses indicate that the parties and some witnesses had been questioned by a Master William Says (possibly a cleric who had been deputed by the Consistory to deal with the dispute) in the cloister of the hospital of St. Thomas de Acon and in the Abbot of Waltham's Inn.[10] Arbitration may in fact have been much more deeply embedded in the formal process than the records indicate. In the ecclesiastical court of the Abbey of Whalley, which held a peculiar jurisdiction over parts of Lancashire, at least one case of 1524 was committed by the Commissary to arbitration by a panel of laymen, and the judgment in the case was given "with the counsel, assent, and consent [*cum consilio, assensu, et consensu*]" of the arbitrators.[11] Such practices were desirable because they were relatively inexpensive and possibly because a local solution might prove more effective than one that came from those who did not know the situation on the ground. At the same time, arbitration also reinforced local power structures, as the arbitrators, prominent men of the neighborhood or town, were unlikely to make decisions that would challenge patriarchal authority or greatly disturb local hierarchies.

Litigation

The litigation process also favored local power and influence. While both men and women friends played important roles in the courtship process, in launching a suit in an ecclesiastical court (or indeed any court), it was the older male friends whose expertise and material resources were most frequently called upon. Thus even a woman of lowly status and little legal experience could launch a marriage suit, if she had connections to men with legal resources and wealth who were willing to help her. This might have been the case in *Joan Chylde c. Thomas Rote*. In 1473, because of their open fornication, Joan Chylde and Thomas Rote had been summoned to appear before the wardmote inquest, a court of inquiry in each City ward held before the alderman and local men chosen as jurors. When the jurors asked him why he consorted with Joan in this way, Thomas answered that he intended to marry her. Calling his bluff, the jurors insisted that Thomas and Joan exchange vows of present consent there at the inquest. Although it seems improbable that Joan Chylde was a woman of much standing, when Thomas refused to live up to the contract of marriage she was able to launch a case against him in the Consistory court. The identity of her witnesses—all members of the wardmote inquest jury—suggests that they supported her in her case and, indeed, that they may have helped her bring it to court.[12]

Although the surviving records of litigation from the diocese of London are not as full as, for instance, the York Cause Papers, the depositions frequently give indications of how litigants organized their cases, or, in some cases, how other people organized their cases for them or helped them to do so.[13] In many cases it becomes clear that the parties named in the litigation were each backed by a host of supporters. Two people from the diocese of London, for instance, who wished to marry but were aware that an impediment of spiritual relationship between them needed to be dispensed, commissioned a friend "who had many acquaintances in the Roman court" to obtain a dispensation from the apostolic see.[14] A weak case, such as that of Agnes Eston, who had no witnesses to an actual contract with John Crosby, might be taken further than its basis warranted because of the support of powerful friends (in her case, papal notary William Dawbeney).[15]

Rose Langtoft, who was apparently caught in the middle between her own desires and her family's wishes, had considerable support from her friends when Robert Smyth, with whom she had allegedly made a contract, sued her in the Consistory court in 1472. The case *Smyth c. Langtoft* gives us insight not only into the importance of the support given by friends in marital litigation but also into the possible motivations of these friends. When Robert Smyth launched his case to enforce a present-tense contract he claimed had been made between him and Rose, he brought forward a number of witnesses. Chief among them were Thomas Hynkley, a twenty-four-year-old sherman (a man who sheared woolen cloth) and former fellow apprentice with Robert Smyth, and Thomas's nineteen-year-old wife Alice. They both deposed that one August afternoon on the vigil of a feast day, as Alice lay sick in her bed and Thomas attended her, Robert Smyth and Rose Langtoft both came to visit. As all four gathered in Alice's bedchamber, the conversation turned to previous promises of marriage made between Robert and Rose. After some urging on Robert's part, Robert and Rose exchanged vows of present consent. This version of the afternoon's events offered by Thomas and Alice Hynkley was disputed by Rose Langtoft; when summoned to respond to the suit, she implicitly denied that she had even been present in the Hynkleys' house on that day. She admitted only that although she had, several times, given a promise to marry Robert, it was always on the condition that her parents consent to the marriage. Robert then brought forward three more witnesses, none of whom had been present at the exchange of vows, but each reporting that there was voice and fame regarding the contract in their parish of St. Mary Abchurch, the rumors originating from a number of directions, including the word of Rose's own employer Thomas Howdon. The three further witnesses also provided a crucial piece of information: Rose's parents, they all agreed, were much richer than Robert's. Rose's parents had presumably refused to proffer their consent to the match because Robert, a sherman (a lower status clothworker), had neither good antecedents nor good prospects.

Robert nonetheless had a good case: he had two eyewitnesses and evidence of fame regarding the contract. But soon after, in early November, a countersuit was launched in Rose's name against Robert. The first witness to appear was Thomas Howdon, a thirty-eight-year-old tailor and Rose's employer. In a long deposition, he testified that on the day and time in question, Rose could not have been standing by Alice Hynkley's bedside, because for the whole day she had been working in his house preparing for the feast the next day. He described in detail what she had been doing: washing clothes at one point, preparing food; sometimes she walked around, he said, sometimes she sat. Besides, throughout the day she was wearing an old gown of murrey, not the red gown described in the Hynkleys' depositions. Thus, Thomas Howdon said, Thomas and Alice Hynkley had perjured themselves, because Rose could not have been in two places at once. At the end of his deposition, when asked if it would be suitable for Robert to have Rose as his wife, he answered no, that it would not be appropriate.

Howdon's testimony was followed and corroborated by a number of other witnesses. Two of his apprentices, William Taylbos and Ralph Nowell, each deposed that Rose never left the house; they would have seen her, they said, since the only way out was through the shop, and they were there working the entire day. Alice Calcote, an eighteen-year-old neighbor living with her widowed mother, testified that she had been working with Rose in the kitchen at the crucial time on the day in question. Unlike Thomas Howdon, the younger deponents all said that they thought it would be suitable for Rose and Robert to be joined together in marriage.[16]

Like many cases for which we have depositions from the Consistory court of London for the later fifteenth century, the two parties presented opposed and mutually exclusive stories: according to Robert's case, the two were married; according to Rose's, they were not. If Robert's witnesses were telling the truth and the contract had taken place, we might interpret this as an attempt to save Rose from a marriage of which her parents clearly did not approve. If, on the other hand, Rose's witnesses were the truthful ones, then instead we see a gold-digging Robert unscrupulously trying to trick a wealthier, and probably naïve, young girl into marrying him. Unlike most other such cases, though, we have a further installment. In January 1473, Rose Langtoft appeared again before the official in the Consistory court. In Robert Smyth's presence, she admitted that about six weeks previously, after both the suit and the countersuit had been heard, she and Robert had exchanged vows of present consent. Moreover, she admitted, she had in fact been in Alice Hynkley's bedchamber on that August day, just as Thomas and Alice had originally deposed, and on that day she had made the contract.[17] So, if Rose was finally telling the truth this time, it seems that a perjured countersuit was engineered in order to prevent a valid marriage. Rose herself might have orchestrated it, but given her youth and probable inexperience, a more likely candidate is Thomas Howdon, her employer, perhaps acting on behalf of her parents.

Why might Thomas Howdon have done this? His motives were

probably relatively common ones: to save a young woman under his care from making an unsuitable marriage. Indeed, as we saw in the previous chapter, his duties as employer of a young female servant included supervision of her social life, in order to prevent just this sort of scenario from developing; he was lax in allowing the relationship with Robert Smyth to develop freely (as it obviously did—Rose spoke of meeting with Robert frequently). Perhaps, even, he had not originally objected to the marriage—hence the testimony that he had spread word about the contract—but had later found that Rose's parents were unhappy about the situation. He apparently tried to solve the predicament through organizing the suit. By the standards of his time and position, the sin of perjury might have been forgivable if it prevented what were even greater wrongs: Rose's marrying below her station and Howdon's own dereliction of his duty to prevent such a thing. And indeed it seems that if Rose had not later decided to admit to the contract, it would have worked.

Howdon's organization of the case involved not only his own testimony but probably also the testimony of the other witnesses who were brought forward. Here Thomas Howdon's economic and social position were almost certainly instrumental. Thomas Howdon's apprentices, presumably, had little choice but to testify as their employer wished them to. Similarly, the testimony of the young neighbor Alice Calcote may have been offered as a favor to a powerful man in the parish, or perhaps on the order of her mother who likewise may not have wanted to offend Thomas Howdon. The stories Rose's witnesses offered were detailed, consistent, indeed probably rehearsed; the one difference—in their opinions as to the suitability of the marriage (Howdon claiming that it was not appropriate, the other witnesses saying that it was)—could have been either a genuine difference of opinion, or perhaps a change in tactics. Thomas Howdon may have thought better of his original answer, given that it impugned his objectivity in the case, and thus he or perhaps their proctor may have told the other witnesses to answer differently.

Success before the law might have derived in some cases from the justice of the claims, but just as clearly it sometimes accrued to the party with the most access to money and influence. The story of Elizabeth Baxster and John Croke gives interesting insights into the processes of both marriage and the law. Some time in or before 1480, Elizabeth Baxster and John Croke contracted marriage and lived together for five or six months, "with love and charity" according to Baxster's later report. After this short period, however, the marriage was dissolved because of a successful divorce on the grounds of precontract. John Croke had allegedly previously made a marriage with a woman named Elizabeth Cotton, who was judged by the Consistory to be his wife rather than Baxster. (The Consistory court records for the late 1470s and early 1480s unfortunately do not survive, and thus this case is only known to us through references in other legal documents.) Both before and probably after this Consistory court litigation, other ecclesiastical fora were involved, illustrating the rather more elaborate array of legal remedies available than is apparent from straightforward readings of the surviving ecclesiastical court records. Even on the day of the solemnization of Croke's and Baxster's marriage, Croke "swore upon a book before the Archdeacon of Westminster in the presence of other credible persons that he then stood and was clear from all earthly women" except Elizabeth.[18] After the Consistory court decision, Elizabeth Baxster appealed the judgment to Canterbury, and at some point the court of the dean of Arches also heard the case at Baxster's instance, apparently finding in her favor. Both Elizabeth Baxster and John and Elizabeth Croke also made petitions to the papacy.[19] While the papal court's findings are not recorded, Croke remained married to Elizabeth Cotton, and thus Baxster's case evidently did not succeed.

Many disputes involving matters under ecclesiastical jurisdiction were fought in oblique ways in the secular courts as well: parties could harass each other by suing for trespass or debt until the opposing side threw in the towel. Some evidence of this is seen in Elizabeth Baxster's petition to the chancellor, probably dating from late 1481 to 1483. Her complaint suggested that Croke was using both legal means and more questionable tactics in his dispute with her (Baxster, too, may have played rough, but her petition naturally focuses on his misdeeds). Baxster told the chancellor that after Elizabeth Cotton, through the "steering and enticing of certain evil-disposed persons," had successfully sued John Croke in the Consistory,[20] Croke "put her [Baxster] shamefully from him," but kept all her goods. Later, Croke met Baxster as she was on pilgrimage to the shrine of the Virgin at Holywell Priory near Shoreditch, and he grievously beat her. (What Baxster's version of the story does not report is that Croke had property at Holywell,[21] and thus Croke perhaps thought she was in the neighborhood less because of her devotion to the Virgin than to harass him.) Moreover, in order to ruin her and "her poor friends," Croke undertook various untrue actions of debt and trespass against her and against her mother and father, and as a result Baxster and her mother were imprisoned. This last salvo was the proximate cause of Baxster's complaint to the chancellor. Her petition asked both for a writ of *corpus cum causa* to have her and her mother brought to the court of Chancery and the charges against them heard, and for a writ of subpoena directed to John Croke in order that the question of the return of her goods be addressed.

Baxster was, by her own description, not a wealthy woman: according to the petition to the pope, "it is very hard for the said Elizabeth Baystre, who is poor, to litigate in the Roman court," and the Chancery bill similarly noted that she was "a poor woman, not able to sue the common law."[22] Yet she did have friends—her parents, at least, and possibly others unnamed who, though "poor," nonetheless may have helped her negotiate the legal mazes through which her marital difficulties led her. But Baxster's attempt to reclaim Croke as her husband was ultimately unsuccessful (the success of her Chancery suit is unknown).

Who had the technical legal right is unclear, but undoubtedly John Croke would have won any battle of influence: he was the eldest son of a wealthy London alderman, also named John Croke, who had died in 1477 leaving significant property to his five sons. His mother, Margaret, was the daughter of William Gregory, longtime alderman and mayor in 1451–52.[23] Two of the alderman's daughters were already at the time of his death married to prominent men: one sister, Elizabeth, was married to London merchant Thomas Ryche, and then subsequently to Oxfordshire gentleman William Stonor, while another sister, Margaret, was married to Sir William Stokker, who became mayor of London in 1485.[24] John Croke himself did not move into civic life, but took the same path as his sister Elizabeth Stonor into the landed gentry. His wife Elizabeth Cotton was the daughter of a Warwickshire gentry family, and when John Croke himself died in 1485, leaving the former Elizabeth Cotton as his widow, his will styled him "gentleman," although he retained his principal residence in London.[25] John Croke's youngest brother, also named John, similarly became embroiled in a marriage suit in 1487: he sued Agnes Hill, the daughter of the late Sir Thomas Hill, former alderman, apparently to enforce a contract of marriage.[26] The younger John's use of the ecclesiastical court was probably successful, just as his older brother's had been: his marriage to Agnes Hill went ahead, although it took a few years, and was an advantageous one for him (and conversely one that her family apparently opposed).[27]

It could cost a tremendous amount of money—or, as one Chancery plaintiff put it, "great cost, labor, pain, and charge"[28]—to launch a marriage case, especially for those whose economic status was low.[29] In several cases references are made to friends of the litigants being willing to spend large sums of money in order to obtain victory. Sometimes this willingness served as a rhetorical insistence that the friends would do anything in order to see justice done. John Myddylton, a witness in the 1471–72 case *John Holder c. Agnes Chambyrleyn*, admitted that he had said, "I will spend twenty nobles rather than that John Holder should have Agnes as his wife contrary to the law."[30] Another witness similarly said, "I will rather spend some silver of mine own purse in her truth than she should be wronged."[31] In *John Yonge c. Joan Blacman* in 1468, Simon Wryxworth, Joan Blacman's employer, was said to have stated that he would rather spend forty pounds (or a hundred pounds, depending on the witness) rather than see John Yonge married to Joan contrary to justice.[32] Although in these cases the spending of money functioned rhetorically only to achieve the correct and just verdict, other references to the bottomless purses of friends suggested that justice could be bought: Nicholas Vavecer's witnesses complained in 1474–75 that Alice Cademan's friends "would spend one hundred pounds" in the illegitimate case that she was waging against Nicholas.[33] As Margery Kempe remarked regarding a different sort of ecclesiastical legal dispute, those who pursued the matter "were rich and powerful men, respectable merchants, and had plenty of money, which in every necessity will lead to success—it is a pity that money should succeed before truth."[34]

As those with the most powerful friends had a greater chance of using the law successfully to gain their ends, so also were those whose friends opposed their marital choices likely to be unsuccessful. Most such cases undoubtedly never made it to litigation; opposing the wishes of one's family or friends to the extent of being willing to suffer through ecclesiastical court litigation in which a number of one's family members or friends testified in favor of the opposing party's side took a kind of fortitude (or stubbornness) that most probably did not possess. Yet a surprising number of female parties, such as Margaret Heed, did suffer through precisely that experience.[35] Litigation was one of a number of tools at the disposal of parents and other guardians to enforce their authority.

The use of ecclesiastical court litigation in marital strategies forms part of an overall pattern that is characteristic not only of marriage and courtship but of medieval social interactions generally—while English society was clearly hierarchical, ties of patronage, protection, and influence between those more powerful and those less powerful make any simplistic assessments we try to make of that society very unsatisfactory. While a person's own socioeconomic status and gender were clearly important factors, his or her access to the influence, protection, and advice of those with more social, political, and economic capital was crucial in determining what that person could do. In a sense, then, the disabilities that a person's status or sex conferred could be offset—a poor woman, for instance, could successfully bring a case to an ecclesiastical court if for some reason a powerful man chose to support her. And social organization was such that it was by no means impossible that such a man would choose to do so: with the identity of the powerful man came the duty and responsibility to protect or advise those in his sphere of influence. This is not to say that gender and status were irrelevant in fifteenth-century England, but rather that their workings were complex and subtle and in some ways even more pervasive than we have yet been able to recognize.

5

Place, Space, and Respectability

RECENTLY, MEDIEVALISTS, inspired by sociologists, geographers, and other social scientists,[1] have begun to explore how space and place both shaped and were shaped by social relations in the Middle Ages.[2] Space in the late medieval city was socially complex, resisting easy categorization by gender or station. The model of a private, domestic female sphere and a public, exterior male sphere[3] cannot take account of households where the male workplace (the shop) was integral to the home, nor can it accommodate more generally the central importance to the identity of the paterfamilias of the governance of the household. Anna Dronzek, for instance, has argued that contemporaries viewed the aristocratic household as masculine space. As she contends, the control of the household was constitutive of masculine identity.[4] Moreover, the contingent circumstances surrounding a social act could be as important as the place in which the act occurred in determining the degree to which it was public and the perception of what that act meant to and for the men and women involved. Similarly, living in a world in which the sacred was immanent, medieval people saw nothing unusual about undertaking a sacrament, a vow "before God" (as deponents often put it), in a space we might regard as obviously profane, such as a tavern.[5]

The location where couples exchanged consent underscores the gendered nature of the entry into marriage. In this chapter I look at the theme of social space in the late medieval urban environment by examining where contracts of marriage were made. Records of marital litigation in London's ecclesiastical courts provide a surprising amount of detail about precisely where and when various episodes leading to the making of a marriage took place. This detail was recorded precisely because it meant something: whether a contract of marriage was made in a chamber or in a hall, in a tavern or in the street, in the house of the woman's employer or her father, in her own house, or in the house of the man—all were locations with social meaning.[6] Studying these nuances more closely yields new understandings of the nature of marriage in fifteenth-century England and of our conceptualizations of privacy and publicity in late medieval social relations.

Domestic Contracts

Reflecting the general patterns of marriage formation in late medieval England—that is, men as active and women as reactive players—an overwhelming majority of men and women who made domestic contracts did so in the house in which the woman or her close family lived (in almost 90 percent of domestic contracts where the householder is identifiable). The single most common site of the exchange of consent to marry was the house of the woman's parents. Although the exchange took place in a home, it was an open, public transaction. Ideally a number of important men were present as witnesses, increasing the solemnity of the occasion and decreasing the likelihood that one of the partners would later try to repudiate the contract. William Clerk of Woodchurch, Kent, for instance, testified in 1469 that in late June of the previous year, about noon, he had been in an upper chamber of the house of the gentleman Alexander Clyfford of Bobbing, Kent, along with Stephen Robert; Ann Clyfford; Alexander Clyfford and his wife (Ann's parents); Sir John Culpeper, knight; Richard Culpeper, gentleman; John Edyngham; Walter Robert; William Salt; William Hochon; and others. After discussion among all those present about the making of a contract of marriage between Stephen Robert and Ann, the daughter of the house, Stephen took Ann by her right hand and said, "I Stephen Robert take you Ann Clyfford as my wife, and thereto I give you my faith," and they unclasped their hands. Ann then took Stephen by his hand and said to him, "I Ann take you Stephen as my husband, and thereto I give you my faith."[7] While the home of the woman's parents was the most common locus for the exchange of consent, in a substantial number of other cases, contracts were made in the home of the woman's employer[8]—not altogether surprising, given that employers often acted in loco parentis for young female servants. Not all women making marriage contracts were young or marrying for the first time: many medieval marriages involved widows. This probably explains the relatively large number of marriage contracts that were undertaken in the house of the woman herself: almost as many took place there as in the woman's parents' home.[9] Although some may have been property-holding single women,[10] in most cases the women undertaking marriage contracts in their own houses had clearly been married before.

Whether the contract took place in the bride's parents' house, or her employer's house, or her own, the predominance of the woman's residence as the venue for the contract underscores in several ways the gendered nature of the entry into marriage. In the case of women making marriage contracts in the houses of parents or employers, a wife's proper dependence on her husband was anticipated and demonstrated by the woman's reception of an offer of marriage under the roof of those to whom she was subject, implicitly or explicitly with their supervision. This show of dependence was less obvious in cases where women were autonomous enough to be householders, but even in some of those cases, as I have discussed, theoretically independent widows could be seen to rely explicitly on the advice and sometimes the consent of others before entering a marriage.[11] While men, too, sought or required advice and, less often, consent, this was much less emphasized in the structure of the marriage process. A man entering into marriage was expected to demonstrate his independence, not his reliance on others. Thus exchanges in the houses of men's parents, relatives, or employers—people on whom a man might depend—are rarely found in the records.

The location of the marriage contract in the woman's space had another significance related to gender and agency: men were literally the ones who had to make the move, to make the effort to go to the woman. Even when the man was an independent householder, his own house was hardly ever used. This said less about the man than the woman: for a woman to undertake a marriage contract or, more generally, to socialize in the man's space, for her to go to him, imparted to her an air of disreputability. In the one case where a contract was allegedly exchanged in the home of a man's employer, the woman was accused of having seduced the man from his employer's service, and the woman's friend who had promoted the relationship was characterized as a bawd.[12]

While the propriety of a contract depended to some extent on whose house it was made in, the precise location within the house was also significant, conferring on the event greater or lesser publicity and respectability. In many houses, the hall was both the largest and in some ways the most public of rooms, and predictably it was the most common venue for the exchange of marital consent. Halls were public enough places that in some cases deponents did not even know the name of the person whose house they entered to witness a contract of marriage.[13]

Halls were employed especially in cases where there was a significant number of people present to act as witnesses.[14] Maude Knyff, a widow of some substance courted by men who were also of high status,[15] contracted marriage with Thomas Torald in the hall of her house in the parish of St. Sepulchre. There were ten people besides Maude and Thomas present, invited for the purpose of witnessing the contract. One witness testified that when he first entered the room, Maude, sitting at the high table next to Thomas Torald, said "publicly" (*publice*) to those gathered that they should not believe the rumors that she would take Robert Grene as her husband; instead, Maude announced to her guests, "Behold, I would have you know that this gentleman Thomas Torald sitting here is my husband, because we two have contracted marriage together."[16] Her guests then prompted her to make this more certain by contracting again, and Maude and Thomas proceeded to exchange words of present consent several times in the course of the afternoon before a number of different sets of witnesses.[17] This was a contract undertaken with the specific intent of making the union as public as possible—due, no doubt, to Maude's surmise that she would later be sued by the said Robert Grene, whose own claim to having made a contract with Maude will be discussed later.

Apart from halls, the shop, another of the more "public" areas of the house, occasionally saw the exchange of marital consent. Four London contracts were made in shops, although interestingly, in three out of four cases these occurred on a Sunday or holiday when the shop was presumably more a social space than a work space. Thomas Berford, for instance, testified that on a Sunday afternoon in July 1464 or 1465 he was in the shop of John Saunder in the parish of St. Dunstan in the East when he saw John Barnet and Agnes Saunder, the daughter of the house, talking and flirting together, eventually exchanging vows of future consent.[18] Similarly, deponents testified that Robert Arwom and Joan Deynes exchanged consent before a number of witnesses in Richard Reynold's shop on the afternoon of the feast of the Assumption in 1467.[19] The (sometimes variable) sociability of the space and the contingency of the particular situation suggest that spaces and situations could be public in different ways.

So also were there different ways in which spaces could be private. Two other common locations for marriage contracts, the parlor and the garden, have been described as the "most private" spaces in a late medieval house judging by access patterns (which measure the distance and number of thresholds that must be crossed to reach different parts of the house),[20] but as they were designed at least partly for the entertainment of guests, they were quite suitable for discussions related to marriage and for the formal witnessed exchange of consent. Parlors were less public than the hall and generally smaller, but served much the same purpose of receiving social visitors. John Thomas, for instance, testified that on a Monday in March 1469, between three and four o'clock in the afternoon, he had been present in a lower parlor in Isabel Palgrave's house in the parish of St. Botulph without Bishopsgate, together with Isabel, William Barker, and John Taylour of the parish of St. John Walbrook, when John Taylour told those assembled that he wanted to take Isabel as his wife. After some discussion, John took Isabel's hand and they exchanged vows of future consent.[21] Similarly, some contracts exchanged in rooms called "chambers" could be highly respectable and formal exchanges of consent witnessed by a number of people, as we saw earlier, for instance, with the exchange between Stephen Robert and Ann Clyfford in a chamber in the home of Ann's father, Alexander, a gentleman. As there were at least twelve people in the room and it was a highly formal occasion, it was probably not a bedchamber, but one of the "great chambers" (social rooms commensurate with halls and parlors) that could be found in some larger English houses by the end of the fifteenth century.[22]

Some more elaborate urban properties also had gardens that functioned as social spaces. Although these were in some ways especially intimate spaces judging by access patterns (one could often reach them only by walking through the house from front to back),[23] a flowering garden was then, as now, both a space for entertaining guests and an attractive place in which to make a solemn vow. William Prudmay, for instance, deposed that in late September 1469 he was in the hall of Thomas Nicholas's house, together with Thomas; his wife, Joan; their daughter, Elizabeth; and John Bedeman. After William Prudmay and Elizabeth's parents discussed and came to an agreement about making marriage between Elizabeth and John Bedeman, and Elizabeth and John themselves indicated that they were willing, they all got up and went out into the garden. There, in a bower, under a vine, Elizabeth and John exchanged vows of future consent. Afterward they all drank good ale.[24] The movement from one part of the house to another (seen in a few other cases)[25] marked the separation between the discussions preceding a marriage contract and the making of the contract itself, increasing the sense of solemnity that should accompany such a meaningful exchange of words.

Thus the privacy and publicity of a space were to a certain extent contingent on the occasion as much as the categorization or accessibility of the space. But the categorization of the space was not entirely irrelevant: some other spaces in a house were private in a way that a garden was not, intimate and unsuitable for social intercourse with those outside the household. Although some marriage contracts were made in such spaces, those contracts were usually in some way problematic, undertaken in secret, often in specific contravention of the wishes of the woman's or man's parents, guardians, or employers. In one unusual circumstance a contract was made furtively in a buttery before a single witness and was meant to be kept secret from the woman's mother.[26] Similarly, a contract in a bedchamber—as in the case of *Parker c. Tenwinter*, discussed in Chapter 2[27]—with the bedroom's associations with sexuality and intimacy, was less than ideal. Literary allusions to contracts in chambers imply that such contracts were not entirely open or legitimate; when the deceptive Walter first weds Griselda in Chaucer's *Clerk's Tale*, for instance, he does so by ambiguous words, with only one witness, in a bedchamber.[28] Bedchamber contracts raised too many questions about the porous boundaries between premarital sexuality and the kind of fornication that could never lead to marriage.

In other cases, contracts in bedchambers were neither so evidently associated with sexual impropriety nor undertaken while the two were alone, but they were nonetheless reflective of awkward or improper situations. In three cases, a man and a woman came to exchange consent in a bedchamber because either one of them, or a crucial witness, was confined to bed because of illness or childbirth. Robert Smyth and Rose Langtoft, estranged lovers, met one another in the bedchamber of their sick friend Alice Hynkeley and reconciled there and exchanged consent before Alice and her husband.[29] John Crote, the servant of a parish priest, lay ill in a room in the bell tower of the church, where he was visited by his former sweetheart, Beatrice Smyth, who was moved by his weak condition to promise him marriage.[30] Mark Patenson and Margaret Flemmyng exchanged vows of marriage before Alice Martyn and a number of other women as Alice lay in her chamber in childbed.[31] While the contracts took place in the chamber because one of the participants or witnesses was bedridden rather than because of some sexual impropriety, it must also be noted that in each of these cases, the marriages were far from being open and public exchanges of consent: the marriages were opposed by the parents, guardians, or employers of one or both of the parties.

At the same time that certain spaces were not suitable as venues for appropriately public contracts, spaces that in some circumstances functioned publicly could also witness private and surreptitious activity. Secret conversations could take place in halls, parlors, or indeed on the street outside the house. But intimate exchanges sometimes became more public than the speakers intended. Medieval houses were much more permeable, the walls thinner, and the borders between a house's interior and exterior more porous than modern domestic spaces. Witnesses in ecclesiastical courts testified about what they had seen when looking through a window or peeking through a hole in the wall, or what they had heard when deliberately listening at a door, or inadvertently because the walls were far from soundproof. On a few occasions witnesses to marriage contracts were not even in the room where the words were exchanged. Sometimes these eavesdroppers were teenagers—probably not originally invited to witness the contract because their admissibility as legal witnesses was doubtful—driven by their own curiosity to listen in. Ralph Penne, for instance, the seventeen-year-old brother of Angela Harewe, stood outside the parlor door eavesdropping while his sister and Stephen Robert contracted marriage.[32] Agnes Hedy, the teenaged stepdaughter of the householder, and Joan Bakby, a teenaged servant, were perched on the stairs leading from the hall to the upper chamber while they listened to Robert Pope and Lucy Braggis exchange words of present consent.[33] Sometimes conversations were meant to be overheard, open windows extending the social space of an interior room into the street. In 1470 Arnold Snorynge and John Pomeys deposed that Robert Grene asked them to go to the house of the wealthy widow whom we met earlier, Maude Knyff, between six and seven o'clock on a July evening, where they would witness a marriage contract Robert Grene would make with Maude. When Snorynge and Pomeys arrived at Maude's house, instead of entering the building they put their heads through the window of a lower parlor, where they could clearly see Maude and Robert. The two, presumably seeing that their witnesses had arrived, proceeded to exchange vows of future consent.[34]

The liminal spaces, in the literal sense, were often locations where the most private conversations were held, although of course the reason we know about them is that they were overheard.[35] Margaret Pevy, the employer of a young woman named Agnes Moyne, promoted a marriage between Agnes and Christopher Kechyn, an older man in the market for a younger wife. One Sunday evening in September 1496, when Agnes and Christopher were talking alone together on the threshold of the Pevys' house, Margaret overheard that they were discussing marriage. She whispered to two other young servants that she wanted to listen to what they said to one another, so the three of them concealed themselves

behind an interior door in order to hear Christopher and Margaret exchange consent.[36]

But if a number of contracts were exchanged on the threshold or on
the street just outside the house where the woman lived, it is striking how
rarely marketplaces or public streets beyond the area just outside the
doorway served as locations for the exchange of contracts, or indeed
(from the evidence of witness testimony) for courting activity at all.[37] This
might reflect generally severe constraints on women's movements around
the late medieval English city:[38] perhaps women did not court on the
streets because they were rarely there. As a fifteenth-century conduct
book suggested, "a virgin and a maid . . . ought not to be vagabond nor
running about, but the most part of the time ought to keep her at home
in following the blessed virgin Mary."[39] But this advice could not have been
followed by all virgins and maidens given what we know about the working patterns of lower-status women. As Jeremy Goldberg has argued, restrictions on women's ability to walk about unaccompanied were highly
dependent on social station, such constraints being virtually impracticable
for the working servant who needed to shop and do other tasks around
the neighborhood.[40] Indeed, daughters who lived with their parents also
contributed to the household economy through running errands: in a
Chancery petition, the parents of Elizabeth Mappulton, who had been seduced by the wicked Spaniard Francis Derbyet, lament that they must keep
her inside the house "and durst not send her further about their businesses,
to their great hurt and damage."[41] Indeed, depositions in London marital
litigation mention servant women on the street running errands or carrying clothes to the Thames to launder[42]—but those women did not court
or contract there. Streets and marketplaces were not respectable venues
for the kind of social activities that might lead to marriage; as quotidian
and necessary as women's presence there was, negotiating a relationship
in such a place may have carried too strong an association with prostitution, an association directly contrary to the chaste and respectable self-
presentation of the prospective wife.

Marriage Contracts in Drinking Houses

Yet not all spaces outside the household were inherently improper for the
pursuit of marriage in fifteenth-century London, and even respectable
women were not always confined to the household in which they lived.

Outside of homes and churches, the most common location for the making of a contract of marriage was the drinking house, an important and socially complex part of late medieval urban life. The importance of the drinking house as a site of socialization has been somewhat obscured by recent tendencies to emphasize the seediness of the late medieval tavern. [43] Certainly some late medieval drinking houses were sites of crime and prostitution,[44] but the evidence of courtship and the making of marriage contracts in alehouses, inns, and taverns makes it clear that it was not universally so.[45] Indeed, there is no sense from depositions in marital litigation, either from those who are testifying in favor of a contract or those testifying against it, that there was anything inherently disreputable about being in a tavern. The ways in which drinking houses were employed as the setting for an exchange of consent to marry highlight the function of such establishments in the social life of late medieval Londoners, especially for those of lower status. The drinking house often functioned as a home-away-from-home, especially for those who did not have a domestic space to call their own.

Drinking houses were ubiquitous in late medieval London.[46] Three sorts of drinking establishments flourished there in the late Middle Ages, although the distinctions between them were by no means hard and fast, especially in the sources I have used here. There were inns, large establishments, sometimes former aristocratic houses, that offered lodging facilities in addition to drinking and dining; taverns, which were not as large as inns and focused more on drink and food than on lodging, although they often had bedchambers for hire; and alehouses, the smallest and least formal of the drinking establishments.[47] Unlike inns and taverns, where wine was sold, alehouses sold only ale, and although some had rooms to let for lodgers, the sale of drink and simple food was their main business. In the fifteenth century, London also saw the proliferation of brew houses or beer houses, which sold, of course, beer.[48] Drinking establishments in late medieval London were marked by poles (or "alestakes") outside their door, from which often hung a sign depicting the name of the house (such as the Saracen's Head, the Cardinal's Hat, the Miter, the Sun, etc.).[49] Many drinking houses had a number of small rooms, primarily on the ground floor, but sometimes also in undercrofts or cellars or on upper floors. Smaller taverns and alehouses closely resembled residences.[50]

Witnesses in Consistory court cases recorded various sorts of conversations and meetings that took place in drinking houses—for instance, witnesses were sometimes persuaded to come forward to testify after one of the parties took them out for a drink,[51] and in one case a parish priest attempted to reconcile an estranged husband and wife in the Saracen's Head tavern in Carter Lane.[52] By far the most common function that drinking houses serve in Consistory court depositions of the later fifteenth century, however, is as the location of a courtship or a marriage contract. In these cases, the drinking house is part of the larger pattern in which marriages were first contracted and announced to those close to the couple in a domestic or quasi-domestic setting, with the circle of publicity subsequently widening.

Drinking houses played an important role for many people in all stages of the marriage process, from the initial conversations to the actual exchange of consent. Courting was often conducted while a man and woman shared one another's company in the course of eating and drinking together, most often in homes—around a table or sitting before the fire in the hall of the house of the woman's father or her employer—but also in inns, taverns, and alehouses. The sharing of food and drink was integral to social interaction and clearly served the purpose of providing an occasion for a man and a woman to come to know one another and to talk about the things that needed to be discussed prior to making a marriage. Some of this courting behavior in drinking houses can be glimpsed, somewhat ironically, in testimony given by women who denied that they had made marriage contracts. Cecily Judde, for instance, admitted that she and Humphrey Gogh ate and drank together many times and had been drinking together at the sign of the Sun in Lombard Street when he asked her to marry him. She testified that she gave him an equivocal answer but did not contract with him.[53] Similarly, Joan Blacman denied that she had ever contracted with John Yonge, although she admitted that she drank with him many times at the sign of the Ave Maria.[54] Although Cecily and Joan each claimed that she could drink with a man in a tavern without committing herself to marriage, their opponents introduced the evidence because they alleged that such behavior did, in fact, indicate intention to marry.

Much more striking than the indications of courtship in taverns is the evidence in witness testimony that a good number of marriage contracts were made in drinking houses: the drinking house was the site not only for the informal socializing of courtship but also, in some cases, for the definitive moment, the point at which the marriage was actually made. Taverns, inns, and alehouses functioned as places in which an important—and respectable—occasion could be celebrated. Robert Jonson, for example, testified in 1472 that one morning in January two years earlier he was in the tavern at the sign of the Greyhound in East Cheap, sitting on a bench, together with his sister Ellen Grey, William Forster, and a number of other men. William Forster and Ellen Grey were discussing marriage between them, and during the discussion the deponent Robert Jonson asked William to affirm that he had previously contracted with his sister Ellen, and William declared that he had indeed done so. Robert then requested that they repeat their vows then and there, so that he and the other men present could bear witness to the marriage. William and Ellen exchanged vows of present consent, and afterward they all drank red and white wine in celebration.[55] Similarly, William Queldryke testified in 1470 that on a June morning fifteen years before, he had been in a tavern called the Green Lattice, right next to the king's palace at Westminster, together with John Jenyco, Puttance Eustas alias Reve, and a number of other men. They were all eating and drinking together, when John Jenyco asked Puttance if she would keep the promise that she had made to him, and she answered yes. They then exchanged vows of present consent, and John took a little gold ring out of his purse and gave it to Puttance.[56] In this example, as in many other cases, John Jenyco's readiness with a gift as a token of the marriage indicates that the exchange of vows was prearranged by him or perhaps both him and Puttance together.[57] Other instances of prearrangement are even more explicit. In 1489, for instance, Londoner John Jenyn asked his brother-in-law William Avenyll to come to the tavern at the sign of the George, bringing with him some neighbors, so that they could witness there an exchange of consent between him and Alice Seton. At John's request, William Avenyll and one of his neighbors, John Gaston, went to the George, finding John and Alice sitting in a parlor in the tavern, talking together. John and Alice proceeded to exchange present consent before the two men, and afterward John, Alice, and their witnesses had a celebratory drink.[58] The tavern served as a useful meeting point and as a suitable place for a special occasion, as ale or wine were at hand.

In another complicated case, two competing versions of a story give different insights into the place of drinking houses in the making of marriages in late medieval London. In the first version, offered by the plaintiff John Mendham, he and Elizabeth Seyve made a contract by future consent in the Galley tavern in Lombard Street, following an agreement that had been made previously between him and Elizabeth's uncle. Unlike most other contracts, where it appears that the witnesses were gathered for the express purpose of hearing the exchange of vows, the witnesses he named just happened to overhear the exchange as they were walking by.[59] John's version—which was somewhat implausible for a number of reasons—was challenged by the woman, Elizabeth Seyve, and others who testified on her behalf. In the alternative narrative that can be constructed from their depositions, Elizabeth, who lived sixty miles north of London in Newmarket, Suffolk, was accompanied to London by her uncle's brother so that she could meet John Mendham and talk about a marriage that had been proposed already between John and her uncle. She met John for the first time that day in the City of London in the Galley tavern, and although they talked about the marriage that had been discussed already with her uncle, she did not at that time make a contract with John.[60] In this second narrative the tavern was a site of preliminary discussion, a place for her to meet the man whom her uncle had chosen for her. Although John himself probably lived in London, it would have been inappropriate for Elizabeth to visit John in his own house; the tavern served as a respectable substitute for Elizabeth's own domestic space, as she lived out of town.

Courtship, discussions of marriage, and marriage contracts conducted in London's taverns indicate something about how drinking houses functioned in the social life of late medieval Londoners, perhaps especially for those who were younger and of lower social station, or for those who lived out of town—in other words, those who often did not have their own domestic space. Contracts in drinking houses were somewhat different from those that took place in residences in that they were less prone to have been the outcome of a well-supervised courtship—in contrast to domestic contracts, parents or employers of the woman were almost never present. In one case a woman's mother witnessed a contract in an inn, but the absence of the father was noted by one of the witnesses and may indicate that the contract took place outside of her father's home in order to circumvent his objections to the match.[61] Drinking houses in some cases served, then, as surrogates for the patriarchal household if the patriarch was seen as an obstacle to the marriage. But in most cases, the parties did not contract in drinking houses because of objections from fathers or masters, but rather because fathers and masters were irrelevant: those who made contracts in drinking houses were often apparently of lower status and less strictly under the control of a patriarchal household.

Lack of patriarchal control did not in itself connote disreputability. But standards differed: what might have been chaste and respectable behavior for a poor young woman was not as suitable for the daughter of a wealthy merchant, who ideally was much more closely supervised and thus much more likely to make a marriage contract in her father's house surrounded by relatives and friends of the family. This did not mean a daughter of the *haute bourgeoisie* could not visit a tavern. A young woman of a substantial family, Margaret Heed, visited the Cardinal's Hat in a party that included the man with whom she had recently contracted marriage, her father and stepmother, and Thomas Bryan, chief justice of the Court of Common Pleas, a close friend of her father.[62] Margaret Heed had previously made her contract in her father's own house, surrounded by prominent citizens who witnessed the vows, and very much under her father's direction (or, as she later alleged, coercion).[63] Such a young woman could have a drink in a tavern, but would not contract marriage in one; a woman from a less privileged background was less constrained and could happily, and apparently respectably, make a marriage in such a venue. There are no implications in the testimony offered in marital litigation that marriage vows made in drinking houses were in any way less binding, less honorable, less worthy, or even less sacramental than those made in other places. Just as domestic contracts could follow a respectable path leading from contract to banns to solemnization, so also could one made in a tavern: William Dichand, for instance, contracted marriage with Joan Qualley at the sign of the Swan around the feast of All Saints in 1491, and then in February 1492 the marriage between them was solemnized in the parish church of St. Peter ad Vincula inside the Tower.[64]

Nor was there anything inherently disreputable about simply being in a drinking house. This is illustrated particularly well by instances where women denied that they had made contracts in a tavern: in other ways women who denied contracts tended to construct their narratives in ways that emphasized their properly chaste, obedient, and demure behavior—for instance, as I have discussed, some women claimed that they would never have made a contract without first consulting or seeking the consent of their relatives or friends.[65] Yet women did not deny that they had been in a tavern, nor that they had eaten and drunk with the man in question; they just denied that they had contracted with them. It does seem nonetheless, as Peter Clark has suggested, that women were less likely to have been patrons of taverns or alehouses except when they were accompanied by their husband or a man who was courting them.[66] Witnesses to contracts in drinking houses were much more commonly male than female—typically at most one other woman was present, but often enough the only woman was the bride. If sixteenth-century evidence is anything to go by, men made up a considerable majority of the customers in drinking establishments.[67] At the same time, though, it is important to note that men made up a considerable majority of the witnesses to marriage contracts made in domestic settings as well: in the search to find the most reliable witnesses men were generally favored over women.[68] Thus the evidence from marital litigation suggests that women's patronage of drinking houses was not in and of itself disreputable, but that there were probably powerful inhibitions against women entering them on their own. In this, drinking houses were by no means unusual: as we saw earlier, a woman could also not easily go to a man's house on her own without compromising her reputation.

Considering both in whose house and in what room a couple exchanged their vows reveals important aspects of the nature of late medieval marriage: what were the expected roles of men and women; who was supposed to participate in the process; what made a proper, respectable contract as opposed to a secret and inappropriate one? Marriage was to be an intimate, but not a private, relationship; a man and a woman entered into it through a process that was to be transparent, beginning with an exchange of consent that was public, even if in a domestic setting, and finishing with the ratification of that union in the even more public environment of the parish church.

PART II

GOVERNANCE, SEX, AND CIVIC MORALITY

6

Governance

IN THE LATE MEDIEVAL English urban world, households were ideally patriarchal—ruled by the husband-father. The formation of marriage discussed in Part I reflected assumptions that fathers ruled the households from which the man and woman marrying came and that the new husband would rule the household that would be formed by the newly married couple. Late medieval English patriarchy was not confined to the household, however; the ideal of the father-ruled household extended beyond the family into society as a whole, so that men rather than women, and particularly older men, were seen as the natural rulers and governors of both family and society. Governance was a crucial concept in fifteenth-century notions of appropriate social comportment. Men and women were commonly enjoined by the mayor and aldermen of London to be "of good rule and honest governance," while those who contravened laws and mores practiced "misrule" and "vicious governance."[1] As these formulations imply, governance denoted the individual's ability to master his or her own appetites, but it also denoted obedience to the rule of those to whom the individual was subject. The extent to which a person could exercise governance depended on status as well as gender and age: those with the greatest duties and the most considerable power were those defined in medieval documents as "most honorable," "most worthy," or "most substantial." The duties of the patriarch included involvement in civic politics, governance of social relationships in the neighborhood (especially marriage and illicit sexual unions), and responsibility for the conduct of those living in the patriarch's household. Governance in late medieval English society was practiced by many different people and institutions, ranging from the rule of parents over children, and husbands over wives, to the authority exercised by ward and civic officials, crafts, the royal government, and the church.

Governance and the Household

Good rule began at home: the properly governed household was the model both of and for the government of the realm.[2] Households were to be model kingdoms, the subjects recognizing and obeying the benevolent rule of its head as a God-given authority, exercising a paternal or semipaternal rule over all members of the household.[3] At the same time that dependents were to submit cheerfully to the householders' authority, householders themselves should "wisely govern"[4] the household rather than exercising "a shrewd [depraved] rule and an untrusty rule."[5] This ensured that both those who lived in the household and those who entered it behaved. Householders were to be respectable, temperate, mature men: when the author of the *Great Chronicle of London* sought to cast aspersions on rioters who attacked immigrant merchants in 1494, he noted that out of the dozens of riotous persons there was "not one householder of them all."[6] In 1491, following "great misrule . . . used by men's servants and other[s]" in the City, the mayor commanded that all the fellowships assemble "to warn and charge their fellowship that every person, householder and other, to keep good rule as well themselves as among their servants."[7] In 1493, the Lord Chancellor, following similar unrest in the City, charged the members of the livery companies that "none of them [were] to have and keep any person, servant or other, but such as he will answer for [and] shall be of good rule."[8] Houses themselves took on an air of good or evil rule, almost as if governance had a miasmic quality. The atmosphere of good rule came, of course, from the wise governance and thus godly behavior of those who lived in the household, subject to the householder. Householders who did not fulfill these duties of good rule might be cited before the wardmote inquest or the Commissary court, such as Edward Newton, who was described to the Commissary as a "man of evil disposition, fostering evil rule in his house."[9]

The center of the model household was the conjugal relationship between the master and his wife. The subjection of the wife to the husband was deeply ingrained in the late medieval ideal of marriage; as the Sarum marriage liturgy had it, the husband was to love and honor the wife, while she was to obey and serve him.[10] The woman, who sometimes professed herself to be "governed by her parents and her friends" in making a decision to marry,[11] was transferred from the governance of her family and friends to the governance of her husband upon marriage, symbolized in the marriage liturgy by the giving of the woman to the man by her father or other male guardian. After the wedding, the husband was to "rule" his wife "fair and easily," as the Wise Man taught his son in the fifteenth-century poem,[12] while the wife, in turn, should cheerfully perform her conjugal duties in such a way as to require little in the way of explicit correction. As the fifteenth-century moralist Peter Idley advised husbands:

Thy wife thou love in perfect wise
In thought and deed, as heartily as thou can,
With gentle speech the best thou can devise;
This shall make her a good woman,
And also to love the best of any man,
And dread thee also and loath to offend,
Thy goods keep, neither waste nor spend.[13]

No doubt few couples fulfilled these ideals, but the assumptions that the wife was subject to the husband's authority, and that he in turn was responsible for both her sustenance and her behavior, are pervasive in the records of the fifteenth century. A female plaintiff in Chancery could plausibly assert that in being bound for a debt of 40s. she did only her wifely duty to her husband, "to whom she might not say nay."[14] A witness in a Consistory court marriage case could cite a woman's calling a man "her husband and master"[15] as evidence that they had contracted marriage. A woman who had abandoned her marriage was described as "at her own guiding and out of the governance" of her husband,[16] lacking any of the normal checks on the wild behavior to which an ungoverned woman was wont. Perhaps the most extreme manifestation of the husband's authority over the wife was the offense of petty treason, whereby a wife who killed her husband was subject to the penalty for treason rather than murder because the severe abrogation of authority was akin to betraying one's king.[17] As the eighteenth-century legal commentator Blackstone put it, such a murder so upset the natural and legal rule of the husband, "so abuses that confidence, so forgets the obligations of duty, subjection, and allegiance," that a guilty wife was burned (the style of execution used for female traitors, and reminiscent of the penalty for heresy) rather than hanged.[18]

At the same time, the limits on both the agency of the wife and the rule of the husband were complicated and contested. The husband had a right and a duty to chastise his wife if she was disobedient, physically if need be, but this right was not absolute.[19] When Thomas Hyll threatened his wife with a dagger, she fled to the home of her sister's husband, Richard Vergeons, with her husband in hot pursuit. Vergeons, seeing the imminent danger in which his sister-in-law stood, took her into his house and went out to speak to Hyll on the doorstep. Vergeons "entreated and desired" Hyll to take his wife back, but "to guide her and chastise her under a due manner and not to draw his dagger to her."[20] Chastisement duly given was appropriate; daggers, on the other hand, were not.

In cases where abuse had become life-threatening, a wife could obtain a legal separation from her husband, a divorce *a mensa et thoro* on the grounds of cruelty. The bar was, by modern standards, high: depositions in cruelty suits—harrowing descriptions of conjugal violence—emphasize the shedding of blood and the threat to life, as only the most serious physical abuse would warrant a separation. The terms in which the violence was described suggested that the husband's rule had become unreasoned, the chastisement not given in a "due manner"; the husband no longer exercised godly rule within the marriage.[21] Out-of-control rage was emphasized, as in William Saunder's testimony in Eleanor Brownyng's 1473 suit to divorce her husband Alexander Brownyng:

On a day in summer seven years ago, this deponent, coming with a repaired gown to the home of a man named Burgoyn situated in the hospital of St. Bartholomew, saw Alexander with a naked dagger in his hand chasing after Eleanor, who was running in her tunic, with her head uncovered and her hair streaming behind her. Out of fear Eleanor ran to the house of the man named Burgoyn, where Eleanor's sister was. Eleanor's sister took her into the house and closed the door. Alexander, seeing this, shouted in a loud voice, swearing that he wanted to kill Eleanor the next time he saw her unless those in the house gave her up to him. When they would not do this, Alexander left. This deponent says in his conscience that Eleanor would have been killed or at least mutilated if she had not escaped into the house. He says moreover that within the last five years on a certain day, exactly when he does not recall, Alexander entered the tavern at the sign of the Sun on Lombard Street, London, where, in the presence of this deponent, he held a naked dagger in his hand and threatened Eleanor with it. On account of his threat, Eleanor jumped at least the distance of four men long, which this deponent saw with his own eyes.[22]

Such a man could no longer govern others, as he could not govern himself.

When a woman was in imminent danger from her husband, she might flee to the home of a relative, as did Eleanor Brownyng and Thomas Hyll's wife, and she might be taken in. But in allowing the abused wife to take shelter in their houses, these relatives committed a trespass: no person was to receive a man's wife without the husband's permission.[23] Thomas Hyll retaliated against Richard and Isabel Vergeons after they received his wife, according to Isabel's Chancery bill, by having Richard murdered, "slain at his own door," and Isabel arrested and imprisoned for trespass.[24] A number of other petitioners sought the chancellor's help after they had been jailed at the suit of a husband whose abused wife they had taken in.[25] Although petitioners emphasized the cruelty and rage of the husband and his inability to rule his wife properly, and thus his forfeiture of his privileges as a husband, the duty of the wife to live in the husband's household, and the duty of all other householders to ensure that she could not live elsewhere, were so strong as to be broken only in the most extreme of circumstances. Plaintiff Matthew Petit of London, a merchant stranger, complained to the chancellor between 1475 and 1485 that Joan Gybson, wife of Robert Gybson and a relative of Petit's wife, came to him "being great with child and sore beaten and hurt and so sore stricken upon her right eye that the blood issued out." She asked him for aid and succor, since her husband was in Ludgate Prison for debt, and she had been left with nothing to live on. She had been to visit her husband in Ludgate, "showing to him her grief," she told Petit, and because of that he had beaten her. She asked Petit "in the way of alms and charity" to help her, "that she might be relieved with leechcraft" and have food and drink. Moved with pity, and because Joan was his wife's cousin, he sent her to see a surgeon, but he said that "as much as the same Joan was a man's wife," he could not receive her in his house nor keep her, saving only that if she were about to perish he would give her sustenance "for the love of God."[26] Petit presented himself in the petition as a man who recognized his Christian duty to his wife's relatives and was moved by Joan's plight, but not to the extent that he could take into his house another man's wife.

If husbands sometimes had become so intemperate that they could no longer properly govern their wives, so also could wives prove impossible to govern. Isabel Newport of London was the very paragon of ungovernability, or so the witnesses in her husband William's suit for separation from her alleged. They detailed her open adultery and her taunting of her husband as a cuckold, her physical violence against him (she attempted to cut him with a knife and on another occasion threw him into Houndsditch), her burglary of William's house, and her incestuous relationship with one of her blood relatives.[27] Although Isabel's ungoverned behavior was in some ways little different from that of abusive husbands whose acts were described in testimony and chancery petitions, the underlying problem was perceived to be different: while an abusive husband could not govern himself, Isabel's fault was that she refused to submit to her husband's rule. As witness John Mader testified, "he believes in his conscience that it is dangerous for William to live with her because he cannot govern or rule her."[28]

Isabel Newport taunted her husband that she had made him a cuckold, an insult that cut to the heart of conceptions of governance in a marriage: while it was the wife who committed the sin of adultery, the insult highlighted the husband's inability to control and govern her. A husband's adultery, on the other hand, was not commensurate; while, as I will argue at length later, a man's adultery could affect his reputation, sometimes deeply, it called into question his own self-governance rather than his wife's ability to affect his behavior. There was no feminine equivalent of cuckold, no label for a woman whose husband committed adultery. The wife might have been wronged (and indeed she might even complain publicly),[29] but her husband's adultery did not reflect directly on her, as she could not be presumed to govern his actions. For men, on the other hand, an adulterous wife spoke loudly about his failures as a husband. An accusation of cuckoldry would from time to time be thrown into an omnibus insult against a man; as Elizabeth Hertford allegedly shouted out to John Calle as he walked by her house, "thou art a false errant thief, a tainted thief, a cuckold, and a witwold [a man contented to have his wife cuckold him]."[30] But it was still a two-edged insult, and the sharper edge could be directed against the wife. Most citations involving accusations of cuckoldry that came before the London Commissary court involved an attack on the fame of the wife rather than the husband, suggesting that in some cases the insult reflected at least as much on the wife's refusal of proper governance as on the husband's inability to rule. Elizabeth Cordener, for instance, was accused of having made her husband a cuckold on the day after the solemnization of their marriage.[31] Alice Yong was cited as a prostitute who had made her husband a cuckold.[32] John Davy allegedly defamed his neighbor Elizabeth Bowman by saying that her husband "is a stark cuckold, for a soldier had to do with her while her husband went to the siege parts."[33] Margaret Andrew defamed Alice Holte by calling her a "cuckold's-wife,"[34] an interestingly reflexive formulation.

Collections of edifying moral tales—such as *The Book of the Knight of La Tour Landry*, printed by William Caxton in 1484—featured salacious tales of incest and adultery, which often ended in the betrayed husband, brother, or father killing both the deceiving woman and her partner (often a cleric) in some terrible way, such as burning them or cutting them into small pieces.[35] A roper's wife, for instance, was able to fool her incredibly gullible husband while having an affair with a prior literally right under the roper's nose, the guilty pair having sex while they lay together in the same bed as the sleeping roper. Suspicious as he was, his wife, the prior, and their accomplice (the wife's godsib—a companion tied through godparenthood—acting as procuress) were always able to pull the wool over his eyes and convince him that his wife's virtue remained intact. At last, though, the roper feigned sleep one night and caught them in the act. On finding that his long-held suspicions were justified, the roper "waxed so much angry and wrathful thereof that almost he was out of his memory and wit, and drew out a great knife with a sharp point, and cast a little straw within the fire [to shed light], and ran to them lightly, and he killed them both at once." This murder was, however, blameless: "And when he had done this deed, he called to him his meinie [retinue] and his neighbors, and showed them the feat or deed, and sent also for the Justice, of which he was excused and had no harm."[36] The lesson, of course, was that wives must resist the temptations of the devil to indulge in the sin of lechery, and in particular they must beware men of religion.

The Knight, in Caxton's translation, laments that while in the good old days an adulteress "was burnt, or stoned with stones," and in some areas of the world in the time he was writing, "men cut off their throats, and in some they be beheaded before the people, and in other places they be mured or put between two walls," in France, England, and the Netherlands such richly deserved penalties are eschewed. "Justice is not done of them as in other realms," although the women do lose "their worship and their estate, the love of God and of their lords and of their friends and world also."[37]

While there is no evidence that, outside fiction, medieval England condoned the honor killings the Knight describes, occasionally the records suggest cuckoldry as a husband's motivation for violence. In 1457, an anti-immigrant riot in London, led by a number of artisan servants who had entered into a sworn confederacy, ended in the death of the Genoese merchant Galiot Scot (Galiut Centurioni). The conspirators had hoped to provoke a widespread revolt against the merchant strangers of London, who were "false extortioners, common lechers, and adulterers, wherefore they thought it a good deed to slay and murder them." Thomas Clement, one of the conspirators, said when questioned later by the mayor and aldermen in a special enquiry into the riot, "that especially he intended to have the said Ga.iot Scot for holding the wife of the same Thomas in adultery, unto his perpetual shame."[38] A number of scholars have suggested that the "real reason" for the attack on Scot was not his lechery but instead a desire to protect the Company of the Staple, the association of English wool merchants who resented Italians' encroachment on their control of wool exports.[39] We need not, however, make this cool separation of economic from sexual factors, this surmise that accusations of lechery and adultery could only have been a cover for more "serious" trade issues. Resentment of foreign merchants' economic intrusions was by no means incompatible with resentment of their sexual conquests of English wives; each fed off the other to create the combustible atmosphere that led to rioting.

While the adultery of the wife reflected badly on both spouses, much more serious abrogation of the husband's duty to govern his wife was implied in the actions of those husbands who acted as bawds for their wives or daughters: the wife or daughter remained under his rule, but the husband was using his power to govern her for evil rather than godly purposes. Many women accused of being whores in the civic and ecclesiastical courts of London were married women, often pimped by their husbands.[40] While the wives were still considered responsible for their own part in the deed, their husbands sometimes came in for even greater opprobrium for their fostering of the crime and sin of prostitution. In 1424, John Leche, fellmonger, was led before the mayor and aldermen by the constable and beadle of Breadstreet ward because he had allowed David Holland, a tailor, to lie naked in a bed with his wife. While all three were committed to the stocks for an hour and from there handed over to ecclesiastical authorities for penance, the heading of the entry in the City's letter book is Leche's name, rather than that of his wife or Holland.[41] A particularly colorful example of a husband bawding for his wife is Robert Sewell, a citizen and grocer of London. He was accused in 1455 by the jurors of Cheap ward both of being a leper who endangered other citizens and inhabitants of London by stubbornly continuing to live among them and of being a bawd and fosterer of the act of fornication committed between his wife, Elizabeth, and his servant, Thomas Martyn.[42] For his misdeeds, the mayor and aldermen expelled Sewell from the city, although they softened the expulsion of a fellow citizen somewhat by allowing him several months to get his affairs in order before he left; while by implication

Elizabeth Sewell was expelled along with her husband, the record does not detail any punishment for her or for Thomas Martyn.[43]

Those who did not supervise their dependents adequately were responsible to some extent for their misdeeds, as it was lack of good rule that allowed evil to fester. The mayor and aldermen might thus enjoin householders to govern their servants better: Nicholas Taillour, for instance, was bound for the large sum of £40 in 1457 to ensure the "good rule" of his servants.[44] Others might be cited before the church court: Roger Maryet and his wife, Agnes, were accused there of fostering lechery in their house, particularly for the servants and apprentices of their neighbors, allowing the apprentices to sit and drink in their house on Sundays and holy days when they should have been at Mass.[45] Maintaining good rule over a household was a battle: a master's governance of his servants was constantly under threat from people like Roger and Agnes Maryet. The formulation of a number of complaints about procurers emphasized the "enticing and steering" of respectable men's dependents into discreditable situations. Agnes a Mylle, for instance, was cited as "a common carrier of men's wives and men's servants to the Steelyard [the Hanseatic merchants' compound near the Thames] and other suspicious places."[46] Henry Whithere was accused of procuring and soliciting young girls and servants "of diverse men" to commit the crime of fornication.[47] The fault was committed as much against the governance of the householder as against the young innocents, seduced into a life of sin.

Good governance meant not only ensuring servants' chastity within the household but also refraining from having sexual relations with one's servants. One of the most frequent reasons for citation to the Commissary court was adultery or fornication with a servant,[48] indicating that this was an ideal often broken, given temptations of close living quarters and power relations between employers and servants. At the same time, the citations themselves indicate that it was not universally accepted that servants were an employer's sexual property. In 1488, for example, a wealthy mercer and former churchwarden of St. Michael Bassishaw, Thomas Shelley, allegedly raped a neighbor's servant and committed adultery (consensually?) with his own servant. In compensation he gave the raped woman the relatively immense sum of £40 for a dowry and offered a man named William Stevyns 20 marks to marry the woman who had been in his employ.[49] The size of these dowries—which can be compared with the standard dowries of £1 or less bequeathed to "poor maidens" by charitable testators[50]—indicates that the actions of Thomas Shelley, something of a troublemaker in general,[51] were not taken lightly. It must also be noted, however, that Shelley, like many men who committed sexual violence, probably escaped any criminal censure: such arbitrated compensation payments were fairly common means of dealing with rape.[52]

Even men of the civic elite were not immune from prosecution, and indeed such charges may have been somewhat useful in political struggles between factions. In late January or early February 1471, Master Robert Bassett, longtime alderman of Aldgate ward, was cited before the Commissary court for committing adultery with his servant Margery, although there is no evidence that he was summoned or ever appeared.[53] It is possible, especially given the timing, that the charge was politically motivated: this was at a high point of drama in the Wars of the Roses—the forces favoring the Lancastrian Henry VI had deposed the Yorkist Edward IV, and Henry sat on the throne once again, if only temporarily. The mayor and aldermen were deeply involved in the struggle between Edward IV and Henry VI, Bassett being a committed defender of Edward IV.[54] Several months after the charge of adultery Bassett, as alderman of Aldgate ward, played a heroic role according to the author of the *Great Chronicle of London* in the defense of the City against the assaults on its gates by the Lancastrian "Bastard of Fauconberg," rallying his people against the rebels, commanding them "In the name of God and Saint George."[55] Bassett's civic career appears to have been unaffected by the church court summons, at least in the long term, as he was later elected mayor; indeed he was something of a reformist mayor, as under his watch ordinances were passed against "masterless men" living within City bounds, against keepers of stews harboring men and women at night, and against the playing of tennis, "cloishe" (a game resembling bowls), and "cailes" (ninepins or bowling) in the City.[56]

Sexual relationships developed not only between male employers and female servants but also between mistresses and their male servants: although less frequently accused in the church courts than men, a significant minority of accusations of sexual misbehavior with servants involved female employers.[57] The accusations in these cases are bald, lacking the kind of detail that might give us a sense of either the development of such relationships or how seriously they were viewed; it is possible, though unverifiable, that women who had sex with their servants were more likely to be cited to the court than men. The somewhat uneasy rule of a mistress

over male servants was rendered even more complicated when she became sexually involved with one of them.

Governance was gendered in many ways, particularly regarding its
internal and external force. For both women and men, absence of proper
rule rendered the individual wild and uncontrollable. Responsibility,
however, fell differently. Men were to govern themselves; even men in a
dependent status (servants or underage boys), who were to submit themselves to the rule of their masters or fathers, must nonetheless learn to
rule their impulses in preparation for the day that they too might exercise
governance. A young man, when sent by his father at a "tender age" to
study law at Thavie's Inn, was bound by his father to govern himself
properly or forfeit £20, a very considerable sum.[58] Another father whose
son was entering Lincoln's Inn asked a friend especially to ensure that
his son "be not conversant nor near among women," as he, the father,
himself had kept away from them until he reached the age of thirty.[59] The
Wise Man of the fifteenth-century poem gave his son the same advice:
"flee all lechery in will and deed/Lest thou come to evil end."[60]

Women, to a much greater extent, would probably experience forms
of external governance throughout their lives: lack of restraint reflected
partly on their own internal self-rule, but it also implied explicitly or implicitly absence of male control, or at least absence of proper, reputable,
and righteous male control. Women who acted in an unruly way were often described as having been "enticed and steered" into such actions by
an evil and unscrupulous person,[61] as they could not be held fully (or often legally) responsible for their own deeds. Sexual misbehavior in women
often implied a turning upside-down of true governance. Herman Ryng,
a Hanseatic merchant living in London, complained to the chancellor in
the 1490s that he had been busy about his work in the Steelyard when he
was approached by a certain Joan White, singlewoman, about whom it
was reliably known that she was "wont to dance and make revel in her
master's house, sometimes in man's clothing and sometimes naked." Just
as her master failed to govern her properly, so also did she offer Herman a
form of perverted rule: Ryng said that she presented herself to him sexually, "to be at his commandment."[62] Although Ryng was himself perhaps
not well governed (he was summoned before the Commissary court several times in 1490 and 1491 to answer to charges of fornication and adultery),[63] he used conventionally gendered notions of governance and rule
to frame his Chancery petition. In a similar way, a husband petitioned the

chancellor because Thomas Hervy, a canon of St. Mary Overie in Southwark, allegedly enticed his wife away; as a result, complained the husband,
she was "only at his [Hervy's] rule and commandment."[64] This adulterous
relationship, the husband implied, made a mockery of true governance,
where a wife was under the rule and commandment of her husband, her
natural ruler.

The patterns of patriarchal household governance, with the deeply
held assumptions about gender that ran through them, also had a strong
impact on how sexual behavior was conceptualized. The sexual ideology
of late medieval London culture appears, from surviving records, to be re-
lentlessly heterosexual: not only were appropriate sexual behaviors conceptualized as male-female couplings within marriage, but even sexual
misconduct was assumed to involve a man and woman. Homosexual relations are almost entirely absent from the late medieval English documentary record,[65] despite considerable concern about male same-sex relations
in other parts of Europe in the same period (the documentary silence
about female same-sex relations is less unusual).[66] Only a few ambiguous
references to sodomy survive in the voluminous records of the Commissary court of the diocese of London, even though records survive for
thousands of prosecutions for sexual misconduct over the last three decades of the fifteenth century.[67] The civic records, which include both
rhetoric reviling the sexually degenerate as well as prosecutions of individuals who contravened sexual codes, are equally silent regarding sodomy
or any kind of same-sex relations.[68] Explaining this silence is both difficult
and inevitably speculative.

It is possible, but unlikely, that late medieval Londoners simply did
not regard homosexual relations as problematic—but given otherwise
close adherence to medieval Christian sexual ideology, this is improbable. It is also possible that there were no prosecutions for sodomy in the
Commissary court simply because there was no homosexual sex—this too
is improbable. It is, in fact, not too difficult to explain the absence of references to sodomy in the Commissary court record: prosecutions for homosexual offenses, as more serious sins, would almost certainly have
taken place in a different venue, probably being heard by the bishop himself, like heresy cases. Records of such proceedings, if any were kept, have
not survived. The bishop may have had good reason to keep such processes discreet; most of the scarce evidence surviving for homosexual relations or sodomy accusations in late medieval England focuses on the
clergy.[69] In Germany, the association between sodomy and the clergy fed

a virulent anticlericalism;[70] it would not be surprising if there were homosexual subcultures among English clerics, and it would equally not be surprising if any prosecutions of such behavior among the clergy were kept out of the public eye in order to avoid scandal.

But the silence on homosexual relations goes beyond the church records to the civic records as well: it is remarkable that when civic officials decried heinous sexual behaviors they, too, focused exclusively on heterosexual couplings (with an occasional tripling).[71] From fornication to adultery to prostitution, even to child sexual abuse—both rhetoric and prosecution of sexual offenses assumed that the sexual activity in question involved both male and female persons. While some modern historians have argued that modern Western heterosexual identities were formed in relation to homosexual identities,[72] in late medieval London the other against which appropriate sexual identity was defined was also heterosexual. The epitome of the misgoverned man, the obverse face of the godly upstanding householder, was the adulterer and strumpetmonger rather than the sodomite. Even the exception can be read to prove the rule: one of the most well-known cases of civic prosecution of sexual misbehavior in medieval London was the mayor and aldermen's prosecution of a male transvestite prostitute named John Rykener, known as Eleanor, in 1395. This case, ably analyzed by David Lorenzo Boyd and Ruth Mazo Karras,[73] raises fascinating issues about sexual identity. One of its most striking aspects, as recorded in the city's plea and memoranda rolls, was that the mayor, aldermen, and recorder appear to have been mystified not only by a man who would dress as a woman but also by the idea of men having sex with men (conceptually he could only have sex with a man "as a woman"). The civic authorities appear also not to have known what to do with Rykener: there is no record of any punishment or further process.[74] The terms in which the Rykener case was written into the civic records, along with the general absence throughout the fifteenth century of prosecution and even rhetorical reference to sodomy, suggest a sexual culture in which the idea of same-sex relations was deeply repressed. This is not to say that men never had sex with men nor women with women, but rather that such relations remained outside public discourse, below the documentary radar.

In this culture of "compulsory heterosexuality," sexual misbehavior was deeply gendered and conceptualized as abrogation of household governance: adultery was a man's trespass on another man's wife; fornication was a trespass on a man's daughter or servant; a woman's wantonness was refusal to be ruled by the proper, usually male, authority. Same-sex relationships could have been inserted into this paradigm of household governance, as they were, for instance, in ancient Rome (a man's seduction of a son of prominent family was an offense against the father),[75] but in fifteenth-century London they were not. Sexual misconduct was fundamentally about men's misrule of women, or women's repudiation of proper male rule; conceptually, it was inseparable from its polar opposite of appropriate sexual relations between the husband and wife within marriage. Ironically, it is possible that in some ways same-sex relations may have been easier to conduct in a culture in which they were publicly unthinkable.

Governance in Neighborhood, Parish, Ward, and Guild

In 1489, Thomas Wulley sued Margaret Isot in the Consistory court of the diocese of London in order to enforce a contract of marriage he claimed had been made eighteen years before. Several witnesses appeared on Thomas's behalf to testify about the circumstances in which the marriage vows had been exchanged. In 1471, they reported, Thomas and Margaret had become sexually involved, much to the consternation of Thomas's parents, who did what they could to break it up. One witness reported that Thomas's mother, finding him and Margaret in bed together one day in Margaret's house, hid Thomas's shoes so that he would have to embarrass himself by walking home in Margaret's footwear.[76] But according to the testimony of John Calton, at that time the local constable, neither his father's nor his mother's influence could deter Thomas from Margaret's company. Finally, Thomas's father had gone to Calton and, telling him that Thomas was associating with Margaret "most suspiciously," asked the constable to arrest the pair for fornication and take them to the Counter, the London sheriffs' prison. The illicit relationship between Thomas and Margaret was not news to John Calton: he reported to the court that he had been hearing for about three months that the neighbors in St. John's Street suspected them of fornication because they spent so much time alone together. Thomas's father told Calton that Thomas and Margaret would be lying together that night in the house of one of Calton's neighbors, John Cracow, if he wanted to catch them in the act.

Later that night, about ten o'clock, Calton went to Cracow's house.

As he reported in his deposition, he brought with him four other men, neighbors who had been his dinner guests that evening. When Calton knocked on Cracow's door there was no answer, but the door was open, so he and the other men with him walked into the house and began to search for Thomas and Margaret. Calton found them eventually in a basement room, both hurriedly trying to put on their clothes—as Calton testified, he spotted Thomas wearing only his doublet, with his gown around his head and his hose and shoes under his arm. Calton took the offending couple, along with Cracow, to his own house to question them in front of the four men who had assisted him in the arrest, and some of their wives (still at Calton's house for the dinner party). Cracow, when accused of having harbored fornicators, claimed that he received them in his house because they were, in fact, husband and wife. Calton, now unsure whether he should take Thomas and Margaret to prison as normal procedure would prescribe, turned to Thomas and asked, "Why drawest thou suspiciously to this woman," when, as he said, "it is not thy father's will thou shouldst have her?" Thomas replied, "For one purpose, to wed her." To ensure that Thomas was telling the truth, Calton prompted the two of them there and then to exchange once more vows of present consent to marry. Even if Thomas had lied about the previous contract, the second contract before a host of respectable witnesses itself created an indissoluble union. As marital intercourse was by no means illegal, Calton had no choice then but to let the couple go.[77]

In *Wulley c. Isot*, Thomas Wulley's father's own authority was inadequate to dissuade Thomas from his undesirable relationship with Margaret Isot: sometimes patriarchal authority was absent, or it failed, or it proved insufficient. In such cases, other resources were available to bolster or stand in for the father's or master's governance. Thomas's father was able to make recourse to the local constable, who stepped in and arrested the fornicating couple, and even took the paternal role in the questioning after the arrest, making it clear that Thomas's relationship with Margaret was not in accordance with his father's will.[78]

Thomas Wulley's father was by no means the only Londoner who called upon other authorities in an attempt to shape the behavior of a dependent. As I argued in Chapter 3, part of the social responsibility of senior men was to supervise marital and sexual relationships among those over whom they had authority; it was the duty and privilege of such men to ensure that suitable marriages were made and unsuitable unions prevented or stopped. Their governance extended beyond the family, and the master-servant relationship, into the community as a whole. Suitable moral standards and publicly acknowledged marriages were of common concern, and senior men, as the patriarchs of the community, felt a responsibility to police relationships outside as well as inside their households. While some attempts to influence the marital and sexual behavior of men and women were fairly clearly informal and ad hoc, they were integrally linked to the more official recourses that were available to them through the church courts, the civic courts, and the merchant and craft guilds. These legal and quasi-legal forums acted as tools for those who were able to wield them. Even the simple possibility that more official sanctions could be brought was sometimes as effective as the actual employment of prosecution or litigation.

In order to exercise their authority and discharge their responsibility to ensure proper behavior, these patriarchs could pursue moral infractions through a number of different avenues. It is important to note, however, that these avenues—the church, the ward, the guild—were mostly complementary rather than competing jurisdictions. Indeed, the process through which prosecutions were brought to the lower-level church court (the Commissary court) and to the lower-level civic forum (the wardmote inquest) may have been handled in many cases by the same men. The acknowledged "worthy men" of the neighborhood often wore several hats: a man who acted as a churchwarden in a parish was likely also to serve as a wardmote inquest juror.[79] The same matter was sometimes brought to the attention of various different bodies, all seen as having an interest in issues of misgovernance. John Palmer, for instance, witnessed adultery one day in August 1471 when he entered the house of another man, Horne Tyler (or Horne, a tiler), between four and five in the afternoon. Going up the stairway leading to a certain upper chamber of the house, he saw William Stevenes and Julian Saunder lying on a bed, having sexual intercourse. Julian heard Palmer and came down from the room and asked him to keep what he had seen there secret, offering him a pair of hose as a bribe. Palmer rejected the bribe and instead reported that William and Julian had committed adultery to a number of different authorities: the parish chaplain and parish clerk of St. John in Walbrook (the parish in which the infraction took place), the rector of the church of St. Mary at Hill (William Wylde, who was also Commissary for the Bishop of London,[80] although Palmer did not state this explicitly), and the twelve men of the wardmote inquest jury. In John Palmer's mind, both church and civic officials would be interested in this information.[81]

Attempts to control misbehavior started informally at the neighbor-hood level. As I discuss in the next chapter, gossip and reputation—exercised by both men and women—were powerful tools of social correction. Somewhat more authoritative interventions were also under-taken below the threshold of formal legal processes: senior men of a neighborhood or parish would sometimes seek to move a misbehaving couple onto a straight and narrow path. John Gosnell of the parish of Walthamstow, for instance, testified that he had confronted Richard Heth "because it was publicly said that Richard too suspiciously frequented the home" of Gosnell's neighbor Agnes Waltham. Gosnell said that he told Richard that he would not tolerate such frequent visits unless he knew whether Richard intended to marry Agnes. At length, Richard admitted that Agnes was his wife, and Gosnell directed them at once, through the ritual questions, to declare before witnesses their vows of present consent to marry.[82] Another example of local outrage apparently prompted one of the few ex officio cases instigated by the London Consistory court.[83] Richard Ellbich had married an excommunicated woman named Alice Trehest clandestinely and outside the parish church and had lived with her and slept with her even though she was excommunicated. John Cruse, a sixty-four-year-old tailor, reported that "most of the neighbors feel and think that this was and is true, and they speak badly of them."[84] Neighbors and parish priests could try to mediate between spouses in the case of a marriage breakdown: in 1476, John Lewys testified that he, an-other layman named Gilbert Horne, and Sir John, the parson of the parish of Lambeth, had several months before brought about a meeting in the Saracen's Head tavern near St. Paul's Cathedral between Katherine Burwell alias Bachelere and her estranged husband, William Bachelere, who had not lived together for five years. Although their attempt to rec-oncile the husband and wife did not succeed—William Bachelere in fact declared he would cut Katherine's throat if he were compelled to live with her—the two laymen subsequently played a role in a different sort of set-tlement of the marriage dispute: they acted as Katherine's witnesses when she sued him for divorce for cruelty.[85] Improper marriages and sexual re-lationships were of wide community concern: they were not only canoni-cally incorrect but also seen as damaging to social relationships. Men like William Hathewey, who married first one woman and then another, often left the first woman in a sorry situation, with a blemished reputation and perhaps a child, unable canonically to remarry. Men like William Bachelere, who went beyond reasonable chastisement into unreasonable cruelty, brought all husbands' authority over their wives into disrepute. It was up to other men to prevent or correct these situations.

Informal pressure did not always work, of course, and in more obdurate cases, leading men of a neighborhood could take a number of tacks. For moral infractions, sins against God, an obvious line of defense was through the ecclesiastical system, in particular the unit through which English Christians practiced their religion, the parish. The parish was in a sense jointly ruled by the parish clergy and the leading laymen of the parish; although evidence for this is somewhat patchy, it is clear that priests and parishioners played a role, and probably an important one, in using parish organizations and the church courts to regulate moral behavior.

In the late Middle Ages all people living in England—where Christianity was the only legal religion—belonged to the parish in which they resided. Although some late medieval English cities had very large parishes (Coventry, for instance, a city of some ten thousand people, had only two parish churches), London parishes were small units. There were more than one hundred parishes in the City, many of which extended over only a few streets, and on average each ministered to about three hundred people.[86] Responsibility for administering the parish and caring for its church building was divided between the parish priest (the parson) and the lay parishioners. The laity were represented by two men who acted as churchwardens, usually for overlapping terms of two years (in the first year a man would be junior churchwarden, the second year moving into the senior position). While the churchwardens acted for the lay parishioners generally, as in other instances in late medieval English society where collective authority was exercised, in practice, the real power lay with a group of "worthy men," the parish elders, most or all of whom had served in their day as churchwarden and continued to act in a supervisory role after their service in this office. Clive Burgess has brought to light a fascinating pyramidical diagram included in the records of the London parish of St. Mary at Hill, which places each of the "significant" parishioners into a defined hierarchy. Those at the top of the pyramid had already served as churchwardens and acted as supervisors of those currently serving; churchwardens of subsequent years came from the middle tiers, indicating that the office was an entry point into the senior levels of the parish worthies. A parishioner's place on the pyramid not only reflected parish service but also correlated significantly with wealth.[87] This was local power, a diagram of big fish in a small pond: interestingly, the name of the alderman of Billingsgate ward in which the parish was located was placed above the pyramid, alongside the name of the parson, indicating both his importance and his transcendence of the parish power structures.[88]

Through the three centuries following the Fourth Lateran Council at the beginning of the thirteenth century, lay parishioners were assigned, and indeed embraced, considerable responsibility in the parish. They were accountable for the upkeep of part of the church, usually the nave, where the congregation sat or stood during the Mass. Together with the parish priest, they managed and paid for the often numerous services for the souls of departed parishioners, in particular administering the properties that had come to the parish through bequests for precisely the purpose of funding these services. Lay parishioners, represented by the churchwardens, had important financial and managerial responsibilities, and it is thus not surprising that the leading men of the parish—who in the urban context were invariably merchants and prosperous artisans—dominated the administration. We know a considerable amount about this side of parish life, for churchwardens rendered accounts of their income and spending on an annual or biennial basis, and a significant number of these accounts survive for the fifteenth century and later.[89]

Another of the duties of the churchwardens is less well documented: their duty to report parishioners' moral infractions to ecclesiastical officials. This duty was fulfilled through reports given during periodic (often annual) visitations by the bishop or (more frequently) a deputy such as an archdeacon.[90] In London it is probable that bishops or their deputies conducted such visitations, but there is no direct indication in surviving late-medieval records of how frequently.[91] Other mechanisms, however, were almost certainly in place for London churchwardens and other parishioners to report misdeeds, for the Lord Commissary of the bishop of London operated a busy court in which he prosecuted hundreds of cases of misbehavior a year related to the City of London, the cases not falling into any obvious annual pattern that might indicate referrals through visitations.[92]

The Commissary court exercised criminal jurisdiction: that is, the Lord Commissary summoned accused misdoers to answer to allegations about sins that had been committed. These accusations or presentments before the commissary were recorded in the act books of the court, which survive for London from 1470. Unfortunately those records rarely indicate how the accusation came to the commissary, but evidence allows us to infer that the cases came to his ears from a number of different routes. Some derived from reports made by the parish clergy: in their pastoral role, parish priests were charged with bringing misbehavers to correction.[93] But it would be misleading to suggest that the ecclesiastical correction system ordinarily pitted the clergy against the laity. Although Chaucer's figure of the Summoner (subtly spying on lechers) might encourage us to see a nosy and eavesdropping church-court functionary attempting to ferret out immoral acts,[94] there is little evidence of such church-police figures operating in London in the fifteenth century.[95] As Richard Wunderli and L. R. Poos have suggested, all indications point to lay parishioners, through the churchwardens, rather than ecclesiastical investigators as the conduit through which most misconduct was revealed to the commissary.[96] (This is similar to the process by which misdemeanors, often the same kinds of sexual offenses, were prosecuted in the local civic forum, the wardmote inquest, as we will see later.) Some act book presentments included the kind of detail that could only have come from inquisitive neighbors, as when Joan Macheynce of Shoreditch was cited for committing adultery with John Lectum. She was said to provide him with food, drink, and money; he lay at her house during the day and on nights when her husband was absent; and calling himself her husband he bought hens, roosters, eggs, and other food and brought them back to the house.[97] Neighbors unhappy with a woman and man who mocked the social conventions could avail themselves of the Commissary court as a tool of correction, directing their complaints through their parish priest, through their churchwardens, or perhaps directly by complaining to the commissary (as, for instance, John Palmer seems to have done when he witnessed the adultery of William Stevenes and Julian Saunder).[98]

Parish guilds or fraternities also played some role in the regulation of morals within the parish. From the second half of the fourteenth century, most London parishes had established at least one religious fraternity, an association of parishioners (usually a broad cross-section, although likely not the very poor) dedicated to collective religious devotions and to providing for members during hard times; these religious guilds were closely related to, and sometimes indistinguishable from, the craft guilds that regulated particular occupations but that also had important religious functions. Fraternities usually supported an altar and a chaplain in the parish church, where masses were said for the souls of departed parishioners, and brothers and sisters of the fraternity participated in an annual mass dedicated to the guild's patron saint, followed by a feast.[99] Guilds served an important function both in creating ties among parishioners of different social rank and in building and reinforcing vertical hierarchies within the parish; as Gervase Rosser has put it, the annual fraternity feasts were "social politics in action."[100] Members of fraternities were to follow particular rules of conduct, to live Christian lives. If they did not—if they were found to be, as the rules of the fraternity of St. Peter in the parish of St. Peter Cornhill put it, a "common contecker [one who is quarrelsome], hazarder [gambler], lecher, chider, [or] false usurer"[101]—they were to be expelled from the fraternity. We know little about how such rules were applied in practice, but they suggest that the parish fraternity was yet another way that neighbors supervised and shaped moral conduct, probably, as in other collectivities, most often according to the hierarchical social structures of neighborhood and parish.

Closely tied to the ecclesiastical system of correction were the civic courts. The relationship between the two jurisdictions, ecclesiastical and secular, is not entirely clear, but it does not appear to have been unfriendly. Civic officials routinely turned over clerical offenders to the ecclesiastical ordinary in the late fourteenth and fifteenth centuries.[102] Similarly, the London Commissary court frequently noted that accused wrongdoers had been arrested by civic officials when it prosecuted adulterers, bawds, and prostitutes, suggesting that the arrest itself had prompted the citation before the ecclesiastical court.[103] The two jurisdictions—both reflecting in different ways the power and authority of leading men of a neighborhood—were apparently wielded in concert more than in competition.[104] Indeed, the double jeopardy under which a fornicator, prostitute, or bawd stood may have made up for the relatively puny sanctions available in either forum.

Although the two jurisdictions were connected, the civic forums were even more directly than the ecclesiastical courts an extension of the patriarchal authority of the leading men of a neighborhood. Just as a citizen of London reasonably expected the mayor and chamberlain of the City to act as guardian for any orphans he might leave, so also did men look to their civic government as an extension of their fatherly authority in other ways. The wardmote juries, to whom constables might report wrongdoers such as Thomas Wulley and Margaret Isot after they had been arrested, were particularly active in attempting to shape the behavior of the inhabitants of the local civic districts, the wards. Wardmote inquests were normally convened once a year, usually in December or early January.[105] Twelve or thirteen men appointed by the alderman (or, according to some sources, elected by the honest men of the ward from amongst themselves) formed the wardmote inquest jury. One witness before the Consistory court in 1472 described the gathering of such a body: "on a certain day within twelve days immediately following the feast of Christmas, . . . [at] a certain place commonly called Hewlyn's Place," there came "thirteen persons named and elected by Sir George Irlond, alderman of Cordwainer Street Ward." As the witness explained, their purpose was "to inquire into and investigate crimes perpetrated in the said ward and to expell criminal persons because of their misgovernment and their crimes."[106] Wardmote inquest juries served a purpose similar in many ways to other late medieval legal bodies, such as leet juries of market towns and tithing groups (especially as the latter survived after the Black Death), which exercised a form of mutual supervision of behavior: neighbors policed neighbors. As in the parishes, such supervision tended to be a top-down affair, the more substantial (and therefore respectable) men bearing the responsibility to govern and correct the behavior of their social inferiors.[107]

Although fornication, adultery, and other sexual sins were theoretically under ecclesiastical jurisdiction, from at least the end of the thirteenth century, wardmote inquests had made sexual misbehavior committed by the inhabitants of the wards their business, along with such matters as keeping the roads clear and cleaning the ditches. Regulations from the reign of Edward I forward provided that wardmote inquest juries were to present common adulterers, bawds, and prostitutes to the alderman's attention, and that the alderman was to order the removal from the ward of persistent offenders.[108] As the journal of the Court of Common Council recorded in 1473, inquest juries were enjoined to present the names of "all common bawds, common strumpets, and common strumpetmongers, or common putours [fornicators], as well men as women, dwelling, coming, or repairing unto your said wards. Ye shall furthermore present the names of all persons within your said wards which late hath committed or done any adultery, and the names also of all such persons with whom such adultery is done, whether they be common adulterers or not."[109]

In the later fourteenth century, civic officials established detailed regulations for the arrest and punishment of such persons, and the City continued to use these provisions through the fifteenth century.[110] The actual procedure in all cases is not entirely clear, but records indicate that normally the beadle or one of the constables of a ward[111] arrested offenders and took them to a jail (usually one of the two sheriffs' prisons, called the Counters), where they remained for a short time while officials decided how to proceed with the case. Some were forwarded to the ecclesiastical courts, which had a considerable business in the prosecution of sexual offenses, whereas others would later come before their local wardmote inquest. After an appearance before the inquest, "criminal persons," including bawds, prostitutes, fornicators, and adulterers, could be presented before the court of the mayor and the aldermen.[112] The wardmote inquest juries themselves may have come to the Guildhall to present their findings, at least until the 1480s, when the mayor and aldermen decreed that henceforth only the alderman should appear with the inquests' verdicts, "eschewing of the great jeopardy and perils that have grown by coming of the multitude of the same inquests to the said hall in times passed."[113] If convicted before the mayor and aldermen, the miscreants were subject to a number of punishments, including, for the most egregious cases, imprisonment and banishment from the city.[114]

The few wardmote inquest presentments that survive from the fifteenth century—the Portsoken ward records for 1465–82 being the most extensive—tell us that arrests for sexual misbehavior were by no means unusual.[115] The Portsoken presentments may tend to mislead us, though, into thinking that ward officials were only interested in prostitution and procurement—the juries there presented women and occasionally men as common strumpets, harlots of their bodies, bawds, and strumpetmongers. Other records, including the church-court deposition evidence, make it clear that in other wards beadles and constables also pursued simple fornicators and especially adulterers. This may indicate that Portsoken had a particular prostitution problem or that designating someone as a "strumpet" or a "harlot of his/her body" was to mark them as sexually promiscuous rather than or in addition to accepting money for sexual favors.[116]

The laconic civic records of the proceedings give us little sense about how the arrests were made,[117] information that is crucial for understanding how constables and beadles attempted to regulate behavior and in whose interests they were acting. More detailed evidence about how such disorders came to the attention of civic officials comes from ecclesiastical court depositions. In a few cases, we learn how the beadle or the constable came to know that a couple would be engaged in illicit activities at a particular time and place; in *Wulley c. Isot*, for instance, Thomas Wulley's father informed the constable where the couple would be.[118] In most cases, ward officials probably came to know about sexual irregularities and their likely time and location through the rumor networks active in every ward and parish. Witnesses offered testimony regarding civic attempts to control sexual misbehavior in order to impugn the trustworthiness of other deponents, or in suits involving defamation or marriage where actions by ward authorities were part of the case. These records can tell us a good deal about how relatives, neighbors, and ward officials handled misbehavior.

In the case of Thomas Wulley and Margaret Isot, the constable John Calton, by virtue of his office, entered a neighbor's house without his permission, late in the evening, because he had reasonable cause to suspect there were fornicators on the premises. Other constables and beadles also burst into people's houses—even at four o'clock in the morning[119]—to catch offenders in the act. Robert Serle, constable in Aldgate ward, for instance, entered into Margaret Hordley's home at ten o'clock in the evening, where he found Herbert Rowland and Margaret together alone; they, like Thomas Wulley and Margaret Isot, escaped a trip to the Counter by claiming that they were married.[120] One man caught committing adultery was dragged out of a window before being taken to the Counter.[121] Other men tried unsuccessfully to escape arrest and were found hiding under the women's beds.[122] In testimony in a Consistory marriage case, we catch something of the technique of surprise used in these arrests: two deponents seeking to discredit previous witnesses reported that one man guarded the door while the beadle and another man marched into the house and up into the chamber, where they discovered an unmarried couple alone together.[123] In this case, as in the arrest of Thomas Wulley and Margaret Isot, other men from the neighborhood aided the beadle or constable in the apprehension of the wrongdoers.[124] It was important, if not always imperative, that those seeking to impose a standard of morality have an official and public role: on a number of occasions Londoners claimed that those who broke into homes to arrest wrongdoers did so "without any constable or other officer or any manner of lawful authority."[125]

A wardmote inquest jury could exert considerable pressure on misbehavers to regularize their lives. In early 1472 two fornicators, Joan Chylde and Thomas Rote, were called before their local wardmote inquest to answer for their crime. Thomas Rote, examined first, was asked by one of the twelve members of the jury why he associated with Joan Chylde in this way, and Rote answered that he wanted to make Joan his wife. Joan, too, indicated that she wished to marry, so then and there they exchanged consent in front of those gathered for the inquest. They kissed, and from then on they were publicly regarded as contracted to one another.[126] The "community of the ward," as represented by the twelve men, clearly felt that their illicit relationship was its business. The pressure brought by the senior men upon the couple did not successfully effect a valid marriage in this case—we know about it because Thomas Rote failed to keep the contract. But while Thomas Rote did not wish to honor his vow (which he later claimed was conditional), he never questioned the jury's jurisdiction in his sexual relationships.

Even when official channels were not actually used, the possibility that they might be invoked gave some men's attempts to shape behavior more authority and force. The threat of an indictment before a London civic court and the shame that would accompany it could in itself prove decisive. As we saw at the beginning of this book, when John Wellys attempted to force William Rote to marry his daughter Agnes, attacking him with a knife and threatening to bring him in front of the mayor and aldermen, Rote later claimed in the Consistory court that he contracted marriage with Agnes Wellys that afternoon "as much out of fear for his body as out of shame of appearing before the mayor and aldermen."[127]

All men did not share equally in access to formal means of regulation: status and "substance" (wealth) as well as gender were important factors. Fifteenth-century civic and ecclesiastical documents are full of descriptive phrases that are, to us, vague and ill-defined, but which, to medieval people, were nuanced and perhaps even precise: "fideidigni" (the trustworthy), "plus sufficeauntz" (the more substantial), "valiores" (the more worthy), "boni et graves" (good and serious men or people).[128] Clearly it was those men of "good fame" rather than those of "ill fame" who were to share in offices; gradations of wealth and status determined where in the official hierarchy men were to serve, reflecting both the obligations and the benefits of greater affluence.[129] The phrasing of the warrant issued to aldermen to call their wardmote inquests reminds us that subtle distinctions determined the roles men were to play in the ward: the representatives chosen for the city's Common Council—the highest political post below alderman—were to be the most "sufficient men of good and wisest discretion"; the wardmote jury was to be staffed by "the worthiest men of all your Ward"; and beadles, constables, and scavengers, important if lower-status ward officials, were to be "honest persons."[130] Those filling the higher offices at least, from alderman through the wardmote inquest jury, often served year after year.[131]

The City exercised a general jurisdiction over those who lived within its boundaries, but other organizations also sought to regulate behavior. The guilds, in particular, hoped to keep their members' disputes and misbehavior out of the civic courts, dealing as far as possible with any problems internally.[132] As the Merchant Taylors put it, "great infamy" would accrue to the fellowship of tailors as a whole if various misdeeds were to "be published and come to light before the Chamberlain of this city and further . . . before the mayor and aldermen of the same city."[133] The Society of Lincoln's Inn similarly noted a close call of collective embarrassment when the Society was able to convince the alderman of the ward of Farringdon Without not to commit William Elys, one of their members, to Newgate prison after Elys had been caught by the beadle and constable of the ward in a house of ill-fame with a woman named Grace. The Society expelled Elys, although they readmitted him on payment of a relatively small fine (6s. 8d.) and on condition that he never again communicate in any way with Grace.[134] Other occupational organizations also responded to acts taken by the City against their members by expelling brothers who had been publicly indicted for sexual misdeeds. Several years before Robert Sewell, notorious bawd and leper, was expelled from the City for pimping his wife, he was also expelled from the Grocers' Company, "for obstinacy . . . and breaking of good rules." He had to pay the considerable fine of £6 13s. 4d. to be readmitted.[135] Even a serious case encompassing a plot to murder a man in order to marry his wife could be dealt with at the level of the livery company. In 1480, Edward IV wrote to the Mercers' Company and asked them to deal with two of their members, Thomas Wyndoute and John Lewellen, who had made "a sinister bargain" that 540 Flemish pounds would be paid by Wyndoute to Lewellen upon Wyndoute's marriage to the wife of Thomas Shelley, another mercer. What separated this from a standard, if expensive, marriage brokerage fee was that Thomas Shelley was still very much alive; as the king put it in his letter, obviously such a bargain could only be kept by conspiring to kill Shelley.[136] No doubt there was more to this odd story than now meets the eyes—Thomas Shelley was a quarrelsome man who had been chastised at least twice by the Mercers' Company and would later be accused of rape.[137] But even so, both the king's letter and the Mercers' Company's own court minutes suggest that such a matter could be dealt with appropriately through the private arbitration of the Mercers' Company.[138]

While both men and women could participate in the attempts to shape their neighbors' behavior through public talk and through reports to bodies such as the wardmote inquest and the Commissary court, only men could play a formal and official role as jurors, craft officials, and churchwardens.[139] A London man's participation in the parish, craft, and city, at whatever level was suitable to his status, was one aspect of his patriarchal duty and privilege of governance. At the same time, such public service helped to define and reflect his identity as a respectable and worthy man.[140] Through formal and informal means, senior men sought to oversee the relationships of those for whom they held responsibility, including their children, their servants, and sometimes their neighbors. These ideals of governance and patriarchy were by no means unproblematic, however, as I discuss in the next chapter: sex and its relation to reputation, for instance, was a particular site of conflict.

7

Gender, Sex, and Reputation

MAINTENANCE OF REPUTATION was of the utmost importance in late medieval society. The concepts of honor and reputation were, however, gender-specific values: women's value and identity were more closely tied than men's to marital status, marriageability, and above all, sexual repute. But this does not mean that men's sexual acts and attitudes were irrelevant to their good name. Male sexual reputability was contested territory, as notions of self-governance, Christian morality, and honor battled with an ethic in which male status and identity were defined by the sexual conquest of women.

"Her Good Name"

Complicated stories about sexual reputation and its relationship to a person's good name abound in the records of fifteenth-century London. A particularly interesting one involves the story of a woman whose fame (she claimed) was unreasonably besmirched. Sometime about 1480, two Londoners, Joan Bawde and her husband, Humphrey, submitted a petition to the chancellor of England in which they told a story of attempted seduction, outraged virtue, and justifiable beating.[1] The villain of the piece was not the seducer but a woman named Maude Olyff, who tried to take advantage of Joan when she knew Humphrey was working and residing in another part of London. According to Joan and Humphrey, Maude, "knowing the same Joan was dwelling in the house alone, . . . labored subtly to the said Joan, saying that there was a man the which ought to be her heartly love and gladly would be with her acquainted." But Joan, a virtuous woman, refused any acquaintance "by the which she in any wise might be hurt of her good name." Maude, a woman of "uncleanly disposition" and some persistence, nonetheless fully intended to help the man "to have his foul lust and will of the said Joan." To that purpose Maude secretly brought the man to Joan's house while Joan was out working in a shed in her yard; when Joan returned to the main house, she found him lying on a bench in her kitchen. When he saw her, he started up and "took the said Joan in his arms, saying that he would have and do with her or else he would die for it." Joan struggled against him, and "by the help and grace of our lady, that blessed virgin, she broke from him" and remained a "woman not defiled." She took a staff and "there gave to the said man a dozen stripes and drove him out of her husband's house." When Joan next met Maude, she gave her a slap on the cheek and told her never to bring such a man to her house again. But Maude subsequently sued Joan for trespass, alleging that Joan had assaulted her, not just with the slap but with a staff. Joan admitted that she had slapped Maude (and indeed she did not explicitly deny that she had beaten her with a stick), but felt that this assault was justified because of Maude's outrageous insult to her virtue and to her reputation.

Joan's story offers us an opening into a discussion of notions of sexual impropriety, virtue, and reputation in late medieval London. The petition to the chancellor foregrounds not the unnamed male attacker but Maude Olyff's role in attempting to procure a partner for this man; Maude, a sinful woman herself, attempted to seduce the vulnerable Joan into adultery while her husband was absent. Joan's role is that of the virtuous woman, ever watchful of her good name, a fragile possession always open to attack from the unscrupulous. Her escape from her attacker is depicted in remarkably physical terms—she "struggled sore with him," and then after she broke away from him she drove him out of the house by beating him—yet her escape is not due entirely to her own strength but instead was assisted by the power of the Virgin, who comes to the aid of the virtuous woman. Joan's report that she invoked the Virgin to protect her, conventional as it may seem in the context of late medieval religious culture, is in fact unusual in English legal materials; explicit references to the intervention of God or the saints in the sexual or marital activities of the late medieval English laity are rare in the records of the secular or ecclesiastical courts.[2] Although Joan emphasizes her status as a virtuous woman, her role as wife is stressed less; while the attacker was driven out of Joan's "husband's house," after having presumed to trespass on both Humphrey's wife and his home, Humphrey is completely absent from the scene of the attempted rape and then apparently also from the retributory attack on Maude. Although Humphrey, as a baker's servant, would probably by necessity have lived away from the marital home through the week,[3] his lack of action to protect his wife is a weak link in the petition and is not satisfactorily explained. Despite the mysteries of the petition's interstices, Maude and Joan are, in the narrative of the petition, two faces of the fifteenth-century woman: one is of "uncleanly disposition" and through wily methods attempts to bring other women to sin, presumably for a price, while the other is the very picture of modesty, probity, and above all, reputability.

Joan's anxiety about "her good name" points to a central concern of late medieval people: maintenance of their reputation or fame. While Joan's petition highlights the differences between her virtuous nature and Maude Olyff's sinful nature, the unnamed man is also characterized in sexual terms: he is the epitome of the ungoverned man, his "foul lust" uncontrolled. A reputable man did not act in this way.

Philandering Physicians: Men and Sexual Reputation

In 1476, Alice Hobbys sued her husband, Master William Hobbys, doctor of medicine and surgery and principal surgeon to the king,[4] for divorce on the grounds of adultery.[5] On being questioned by the official presiding over the Consistory court, William admitted that despite twenty years of marriage and five children he had committed adultery from at least 1462, sleeping with many different women in Calais, Saint-Omer, Southwark, the City of London, and other places. Alice, however, had been unaware of his infidelities, he said, until she came to hear of it around Christmas 1475, first from their neighbors and then from his own confession. Since then, he complained, Alice had contemptuously rejected his embraces, refusing to fulfill the marital debt (i.e., the duty that each spouse owed the other of having sex when asked).

Following William's examination, several witnesses came forward to testify in the case. Two fellow surgeons, Richard Chambyr and John Staveley, who had joined Hobbys as part of Edward IV's military expedition to France in the summer of 1475,[6] testified that Hobbys had misbehaved while overseas. Chambyr deposed that while both he and William Hobbys were in the town of Péronne in Picardy, he saw William lying on a bed with a prostitute, both of them naked. Upon finding William in this situation, he later testified, he spoke to him, telling him that he marveled ("mirando") that William would want to commit adultery with a prostitute. John Staveley testified that he had seen William Hobbys entering brothels on many occasions in Calais, Saint-Omer, and Péronne and that William used to stay there suspiciously, committing adultery, as Staveley believed, with the said prostitutes.[7] William also resorted to prostitutes while at home, according to other witnesses. Thomas Rolf and Robert Halyday, also barber-surgeons, both told the official that a year ago the previous June, they had been called to a brothel in Southwark to minister to the brothelkeeper, who had been wounded, presumably in a fight. While there, Rolf and Halyday happened to look through a hole in the wall into another room, where they saw William Hobbys lying on a bed with a prostitute, described as a "young girl" ("juvencula"). Like Richard Chambyr, they too "marveled" at William's illicit deed. Soon after, the older of the two, Robert Halyday, who was at that time master of the Barber Surgeons' Guild,[8] confronted William Hobbys and upbraided him for his nefarious deed, with the intention, he claimed, of persuading William to eschew such behavior in future. After hearing these witnesses and considering the motions put forward by the lawyers for each of the parties to the case, the official granted a decree of divorce *a mensa et thoro*, noting that William had rashly violated the matrimonial bed by committing adultery. Henceforth, Alice would not be required to consort or cohabit with William, nor to render the conjugal debt.[9]

Alice Hobbys's grant of divorce from her husband, William, opens up a number of questions about attitudes toward sexual morality and masculinity in late medieval London. Adultery was by no means unusual in late medieval London; why in this case could it serve as the grounds for divorce, as a sin heinous enough to break asunder what God had joined together? How can we understand the response of Hobbys's fellow surgeons to his behavior? Was Hobbys's occupation as surgeon and physician—the juxtaposition of the filth of his sin and his supposed dedication to health—a crucial element in the apparently overblown reaction to his adultery? Is it significant that Hobbys was a married physician, one of the first English laymen to become an academically trained medical doctor? Were his status as royal servant and his connections to the king's court important?

The reaction to Hobbys's behavior probably derived at least in part from a conflict between different styles of masculinity and the ambiguous part played by sexuality in defining appropriate manly conduct. Recent work on medieval and early modern masculinity has emphasized that we cannot think of masculinity as a unitary phenomenon.[10] To put it simply, there were many ways to be a man in the Middle Ages: city men were different from country men; aristocrats were different from merchants; university scholars were different from the unlearned; apprentices were different from masters; young men were different from old. For those who had fingers in a number of different masculine subcultures, inevitable conflicts of expectations and values could result. In an attempt to explain the reactions to William Hobbys's adultery, I will look first at the phenomenon of divorce itself and then move on to look at some of the models of masculinity and sexuality Hobbys experienced in his life as surgeon, as court physician, and as London citizen.

In medieval ecclesiastical courts, the divorce *a mensa et thoro*, from board and bed, was the equivalent of a modern judicial separation. The fact of the marriage itself was not denied, but on the grounds of cruelty, adultery, or "spiritual fornication" (adherence to heresy), the couple was allowed to live apart and to cease rendering the conjugal debt, although neither could remarry. This sort of divorce was not at all common in the late Middle Ages (or indeed at any time in the medieval period). For example, only about ten marriage cases from the surviving records of the late medieval diocese of London are suits for divorce *a mensa et thoro*; all but one of these were brought by wives against husbands; and all but *Hobbys c. Hobbys*, and possibly one other, were brought on the grounds of cruelty.[11] Divorces *a mensa et thoro* sought on the grounds of adultery were very rare in medieval Catholic Europe generally, those sought by the wife even more so.[12] Obviously many people had the grounds to seek divorces on the grounds of adultery, but very few did. Richard Helmholz has speculated that formal ecclesiastically granted divorces were rarely sought because unsanctioned "self-divorce" was so frequently practiced—that is, either abandonment of one spouse by another or mutually agreed-upon informal separation.[13]

Why, then, would Alice Hobbys have pursued this unusual course? Alice herself gave no deposition in her divorce suit and we know almost nothing about her. The only record of her outside the testimony offered in her divorce suit that I have been able to locate is a laconic and difficult to read entry in the records of testamentary proceedings in the Commissary court of London, which indicates that she died in December 1495 or 1496, and that there was some dispute about whether she died intestate.[14] Her motives in the suit can thus only be inferred conjecturally from the testimony offered by the witnesses in the case. As the wife of a wealthy man, she may not have felt that it was possible simply to run away from her husband, as some women in her situation evidently did; she would almost certainly have lost a great deal materially from such an action. William, from the evidence of his own deposition, seems not to have been willing to agree to an informal separation, probably the most common solution to marriage breakdown, and particularly seems to have been insistent on his sexual rights. One might guess, again from the evidence of William's deposition, that Alice felt driven to pursue this course by her repugnance at having sexual relations with the man she had just learned had slept with an unknown number of prostitutes.

Alice's evident refusal to render the conjugal debt because of William's adultery, and the shock and dismay that the witnesses in the case expressed regarding his sexual misbehavior, are topics that bear further discussion. First, however, let us turn to William Hobbys's career as a physician and surgeon and his professional relationship with the witnesses who testified on Alice's behalf, as they bear on the interpretation of the case.

William Hobbys rose to considerable prominence as surgeon and physician in the second half of the fifteenth century.[15] Following in the footsteps of his father, John, a surgeon who had been warden of the Company of Surgeons of London in 1448, William served as warden twice, in 1458 and 1461.[16] Unlike his father, however, William moved from surgery into medicine. Although it was then still unusual in England for married laymen to pursue academic medicine, he trained as a physician at Oxford and Cambridge in the 1450s, receiving his M.D. from Cambridge in 1461–62.[17] Perhaps even more unusually, he combined the arcane formal academic training of the physician with the more practical skills of the surgeon.[18] First working for the Duke of York in the 1450s, he entered into the service of the duke's son, Edward IV, by the early 1460s and apparently served as royal physician and surgeon through the reigns of Edward IV and Richard III. A position at the royal court was the surest avenue to riches and professional recognition for medical men in the fifteenth century; like other royal physicians, William Hobbys was granted the considerable salary of 40 marks per annum by Edward IV in 1470, a sum that was increased to £40 per annum by Richard III in 1484.[19] Hobbys obviously greatly valued the favor that he had been shown by the house of York, for when he lay dying in 1488, he ordered that a marble stone be placed over his tomb, inscribed thus: "Here lies William Hobbys, formerly physician and surgeon of the most illustrious duke of York, and his sons the most illustrious kings Edward IV and Richard III, whose souls may God protect, amen."[20]

William Hobbys was thus a highly educated and wealthy man, at the peak of his profession. While nothing in the surviving evidence regarding his medical career suggests that the 1476 divorce harmed his professional standing as court physician and surgeon, his notorious behavior could well have adversely affected his relationships with other surgeons in London. It is curious that the men who testified on Alice's behalf all worked in the surgical profession. One was the master of the London guild of barber-surgeons, while two of them worked under William on the military expedition in France and had possibly been his apprentices. One may even have subsequently become William's (and Alice's) son-in-law.[21] Why would they have testified against William? There are any number of reasons why they might have done so, but the reason explicit in their depositions is that they strongly disapproved of William Hobbys's behavior. They all took pains to insist that they had not themselves been patrons of the brothels where they saw William Hobbys. Whether they actually felt strongly about his adultery is unknowable at this remove, but the sentiments they expressed would have had to be credible to be effective as testimony.

Hobbys's neighbors may have been particularly concerned about his open adultery because of his occupation as physician. Hyperbolic reactions by Londoners to two other philandering medical men in the second half of the fifteenth century suggest that some were uncomfortable with the juxtaposition of sexual sin and the health professions. In 1474 the mayor and aldermen of London arrested and imprisoned a barber-surgeon, John Denys, on a charge of bawdry, or pimping. Neither the charge nor the arrest were in themselves unusual, but the rhetoric in which the charges were presented was. In answer to a chancery writ of *corpus cum causa*, the mayor and aldermen defended their arrest and imprisonment of Denys. The tone of the London city fathers' answer to the chancellor, interestingly written in Latin rather than the usual Chancery English, was high-flown: "Just as crows and eagles, by the instinct of their nature, converge on places where dead bodies lie [*sicut corui et aquile ex sue instinctu nature ad loca ubi cadauera mortua iacent convolant*]," the mayor and aldermen wrote, so also do bawds attract to their bawdy-houses, by their nefarious vice of lust, other evildoers, whence comes murder, robbery, felonies, litigiousness, dissensions, and other evil deeds against the king's peace and the healthy (*sanum*) and politic rule of the kingdom.[22] Death, crime, and prostitution are opposed to order, good rule, and health.

Even more suggestively, Hobbys's Tudor successor as court physician, Lewis of Caerleon, was presented to the Commissary court of London in 1491 on a charge of adultery. The charge was ordinary enough: as we have seen, each year, hundreds of Londoners were accused before this lower-level church court by their churchwardens, fellow parishioners, or parish priests of sexual sins of one kind or another. The presentments of those accused were recorded in act books, normally in a brief and bald fashion: "William Keynys committed adultery with Elizabeth his servant and impregnated her."[23] But the citation of Lewis is unusually elaborated, ringing with indignation:

Master Lewis Kaerlon, in greatest contempt of Christianity, impregnated his servant Margaret; he sent her to the country to wait there until she gave birth; afterwards, she returned to his house. He impregnated her a second time and again sent her outside the city and she is pregnant now. He cares neither for God, nor for the lord king whom he serves, nor for the law, nor for the ministers of the law. He has a young wife who is certain of these things, as are all his neighbours.[24]

As the presentment hints, Lewis of Caerleon was a man of considerable prominence and high political connections: he was royal physician to Henry VII and England's leading astronomer and mathematician of the fifteenth century. Despite, or perhaps because of, his standing, Lewis's commonplace sexual misbehavior, impregnating a household servant, was presented in an unusual way, as an attack both on Christianity and on the crown. Not only do the presenters invoke Lewis's status as royal servant, but they also mention his "young" wife: the implication is that he had no reason to seek extramarital sex. The presentment apparently derived both from the discontent of his wife and from his neighbors' feeling that his behavior was beyond the pale. While it is unclear whether Lewis was even summoned as a result of the accusation against him and there is no record of any appearance, the record of the citation itself is a fascinating document.

Like Hobbys, Lewis of Caerleon was a man whose life's journey brought him into contact with a number of different models of masculinity: possibly (although this remains obscure) ethnic differences between his native Wales and England; between the academic world and the royal court; between scholarly and aristocratic circles and the rather different world of late medieval London civic life. Although little is known about his life before the 1480s, Lewis was Welsh and was probably born, as his name suggests, in Caerleon, Monmouthshire and had moved to London by the late 1470s.[25] In addition to his training as a physician, he wrote a number of important astronomical treatises and was considered the most famous English mathematician of the later fifteenth century. Although his scholarly writing focused on astronomy and mathematics, he also practiced as a physician throughout his professional life. Ambitious physicians with astrological skills—men with arcane knowledge and possibly predictive powers—were well placed to play important roles in the highly uncertain political scene of the day,[26] and by the 1480s Lewis had come to the attention of the high aristocracy. Lewis served as physician to Elizabeth Woodville, wife and then widow of Edward IV, as well as to Margaret, countess of Richmond, and to the latter's son, Henry Tudor—in other words he ministered to representatives of both the house of York and the house of Lancaster. The Italian chronicler Polydore Vergil credited Lewis with using the intimate access afforded him as physician to pass secret messages between Elizabeth and Margaret, allowing Lewis to play an important role in the arrangement of the marriage between Henry Tudor and Elizabeth of York.[27] Moreover Lewis may have been involved in Buckingham's Rebellion against Richard III in 1483; he was certainly imprisoned in the Tower by Richard as a supporter of Henry Tudor in 1485. Bosworth Field changed Lewis's luck as well as Richard's and Henry's: when Henry VII came to the throne in 1485, Lewis became royal physician and was granted 40 marks a year, later raised to £40. Henry appointed Lewis as a knight of the king's alms in 1488, and in 1494 he was still acting as physician to Elizabeth of York. He died in 1494 or 1495.[28]

The Commissary court entry appears to be the only record that Lewis of Caerleon was married, still unusual for physicians and for men with academic pretensions: apart from their positions at the court, this was another point that Hobbys and Lewis had in common.[29] Unfortunately, we know nothing about Lewis's wife's background or identity, other than that she was young. The Commissary court entry also indicates that he lived in London, in the parish of St. Leonard Foster Lane, which lay just to the northwest of St. Paul's Cathedral, north of Cheapside. Lewis thus occupied a liminal position in a number of different ways—between normally unmarried (but not necessarily chaste) academic and married paterfamilias, between royal courtier and Londoner. We can guess that other factors might have influenced his neighbors' accusation against him: perhaps his Welshness, maybe his astrological interests (a bit too close to necromancy for some?), possibly resentment against his Lancastrian political loyalties in the predominantly Yorkist city.

The heightened response to Lewis's, Denys's, and Hobbys's sexual misbehavior may be partly attributed to their profession: the mayor's and aldermen's answer to the Chancery writ regarding Denys's arrest particularly suggests that the sordid sinfulness and disease of the brothel was the very opposite of cleanliness, health, and godliness. For Lewis and Hobbys, the new phenomenon of the married physician posed particular diffi-culties: physicians were still normally clerics, celibate if not chaste. As physicians integrated into the world of the married layman, of the house-holder, they may have been confronted with expectations of sexual behav-ior for which they were not prepared.

Or it may have been the conflict between the values of the court and the city that caused Lewis's neighbors and Hobbys's fellow surgeons to view them with suspicion. As royal physicians who lived in London, both Lewis and Hobbys had to negotiate the differences between the civic cul-ture of London and the court culture of the households of Edward IV, Richard III, and Henry VII. From the courtly point of view, it is plausible that the two physicians' sexual adventures were quite ordinary: a man's adultery would not have seemed at all shocking to the court of the noto-riously licentious Edward IV nor even to the court of Henry VII. Cer-tainly the uncovering of their extramarital sexual adventures had little or no apparent effect on either Hobbys's or Lewis's standing as royal physi-cians. But open flaunting of patronage of prostitutes or of the mainte-nance of concubine-servants was much less tolerated in the City. As I discuss further below, bourgeois and aristocratic moral values regarding men's sexual behavior differed significantly in the fifteenth century. While marital infidelity was likely common and accepted among aristocratic men, tendencies were different in urban society: later fifteenth-century civic rec-ords show an attempt by elite men of the larger cities to redefine their roles to include proper sexual behavior as integral to the governance of the re-spectable patriarch.[30]

Certainly William Hobbys and Lewis of Caerleon were not the only adulterers living in London in the fifteenth century, and although the re-sponse to their misdeeds may have been heightened, hundreds of other people, women and men in about equal numbers, were charged with adultery each year in the lower-level London ecclesiastical courts,[31] and adulterers were prosecuted in the civic courts as well, even though such offenses were theoretically under church jurisdiction.[32] This indicates two things: first, that adultery was by no means uncommon, a conclusion that will cause no great surprise. But second, the frequency of prosecution of adultery in this period in both church and civic courts—the impetus for prosecution in both jurisdictions coming from the presentments of local laypeople, not as a result of "social control" by the church or other distant authorities—indicates that it was by no means universally tolerated behavior. Adultery of both husband and wife disrupted the good governance of the household and, by extension, of society. On a number of occasions, adultery allegedly drove husbands to beat their wives and expel them from the conjugal home, "out of love [*ob amorem*]" for the other woman.[33] Adultery could also cause severe heartache for the deceived spouse: Philip Cruce of Shoreditch died "of sadness [*pre tristiciam*]" after he had caught his wife committing adultery with John Herford, while George Sayer's wife apparently also died because of his adultery.[34]

While it seems improbable that all late medieval Londoners would have agreed with the witnesses in *Hobbys c. Hobbys*, that William's adulterous behavior was shocking and nefarious, many of those whose voices are heard in the civic documents of the later fifteenth century apparently would have thought so. The rhetoric of the deponents in *Hobbys c. Hobbys* was not outside the mainstream, but rather reflected a particular moral climate in London and other English urban milieux in the second half of the fifteenth century. The witnesses' wonderment at William Hobbys's adultery is typical of the articulation of a notion of masculine respectability that included appropriate and controlled sexual behavior. In light of other cases in late fifteenth-century London in which sexually misbehaving men were marked out as disreputable and misgoverned, the condemnation of William Hobbys's behavior becomes more comprehensible: it was offensive, according to this rhetoric, because he was not fulfilling his responsibilities of self-governance as a man of considerable standing, as a husband and father and head of a substantial household, and as a respectable citizen of London.[35]

It is clear that disapproval of irregular sexual unions was more than rhetoric designed for the ears of ecclesiastical officials: as we saw in the last chapter, for instance, Thomas Wulley's father and mother took considerable pains to end his fornication with Margaret Isot, a relationship that they clearly felt was dishonorable to him and to them. Moreover, when parental dissuasions were shown to be ineffective, Thomas's father could rely on the local constable and a posse of neighbors, a group that apparently did not find his objections to his son's fornication foolish or irrelevant, to arrest the misbehaving couple. Sexual impropriety, such as that evinced in the cases of William Hobbys and Thomas Wulley, was damaging to men's good names, just as it was to the good names of women—although not in the same way. Governance brought with it not just the rule of men over women but also the responsibility of men to use that rule wisely. In addition, each man was expected to rule himself and contain his own lustful will. A man such as Joan Bawde's unnamed attacker, who was out of control of his faculties, swearing that he would have "his foul lust and will . . . or else he would die for it," was as disreputable as the woman who tried to procure him a partner. The limits of respectable behavior were placed differently for men and for women, but by no means was a London man's sexual life irrelevant to his good name.

A crucial aspect of sexual misbehavior was its publicity or notoriousness; indeed, it was one's *reputation* rather than one's actions that was important in a society that placed huge importance on rumor and fame—knowledge that embraced, in other words, both what other people knew about a person and what they thought they knew. For women, acting in the public realm was frequently associated in such rumors with sexual misbehavior. This was particularly true, of course, for the most public of women, the prostitute.[36] In general, a woman's unguarded tongue and loose sexual behavior were seen to be strongly correlated: women who were loud in the streets were generally ungovernable.[37] Conversely, a sober and honest man had a duty and privilege to play a public role in his society, a role that was itself constitutive of his respectable masculinity. In 1494, for instance, William Huntyngfeld defamed a woman named Cecily Clerk by calling her a "strong whore of her tongue" and suggesting that Cecily's husband, John, should cede his place at the wardmote inquest to his wife. This both challenged John Clerk's right as a man of a certain status to act publicly and at the same time impugned Cecily's reputation as a respectable woman, because women normally appeared at the wardmote inquest only when charged with a sexual offense. As a result of Huntyngfeld's words, Cecily was forced to purge herself of adultery before the Lord Commissary.[38] As this case shows, a woman's reputation for chastity and respectability depended not only on her physical integrity but also on her representation in public by a man; a man's reputation for honesty, good fame, and status conversely depended on his ability to protect and control his dependants and to act for them in the political arena.

The strictures placed on women's behavior were different from those placed on men: a woman's good name was constructed largely[39] through others' knowledge about her sexual behavior, which in turn was related to her governance by a properly constituted male authority. But men also had to guard against public sexual misbehavior if they wanted to retain good reputations. As fifteenth-century moralist Peter Idley instructed his son: "He that willfully his body abuseth/And past is all dread and shame/ Loseth a precious jewel, which is his name."[40] Men's governance, like that of women, could be related to their submission to proper authority, but men's rule much more frequently took the form of self-governance. Sexual misbehavior that showed their lack of control of themselves, their misgoverned state, could result in disreputability and ill fame. Men accused of misdeeds or bad behavior commonly pledged significant sums of money to the chamberlain of the City that they would henceforth be "of good rule and honest conversation."[41] Respectable people shunned men charged with sexual misconduct: when Anastasia Reygate accused Thomas Hay of committing adultery in the home of a local bawd, witnesses reported that many people, including his wife, avoided his company, and there was a good deal of murmuring against him.[42] Similarly, when William Boteler told people that John Stampe had carnally known Joan Folke, the "status and good fame of both Joan Folke and John Stampe were greatly injured."[43] Indeed, a man's sexual misbehavior might provide his wife with justification to withdraw herself from his governance: a Cornish woman, told by three men that her husband, away serving his master, was enjoying the embraces of other women, refused to obey her husband any longer.[44] Male adultery could apparently occasion a man's loss of his rights to govern, and indeed it could even serve (if infrequently) as the grounds for a divorce *a mensa et thoro*, as we have seen already in the case of *Hobbys c. Hobbys*.

The terms used to describe women and men who sexually misbehaved are also revealing. As Ruth Mazo Karras has shown, the Latin *meretrix* (best translated into modern English, as she has argued, as "whore" rather than "prostitute"), was a highly gendered term, a grammatically and culturally feminine noun with no precise masculine counterpart. It combined notions of sexual licentiousness with an underlying venality: although a medieval whore did not have to accept payment for sex in order to be labeled a *meretrix*, the assumption that women's essential natures combined the mercenary with the promiscuous underlay the terminology.[45] Although there was no precise masculine counterpart to *meretrix*, there were terms to describe men who sexually misbehaved, although they had somewhat different valences. A man might be accused before a wardmote inquest of being a "harlot of his body," an interesting composite term: "harlot" could mean a number of things connoting misgovernance (rogue, untrue man), but the modifier "of his body" (especially in the context of other indictments for sexual crimes) clearly meant that his misdeed involved illicit sex.[46] Fifteenth-century documents also record the term *putour*, the male form of the Anglo-French word *putayne*, or whore; although *putayne* is not used in the fifteenth-century English-language civic records (English equivalents, notably "whore" and "strumpet," were at hand), *putour* did enter into English usage, perhaps because it filled a need that English vocabulary could not. About 1400, the word appears in French-language London civic records as the male counterpart to *putayne*, in a city ordinance directed against "ascuns homes pur comunes putours . . . et auxi femmes pur comunes putaynes [any men (taken) for common *putours* and also women for common *putaynes*]"[47] and thereafter appears in the English-language civic records to designate a number of men.[48] In 1421, for instance, the parson of St. Leonard's Foster Lane was called "a common putour" of his parishioners when he was accused of seducing women through the sacrament of confession.[49] The term carried with it connotations of both a man's own sexual licentiousness and his fostering of sexual misbehavior of others: it could mean both fornicator and pimp. Whereas accusations of women's sexual licentiousness shaded into venality, men's shaded into misgovernance. Both men and women could be called "bawds," but only men were ever labeled "strumpetmongers" or "whoremongers,"[50] probably because the latter term indicated a measure of governance over the strumpet that a woman could not be supposed to exercise over another woman.

Sexual misbehavior was thus understood in gendered ways: that much of the double standard holds true. And quite probably allegations of sexual misbehavior were more damaging for women than for men. Witnesses in several cases where women claimed defamation swore that these women lost value on the marriage market because of allegations of sexual misbehavior.[51] In the later fifteenth century when women had few economic options apart from marriage,[52] such attacks were potentially very damaging. For men, marriageability was not at issue, or at least not in the same way; the sources do not indicate the same direct relationship between a man's marriage prospects and his sexual reputation as applied to women. While virginity per se may have been less important to men on the marriage market than to women, a reputation for misrule rather than serious and sober behavior certainly harmed men's overall good names.

Witnesses regarded both men and women accused of inappropriate sexual behavior as generally disreputable; male adulterers and fornicators were mentioned in the same breath as thieves, criminals, oath-breakers, the indigent, and the idle. John Waldron, who described himself as a sawyer living in the precinct of the hospital of St. Katherine by the Tower, testified in the London Consistory court case of *Gilis c. Broun* in October 1491.[53] In December of the same year, a number of witnesses were brought forward to impugn Waldron's testimony. In attempting to convince the court that Waldron's testimony was unreliable, the deponents focused on a number of different kinds of misconduct that included poverty, dishonesty, and sexual irregularity, calling him a perjurer, a vagabond, a bawd, and an adulterer. They testified that he had been the landlord of Stewside brothels in Southwark and that he lived there adulterously with a woman named Joan who had another husband. After the bishop's official of the diocese of Winchester had summoned them for their adultery and enjoined penance on them, Waldron and Joan fled Southwark and went to live together in the precinct of the hospital of St. Katharine by the Tower. There, the witnesses reported, Waldron continued his bawdry, took up with another woman, and consorted with whores, vagabonds, and thieves, gaining a reputation as an adulterer and a thief himself. He also associated with a band of infamous and perjurious men in Westminster—in effect witnesses for hire—called the "Knights of the Post."[54] Waldron's fellow witness William Alston was also discredited as a man of ill fame, a vagabond, and an adulterer; he had deserted his wife to go to live in St. Katharine's precinct, leaving her to make her living by shameful means. In St. Katharine's precinct he committed adultery with many women, as he himself had admitted before the honest men of the neighborhood.[55] His adultery and his abandonment of his wife to a life of prostitution—his refusal to be a responsible householder—were primary signifiers of his shiftlessness and lack of trustworthiness.

Sexual impropriety in men was seen as part of a complex of generally bad behavior; for men, it was related especially to the sorts of faults associated with men who refused the responsibility of governing their families and households and who threatened other men's rule over their dependents.[56] These associations dovetailed with the conventional discourses of sin, where gluttony led to drunkenness, which in turn made people fall into lechery and all other vices: "It is pity of lechery," Jacques Legrand's *Boke called good maners* said, "which is on this day so common and causeth people to go out of the way, and to languish in sin and in dissolute life."[57] The public humiliation of an indictment for adultery or fornication—often accompanied by several mortifying hours in the stocks—could not have improved a man's (or a woman's) position in a town. Witnesses discrediting the testimony of Thomas Carpenter of Enfield disdainfully reported not only that he was poor and out of work but also that he was widely known to have done time in the stocks in Stratford Langthorne for his adultery with two women.[58] Readers of Caxton's translation of La Tour Landry's *Book of the Knight of the Tower* found an extreme version of the shaming of sexual misbehavers. When a man named Perrot Lenard lay with a woman in a church, under an altar, a miracle occurred: "they were joined together as a dog is to a bitch, and in this manner they were found and taken. And so joined and knitted together they were all the whole day, insomuch that they of the church and of the country had leisure enough to see and behold them, for they could not depart one from the other." The parishioners formed a procession to pray to God for them, and at last the couple was "loosed and departed that one from that other." The church had to be newly blessed after the blasphemy, and Perrot, for his penance, had to process around the church, "all naked," on three Sundays, beating himself and "rehearsing and telling his default and sin." As Caxton finishes the story, "here is to every man a good example, how that he should hold him cleanly and honestly in holy church."[59]

Unquestionably, both men and women were liable to prosecution for sexual misbehavior, although the focus of official interest might shift from men to women at different times. London secular and ecclesiastical officials charged both men and women in the fifteenth century with adultery and fornication through a process of presentment by local juries and other such bodies.[60] Civic juries were not consistent throughout the fifteenth century in their presentments; as Marjorie McIntosh has shown, concern about misbehavior of various kinds tended to ebb and flow over the years.[61] In London, some mayoral administrations probably pursued sexual misbehavior more vigorously than others: as the author of the *Great Chronicle of London* put it, in 1473, "the mayor [William Hampton] did diligent and sharp correction upon Venus's servants, and caused them to be garnished and attired with ray [striped] hoods, and to be shown about the City with their minstrelsy before them by many and sundry market days," an attention to prostitutes borne out by a large number of presentations for that year in the civic records.[62] As Stephanie Tarbin has argued, civic officials' attention to sexual misbehavior could also vary in its target: at some points, officials were apparently more interested in men's sexual misconduct than in women's, whereas at other times the focus reversed.[63]

Even at times when civic officials targeted men, were all men equally liable to indictments for sexual misbehavior? Was all extramarital sexual activity in men seen as disreputable? Were lower-status men, for instance, more or less likely to find rumors and accusations about sexual misbehavior damaging to their fame, or were they more likely to be cited before ward-mote inquests or the Commissary court for their offenses? It is certainly plausible that men with little influence were more vulnerable than men of higher status: disreputability was frequently connected with poverty, and honesty with affluence and substance (the word "substance" connoting both material and moral weight).[64] At the same time, because a poor man (or woman) was already assumed to have less reputability than a more substantial person, the standard penalties employed by both church and civic officials for sexual offenses would often have had less effect on those who were marginal rather than deeply embedded in civic social networks. To punish sexual offenders, both church and civic bodies imposed penalties that humiliated the offender and caused his or her reputation to suffer or fall: those convicted of sexual offenses might be ordered to process penitentially through the main streets of the city or to spend an hour in the pillory at Cornhill after a civic officer had announced to those gathered the nature of the offense.[65] But if one did not have a reputation to lose, such humiliation may have had little effect. It is possible—although difficult to trace—that sexual morality among London's underclass was quite different from that expressed in London civic records and implied by church court citations, both of which mainly reflect the views of more substantial inhabitants of the City of London. Among the poor, sexual relationships may not have been confined, even in theory, to marriage; households may have been less likely to be headed by men or structured in the same patriarchal way; the construction of reputation or indeed of the self may have depended on entirely different terms.[66] These are all plausible, but the only hints of such an alternative sexual culture come from ambiguous evidence such as repeated arrests or continual church court citations for sexual misbehavior, which indicates only that for those repeat offenders the standard shaming penalties did not hold sufficient deterrent effect to prevent subsequent misdeeds.

If the poor were more vulnerable to accusations of sexual misbehavior, wealthier men were nonetheless far from immune, as Master William Hobbys found out. Other wealthier, high-status men also found themselves subject to prosecutions of various kinds. In a 1445 case, the wardmote inquest of Farringdon Without indicted George Fynse, "esquire," for "open fornication and adultery," and he was imprisoned for some time.[67] Alexander Marchall, whose father had been a wealthy grocer and sheriff of London and whose son-in-law was styled "gentleman," was, despite his status, also arrested and imprisoned for adultery in 1471. Witnesses to the case testified before the mayor's court that the beadle of Candlewick Street ward, "about eleven of the clock before midnight found a woman in the chamber of the said Alexander, sitting by his bedside, and no more persons being with them, whereupon the same Symon [the beadle] brought the same Alexander and the said woman into the Counter."[68] This behavior was not appropriate to his station, and Alexander's father, Robert Marchall, a man of considerable wealth, had in fact made Alexander's good and virtuous governance a condition of inheritance. But as the executors of Robert's will said, "the governance of the said Alexander after the decease of his said father was neither good nor virtuous but gave him to riot and vices," including adultery "with diverse women," so they argued in the mayor's court that he should not have been able to inherit his father's estate.[69] Ironically, John Lambert, Robert Marchall's son-in-law and one of his executors who made this argument in 1471, was the father of Elizabeth Shore, who later became famous as the merriest mistress of Edward IV.[70]

At what point did sexual activity outside the marriage bed become "misbehavior"? Was occasional and discreet fornication more acceptable than notorious or excessive sexual adventures (as in the cases of Alexander Marchall, George Fynse, or William Hobbys)? Letters from the Celys, the late fifteenth-century merchant family, suggest that it was common for young unmarried merchants of the Staple to keep mistresses in Calais, where they often spent several years in their twenties learning the trade. The Cely letters seem to indicate (although by no means conclusively) that such philandering ceased upon return to England and marriage.[71] Perhaps what was tolerable at one stage of life ceased to be suitable after crossing over into the next. Or perhaps it was the fact that this activity was away from home, out of the sight of London society, that made it acceptable. Marchall's and Fynse's misbehavior, on the other hand, was local and apparently very public and notorious. As the mayor and sheriffs of the City of London argued in 1446, the City had jurisdiction over various disturbances of the peace, including *public* adultery, perhaps making a distinction between the sin (a matter for ecclesiastical correction) and the threat to order constituted by open and notorious sexual misbehavior.[72]

It is also possible that the stricter attitudes toward male sexual misbehavior seen in London were particularly characteristic of London, or of
urban society. There are signs that the second half of the fifteenth century
witnessed a growing rift between "bourgeois" and "aristocratic" moral
values in relation to extramarital sexual behavior for men. As Barbara
Harris has suggested, marital infidelity among men of the landed classes
was common and tacitly accepted in aristocratic society and expected by
wives.[73] Tendencies were different in urban society. Civic ordinances of
1492 from the city of Coventry, for instance, enjoined mayors, past mayors, and members of the ruling Common Council to maintain flawless
personal conduct or to face removal from office. Indeed, higher standards
of behavior were applied to those of more elevated political position, indicating that the Coventry civic leaders felt that their status behooved them
to lead an exemplary life.[74] Londoners may have practiced the same ideas
even if they did not codify them: a number of London officials were removed from office because of sexual misbehavior.[75] A similar heightening
of anxiety about sexual misconduct in the decades following 1450, perhaps
related to a tightening of the English economy, also characterized England's smaller market centers, according to Marjorie McIntosh.[76]

William Hobbys and Lewis of Caerleon, both living in London at the
same time that they frequented the royal court as king's physician, thus
may have been caught between the strict moral climate of later fifteenth-
century London and the rather looser environment of the court of the
notoriously dissolute Edward IV, a man said by Polydore Vergil to "read-
ily cast an eye upon young ladies, and love them inordinately,"[77] and the
milder but still far from monastic court of Henry VII. Objections to no-
blemen or gentlemen who used London as a sexual playground may have
lain behind presentments of men such as Marchall and Fynse in the civic
court, or Londoner William Campion's petition to the chancellor about
Piers Boteler, "gentleman, neither godly nor well disposed," who had enticed Campion's wife away with subtleties and blandishments and kept
her at his pleasure.[78] But while a few notorious evildoers were prosecuted,
the realities of power politics made the presentment of nobles or gentlemen in London courts very difficult, and frustration with this situation
can sometimes be read in the records. In 1459–60, a citizen chronicler
complained about the "misrule of the king's gallants," who wrought
havoc in the city after having drunk too much wine, robbing houses, and
"defoul[ing] many women."[79]

Perhaps because their lower-status female partners were more acces-
sible, the local church and civic courts and even the networks of neighborhood gossip sometimes focused on the women rather than the nobles
or gentlemen with whom they consorted. In 1483, a woman and her husband claimed that she had been defamed when neighbors spread the following story about her and Master William Paston, probably either
William Paston II or William Paston III of Paston letters fame: "Maude
Nesche is a strong whore and a strong strumpet, for Master William Paston should live in adultery with her, and had to do with her in her house,
and sent his meinie [retinue] down to keep the door, and he keepeth her
in a house in St. George's field, as a strong whore and harlot as she is."[80]
While the defamatory story was told about Maude Nesche rather than
William Paston, and the venom is directed primarily at her, there is
nonetheless an air of resentment against such men and their ability to call
upon a "meinie" to guard the door when they engaged in their adulterous activities.

The differences between bourgeois and aristocratic values may have
become particularly tricky to negotiate in the later decades of the fifteenth
century. In other ways during this period London civic culture came more
closely to emulate and participate in aristocratic and, particularly, court culture. London citizens from the 1460s, especially at the most elite level, began to attend tournaments, came to be knighted in greater numbers, and
married into the gentry and aristocracy more frequently. From the late
1470s onward, their reading habits also changed to reflect new cultural
directions, as they began to consume the chivalric literature coming off
Caxton's presses.[81] Although both Hobbys's and Lewis's careers were unusual, many other Londoners must have experienced some of the culture
shock that these social changes brought with them, including a clash of
sexual ethics.

If aristocrats were regarded suspiciously by Londoners, so also were
foreign merchants; the medieval equivalent of salesmen on the road, they
were apparently an important market for London bawds and prostitutes,
some of whom catered especially to "Spaniards, Lombards, and Easterlings."[82] Inhabitants of the Steelyard, an enclave for Hanseatic merchants
("Easterlings"), were particularly suspect.[83] While Londoners may have
looked indulgently upon their young men keeping mistresses in Calais,
they were not so happy about foreign merchants doing the same in
London, at least not when the merchants tried to seduce respectable

young women. John and Margery Mappulton petitioned the chancellor in the 1490s because one Francis Derbyet, a Spaniard, had come to their house continually over the previous year and "there craftily hath moved and stirred one Elizabeth, daughter unto your said orators [petitioners], to go with him and hath procured her to be of vicious living of her body, contrary to the laws of God and to the utter destruction of her body forever." Elizabeth told her parents about this, and so they charged Francis "to cease of his unlawful desire," but he refused, instead offering them £20 "so that they would suffer him" to have their daughter as his concubine. In revenge for their refusal to acquiesce, Francis pursued cases of debt against each parent, and both were imprisoned, so that he could get "them to agree to him that he might have his desire."[84] Francis Derbyet fulfilled the stereotype of the licentious foreigner: he was crafty, ruthless, and intent on fulfilling his sexual desires regardless of the costs.[85]

No doubt Londoners of whatever station or ethnicity disagreed about the appropriateness of extramarital sexual activity for men: the limits seem to have been contested territory, some seeing sex outside marriage as a blameless natural tendency in men, others viewing it as a venial sin, and yet others regarding it as a very serious fault. On the one hand, London and environs abounded with prostitutes and brothels, designed to service male needs and, as Ruth Karras has argued, in many ways tolerated by the authorities.[86] Moreover, as Lyndal Roper has reminded us, the wild, uncivilized, out-of-control male behavior that civic ordinances sought to contain was nonetheless integral to constructions of masculinity and, indeed, of governance.[87] A case appearing before the Court of Aldermen in 1515 shows the importance of virility and sexual prowess in male reputation: Robert Harding testified that he had bedded the "whore" Katherine Worsley simply to prove that he could, because otherwise Katherine might tell women in the parish that he was impotent and scuttle his courtship of a wealthy widow.[88] Some men boasted about their sexual adventures—John Metecalfe, for instance, was cited to the commissary because he had bragged that he had carnally known Joan Snawis, while John Caryk said that he was always being pestered by other men's wives for his sexual favors.[89] Clearly there was a certain ambiguity about the exercise of male sexual prowess. For some, the sexual conquest of women was a powerful demonstration of masculinity. For others, promiscuity was simply not acceptable: male fornicators and adulterers were presented by local juries and churchwardens to ecclesiastical and secular authorities, just as female misbehavers were, indicating that at least some men thought that male sexual misbehavior was a problem to be corrected. A respectable man, perhaps, was one who had a healthy sexual appetite but who could control it; his mastery of himself showed his ability to master others.[90] For women, on the other hand, there was no ambiguity: the effect of licentiousness on their reputation was much more clearly negative. Tellingly, there are no records of women boasting about their sexual adventures.

Precisely what lies behind the ebb and flow of what we might call "public opinion" regarding what constitutes serious transgression of sexual codes is even more difficult for us to discern in the distant past than it is now. We may, however, be able to link the stricter attitudes toward sexual misbehavior discussed earlier with certain tendencies in late medieval religious culture, especially in the urban milieu of London. In London—differing from the local courts of England's smaller centers, as Marjorie McIntosh has shown—disapproval of misbehaving persons was usually couched in both religious and social terms, as breaches both of God's law and of earthly edicts: according to civic ordinances, those guilty of "the detestable sin [of] lechery" acted "in displeasing of almighty God and against the laws of this City."[91] Late medieval civic culture was integrally intertwined with late medieval religious culture. Religious processions functioned also as expressions of civic solidarity and hierarchy, while certain fraternities doubled as social-political clubs for the ruling elite.[92] The fifteenth century saw the creation of a style of Catholicism, primarily lay-centered, that suited the civic ethic of the merchant classes.[93] This civic Catholicism might be described as "puritanical"—sexual morality became caught up in questions of honesty, respectability, and good fame, all civic as well as Christian virtues,[94] reminding us that the phenomenon described as the Puritan "reformation of manners"[95] of the late sixteenth and seventeenth centuries was neither new nor peculiarly Protestant. The respectable, honorable, sexually well-governed man was thus not only a civic ideal but also a Christian one.

Although it would make little sense to posit that all late medieval Londoners, or even all late medieval London citizens, shared these views in their entirety, the ideals took on immense rhetorical power in the political struggles in the latter part of the fifteenth century. As David Santiuste has suggested,[96] Richard III especially employed a version of this civic ethic that fused godliness, sexual propriety, and proper governance. Richard's "Proclamation for the Reform of Morals" of October 1483 denounced the leaders of Buckingham's Rebellion in unusual terms compared to previous royal proclamations and other sorts of royal propaganda. Some historians have characterized the language as either fanatical or hypocritical and have found it difficult to comprehend why Richard would have chosen to use it,[97] but the answer to that question seems clear when one looks at it from the London perspective: it perfectly matched the kind of rhetoric coming from London civic documents. Those rising against the crown were "horrible adulterers and bawds, provoking the high indignation and displeasure of God"; Thomas, marquis of Dorset, "not fearing God, nor the peril of his soul, hath many and sundry maids, widows, and wives damnably and without shame devoured, defloured and defouled."[98] Throughout the proclamation, treachery and sexual misgovernance are linked, Buckingham and his cronies several times identified by the triple epithet "Traitors, Adulterers, and Bawds."[99] Richard continued using these themes in subsequent propaganda efforts: the January 1484 act of parliament that settled the crown on Richard, for instance, decried in unmistakable terms the effects of his brother's sexual life on the well-being of the kingdom. As a result of Edward's "sensuality and concupiscence" and his marriage to the sorceress Elizabeth Woodville,

the order of all politic rule was perverted, the laws of God and of God's church, and also the laws of nature and of England, and also its laudable customs and liberties, to which every Englishman is heir, were broken, subverted and disregarded, contrary to all reason and justice, so that this land was ruled by self-will and pleasure, and fear and dread and all equity and law were laid aside and despised, as a result of which many calamities and misfortunes ensued, such as murders, extortions and oppressions, particularly of poor and powerless people, so that no man was sure of his life, land or livelihood, or of his wife, daughter or servant, with every virtuous maiden and woman standing in dread of being ravished and defiled.[100]

The ever-canny Richard may have deliberately chosen to vilify his opponents in terms especially reprehensible to the powerful London civic elite: those who opposed him were godless sexual deviants.

This brings us back to the story of William Hobbys. William died in September 1488, about twelve years after his divorce, leaving behind wills that were registered both in the Prerogative Court of Canterbury and in the Court of Husting in the City of London. The lengthy and detailed will registered in the Prerogative Court of Canterbury gives us some rather surprising evidence about the last years of his life. First of all, it is prefaced by a lengthy section in which William bequeaths his soul to God, the Blessed Virgin, and all the saints—in itself an ordinary and indeed usually formulaic proem to the wills of this period. But William's will departs significantly from the standard laconic form of the bequest of the soul ("I bequeath my soul to God, to the blessed Mary, and to all the saints, and my body to be buried . . ."):

In the name of God Amen, to whom I, William Hobbys, bequeath my soul, because it belongs to him through prayer, and I beseech the Most Blessed Mary, mother of Jesus, and all the saints, that they aid me in the departure of the spirit of my soul, and thus I trust in [them] against all the shackles of demons and also because the true light expels all darkness and all the saints are in the true light because they are in God and God is in them. Because of this I have beseeched your aid and thus I am certain that no demon will dare to approach such a presence, because all darkness is as nothing compared to this power, [on account of] which all things are able to exist and act. God is powerful and all creatures have power from him, and thus it follows that the power of the saints has always and without interruption surpassed the power of demons, by which my heart is comforted through the hope I have in the wounds of Christ and in Mary, his mother, and in all the saints.[101]

William's will suggests that he found religion in the last years of his life. Other provisions of his will corroborate this impression. He seems to have had a particular association with Holy Trinity Priory (a house of Augustinian canons in London); he directs his body to be buried in the priory church and the prior himself to arrange the funeral, and he names various specific members of the house for bequests. And while he makes various other smaller bequests to individuals, he leaves the bulk of his estate to the priory and to the house of minoresses of the Abbey of St. Clare, just outside the London Wall near Aldgate.

William's former wife, Alice, who was still alive at the time, is mentioned only when he leaves money for the canons of Holy Trinity to pray for both his and Alice's souls—presumably a division of the marital property was made upon the divorce, and she thus had no claim on his estate, but this provision suggests goodwill, at least on his part. While his testimony in the divorce case indicated that they had had five children together, only one child, Agnes, who was a nun, is explicitly mentioned in his will, although it seems probable that another woman mentioned in the will, Mercy Staveley, was also his daughter. Two other people associated with the divorce case are mentioned in the will. Mercy Staveley's husband was John Staveley, who as a young surgeon had testified against William in 1476. Both Mercy and John received bequests of chattels, and

William Staveley, probably their son and William's grandson, is bequeathed two books, one a book that "teaches general arts" and the other a primer or prayer book. While we can only imagine how it was that John came to marry William's daughter (assuming that they were not already married at the time of the 1476 case), even more interesting is the naming of Robert Halyday as executor of the will. Robert Halyday, one of the men who testified that he saw William with the young prostitute in Southwark, was one of the more prominent surgeons working in London in the last thirty years of the fifteenth century, acting as master of the guild five times from the 1470s until the 1490s.[102] His being named as executor of William's will in 1488, in addition to several bequests that were made to the guild of barber-surgeons, suggests that William was on good terms with Halyday and the guild at the time of his death. So if the divorce case caused a rift between him and the surgeons who testified on Alice's behalf, that rift had apparently healed by the time of William's death.

Although one cannot make too much of a will, even one that eschews the formulaic as this one does, it is tempting to link William's apparent religious conversion and friendship with those who had previously testified against him with a radical change in his sexual behavior, and to link that in turn with remorse following his divorce or, more specifically, the shock of the public revelation and condemnation of his sexual habits. While we will probably never know what precisely happened to William or to Alice Hobbys after their divorce, it is plausible in the context of later fifteenth-century London culture that a movement away from William's previous life of licentiousness would take an explicitly religious form.

For both men and women, then, perceptions of sexual behavior were an aspect of reputation. Sexual misbehavior was an important element in the construction of the disorderly and misgoverned man. Reputation, like gender identity, was continually forged both by the individual and by others through their reaction to their knowledge about the individual's actions; in a sense, reputation was a story that assigned meanings to actions, written and rewritten by those who told and heard it. The same actions might be interpreted differently depending on the actor, on the interpreter, or on the circumstances. The construction of reputation and the meaning assigned to sexual activities (rendering them proper or improper, reputable or disreputable) were shaped particularly by the gender of the actor; but this double standard did not create a completely asymmetrical moral code where men's sexual activities were irrelevant to their reputations. For women and for men, the gendered notions of publicity and especially of governance shaped the concept of sexual impropriety. Women who notoriously transgressed sexual codes were out of any man's real control, disrupting the proper social order where women should be governed by the male head of their household. Public male adulterers, fornicators, and patrons of prostitutes contributed to this misrule and were also themselves "misgoverned" and to some, at least, disreputable.

Crucial to understanding the nature of respectable masculinity in late medieval London civic culture are the relationships between patriarchy, governance, and sexual reputation. A respectable man supervised the relationships of those in his sphere of influence, a sphere that included both his household and others who lived around him in his neighborhood, parish, and ward. Just as he might act as a mediator between a courting couple and a presider at the exchange of marriage vows, so also might he intervene either informally or officially when a couple engaged in a relationship he regarded as inappropriate, illicit, or sinful. While the extent of responsibility and the power to police relationships depended a good deal on the status of the man, all householders owed this duty at least to some extent. Those who refused it (for instance, men who pimped for their wives or who maintained prostitutes—bawds or strumpetmongers) were challenging the social order as surely as women who refused proper governance. Similarly, men who fornicated or committed adultery were refusing the responsibility to govern themselves and to respect other men's women. Sexual ideologies was inseparable from the structures of household governance.

Conclusion: Sex, Marriage, and Medieval Concepts of the Public

In 1985, Georges Duby and Philippe Ariès launched the five-volume *Histoire de la vie privée*. Both in its original French version and in translation into various other European languages, the series achieved that rare combination of commercial success and scholarly acclaim.[1] *A History of Private Life*, as one reviewer put it, "inaugurated one of the great historical enterprises of our time":[2] the series opened many new territories of enquiry and the volumes remain, almost two decades later, highly readable and often insightful. But the underlying premise of the series—"to isolate that sphere of social relations corresponding to what we *nowadays* call 'private life'"[3]—seems more problematic today than it did in the late 1980s, as some recent critics have noted.[4] In the medieval volume (titled in its English translation *Revelations of the Medieval World*), Georges Duby admitted that the adoption of modern definitions of the boundaries between public and private was anachronistic.[5] Despite this acknowledgment, however, the structure and content of the series naturalized the modern liberal public/private dichotomy. "Private life" is gendered female and lies outside the realm of politics. Interiors of homes are by definition "private space," and throughout the medieval volume we are reminded that "the family was the heart of private life."[6] The reification of the liberal paradigm becomes particularly clear in Duby's general comments about the later Middle Ages in the preface, where he describes the mushrooming of documents that touch on hitherto obscure details of everyday life, especially the records of the ecclesiastical courts. Documents such as Jacques Fournier's register, which Emmanuel Le Roy Ladurie made so famous in his reconstruction of the fourteenth-century French village of Montaillou, illustrate for Duby the desire of "public authorities" to penetrate "the secrets of private life." "The state," he goes on to say, "conceived the ambition of total control over the population";[7]

by implication, he argues that medieval authorities exceeded their proper role of dealing with the res publica, extending their reach into the private realm where the state had no business. Duby's error here is in assuming that the aspects of life that came under investigation by secular or ecclesiastical officials, and that provide us with such interesting evidence for the late Middle Ages—investigations of heresy, sexual misdemeanors, marital irregularities—can helpfully be understood as "private" in the late medieval context. Officials of church and state investigated heresy, sexual misbehavior, and marital problems not because they wanted "total control" (although perhaps they wanted that too) but because these were issues of *public*, and not just private, import.

The study of the household, marriage, sexuality, women, children, diet, dress, and a host of other subjects that Duby and his fellow contributors included in *A History of Private Life* no longer requires apology or legitimation, partly because of the very success of that series. History as a discipline in the twenty-first century is no longer confined to subjects falling under the nineteenth-century definition of "public affairs." But we still have not entirely accepted that some of those arenas of life that seem obviously "private" to us were not so categorized in the Middle Ages. Recognizing that in our conceptualizations of privacy and publicity we are inheritors of liberal Enlightenment thought helps us to see that our public/private dyad is neither natural nor universal.

Although modern liberal paradigms have taught us to think of homes as private and streets as public, and of sex, marriage, and family as aspects of "private life," thinking in this way obscures our understanding of late medieval society. Marriage in late medieval England was properly an intimate, but not a private, relationship, even when it was initiated in a domestic setting. A man and a woman entered into it through a process that was to be transparent, beginning with an exchange of consent that was public and finishing with the ratification of that union in the even more public environment of the parish church. Other kinds of sexual relationships were also subject to public scrutiny, but of a different kind. The ways in which sexual relationships were policed, particularly by London civic rather than ecclesiastical officials, help us to refine further medieval concepts of the public and the private, and their relationship to space and place.

In 1474, the beadle (a lower-level law enforcement official) of the London ward of Farringdon Without had reason to suspect that Joan Salman and Walter Haydon, both unmarried, were alone together in a house situated in the street called the Old Bailey. Accompanied by two neighbors, the beadle approached the house; one of the neighbors stayed outside on the street, guarding the doorway in case one of the miscreants tried to escape, as the beadle and the other man proceeded up the stairs to the chamber where the couple was rumored to be. In the chamber, Walter was found lying on the bed and Joan, "reputed as a woman of evil life and conversation," was standing beside it. Because they were found together in such suspicious circumstances, they were arrested and taken to the Counter, the sheriffs' prison in London.[8] Such arrests were relatively routine in late medieval London, as we have seen;[9] as another London beadle described in 1386 when accused of trespass in a similar case, it was the custom of the City for law enforcement officials to enter a man's or a woman's house if word came to his ears that fornication, adultery, or similar infractions were taking place there and to search diligently (*perscrutari*) through all parts of the house to find, and expel, any suspiciously lurking (*latitantes*) there.[10]

Contrast this late medieval arrest for sexual misbehavior with a modern one. In 1998, local police officers in Houston, Texas, entered the home of a man named John Lawrence after having been tipped by a neighbor who claimed to have seen an armed man behaving erratically outside Lawrence's apartment. The officers entered the unlocked door of Lawrence's apartment, weapons drawn, and searched the apartment. Although they found no man with a gun, they did find Lawrence in his bedroom, having sex with another man named Tyron Garner. The officers arrested the two men, charging them under the Texas "Homosexual Conduct" statute, which made "deviate sexual intercourse" a criminal offense. The two men spent the night in jail and later pleaded no contest to the charges (reserving the right to appeal) and were each fined $200.[11]

There are a number of striking similarities between the arrests of Salman and Haydon in 1474 and of Lawrence and Garner in 1998. Here, however, I would like to emphasize one of the differences. Lawrence and Garner appealed their conviction to the U.S. Supreme Court, which rendered its judgment in June 2003. The petitioners' appeal, based on their right to equal protection under the laws and their right to privacy, emphasized the unjustifiable invasion of Lawrence's private home.[12] In its judgment, the Supreme Court concurred: it found that the laws under which Lawrence and Garner had been charged and convicted inappropriately targeted "the most private human conduct, sexual behavior, and in the most private of places, the home."[13] When antihomosexual laws were repealed in many other Western countries in the 1960s and 1970s, the distinction between the private and the public was often invoked. As Canada's then minister of justice, Pierre Elliot Trudeau, quipped in 1967 when he introduced criminal code amendments that removed legal sanctions from private consensual homosexual acts, "The state has no place in the bedrooms of the nation."[14]

In England in the later Middle Ages, this divorce between public and private would have been wholly foreign, especially in the realm of sexuality, which could never be conceptualized as a thoroughly private relationship in which the state or the church had no role. Joan and Walter could not claim that their right to privacy had been violated when the beadle and his companion broke into the chamber, because they had no such right. We do not know how or if Joan and Walter defended themselves: they may simply have accepted the relatively light, if humiliating, penalty for a first offense (a night in the London sheriffs' prison and perhaps an hour or two on the pillory).[15] Others caught in the act had few possibilities for defense: they might accuse the constable or beadle of trespass (a forerunner of the right to privacy, but conceptualized as a crime against property), or, more commonly, the couple could claim to be married, legitimizing their sexual relationship.[16] But a medieval person could not claim that the sexual relationship, whether inside or outside marriage, was no one else's business, because it was. There was no such thing as a private sexual relationship: it was either a publicly recognized appropriate relationship (marriage) or an inappropriate and illegal one (fornication, adultery, sodomy).

This is not to argue that all things were public domain. Late medieval English people did feel that some things were intimate and should properly be kept so. By means of the Assize of Nuisance in the fourteenth and early fifteenth centuries, Londoners (mostly of high station) regularly complained that neighbors had constructed windows overlooking their property or peered over the tops of or through holes in walls into their gardens and houses in order to see their "secrets."[17] As Robert Ottele of London complained in 1431, his neighbors William and Joan Warde and John Fan "have two large windows in their tenement overlooking [Robert's] garden, through which when they are open the tenants and the tenants' servants can see the intimate affairs [*secreta*] of Robert, his servants, and his tenants, to the serious nuisance of Robert, and against the above said custom [of the City of London]."[18] The records do not reveal what is meant by *secreta*, although in most cases the word appears to relate to the personal aspects of domestic life (complaints were made about neighbors' being able to see into chambers and privies).[19] Diane Shaw has used the published calendar of these records (where the word *secreta* in the assize rolls is translated throughout as "private business") to argue that late medieval Londoners had a remarkably keen sense of their "right to privacy."[20] Shaw's conceptualizations are somewhat anachronistic: the notion of privacy as a right was a product of Enlightenment liberalism, and she has imposed on her sources much too sharp a line between "private" homes and "public" streets.[21] But she is right to argue that at least some Londoners wanted to keep certain aspects of their lives—perhaps better translated as the "intimate" things?—away from outsiders' eyes, even if they lacked the conceptual framework to articulate this desire specifically as a right.

Nonetheless, a medieval Londoner would not have made the same assumption that Shaw and many other scholars have made—that an event that takes place in a domestic setting is, by the very fact of its taking place in a "private" home, a private affair. Nor would they have recognized an ideological framework that places sexual relationships beyond public scrutiny. The public/private dyad, as theorized by John Locke and crystallized in nineteenth-century social and political theory, becomes too easily naturalized, so that marriage, the family, and sexuality become part of "private life." The liberal paradigm has never entirely reigned in Western countries, and its assumptions have been subjected for decades to attacks from various quarters,[22] but its influence on historical scholarship is profound. As Fredric Cheyette has recently remarked, when we assume that issues of love and sexuality are outside the public arena, "we are, of course, the children not just of Darwin but of Locke and the Enlightenment, and true to their teachings we easily project the same expectations back onto earlier societies as their true reality."[23] As Mary Hartman argues, it also diverts us away from considering the household, marriage, and sexuality as motors of historical change.[24] To understand the ways in which medieval people saw their world, we have to consider that premodern understandings of the public and the private were fundamentally different from those we have inherited from the eighteenth and nineteenth centuries. And to appreciate fully the nature of historical change since the fifteenth century, we must think about how late medieval Londoners' marriages, sexual relationships, and patterns of family authority were integral to the subsequent development of Western history.

Appendix: Legal Sources

Ecclesiastical Court Records

Much of this study is based on the records of litigation in the fifteenth-century diocese of London church court known as the Consistory.[1] The Consistory was the bishop's highest court. Its judge was called the bishop's official, who was a man university trained in canon and civil law. The diocese of London comprised Middlesex, Essex, and parts of Hertfordshire as well as the City of London; litigants from London made up roughly half the number pursuing suits at the London Consistory court, with a higher number of Londoners serving as witnesses (litigants from out of town, who often paid the travel expenses of their witnesses, probably sought to cut costs by choosing Londoners as witnesses if they had a choice). Of particular interest are the two types of suits women and men launched most frequently in the church courts of the diocese of London in the second half of the fifteenth century: they sued one another in church courts to enforce or, less frequently, to dissolve a contract of marriage, and they sued one another for defamation (an allegation that a statement one person made about another damaged the second person's reputation). Both of these types of suits provide a good deal of evidence about how people entered into marriage and sexual relationships, and how reputations (which had a significant sexual component) were formed, maintained, and damaged. This study relies on about 950 examinations of parties and witness depositions offered in about 230 cases of marriage and defamation litigation in the diocese of London in the second half of the fifteenth century.[2] This book has emphasized the cases deriving from the City of London.

Litigants were assisted through the legal intricacies of the court by lawyers who were called advocates, usually university graduates in law, or proctors, often not formally trained. The presiding judge usually examined the witnesses (appearing for either the plaintiff, the person suing, or the defendant, the person being sued) individually, in a private house (the house of the scribe was frequently used) or in a room in St. Paul's

Cathedral or elsewhere. In each case he questioned the witnesses according to series of articles, questions, charges, and challenges that were set out by the lawyers of the parties involved in the suit to the court. A plaintiff or defendant in a case could also appear to answer the allegations of his or her opponent. After the official had heard the various witnesses, he rendered a judgment; unfortunately these were only rarely recorded in the deposition books, instead being recorded in separate books, none of which survive for the period in question. Should a party be unhappy with the judgment, he or she could appeal the decision to the archbishop of Canterbury, or to the highest earthly authority, the pope. While the records of appeal to the archbishop have not survived, the records of some cases that were appealed beyond the Consistory court of London to the papacy have survived in Rome and are helpfully summarized in a modern printed edition.[3]

At the Consistory itself, a scribe or registrar recorded depositions in a book. Two such books survive for the years 1467–76 and 1487–96. The relationship of the surviving record to the actual hearing is indirect. At the actual hearing, the scribe probably took notes which he later wrote in a more formal style in the books we now have. He did not record the actual article or question to which the witness responded in their testimony; presumably anyone wishing to refer to the deposition was assumed to have a copy of those documents as well (although they have not survived). The clerk translated the depositions, which the witnesses gave in English, into Latin. During the period under study here, the second half of the fifteenth century, ecclesiastical court clerks all over England began more frequently to insert English words into their records, especially in quotations, reflecting the legal importance of knowing the exact words spoken in marriage contracts and defamations.

The questions witnesses were asked in marriage cases centered around points essential to the case and the canon law of marriage, but the court gave witnesses room to tell fairly lengthy stories in some cases. In most marriage cases, the most important issue for the court was usually whether or not the principals had properly exchanged consent. Sometimes priority was the matter at hand: which exchange of consent came first? At other times, the exact words spoken and whether they constituted free and unconditional consent were in question. The court was also interested, however, in the events that surrounded the actual exchange of words, as other factors could influence whether or not both parties participated of their own free will. Suits where consent was not the question—for instance a suit for separation on the basis of cruelty—obviously elicited other sorts of questioning and testimony. Defamation suits usually revolved around the context in which the damaging words were allegedly spoken and their effect on the fame of the plaintiff.

Litigants in marriage suits came from a fairly broad cross-section of London society, as far as we can tell: all too frequently there is little evidence about a litigant's or a deponent's socioeconomic status. Some cases involve aldermen and gentlefolk; other cases involve very poor people living on the margins of London society. It seems probable, however, that more substantial inhabitants of the City are more frequently represented than other social groups: litigants and deponents, or their families, turn up often (either through internal evidence or through other records) as citizens. Others probably came from the socioeconomic groups below the citizenry but still in the upper half of the urban social ladder. Both the financial means and the legal know-how required to pursue litigation were much easier to access if one belonged to a wealthier and better-connected social group. At the same time, relatively poorer people could and did sue cases in the Consistory.

I have also used other kinds of church court evidence that bears on issues of marriage and sex, and some of these records more obviously included Londoners from lower socioeconomic stations. A lower-level church court known as the Commissary court was also important, and a significant run of London records survive from those tribunals from the 1470s onwards.[4] This court dealt with what lawyers call "office" cases: rather than one party suing another, the procedure resembled a criminal process by which suspects were summoned to appear before the judge (known as a commissary) to answer for a sin that had been alleged against them. The alleged misdeeds were often sexual—hence its later nickname, the "bawdy court"—and sometimes involved marital problems. The recorded entries from the Commissary court are usually brief and undetailed—in contrast to the sometimes fairly lengthy record of witness testimony in Consistory marriage litigation—but all together the evidence the records of these courts offer is invaluable for our understanding of late medieval London life. Other church courts,[5] such as archdeaconry courts and the Court of Arches, an archdiocesan appellate court, also heard marriage cases in London, but no documentation survives from them, although on occasion echoes of their business show up in the records of other legal fora. In addition, the church courts had jurisdiction over most testamentary business, and I have used various will registers coming from the local London Commissary courts as well as the Prerogative Court of Canterbury (where the wills of wealthier people were proved).[6]

Records of Civic and Royal Jurisdictions

While marriage, as a sacrament, and extramarital sex, as a sin, were theoretically under the church's jurisdiction, the lay leaders of late medieval London—the civic elite, the neighborhood "probi homines," the heads of households—were by no means content to leave marriage and sex to the church's sole supervision. Thus other kinds of records from the civic archives and from the system of royal justice are also replete with evidence that bears on the issues this study discusses.[7] The records of the civic government now housed at the Corporation of London Record Office— ranging from the letter books, the journals of the Court of Common Council, the plea and memoranda rolls (records of the mayor's court), a few surviving wardmote inquest records, and other documents such as wills—have proven fruitful, and references to them will be seen frequently in the notes. Copies of petitions sent to the chancellor, kept now in the National Archives, have also yielded a good deal of fascinating material. Medieval English people petitioned the chancellor when the common law could give no remedy, either because the particular issue was not governed by common law or because the functioning of the common law was in some way defective (for instance, through corruption of the sheriff or the local jury).[8] In making his or her complaint, the petitioner told a story about the wrongs that had been done him or her. The results are often gripping narratives, which must nonetheless always be treated with an eye both to the legal forms a Chancery petition had to follow and to the hyperbole that the process encouraged. The complaints are useful in revealing the concerns and assumptions of the petitioner and what he or she expected would be most persuasive to the king's chancellor.

Abbreviations

BRUC	A. B. Emden, *A Biographical Register of the University of Cambridge to 1500* (Cambridge: Cambridge University Press, 1963).
BRUO	A. B. Emden, *A Biographical Register of the University of Oxford to A. D. 1500*, 3 vols. (Oxford: Clarendon Press, 1957–59).
Cal. Husting	Reginald R. Sharpe, ed., *Calendar of Wills Proved and Enrolled in the Court of Husting, London, A.D. 1258–A.D. 1688*, 2 vols. (London: Corporation of the City of London, 1890).
Cal. Inq. P.M. Hen. VII	*Calendar of Inquisitions Post Mortem . . . Henry VII*, 3 vols. (London: Public Record Office, 1898–1955).
CLBG, CLBH, CLBI, CLBK, CLBL	Reginald R. Sharpe, ed., *Calendar of Letter-Books Preserved among the Archives of the Corporation of the City of London at the Guildhall*, 11 vols., *Letter Books G* through *L* (London: J. E. Francis, 1899–1912).
CLRO	Corporation of London Record Office
CPMR	A.H. Thomas and Philip E. Jones, eds., *Calendar of Plea and Memoranda Rolls Preserved among the Archives of the Corporation of the City of London at the Guildhall, 1323–1482*, 6 vols. (Cambridge: Cambridge University Press, 1926–61).
EETS	Early English Text Society
GL	London, Guildhall Library
HMSO	His/Her Majesty's Stationery Office
LMA	London Metropolitan Archives
ODNB	*Oxford Dictionary of National Biography* (Oxford: Oxford University Press, 2004), available at http://www.oxforddnb.com.
OED	*The Oxford English Dictionary Online* (Oxford: Oxford University Press, 2005), available at http://dictionary.oed.com.
PCC	Prerogative Court of Canterbury
P&MR	Plea and Memoranda Rolls
PROME	Chris Given-Wilson, et al., eds., *The Parliament Rolls of Medieval England*, CD-ROM (Leicester: Scholarly Digital Editions, 2005).

RP	J. Strachey, ed., *Rotuli Parliamentorum; ut et petitiones et placita in Parliamento . . . 1278–1503*, 6 vols. (London: n.p., 1783).
TNA, PRO	Kew, The National Archives, Public Record Office

Notes

Introduction

1. LMA, DL/C/205, fols. 266rv. "[Wellys] dixit quod nisi iste iuratus vellet ibidem contrahere matrimonium cum prefata Agnete filia sua quod ipse vel alius pro ipso et nomine ipsius daret huic iurato tale signum quod secum adduceret usque sepulcrum suum. Et dixit ulterius ibidem quod ipse idem Johannes vellet cum rubore adducere istum iuratum coram maiore et aldermannis ubi tali erubescencia confunderetur, quod pudor sive erubiscencia et necessitas compellerent istum iuratum ad contrahendum matrimonium cum prefata Agnete. Unde iste iuratus tam timore corporis sui <quam> pudore comparacionis coram maiore et Aldermannis, iste iuratus contraxit ibidem matrimonium cum prefata Agnete."

Throughout this book, when material quoted is in Latin in the original manuscript source, I have translated the passages into English in the text and provided the original Latin in the accompanying note (as in this case). When the original material was recorded in Middle English, I have modernized the spelling and on rare occasions changed the wording slightly to facilitate the reading and comprehension of nonspecialists. I have also used modern dating conventions: in late medieval England, the calendar year began on 25 March (Lady Day, the feast of the Annunciation), but I have adhered to the modern practice of using 1 January as the first day of the year. This means that in the case of a document dated 1 February 1476, I report the date as 1 February 1477.

2. LMA, DL/C/205, 265v–266v.

3. P. J. P. Goldberg, *Women, Work, and Life Cycle in a Medieval Economy: Women in York and Yorkshire, c. 1300–1520* (Oxford: Clarendon Press, 1992), 6–7.

4. Mary S. Hartman, *The Household and the Making of History: A Subversive View of the Western Past* (Cambridge: Cambridge University Press, 2004).

5. John Hajnal, "European Marriage Patterns in Perspective," in *Population in History: Essays in Historical Demography*, ed. D. V. Glass and D. E. C. Eversley (London: Edward Arnold, 1965), 101–43.

6. Hartman, *Household*, ch. 3.

7. Goldberg, *Women, Work, and Life Cycle*, esp. 234, 243–54, 273; also on York and Yorkshire, see Frederik Pedersen, *Marriage Disputes in Medieval England* (London: Hambledon Press, 2000).

8. Michael M. Sheehan, "The Formation and Stability of Marriage in Fourteenth-Century England: Evidence of an Ely Register," *Mediaeval Studies* 33

(1971): 228–63 (quotation at 263), reprinted in his *Marriage, Family, and Law in Medieval Europe: Collected Studies*, ed. James K. Farge (Toronto: University of Toronto Press, 1996), 38–76 (quotation at 76).

9. Goldberg, *Women, Work, and Life Cycle*, 6–7, 155–57, 261–63.

10. Pamela Nightingale, *A Medieval Mercantile Community: The Grocers' Company and the Politics and Trade of London, 1000–1485* (New Haven, Conn.: Yale University Press, 1995), 477–78.

11. Marjorie Keniston McIntosh, *Controlling Misbehavior in England, 1370–1600* (Cambridge: Cambridge University Press, 1998), 13–14, 128, 158–64, 175–77; Goldberg, *Women, Work, and Life Cycle*, 7, 155–57, 261–63, 276–78; Shannon McSheffrey, "Jurors, Respectable Masculinity, and Christian Morality," *Journal of British Studies* 37 (1998): 269–78.

12. This argument resonates with that made by Martha C. Howell regarding the late medieval Flemish city, Douai, although her focus emphasizes property much more than mine does; Howell, *The Marriage Exchange: Property, Social Place, and Gender in Cities of the Low Countries, 1300–1550* (Chicago: University of Chicago Press, 1998), esp. 233–39.

13. The period of the first half of the sixteenth century remains relatively little studied. There is, however, a significant body of scholarship on the Elizabethan period: see, for instance, Martin Ingram, *Church Courts, Sex and Marriage in England, 1570–1640* (Cambridge: Cambridge University Press, 1987); Eric Josef Carlson, *Marriage and the English Reformation* (Oxford: Blackwell, 1994); Anthony Fletcher, *Gender, Sex and Subordination in England, 1500–1800* (New Haven, Conn.: Yale University Press, 1995); Laura Gowing, *Domestic Dangers: Women, Words, and Sex in Early Modern London* (Oxford: Clarendon Press, 1996); David Cressy, *Birth, Marriage, and Death: Ritual, Religion, and the Life-Cycle in Tudor and Stuart England* (Oxford: Oxford University Press, 1997); Diana O'Hara, *Courtship and Constraint: Rethinking the Making of Marriage in Tudor England* (Manchester: Manchester University Press, 2000).

14. See especially Gowing, *Domestic Dangers*.

15. On the population of London, see Caroline M. Barron, *London in the Later Middle Ages: Government and People, 1200–1500* (Oxford: Oxford University Press, 2004), 237–42. This book is now our best guide to the city's later medieval history. See also Barron's useful essay "London 1300–1540," in *Cambridge Urban History of Britain*, vol. 1, ed. David Palliser (Cambridge: Cambridge University Press, 2000), 395–440. Although in a few ways superseded by recent studies such as Barron's, Sylvia L. Thrupp's *The Merchant Class of Medieval London, 1300–1500* (Chicago: University of Chicago Press, 1948; rept., Ann Arbor: University of Michigan Press, 1962) remains indispensable.

16. On London's government, see Barron, *London in the Later Middle Ages*, chs. 6 and 7; Thrupp, *Merchant Class*, 80–85. On concentration of capital and power, see Nightingale, *Medieval Mercantile Community*, 477–78.

17. Barron, *London in the Later Middle Ages*, 273; Barron, "London," 397, 400.

18. Thrupp, *Merchant Class*, 2–3.

19. See Appendix for a more detailed discussion of sources.

20. Joel T. Rosenthal, *Telling Tales: Sources and Narration in Late Medieval England* (University Park: Pennsylvania State University Press, 2003), xiii.

21. I have made extensive and intensive use of the surviving records of marital litigation from fifteenth-century marriage, mostly, although not exclusively, from two deposition books from the Consistory Court of the Bishop of London: LMA, DL/C/205, Consistory Court of the Diocese of London Deposition Book, 1467–76; and GL, 9065 and 9065B, Consistory Court of the Diocese of London Deposition Book, 1487–97. I am preparing editions of each of these books. I have focused on the cases that relate to the City of London (the diocese of London was larger, comprising the City, the counties of Middlesex and Essex, and a part of Hertfordshire). I have also used the act books from the Commissary Court of the Diocese of London. Seven of the eight surviving act books from the fifteenth century (GL, 9064/1–6 and 8) deal with parishes within the City and in the immediate suburbs; GL, 9064/7 relates to cases further afield in the diocese of London. Civic records have also proven very useful (especially the journals of the Court of Common Council; the letter books; and the plea and memoranda rolls, all held in the CLRO), as have bills of complaint made to the chancellor (TNA, PRO, C 1) and testaments registered in various courts.

22. For doubts about the representativeness of marital litigation evidence, see R. M. Smith, "Marriage Processes in the English Past: Some Continuities," in *The World We Have Gained: Histories of Population and Social Structure*, ed. Lloyd Bonfield, Richard M. Smith, and Keith Wrightson (Oxford: Basil Blackwell, 1986), 70–71; Martin Ingram, "Spousals Litigation in the English Ecclesiastical Courts, *c. 1350–1640*," in *Marriage and Society: Studies in the Social History of Marriage*, ed. R. B. Outhwaite (New York: St. Martin's Press, 1981), 36.

23. For discussion of the fruitfulness of church court depositions as historical evidence, see Gowing, *Domestic Dangers*, 41–58, 232–39. In general for legal sources and the interpretation of the narrativity of depositions and other kinds of legal submissions, see Rosenthal, *Telling Tales*; Natalie Zemon Davis, *Fiction in the Archives: Pardon Tales and Their Tellers in Sixteenth-Century France* (Stanford, Calif.: Stanford University Press, 1987), esp. 1–6; Paul Strohm, *Hochon's Arrow: The Social Imagination of Fourteenth-Century Texts* (Princeton, N.J.: Princeton University Press, 1992), 4, 9, 14–15, 18; Garthine Walker, "Rereading Rape and Sexual Violence in Early Modern England," *Gender and History* 10 (1998): 1–25; Cordelia Beattie, "Single Women, Work, and Family: The Chancery Dispute of Jane Wynde and Margaret Clerk," in *Voices from the Bench: The Narratives of Lesser Folk in Medieval Trials*, ed. Michael Goodich (Houndmills, Hampshire: Palgrave Macmillan, forthcoming) (my thanks to Dr. Beattie for sharing this work with me before publication).

24. The best work on this—albeit for an earlier period—is Anthony Musson, *Medieval Law in Context: The Growth of Legal Consciousness from Magna Carta to the Peasants' Revolt* (Manchester: Manchester University Press, 2001). I am currently working on a book called *Londoners and the Law* that will look more closely at the ways in which law was used to negotiate social relationships.

Chapter 1. Making a Marriage

1. Although demographic data for late medieval England are notoriously scarce and unreliable, Maryanne Kowaleski's recent overview of the scholarship suggests that elite women (both aristocratic and mercantile) rarely remained unmarried, while available evidence suggests that a fairly large proportion—about one-third—of nonelite women, especially those who lived in cities, never married. Maryanne Kowaleski, "Singlewomen in Medieval and Early Modern Europe: The Demographic Perspective," in *Singlewomen in the European Past, 1250–1800*, ed. Judith M. Bennett and Amy M. Froide (Philadelphia: University of Pennsylvania Press, 1999), 38–81, esp. 44–51.

2. Barbara J. Harris, *English Aristocratic Women, 1450–1550: Marriage and Family, Property and Careers* (Oxford: Oxford University Press, 2002), 56–57.

3. Frustratingly, although depositions in marital litigation usually give the ages of the witnesses, the ages of the parties in the case—those actually marrying—are not recorded. Few other sources have been found that allow for calculation of ages at first marriage in this period, and those that do allow such calculations (such as indications of orphans' marriages) relate to unusual or atypical populations.

4. Hajnal, "European Marriage Patterns"; Hartman, *Household*, esp. chs. 1, 2; Kowaleski, "Singlewomen," 40, 44–45; Goldberg, *Women, Work, and Life Cycle*, 225–32.

5. Richard M. Smith, "Geographical Diversity in the Resort to Marriage in Late Medieval Europe: Work, Reputation, and Unmarried Females in the Household Formation Systems of Northern and Southern Europe," in *Woman Is a Worthy Wight: Women in English Society, c. 1200–1500*, ed. P. J. P. Goldberg (Gloucester: Alan Sutton, 1992), 27–28, 38–42.

6. Jacques Legrand and William Caxton, *Here begynneth a lytell boke called Good Maners* (Westminster: Wynkyn de Worde, 1498), sig. M3v–M4r. On the intended audience of Caxton's translation, see sig. A2rv.

7. Eileen Power, "The Position of Women," in *The Legacy of the Middle Ages*, ed. C. G. Crump and E. F. Jacob (Oxford: Clarendon Press, 1926), 414; in fifteenth-century Chancery bills, the "sale" of a marriage refers to the right to control the marriage of a minor heir (e.g., TNA, PRO, C 1/6/89; C 1/10/233; C 1/99/16; C 1/102/63). See Harris, *Aristocratic Women*, 44, for language of the marketplace used in arrangements of aristocratic marriages.

8. See, for instance, O'Hara, *Courtship and Constraint*, 190–235, esp. 217–18.

9. As Barbara Harris demonstrates (*Aristocratic Women*, 43–59), while many parents took into account their children's future happiness, material and political advantage were by far the most important criteria considered in the arrangement of aristocratic marriages.

10. Charles Ross, *Edward IV* (New Haven: Yale University Press, 1974), 84–87.

11. E.g., LMA, DL/C/205, fols. 53v–55r; GL, 9065, fol. 194r.

12. E.g., Richard Leighton Greene, ed., *Early English Carols* (Oxford: Clarendon Press, 1935), nos. 452 (275–76) and 453 (276–77). See also, regarding parish celebrations, Gervase Rosser, "Going to the Fraternity Feast: Commensality and Social Relations in Late Medieval England," *Journal of British Studies* 33 (1994): 443; Katherine L. French, *The People of the Parish: Community Life in a Late Medieval English Diocese* (Philadelphia: University of Pennsylvania Press, 2001), 130–39; French, " 'To Free Them from Binding': Women in the Late Medieval English Parish," *Journal of Interdisciplinary History* 27 (1997): 387–412. French describes the ritual of "Hocking," where on Hock Monday in some parishes in late medieval England women took men "captive" in return for a small ransom (a donation to parish funds), with the men's and women's roles as captor and captive reversed on Hock Tuesday. In some parishes it was the unmarried who participated in this ritual ("To Free Them from Binding," 404): although we know nothing about its social implications, there was obvious courting potential in such activities. In other parishes, however, hocking was confined to married parishioners (ibid., 407–9).

13. E.g., Charles Donahue Jr., "Female Plaintiffs in Marriage Cases in the Court of York in the Later Middle Ages: What Can We Learn from the Numbers?" in *Wife and Widow in Medieval England*, ed. Sue Sheridan Walker (Ann Arbor: University of Michigan Press, 1993), 197–98.

14. P. J. P. Goldberg, "Household and the Organisation of Labour in Late Medieval Towns: Some English Evidence," in *The Household in Late Medieval Cities: Italy and Northwestern Europe Compared: Proceedings of the International Conference, Ghent, 21st–22nd January 2000*, ed. Myriam Carlier and Tim Soens (Leuven-Apeldoorn: Garant, 2001), 62–63.

15. The following account of the canon law of marriage in late medieval England draws heavily on the substantial scholarship in the field. Most obviously, I am indebted to Sheehan, *Marriage, Family, and Law*, and Richard Helmholz, *Marriage Litigation in Medieval England* (Cambridge: Cambridge University Press, 1974). See also the important work by Richard M. Wunderli, *London Church Courts and Society on the Eve of the Reformation* (Cambridge, Mass.: Medieval Academy of America, 1981); Charles Donahue Jr., "The Canon Law on the Formation of Marriage and Social Practice in the Later Middle Ages," *Journal of Family History* 8 (1983): 144–58; L. R. Poos, "The Heavy-Handed Marriage Counsellor: Regulating Marriage in Some Later-Medieval English Local Ecclesiastical-Court Jurisdictions," *American Journal of Legal History* 39 (1995): 291–309; Goldberg, *Women, Work, and Life Cycle*; Pedersen, *Marriage Disputes*. For Europe more generally, see James A. Brundage, *Law, Sex, and Christian Society in Medieval Europe* (Chicago: University of Chicago Press, 1987).

16. Sheehan, *Marriage, Family, and Law*, 76.

17. Alan Watson, *Roman Law and Comparative Law* (Athens: University of Georgia Press, 1991), 27–30, 53–57.

18. See J. L. Austin, *How to Do Things with Words*, 2nd ed., ed. J. O. Urmson and Marina Sbisà (Cambridge, Mass.: Harvard University Press, 1975), esp. 4–11, 14–15; Helmholz, *Marriage Litigation*, 27.

19. E.g., LMA, DL/C/205, fols. 8r, 43v–44r, 52v; GL, 9065, fols. 75v, 221v, 250v. A seventeenth-century example shows a man playing on this formula: angry at a woman who untruthfully claimed him as the father of her unborn child, he said he "could find it in his heart to kick her." Bernard Capp, "The Double Standard Revisited: Plebeian Women and Male Sexual Reputation in Early Modern England," *Past & Present* 162 (1999): 76.

20. See Chapter 7.

21. Frederick Pollock and Frederic William Maitland, *The History of English Law before the Time of Edward I*, 2nd ed., 2 vols. (Cambridge: Cambridge University Press, 1968), 2:386–89.

22. In 1475, J. Janyn of Horndon on the Hill appeared before the Consistory, possibly in answer to a summons from the court acting ex officio rather than a suit brought against him, and admitted that three weeks before he had married a woman whose former husband had been Janyn's son's godfather. There is no record of how the court responded. In two other cases heard before the Commissary court in 1494 and 1495, spiritual affinity was cited as an aggravating factor in citations for adultery and bigamy respectively. LMA, DL/C/205, fol. 306v; GL, 9064/6, fols. 72v, 92r.

23. Helmholz, *Marriage Litigation*, 87–90; GL, 9065, fol. 252v (1496); William Henry Bliss et al., eds. *Calendar of Entries in the Papal Registers Relating to Great Britain and Ireland: Papal Letters*, 18 vols. (London: HMSO/Irish Manuscripts Commission, 1893–1955), 13:488. In another suit from 1475, a male defendant appears to have used his impotence as a defense (indicating his inability to marry). *Alice Cademan c. Nicholas Vavecer*, LMA, DL/C/205, fols. 286r–287v.

24. *Calendar of Papal Registers*, 13:488.

25. Rosemary Horrox, "Shore , Elizabeth [Jane] (*d.* 1526/7?)," *ODNB*, available from http://www.oxforddnb.com/view/article/25451, accessed 26 May 2005.

26. GL, 9065B, fols. 2v–3r. For other examples of "marriage before God," see LMA, DL/C/205, fols. 137v–138r, 151r–152v, 167v–168r; GL, 9065, fols. 73rv, 207v, 244rv. For more on Agnes Skern and Piers Curtes, see p. 52.

27. It may at first seem odd that Sir Martin, a priest (clearly identified as "dominus Martinus Jelyf, capellanus cathedrale sancti Pauli London," GL, 9065, fol. 113r), had a son, but it was by no means unknown for widowers to enter the priesthood in late adulthood. R. N. Swanson notes that monitions directed at ordinands warned that men who had married twice or had married a widow could not be ordained, implying that a once-married widower could become a priest. Swanson, *Church and Society in Late Medieval England* (Oxford: Blackwell, 1989), 42–43, 58. It is also possible, of course, that Richard Jelyf was an illegitimate son, but if so, Sir Martin was remarkably open about it (in addition to indicating that Richard was his son, he notes that he customarily ate at Richard's house). Unfortunately, the ordination lists for the diocese of London for most of the second half of the fifteenth century are missing. See Virginia Davis, *Clergy in London in the Late Middle Ages: A Register of Clergy Ordained in the Diocese of London Based on Episcopal Ordination Lists, 1361–1539*, with accompanying CD-ROM (London: Centre for Metropolitan History, Institute of Historical Research, 2000), 2.

28. "Iste juratus [dominus Martinus Jelyf], in presencia eiusdem Johannis Kendall, examinauit eandem Elisabet an ipsa unquam contraxit cum eodem Johanne Kendall, que adtunc respondebat affirmatiue, dicendo in anglicis, '*y haue made a contracte with hym and he is my husband by for god,*' ipso Johanne adtunc dicente hec verba in anglicis, '*and she is my wyfe befor god.*'" GL, 9065, fol. 113r.

29. See Richard Jelyf's deposition. GL, 9065, fols. 113v–114r.

30. GL, 9065, fols. 201rv.

31. See Chapter 2 for further discussion of this case. Assuming that this John Crosby was the son of Sir John Crosby, alderman, he died unmarried and without legitimate issue in 1501. Will of John Crosby, gent, 1501, TNA, PRO, PCC Prob. 11/12, 166v; *Cal. Inq. P.M. Hen. VII,* 3:280.

32. LMA, DL/C/205, fol. 182r.

33. GL, 9064/3, 76v; see also Helmholz, *Marriage Litigation,* 71.

34. "'Ego Johannes Colyn accipio te Johannam Stocton in uxorem meam, et ad hoc do tibi fidem meam,' et retraxerunt manus. Et tunc ipsa Johanna cepit ipsum Johannem Colyn per manum et dixit eidem, 'Et ego Johanna Stocton accipio te Johannem Colyn in maritum meum, et ad hoc do tibi fidem meam.' Et tunc statim Johannes Colyn extraxit de sinu suo unum manutergium in quo erat una bursa de rubeo veluet, quam bursam idem Johannes eidem Johanne dedit, dicens sub hac forma, 'Hanc bursam do vobis ut uxori mee,' et ipsa eandem recepit sic dicens, 'Et ego hanc bursam accipio a vobis ut a marito meo.' Et eandem bursam ipsa Johanna inuoluit in manutergio suo proprio et imposuit in manica sua, et tunc osculati sunt adinuicem." LMA, DL/C/205, fols. 46v–47r. This deposition was offered in what was probably a case for divorce (annulment) by reason of precontract between Joan Stocton and Richard Turnaunt, whom Joan had married about 1459 (ibid., 45v–46r), fourteen years after what would presumably have been a youthful marriage to John Colyn in 1445. One of the witnesses deposed that John Colyn had been seen alive recently (ibid., 47v), which would indicate that the second marriage to Turnaunt was bigamous, but Colyn does not appear to be involved in the case, suggesting that Joan's goal was to end her marriage to Richard. Joan Stocton was the daughter of John Stocton, mercer, who became an alderman in 1463 and was knighted in 1471. Thrupp, *Merchant Class,* 368. She was thus of high status, as was Richard Turnaunt, who was styled "gentleman" in his will. TNA, PRO, PCC Prob. 11/7, fols. 193rv.

35. Bramanger also became churchwarden of his parish, St. Mary at Hill, in 1472, indicating high status within his parish, and he testified in another Consistory court case in 1474. *CLBL,* 167, 173, 174, 214; Henry Littlehales, ed., *The Medieval Records of a London City Church, St. Mary at Hill, 1420–1559,* Early English Text Society, O.S., 125 and 128 (London: Kegan Paul, Trench, Trübner & Co., 1904–5), 18; LMA, DL/C/205, fols. 241v–242r.

36. Katherine Combes, widow of William Combes (the title "Lady" was a common honorific for the wives of prominent London aldermen). William Combes's will (proved 1452; TNA, PRO, PCC Prob. 11/1, fols. 132v–134r, 135r) shows that he left her considerable property. For Combes, see also Josiah C. Wedgwood, *History of Parliament, 1439–1509,* 2 vols. (London: HMSO, 1936–38), vol. 2,

Biographies, 210–11. The William Gregory cited as a witness was not the mayor and alderman of the same name.

37. LMA, DL/C/205, fols. 42rv.

38. *Missale secundum vsum Insignis Ecclesie Sarum* (Westminster and Paris: Wynkyn de Worde and Michel Morin, 1497; STC 16169), sig. E1r-E4v. A handy modern English translation of the Sarum marriage liturgy is available in Emilie Amt, ed., *Women's Lives in Medieval Europe: A Sourcebook* (New York: Routledge, 1993), 84–89.

39. A number of scholars have observed this. Lyndal Roper, " 'Going to Church and Street': Weddings in Reformation Augsburg," *Past & Present* 106 (1985): 44–47, 67–69; L. R. Poos, *A Rural Society after the Black Death: Essex, 1350–1525* (Cambridge: Cambridge University Press, 1991), 133–58, esp. 133; Beatrice Gottlieb, "The Meaning of Clandestine Marriage," in *Family and Sexuality in French History*, ed. Robert Wheaton and Tamara K. Hareven (Philadelphia: University of Pennsylvania Press, 1980), 72.

40. Sheehan, *Marriage*, 137–66.

41. Carlson, *Marriage and the English Reformation*, 91–93; R. B. Outhwaite, *Clandestine Marriage in England, 1500–1850* (London: Hambledon Press, 1995); O'Hara, *Courtship and Constraint*, 31, 42–43.

42. Many scholars use the term "clandestine marriage" to denote extraecclesiastical contracts in this period: Helmholz, *Marriage Litigation*, 27–31, 66; Donahue, "Canon Law"; Gottlieb, "Meaning of Clandestine Marriage," 50–53, 70–71; Outhwaite, *Clandestine Marriage*, xiv. Helmholz, in particular, believes that such contracts were intrinsically problematic, disreputable, out of the ordinary, and both technically and literally clandestine. Recently, Peter Fleming, *Family and Household in Medieval England* (New York: Palgrave, 2001), has extended this argument and made the erroneous contention that marriages performed anywhere but "at the church door" were regarded by late medieval church authorities as illegitimate (49, 51).

43. "Thomas et Margareta contraxerunt matrimonium inter se in villa de Stratford per verba de presenti, ut audiuit dici, et huiusmodi matrimonium solemnisatum fuit inter eosdem in capella infra dictam villam per curatum ibidem, et hoc se dicit scire eo quod tribus diebus solemnis audiuit banna edita inter eosdem per curatum et eciam quod presens fuit huiusmodi solemnisacioni matrimonii, et post solemnisacionem iste iuratus eodem die ianctauit cum eisdem et sic per ii annos proximos sequentes ut credit insimul cohabitauerunt ut vir et uxor, et diuersos proles inter se procreauerunt, et pro talibus fuerunt communiter dicti, tenti, et reputati." GL, 9065, fols. 178rv.

44. In other cases banns followed present-tense contracts: e.g., LMA, DL/C/205, fols. 221r–223r; GL, 9065, fol. 17r.

45. "Katerina, hic stans coram vobis, est uxor mea coram deo et homine, et quamcito ipsa Katerina peperit ego ducam ipsam in uxorem meam." LMA, DL/C/205, fol. 151r.

46. A widow named Margaret Elys, for instance, complained to the chancellor in the 1490s that although "she stondith contracted in marage with John

Melyonek, . . . John in no wyse wold accomplisshe the seid marage." TNA, PRO, C 1/199/64.

47. LMA, DL/C/205, fols. 30v–31r.

48. E.g., GL, 9065, fols. 10v–11v. This is not to say, of course, that all couples refrained from sexual relations until after the solemnization.

49. See below, p. 156.

50. GL, 9064/1–8. A typical presentment was "Willelmus Kildon fornicauit cum Katherina Wright et contraxit cum eadem." (They admitted the charge and paid a fine.) GL, 9064/6, fol. 113v. For other examples, see GL, 9064/2, fols. 151v, 262r; 9064/3, fol. 200r; 9064/4, 68r, 280r; 9064/5, fol. 37r; 9064/6, fols. 19v, 30r, 47r, 90v, 113v, 124r; 9064/7, fol. 63r; 9064/8, fols. 7r, 54r, 101v, 103v.

51. Typically such presentments emphasized the refusal to fulfill the contract: e.g., "Agnes Symson contraxhit cum Willelmo Jakisson et recusat adimplere contractum." GL, 9064/2, fol. 105v. For other examples, see GL, 9064/1, fols. 24r, 105r; 9064/2, fol. 126r; 9064/5, fol. 13r; 9064/6, fol. 122r.

52. F. R. H. Du Boulay, ed., *Registrum Thome Bourgchier Cantuariensis Archiepiscopi*, Canterbury and York Society 54 (Oxford: Oxford University Press, 1957), 92; Sheehan, *Marriage, Family, and Law*, 153–54. At another point in Bourgchier's register, a marriage is called clandestine if it is not contracted before at least two witnesses. Du Boulay, *Registrum Bourgchier*, 22. See also Sheehan, *Marriage, Family, and Law*, 45–47, esp. 47 n. 32, where, although he does not explicitly note the change in the meaning of clandestinity, Sheehan points out that the word usually applied to the improper calling of banns in the fourteenth century and that at least one witness objected to a nonecclesiastical marriage being termed "clandestine," when it had been made publicly and with witnesses. Early modern historians have tended to follow the terminology of Hardwicke's Marriage Act of 1753 ("An Act for the Better Preventing of Clandestine Marriages") to investigate marriage processes in earlier centuries: see, e.g., Outhwaite, *Clandestine Marriage*, xii, xiv, xxii–xxiii, 1–17.

53. See C. R. Cheney, "William Lyndwood's *Provinciale*," in *Medieval Texts and Studies* (Oxford: Clarendon Press, 1973), 158–84.

54. William Lyndwood, *Provinciale; seu Constitutiones Angliae* (Farnborough, Hants.: Gregg International, 1968), 276 (3.4.3).

55. Ibid., 273–77 (3.4.1–3.4.3).

56. For London, I have found four instances in which the word was used: LMA, DL/C/205, fols. 21r (1468); 110r (1471); GL, 9064/6, fol. 27r (1494); 9064/8, fol. 152r (1498). Published records of other fifteenth- and early sixteenth-century ecclesiastical courts dealing with marriage issues show few instances of the word. In the early sixteenth-century act book of the Abbey of Whalley, which held a peculiar jurisdiction over parts of Lancashire, the two citations of clandestine marriage refer to a marriage allegedly solemnized in an unconsecrated chapel and a marriage knowingly contracted within prohibited degrees of affinity. Alice M. Cooke, ed., *Act Book of the Ecclesiastical Court of Whalley, 1510–1538*, Chetham Society New Series 44 (Manchester: Chetham Society, 1901), 52, 67–69. A search through other published records found no instances of the word: E. D. Stone and

B. Cozens-Hardy, ed., *Norwich Consistory Court Depositions, 1499–1512 and 1518–1530*, Norfolk Record Society 10 (London: Wyman & Sons, 1938); E. M. Elvey, ed., *The Courts of the Archdeaconry of Buckingham, 1483–1523*, Buckinghamshire Record Society 19 (Aylesbury: Buckinghamshire Record Society, 1975); *Acts of Chapter of the Collegiate Church of SS. Peter and Wilfrid, Ripon, A.D. 1452 to A.D. 1506*, Surtees Society 64 (Durham: Andrews, 1874); L. R. Poos, ed., *Lower Ecclesiastical Jurisdiction in Late-Medieval England: The Courts of the Dean and Chapter of Lincoln, 1336–1349, and the Deanery of Wisbech, 1458–1484*, British Academy Records of Social and Economic History, new series 32 (Oxford: Oxford University Press for the British Academy, 2001).

57. See below, p. 39, regarding the archdeacon of Westminster.

58. LMA, DL/C/205, fol. 110r.

59. *Calendar of Papal Registers*, 13:310.

60. Helmholz, *Marriage Litigation*, 27–31.

61. Sheehan, *Marriage, Family, and Law*, 59–61; Ingram, "Spousals Litigation," 46; Helmholz, *Marriage Litigation*, 34–38. Note that in the early sixteenth-century litigation from the diocese of Norwich, a much greater range of words of contract were employed (in some cases making for considerable ambiguities about whether there was a contract of marriage). Stone and Cozens-Hardy, *Norwich Consistory Court Depositions*, passim. It is impossible to say whether London depositions reflect more uniformity in the saying of words or simply better advice from proctors about unambiguous words to use in testimony, but there is at least some evidence that concern extended outside the courtroom (see below).

62. The question of exact words spoken and whether they constituted present or future consent was tricky. Helmholz found that the focus was usually on the verb used—"I will take," meaning future consent, and "I will have," meaning present consent. Helmholz, *Marriage Litigation*, 34–38. I have not yet found another case that differentiated between plighting faith and troth, although cf. LMA, DL/C/205, fols. 81v–82v (see n. 65 in the present chapter).

63. GL, 9065, fols. 23rv.

64. There are many other examples; see, e.g., LMA, DL/C/205, fols. 4v–5v, 10rv; GL, 9065, fols. 7r–8r.

65. See also LMA, DL/C/205, fols. 81v–82v, where witnesses to an exchange of consent argued also about the proper form of words. After Margaret Mylsent and Thomas Alcote had said their vows (in the form "Ego volo habere te in maritum meum/uxorem meam"), "then John Clerke [one of the witnesses] said to Margaret that she should contract under this form, 'I will have you *by my faith*,' and she said that this was not necessary because she had had three previous husbands, and she had never given them her faith in her contracts, nor had she ever been false to those husbands [tunc Johannes Clerke dixit eidem Margarete quod deberet contrahere sub hac forma, 'Ego volo habere te *per fidem meam*,' et ipsa dixit ad hoc non erat necessarie pro eo quod per prius habuit tres maritos et nunquam dedit eis fidem suam in contractibus suis nec unquam erat falsa eisdem maritis]."

66. An exception is Beatrice Stoughton, mother of the prospective bride and the only witness present when the couple contracted. GL, 9065B, fols. 2v–3r.

67. LMA, DL/C/205, fol. 16v.

68. GL, 9065, fols. 4r–5r.

69. "Si jura ecclesie veluit dare michi licencia." LMA, DL/C/205, fol. 264v.

70. GL, 9064/6, fol. 71v (1494). A widow of a freeman could inherit her husband's right to trade as a freeman; this did not give her the right to participate in the political aspects of citizenship.

71. "Iste iuratus et prefata Alicia habuerunt multa verba adinuicem de et super matrimonio inter eosdem contrahendo, et tandem prefata Alicia dixit huic iurato, 'ego volo habere vos in maritum meum,' et iste iuratus respondebat eidem et dixit, 'tu non debes eligere habere me in maritum tuum absque consensu et beneplacito meo, nec aliquem alium maritum habebis infra Anglia nisi ego consensiam ad hoc.' Et dicit quod post dicta verba semel cognouit eam carnaliter et alia verba sonancia in matrimonium non protulit eidem ut dicit." LMA, DL/C/205, fol. 285r.

72. LMA, DL/C/205, fols. 312v, 314r–315r.

73. "Cecilia moram trahens le Pewterpote fornicauit cum Johanne Bencham. Citata ad xii diem Aprilis, illo die comparet mulier et negat articulum et dominus induxit ea ad purgandum se 4ᵃ manu die jovis proximo futuro. Illo die comparet cum purgatoribus suis, videlicet Alicia Dale, Elisabeth Dowch, Johanna Eggecote, et Emma Lancelate. Dictus Bencham coram domino commissario recognouit et dixit se contraxisse matrimonium cum dicta Cecilia et dominus super eodem eos examinauit, et mulier fatebatur quod huic ad iiᵒˢ annos elapsos bene dilexit dictum Bencham et in mente sua erat determinata eum habere in virum suum et ea intencione eum diligebat et non aliter nec pro aliqua alia causa, sed dicit quod iam non ita bene eum diligit pro eo quod prodigaliter se habet in suis expensis et in illicitis ludis expendit pecunias suas videlicet at þe dise and þe Kardis." GL, 9064/4, fol. 242r.

74. LMA, DL/C/205, fols. 222v–223r.

75. LMA DL/C/205, fols. 221r–222v. Agnes Rogers denied both the 3 February contract in her house and any request on her part to have banns read; her witnesses alleged the priests' general moral turpitude and specifically their propensity to perjury. LMA, DL/C/205, fols. 224r, 234v–240v. Nonetheless, the procedure the two priests described in their testimony—whether or not they actually issued the banns as they claimed—must have been fairly typical if they were attempting to persuade a judge in an ecclesiastical court, who would be presumed to know the normal procedure.

76. See, for instance, the entry, dated 8–10 September 1490, that Agnes Adam of the parish of St. Sepulchre had made a reclamation against banns read in that church concerning Richard Preston of the same parish. She had been given until the end of August to explain to the parish priest the reasons for her claim, and he now referred it to the Commissary. GL, 9064/4, fol. 139r.

77. GL, 9064/6, fol. 27r.

78. E.g., GL, 9064/8, fol. 17v (1496).

79. LMA, DL/C/205, fols: 27rv.

80. LMA, DL/C/205, fol. 109r; the rest of the case appears at fols. 108v–111v, 115rv, 124r–125r, and the appeal to the papacy in *Calendar of Papal Registers,* 13:310.

81. "Dicit quod circiter festum sancti Andree ultimum, quem diem aliter specificare nescit, iste iuratus venit ad vicarium de Enfeld existentem in ecclesia sua quodam die dominica tempore alte misse, et dixit eidem quod nullo modo ederet banna inter dictos Ricardum Cordell et Margeriam eius filiam quousque dicti Ricardus et Margeria essent melius concordati. Et aliter non reclamauit ut dicit. Et dicit quod auctoritate sua propria hec dixit vicario predicto et non auctoritate seu mandato cuiusvis alterius." LMA, DL/C/205, fols. 136v–137r. Margery's mother, Alice Forde, also objected (ibid., fols. 137rv), but said that she did so at Margery's request, not on her own authority.

82. LMA, DL/C/205, fol. 249r; GL, 9064/1, fols. 24v, 134r, 146v; 9064/3, fol. 15r; 9065, fols. 36r–37r, 9065B, 7rv.

83. GL, 9064/6, fol. 3r (1494).

84. See Chapter 4.

85. ". . . eo non obstante quod bannis matrimonialibus insimul bina vice solemniter editis ac eciam dictus Johannes White habet aliam uxorem in Hibernia viuentem." GL, 9064/8, fol. 130v (1498).

86. On parish clerks, in London by the fifteenth century most often married laymen, see N. W. and A. V. James, *The Bede Roll of the Fraternity of St. Nicholas*, 2 vols., London Record Society 39 (London: London Record Society, 2004), 1:xv–xviii; Peter Heath, *The English Parish Clergy on the Eve of the Reformation* (London: Routledge & Kegan Paul, 1969), 19–20; Swanson, *Church and Society*, 43.

87. GL, 9064/3, fol. 41v (1481).

88. GL, 9064/8, fol. 16r (1496).

89. GL, 9064/3, fol. 48 (1481).

90. GL, 9065, fols. 76v–77r. It is likely that Gilderson meant the Commissary court, whence the case may have been transferred to the Consistory. Gilderson's deposition is the only testimony in the case.

91. See above, p. 32.

92. Du Boulay, *Registrum Bourgchier*, 91. For a short description of the archdeacon's jurisdiction, see E. H. Pearce, *The Monks of Westminster* (Cambridge: Cambridge University Press, 1916), 4–5.

93. GL, 9064/8, fols. 57v, 60v. Master Cutford could be Thomas Cutfolde, doctor of canon law, who was appointed official and vicar general of the bishop of Rochester in 1497. *BRUO*, 1:531.

94. E.g., LMA, DL/C/205, fols. 30v–31r.

95. GL, 9065, fols. 4r–5r.

96. O'Hara, *Courtship and Constraint*, 84.

97. GL, 9065, fol. 279r.

98. GL, 9065, fols. 10v–12r.

99. GL, 9065, fols. 39v–40r.

100. "Multa ornamenta apta et preparata pro corpore Margarete erga nupcias inter eos celebrandas." GL, 9065B, fol. 12v.

101. TNA, PRO, C 1/17/1. For Cawdrey, see *BRUC*, 126–27; *CLBK*, 171, 241–46, 325n; *CPMR*, 5:39, 40, 155–56, 181.

102. Westminster City Archive, Churchwardens' Accounts E2, 1510–11, p. 25. My thanks to Kit French for this reference.

103. GL, 9065B, fol. 10v.

104. E.g., LMA, DL/C/205, fols. 46r, 117r; GL, 9065B, fol. 10r.

105. LMA, DL/C/205, fols. 45v–46r; GL, 9065, fols. 225r–226r.

106. "Duxit dictam mulierem ad ecclesiam et ibi eam dedit dicto fratri ut mors <est> matrimonium sole<mni>santi." GL, 9065, fol. 276v.

107. GL, 9065, fol. 258v.

108. "Iste iuratus tanquam pater eiusdem Alicie dedit eam presbitero, et post missam finitam produxit eam ad domum suam." GL, 9065, fol. 257r. Note that the St. Margaret's Westminster churchwarden accounts show that Robert Raby and his wife Agnes were prominent and active parishioners there from 1479 until their deaths respectively in 1503 and 1524. Westminster City Archives, St. Margaret Westminster Churchwarden Accounts, E1, fols. 158–561 passim; E2, fol. 7 (thanks to Kit French for these references).

109. *Missale*, sig. E1r; LMA, DL/C/205, fols. 27v–29r, 73rv, 107rv, 138v–139v, 218v–219r; GL, 9065, fols. 47v–48r, 78v, 149rv, 222rv, 225rv; Sheehan, *Marriage, Family, and Law*, 158, see also 47.

110. E.g., most famously the Wife of Bath says "Housbondes at chirche dore I have had fyve." Geoffrey Chaucer, "The Wife of Bath's Prologue," in *The Riverside Chaucer*, 3rd ed., ed. Larry D. Benson (Boston: Houghton Mifflin, 1987), 105. Also see Geoffroy de La Tour Landry, *The book of the knight of La Tour-Landry, compiled for the instruction of his daughters*, rev. ed., ed. Thomas Wright (New York: Greenwood Press, 1969), 50: "ye are suoren to God and to youre husbonde atte the chirche dore afore witnesses." For modern commentators, see Christopher Brooke, *The Medieval Idea of Marriage* (Oxford: Oxford University Press, 1989), who devotes a chapter to the architectural manifestations of the church door wedding (248–257); Fleming, *Family and Household*, 46, who divides the "secular" part of the marriage ceremony (the exchange of consent taking place at the church door) and the "sacramental" part inside the church itself. Some other scholars, acknowledging the ambiguity of the phrase, leave it in the Latin original: e.g., Pedersen, *Marriage Disputes*, 106, 162, 172.

111. "*Facie ecclesiae*, i.e. Conspectu Ecclesiae populi se congregati in Ecclesia." Lyndwood, *Provinciale*, 271 (3.4.1). See also R. E. Latham, *Revised Medieval Latin Word-List* (London: Oxford University Press for the British Academy, 1965), s.v. "facies"; Sheehan, *Marriage, Family, and Law*, 47, 158; TNA, PRO, C 1/61/486 (1480–83).

112. E.g., "Iste iuratus, presens in ecclesia sancti Stephani in Walbroke, Ciuitatis London, ante meridiem eiusdem diei inter matutinas et altam missam eiusdem diei celebratas in eadam ecclesia, vidit et audiuit quando quidam sacerdos, cuius nomen aut cognomen nescit iste iuratus ad presens specificare, solempnisabat matrimonium in naui ecclesie predicte inter dictos Thomam Fordell et Johannam Fordell. . . . Quibus verbis sic hincinde prolatis, et dicta solemnisacione prout mors in ecclesia Anglicane in dicta naui ecclesie solempniter consummata et finita dicti contrahentes insequebantur dictum sacerdotem usque ad gradus summum altaris ibidem, et tunc ibidem dictus sacerdos celebrauit missam nupcialem et cetera perfecit que in hac parte incumbunt officio sacerdotali. Et cum eisdem contrahentibus iste iuratus in dicta missa nupciali obtulit ut dicit." LMA, DL/C/205, fols. 140v–141r; see also fols. 45v, 71r, 116v.

113. "Dicit quod die dominico contingenti proximo post festum Assumpcionis beate Marie ultimum preritum ad annum elapsum, presens fuit iste juratus in naui ecclesie parochialis omnium sanctorum de Maldon, et ibidem audiuit quando prefata Alicia et Johannes Grose adinuicem matrimonium contraxerunt in facie ecclesie." GL, 9065, fol. 78v.

114. LMA, DL/C/205, fol. 105r.

115. The following description of the liturgy is derived from *Missale* (see note 38 in this chapter), sig. E1r-E4v.

116. "Ecce, conuenimus hic fratres coram deo et angelis eius, et omnibus sanctis, in facie ecclesie ad coniungendum duo corpora, scilicet huius viri et huius muliere, vt amodo sint vnum corpus, et due anime sint in fide et in lege dei, ad permerendam simul vitam eternam, et quicquid ante hec fecerint." *Missale*, sig. E1r.

117. "N., vis habere hanc mulierem in sponsam, et eam diligere, et honorare, tenere, et custodire, sanam et infirmam, sicut sponsus debet sponsam, et omnes alias propter eam dimittere et illi adherere quamdiu vita vtriusque vestrum durauerit." Ibid., sig. E1v.

118. "N., vis habere hunc virum in sponsum, et illi obedire et servire, et eum diligere et honorare, ac custodire, sanum et infirmum, sicut sponsa debet sponsum, et omnes alios propter eum dimittere, et illi soli adherere quamdiu vita vtriusque vestrum durauerit." Ibid.

119. Ibid.

120. Ibid.

121. "Quodam die mercurii contingenti in eodem mense Junii iste iuratus in capella sancte Marie infra prioratum Monasterii Sancti Bartholomei predicta publice celebrauit matrimonium inter dictos Robertum et Katerinam ut mors est in Regno Anglie. Videlicet dictus Robertus cepit dictam Katerinam per manum et dixit eidem secundum informacionem istius iurati, 'Ego Robertus Dorward hic accipio te Katerinam in uxorem meam et ad hoc do tibi fidem meam,' et retraxerunt manus. Et tunc dicta Katerina cepit eundem Robertum per manum et dixit eidem, 'Et ego Katerina hic accipio te Robertum in maritum meum et ad hoc do tibi fidem meam,' cum aliis verbis et solempnibus in talibus matrimoniis usitatis et obseruatis in Regno Anglie." LMA, DL/C/205, fol. 60r. A number of other witnesses emphasized that the solemnization followed the customs of the realm of England or of the English church, e.g., LMA, DL/C/205, fols. 71rv, 77v–78r, 218v–219r.

122. *Missale*, sig. E3r.

123. LMA, DL/C/205, fols. 27v–28r, 84r, 102v–103r; GL, 9065, fol. 79v. See Heath, *Parish Clergy*, 19–20.

124. LMA, DL/C/205, fols. 105v, 189v–190r.

125. E.g., LMA, DL/C/205, fol. 92v; GL, 9065, fols. 265rv.

126. GL, 9065, fol. 79r.

127. E.g., LMA, DL/C/205, fols. 46r, 50r, 77v–78r, 83r, 105v, 107rv, 117r, 141v, 218v–219r; GL, 9065, fols. 47v–48r, 177v, 178v. Cf. the citation of feasts following a woman's purification as a way of fixing the memory of the birth of a child, as later recalled by witnesses testifying to the age of an heir in inquisitions post mortem. See Becky R. Lee, "Men's Recollections of a Women's Rite: Medieval

English Men's Recollections Regarding the Rite of Purification of Women after Childbirth," *Gender and History* 14 (2002): 224–41.

128. CLRO, Journal 10, fol. 183r.

Chapter 2. Courtship and Gender

1. See Chapter 1.

2. "Dictus Thomas Torald parum ante horam terciam post meridiem venit ad domum istius iurate ubi in aula ibidem communicauit cum marito istius iurate et eciam cum ista iurata, asserendo quod diuersis vicibus communicauit cum dicta Matilda Knyff de matrimonio inter eosdem contrahendo et quod inuenit eam bene dispositam ultimo tempore quo secum communicauit pro huiusmodi matrimonio contrahendo. Et rogauit eos quod venirent secum ad domum eiusdem Matildis ad habendum finalem responsum de huiusmodi Matilde." LMA, DL/C/ 205, fol. 65v.

3. See Chapter 1.

4. LMA, DL/C/205, fol. 55v.

5. "Presens fuit ista iurata in domo Willelmi Gregory situata infra dictam parochiam sancti Nicholai, in parlura eiusdem domus, una cum dictis Roberto Allerton, Katerina Aber, ubi et quando dicta Katerina genuflectans coram eodem Roberto, flendo desiderabat ab eo quod ipsam haberet in uxorem suam et quod ulteriorem dilacionem non faceret." LMA, DL/C/205, fols. 152rv.

6. Geoffroy de La Tour Landry and William Caxton, *Here begynneth the booke which the knyght of the toure made and speketh of many fayre ensamples and thensygnementys and techyng of his doughters* (Westminster: William Caxton, 1484; STC 15296), sig. B2rv. Another fifteenth-century English version of the text (from a manuscript dating from the reign of Henry VI) is slightly different: La Tour Landry, *The book of the knight of La Tour-Landry*, 18.

7. This is another illustration of Deniz Kandiyoti's "patriarchal bargain." Kandiyoti, "Bargaining with Patriarchy," *Gender and Society* 2 (1988): 274–90. For discussions regarding early modern women's strategic use of customs that otherwise appear to restrict their choice, see Natalie Zemon Davis, "Boundaries and the Sense of Self in Sixteenth-Century France," in *Reconstructing Individualism: Autonomy, Individuality, and the Self in Western Thought*, ed. Thomas C. Heller et al. (Stanford, Calif.: Stanford University Press, 1986), 53–63, esp. 55, 61–63; and Gowing, *Domestic Dangers*, 144–46, 151–54.

8. "Presens fuit iste iuratus [Thomas Berford] in domo Johannis Saunder situata infra dictam parochiam sancti Dunstani in Oriente civitatis London, ubi et quando in shopa eiusdem domus prope stratam publicam iste iuratus vidit dictum Johannem Barnet et Agnetem adinuicem communicantes et pendente communicacione huiusmodi dicta Agnes vidit dictum Johannem habentem et utentem in digito suo duobus annulis aureis quem alloquebatur dicta Agnes et dixit, 'Johannes, <.> des mihi unum de istis anulis quibus uteris in digito tuo,' cui respondebat dictus Johannes et dixit, 'tu habebis unum de istis anulis sub condicione.'

Tunc dicta Agnes peciit a dicto Johanne que erat illa condicio qui dixit, 'certa condicio est ista, quod eris uxor mea.' Et tunc dictus Johannes accepit unum de illis anulis a digito suo et tradidit dicte Agneti, post cuius anuli tradicionem dicta Agnes dixit eidem Johanne, 'Ego volo habere vos in maritum meum.' Et immediate dictus Johannes dixit eidem Agneti, 'Et ego volo habere vos in uxorem,' que deponit iste iuratus de visu et auditu suis propriis, ut dicit." LMA, DL/C/205, fols. 117rv.

9. LMA, DL/C/205, fols. 112r–114v, 125r–131v.

10. "Presens fuit iste iuratus [John Holder] in quodam introitu ad domum Cecilie Chambyrleyn situatam infra parochiam sancte Marie Colchirch, Civitatis London, qui introitus est inter limen primi ostii iuxta via sive strata publica et istium aule eiusdem domi, ubi et quando loquebatur iste iuratus cum Agnete Chambyrleyn et in presencia Willelmi Phyppis et Marione eius uxoris, ac Johannis Jonson iam mortui. Et dixit, 'Agnes, vos misistis pro me, scire vellem causam ob quam pro me iam misistis.' Cui dixit dicta Agnes, 'Certe misi pro vobis ad perficiendum et complendum negocium de quo bene scitis.' Et iste iuratus dixit, 'Perficiatis.' Et tunc dicta Agnes cepit istum iuratum per manum et dixit, 'Quid vobis dicam?' Et iste iuratus statim dixit eidem, 'Dicatis, "ego volo habere vos in maritum meum et ad hoc do vobis fidem meam,"' et statim absque intervallo dicta Agnes iuxta informacionem istius iurati dixit eidem, 'Ego volo habere vos in maritum meum, et ad hoc do vobis fidem meam.' Post que verba incontinenti protulit iste iuratus hec verba eidem Agneti, 'Et ego volo habere vos in uxorem meam et ad hoc do vobis fidem meam,' et osculati sunt adinvicem." LMA, DL/C/205, fol. 112r.

11. LMA, DL/C/205, fols. 112v–113r.

12. LMA, DL/C/205, fols. 112v, 125r–131v.

13. See Helmholz, *Marriage Litigation*, 170–72.

14. LMA, DL/C/205, fols. 18v–130r; GL, 9065, fols. 190r, 195v–196r.

15. Spencer's home was used on at least one other occasion for sequestration. GL, 9065, fol. 190r. A household headed by a married man who was also an ecclesiastical court official was an ideal neutral location for sequestration. On Spencer as married man, see GL, 9064/4, fol. 192v; in *Calendar of Papal Registers*, he was called notary public and registrar-principal of the court of Canterbury (14:15–17, 26).

16. GL, 9065, fols. 38rv.

17. E.g., GL, 9065, fols. 22r–24r.

18. Although not named as such in the suit, Curtes was "groom of [the king's] robes" from at least 1463 and keeper of the king's wardrobe in the early part of Henry VII's reign (i.e., during the events at issue in the suit and at the time of the suit itself). *RP*, 5:536, 6:372; TNA, PRO, C 1/88/52, C 1/124/33, C 1/130/13, E 101/412/20, E 101/413/1, E 361/8.

19. As I discovered just before this book went to press, Agnes Skern was likely the "Mistress Annes" to whom John Paston III wrote a courting letter in 1474 (Norman Davis, *The Paston Letters and Papers of the Fifteenth Century*, 2 vols. (Oxford: Clarendon Press, 1971, 1976), 1:590–91, see also 592) and was certainly the "Stokton's daughter" about to marry "Skeerene," to whom John II

disparagingly referred later that same year (ibid., 1:479). Robert Skern, a Surrey gentleman and retainer of the earl of Oxford, died in 1485, leaving Agnes with four children (TNA, PRO, E 150/1065/5; C 1/130/14). I am preparing an article more fully exploring this interesting case.

20. GL, 9065B, fols. 2v–3r.

21. Ibid., fols. 4rv.

22. Ibid., fols. 1r–2r.

23. For Margaret's status as widow, see will of her husband, Robert Niter, gentleman, of London, probated 16 January 1486 (TNA, PRO, PCC Prob. 11/7, fol. 114r); the will does not mention any children.

24. One of the witnesses to the marriage between Margaret Niter and Piers Curtes was Ralph Riplingham, one of the wealthiest members of the Grocers' Company. Riplingham and Clarel became freemen of the company around the same time (probably in the early to mid–1450s). John Abernethy Kingdon, ed., *Facsimile of First Volume of Ms. Archives of the Worshipful Company of Grocers of the City of London, A.D. 1345–1463*, 2 vols. (London: Richard Clay and Sons, 1886), 2:278, 325, 330; see also Nightingale, *Medieval Mercantile Community*, 529.

25. An early sixteenth-century Chancery bill names the four children (C 1/130/14), two sons and two daughters. In her will Beatrice Stoughton made bequests to her two Skern granddaughters. TNA, PRO, PCC Prob. 11/11, fol. 273r.

26. A memorandum written into the flyleaf of a psalter recorded the solemnization of the marriage in January, 1488, immediately in the wake of the Consistory court suit. London, British Library, Additional MS 18,629, fol. IV.

27. GL, 9064/5, fols. 31v–32r. Another instance of an alleged use of witchcraft for the sake of winning love is recorded in the Commissary court act book for 1499: Thomas Goston was cited to appear because he gave a certain young man of London holy oil, which Goston promised would enable the young man to win the love of a certain girl if he gave it to her and she put it on. GL, 9064/8, fol. 177v.

28. LMA, DL/C/205, fols. 230v, 241v.

29. Nonetheless, Nicholas Vavecer eventually defended himself from Alice Cademan's suit in which she claimed a contract of marriage by bringing in three surgeons who testified that he was incapable of having sexual relations. LMA, DL/C/205, fols. 286r–287v. While fecundity may not have that important, sex was still considered integral to the marriage. Nicholas Vavecer died between 1477 and 1479. Littlehales, *Medieval Records of St. Mary at Hill*, 92.

30. See, for instance, widows Joan Cardif and Agnes Skern, each of whom asked for parental consent before remarrying. Unfortunately, we do not know these women's ages, although as both had parents living they were likely relatively young. GL, 9065, fols. 22rv; GL, 9065B, fols. 2v–3r.

31. TNA, PRO, C 1/116/34–35.

32. LMA, DL/C/205, fols. 108v–110v, 115rv, 124rv. Agnes Twytynge is not named as a widow in the deposition book, but within weeks after the case was heard Agnes Twetynge, widow, was recorded in the controlment rolls of the court of King's Bench as having laid a complaint of trespass against Alice Roche before the sheriffs of London (Trin. 11 Edw. IV, i.e., 8 June–8 July 1471). TNA, PRO, KB

29/101, m. 4. See also, regarding the case, *Calendar of Papal Registers*, 13: 310. An Agnes Smalwode was admitted as a laywoman to the fraternity of St. Nicholas in 1492 (James and James, *Bede Roll*, 157), suggesting that in the end, on appeal, declaration was made for Agnes's and Richard Smalwode's marriage (contrary to Richard's wishes, as he had sued to have the marriage declared null).

33. GL, 9065, fols. 20rv.

34. LMA, DL/C/205, fols. 222v–223r, 224r, 225rv, 235v–240v, 257v–258v.

35. "Eo quod noluit quod ipsi scirent quod ista adeo prope tempus mortis prioris mariti sui ad aliud votum conuolaret." GL, 9065, fol. 75v.

36. His will (GL, 9171/8, fol. 25r) was dated 17 September 1491 and probated 26 September 1491.

37. GL, 9065, fols. 6r, 7rv, 98rv.

38. LMA, DL/C/205, fols. 60v–69v. John Knyf's will is calendared in *Cal. Husting*, 2:506; the will was written 10 January 1470 and proved 30 July 1470; see also *CLBL*, 90–91. Wills were usually probated shortly after the testator's death (see, e.g., note 36 in the present chapter).

39. "Dictus Robertus cepit manum suam sinistram a digito sinistra eiusdem mulieris unum anulum aureum, quem dicta mulier rogauit quod bene servaret eundem anulum pro eius amore et pro amore mariti sui premortui." LMA, DL/C/205, fol. 62r, see also 61r.

40. LMA, DL/C/205, fols. 234v–235r. This may be a case of the scribe mishearing the witness or mistakenly writing "days" instead of "months," as other evidence indicates that Baynard's wife must have died some time before this. GL, 9064/6, fol. 55v.

41. John Knyf's occupation is listed in *Cal. Husting*, 2:506. Thomas, the son of Maude and John Knyf, was registered as an orphan of the City following John Knyf's death, on 27 July 1470. *CLBL*, 90–91.

42. GL, 9065B, fols. 2v–3r, 4rv.

43. GL, 9065, fols. 20rv; Will of Agnes Fry, 1502, TNA, PRO, PCC Prob. 11/13, fol. 77v.

44. GL, 9065, fols. 57rv, 61v–62r; cf. MS 9065B, fol. 16v. The will of Richard Alp, tallowchandler, names the four children: TNA, PRO, PCC Prob. 11/8, fols. 2rv. See also *CLBL*, 269.

45. "Dicit quod iste juratus impetrauit prefatam Elisabeth ad custodiendam domum suam eo quod solus stetit, et postea retulit eidem Elisabeth quod bene custodiret domum suam et si bene custodierit haberet eandem domum tanquam suam propriam." GL, 9065, fol. 234v.

46. GL, 9065, fol. 233v.

47. Wedgwood, *History of Parliament*, 2:980; *CPMR*, 4:40–170; *CLBL*, 55–161.

48. TNA, PRO, C 1/46/212 (1467–72).

49. A. H. Thomas and I. D. Thornley, eds., *The Great Chronicle of London* (London: George W. Jones, 1938), 233.

50. TNA, PRO, C 1/198/22, 1493–1500. On Duplage, see Matthew P. Davies, ed., *The Merchant Taylors' Company of London: Court Minutes 1486–1493* (Stamford, U.K.: Richard III and Yorkist History Trust in association

with Paul Watkins, 2000), 13, 289; on Capell, see Thrupp, *Merchant Class*, 328, and Barron, *London in the Later Middle Ages*, 145n.

51. Valentin Groebner, *Liquid Assets, Dangerous Gifts: Presents and Politics at the End of the Middle Ages*, trans. Pamela E. Selwyn (Philadelphia: University of Pennsylvania Press, 2002), 1–14.

52. On tokens in commercial contracts, see David Ibbetson, *A Historical Introduction to the Law of Obligations* (Oxford: Oxford University Press, 1999), 73–76. On gifts and early modern marriage, see O'Hara, *Courtship and Constraint*, 57–98; Gowing, *Domestic Dangers*, 159–64; Lucia Ferrante, "Marriage and Women's Subjectivity in a Patrilineal System: The Case of Early Modern Bologna," in *Gender, Kinship, Power: A Comparative and Interdisciplinary History*, ed. Mary Jo Maynes et al. (New York: Routledge, 1996), 121–22.

53. Christopher Dyer, *Everyday Life in Medieval England* (London: Hambledon and London, 2000), 109. I am grateful to Connie Morgenstern for this reference.

54. "Dixit eidem si potuit inuenire in corde suo ad diligendum eum tanquam maritum suum, ipse Johannes esset sibi et suus pro futuris." GL, 9065, fol. 22r. Some depositions from this case have been translated in Shannon McSheffrey, ed., *Love and Marriage in Late Medieval London* (Kalamazoo, Mich.: Medieval Institute Publications, 1995), 37–40.

55. Ibid.

56. TNA, PRO, C 1/116/34, datable to the period between Elizabeth Kirkeby's death in January 1488 and 1493. For Bulstrode, see *CLBL*, 282, 295. Elizabeth Kirkeby was the widow of John Kirkeby, goldsmith, who died by 1481 (see *CLBL*, 216). Her own will survives (TNA, PRO, PCC Prob. 11/8, fols. 74v–76r, dated 15 January 1488, probated 30 January 1488), in which she names John Heron as her brother.

57. Tuns, pipes, butts, and hogsheads were liquid measures, in the following volumes (see *OED* s.v.): a tun was a large cask of about 210 imperial gallons; a butt was between 108 and 140 gallons; a pipe was half a tun; two hogsheads made a pipe; two barrels made a hogshead.

58. TNA, PRO, PCC, Prob. 11/8, fols. 74v–76r.

59. See Ronald Hutton, *The Rise and Fall of Merry England: The Ritual Year, 1400–1700* (Oxford: Oxford University Press, 1994), 14–15.

60. "In signum huiusmodi matrimonii." GL, 9065, fol. 279r. Apart from Christopher Kechyn himself, the other parties and the witnesses to the case do not appear in the civic records, likely indicating that they were not of sufficient status to serve at the higher reaches of the City's government. Christopher Kechyn was a carpenter who did a considerable amount of work as a contractor for the parish of St. Mary at Hill. Littlehales, *Medieval Records of St. Mary at Hill*, 100–215 passim. He was something of an unsavory character; he was summoned before the Commissary court at least three times on account of adultery (GL, 9064/3, fols. 93v, 94v [1481]; 9064/4, fol. 311r [1491]) and in 1496–97 was enmired in a complicated set of proceedings in which he was alleged to have made contracts of marriage with three young women, including Margaret Broke (GL, 9064/8, fol. 26v; GL, 9065, fols. 268v–270r, 277v–279v). He died in 1499, his will indicating that he did

not leave a great deal at his death (his only child, a daughter, was left £10 and some silver). The will was dated September 1496, just before he embarked on the marital adventures that occasioned the suits against him, and it is unclear whether he was married or to whom when he died in 1499. TNA, PRO, PCC Prob. 11/11, fol. 312v.

61. GL, 9065, fols. 279rv. On the gift of a dead wife's clothes to a subsequent spouse, see Chapter 1.

62. Rings given by men to women, e.g., LMA, DL/C/205, fols. 4v, 12r, 33r, 40r, 73r, 115v, 117v; GL, 9065, fols. 7r, 47v, 64r, 201v–202r; GL, 9065B, fol. 11v; rings exchanged, LMA, DL/C/205, fols. 149v–150r, 215v, 241r; GL, 9065, fols 80v, 249v; GL, 9065B, fol. 1r, 3rv; rings given by women to men: LMA, DL/C/205, fols. 61r, 62r, 224r.

63. GL, 9065, fol. 212r. O'Hara notes sixteenth-century examples of coins being broken in half at the time of the contract. *Courtship and Constraint*, 85.

64. LMA, DL/C/205, fol. 166r; see *OED*, s.v. "groat," for its varying value in the fifteenth century.

65. GL, 9065, fol. 81r.

66. GL, 9065, fol. 224v.

67. The examples are too numerous to list: they are found throughout LMA, DL/C/205 and GL, 9065.

68. E.g., LMA, DL/C/205, fols. 11r, 12r, 16r; GL, 9065, fols. 72v–73r, 200r, 269v.

69. "The Peterborough Lapidary" says that "whoso bereþ þis stone vpone him or one his fynger, he schal get loue." Joan Evans and Mary S. Serjeantson, eds., *English Mediaeval Lapidaries*, EETS, Original Series 190 (London: Oxford University Press, 1933), 77. See also "Sloan Lapidary," in ibid., 125; Albertus Magnus, *Book of Minerals*, trans. Dorothy Wyckoff (Oxford: Oxford University Press, 1967), 81. I owe these references to Kit French.

70. From a man to a woman, LMA, DL/C/205, fols. 53v–54v, 112r; GL, 9065, fols. 10r, 110r, 139rv, 194v–195r, 234v, 277v–278r; from a woman to a man, LMA, DL/C/205, 34r–35r, 36v; GL, 9065, fol. 111v.

71. In about ninety courtships where gifts were given, in fifty-six cases witnesses reported gifts given from the man to the woman only; in five cases witnesses reported gifts given from the woman to the man only; and in twenty-nine cases gifts were exchanged. This includes instances where parties denied that the items in question were gifts or that they were given in token of marriage (as opposed to friendship, payment for sex, etc.). LMA, DL/C/205 and GL, 9065, passim.

72. "Dicit quod post duos vel tres dies post dictum contractum inter eos habitum, ista iurata ad rogatum prefati Nicholai tradidit prefate Alicie medium quarterii de Pepyns et viii poma vocata Orens et unum anulum de auro, que dicta Alicia nomine dicti Nicholai ab ista iurata gratanter recepit tanquam a marito suo prout huic iurate apparuit. Et incontinenter post recepcionem rerum predictarum unum cor auratum dicta Alicia isti iurate tradidit ad tradendum prefato Nicholao tanquam marito suo, quo ut talis ab ista iurata gratanter dictus Nicholaus recepit nomine prefate Alicie ut dicit." LMA, DL/C/205, fols. 230v–231r.

73. LMA, DL/C/205, fols. 196rv; see also a similar case in GL, 9065, fols. 229v–230r.

74. She thought it was either Barnard's Inn (a chancery inn) or Lincoln's Inn (an inn of court).

75. GL, 9065, fols. 55r–56v.

76. See *OED*, s.v. "shep."

77. LMA, DL/C/205, fols. 3r–4r.

78. "Dicit quod ista jurata dicto Johanni Kendall nulla dona contulit seu ab eodem Johanne Kendall aliqua donaria recepit, sed dicit quod quodam die circiter festum penticostis ultimum dictus Johannes venit ad istam juratam et mutuauit ab ea iiii d. ea intencione quod eosdem rehaberet se saltem alios iiii d. pro eisdem. Et quodam die dominico proximo et immediate ante festum pentecostes ultimum contingentim, dictus Johannes Kendall deliberauit huic jurate unum par precularum rogando istam juratam quod easdem preculas restitueret cuidam pinctori videlicet *a stener* manenti iuxta turrim London qui pictor adtunc habuit frequentem accessum ad domum sororis sue manentis iuxta domum habitacionis parentum huius jurate. Ulterius dicit quod ista jurata accordauit eidem Johanni Kendall ii^{os} flammiola anglice *brest kerchefis* pro eo quod camisia eiusdem Johannis fuit multum sordida et deturpata, qui Johannes ad restituendum eadem flammiola per istam juratam sepius requisitus et interpellatus eadem restitue<..> distulit et differt in presenti." GL, 9065, fol. 110r.

79. E.g., LMA, DL/C/205, fol. 16r; GL, 9065, fol. 209v.

80. E.g., LMA, DL/C/205, fols. 36v, 108r; GL, 9065, fols. 83v, 111v.

81. E.g., LMA, DL/C/205, fols. 177v, 251r; GL, 9065, fols. 10r, 20r.

82. E.g., LMA, DL/C/205, fols. 150rv, 196rv, 260v; GL, 9065, fols. 147v, 229v–230r.

83. "Dicit et fatetur quod ipse dedit eidem Agnetem unam par Cultellarum, ix denarios ad comparandam bursam, et i par cerothecarum. Non tamen illa dona dedit eidem Agneti ad intencionem habendi eam in uxorem suam, sed ad complacendum et continuandum sibi in peccata. Et ipsa Agnes dedit huic iurato quoddam ligamen siue zonam de nigro colore et unam singulam de nigro cerico ea intencione ut credit habendi istum iuratum in maritum suum." LMA, DL/C/205, fol. 55v.

84. LMA, DL/C/205, fol. 55v.

85. GL, 9065, fol. 167r.

86. LMA, DL/C/205, fol. 65r.

87. GL, 9065, fol. 20v.

88. "Johannes Songer violenter abstraxit contra voluntatem istius iurate unum anulum aureum a digito istius iurate in die dominica proximo precedente Carnispriuii ultimi preteriti et postmodum ista iurata repeciit anulum suum a prefato Johanne qui tradidit huic iurato unum anulum aureum quem ista iurata recepit credens tempore recepcionis eiusdem fuisse proprium, quem postmodum cum deliberacione ista iurata inspexit et intellexit suum non esse." LMA, DL/C/ 205, fol. 215v.

89. GL, 9065, fol. 171v. William Randolf made a similar claim regarding a ring being forcibly taken from his finger by a woman named Elizabeth with whom he had had sex. Ibid., fol. 253r.

90. GL, 9065, fol. 188v. See also GL, 9065, fols. 52v, 53r.

91. TNA, PRO, C 1/66/203 (1475–80 or 1483–85).

92. Some historians have argued that chastity was not particularly important for late medieval women below the elite. P. J. P. Goldberg writes that there is no reason to assume that women were expected to be virgins when they married (although shrinking of economic options for women outside marriage later in the fifteenth century may have increased the importance of chastity). *Women, Work, and Life Cycle*, 153–57, 232, 330. Barbara A. Hanawalt, *Growing Up in Medieval London: The Experience of Childhood in History* (New York: Oxford University Press, 1993), suggests that female servants—a group including the larger part of adolescent women—were "likely to experience unwanted sexual initiation in the arms of their masters or being sold by their mistresses. Only those females of better classes, who were married relatively early, expected to find sexual initiation only on marriage" (121, see also 186–88). The evidence from London in the second half of the fifteenth century suggest that attitudes toward female chastity were somewhat more complex than this.

93. "Dicit quod si iste iuratus esset solutus et liber ad matrimonium contrahendum, adhiberet eidem Johanne minorem fidem et favorem et ipsius matrimonium cicius recusaret pretextu dicte criminis imposicionis." GL, 9065, fol. 267r. There are other examples: in *Joan Ponder c. Margaret Samer*, a woman defaming another of having given birth to an illegitimate child was said to have ruined the chances of that child's making a good marriage. GL, 9065, fols. 70rv. In the Consistory court case *Marion Lauson c. Laurence Gilys*, several witnesses insisted that Marion was more worthy than another woman to have Laurence as her husband, because she was an "honest woman" and the other woman was a whore. Even the scribe seems to have agreed: he wrote as the heading for the case, "For the party of the honest woman, Marion Lauson, against Laurence Gilys [ex parte honeste mulieris, Marione Lauson, contra Laurencium Gilys]," an editorial comment that is unique in the case headings in the fifteenth-century London deposition books. GL, MS 9065, fols. 85r, 86v.

94. "Credit in consciencia sua quod dicta Johanna Sebar que mulier juvenis est et apta marito tamen leditur ex prolacione verborum predictorum quod vix aut nunquam evadet huiusmodi lesionem sue fame." GL, 9065, fol. 267r.

95. *Alice Brigge c. William Markis*, GL, 9065, fol. 184r.

96. E.g., cases where men sought to marry women who had clearly had previous sexual partners (and sometimes children outside wedlock): GL, 9064/1, fol. 8v; 9064/2, fol. 224v; 9064/4, fol. 238Av; 9064/5, fols. 81r, 106v.

97. See, for instance, CLRO, Letter Book L, fol. 83r (*CLBL*, 103), where a girl under the age of fourteen received £40 in compensation for having been raped, to be held in trust for her by the chamberlain of the city until she came of age or married; or Chancery cases complaining that such a compensation payment was not made or afterward illegally seized: TNA, PRO, C 1/29/254 (1459–64); C 1/45/24 (1432–43 or 1467–72); C 1/461/19 (1518–29). On arbitration of legal disputes generally, see Edward Powell, "Arbitration and the Law in the Later Middle Ages," *Transactions of the Royal Historical Society*, 5th ser., 33 (1983): 49–67.

98. Judith M. Bennett, "Ventriloquisms: When Maidens Speak in English Songs, *c.* 1300–1550," in *Medieval Woman's Song: Cross-Cultural Approaches*, ed. Anne L. Klinck and Ann Marie Rasmussen (Philadelphia: University of Pennsylvania Press, 2001), 187–204.

99. See, e.g., William Love, parish clerk of St. Botulph Billingsgate. LMA, DL/C/205, fols. 33r, 34r.

100. Greene, *Early English Carols*, no. 453 (276–77).

101. Charlotte D'Evelyn, ed., *Peter Idley's Instructions to His Son*, The Modern Language Association of America Monograph Series, 6 (Boston: D. C. Heath, 1935), 135.

102. Ibid.

103. Bennett, "Ventriloquisms," 195.

104. GL, 9064/1, fol. 134r; GL, 9065, fols. 48v–49v, 53v–55r.

105. "Nan Hop violatrix fidei et periura eo quod contraxit matrimonium cum Thoma Robardson calcifice, et banna matrimoniales per tres dominicas continuas legitime inter eosdem edita; premisso non obstante iam renuit et recusat huiusmodi matrimonium. Et ut dicitur per suasionem Johannis Norfolke qui eandem in concubinam tenet sic exortata est et pluries apud stufas pernoctauit. Et contumatrix curie qui dicit et dixit 'cursse and blisse, I set not a straw by the cursing ther.'" GL, 9064/5, fol. 106v. John Norfolk was convicted in 1494 by the mayor and aldermen of bawdry and "for conveyng of one Alys Wilson of thage of xiii yeres to his house to one Aleyn Redeman, by whom the same Alys was Ravisshed and devoured." CLRO, Journal 10, fol. 31v. His punishment (although not the full extent of his alleged crime) was recorded in some London chronicles: "MS Vitellius A XVI," in *Chronicles of London*, ed. Charles Lethbridge (Oxford: Oxford University Press, 1905; rept., Gloucester: Alan Sutton, 1977), 200; Robert Fabyan, *The New Chronicles of England and France, in Two Parts* (London: F. C. and J. Rivington, 1811), 685.

106. See above, p. 19.

107. GL, 9065B, fols. 2rv (quotation at 2r).

108. GL, 9065, fols. 201r–202r, 207r–208r.

109. John Crosby, son of Sir John Crosby, was likely born in 1476 as the inquisition post mortem on the former noted that he was a posthumous son (*Cal. Inq. P.M. Hen. VII*, 3:280). Sir John Crosby's own will, which was written in 1472 but not probated until shortly after his death in 1476 (TNA, PRO, PCC Prob. 11/6, fols. 182r–188v; Pamela Nightingale, "Crosby, Sir John [d. 1476]," *ODNB*), does not indicate any children but refers repeatedly to the possibility of a child being in his wife's womb; if written in 1472 this was presumably a previous pregnancy. Confusingly, however, the 1487 Inquisition Post Mortem for Sir John Crosby's widow names her son and heir as John Crosby, age seventeen (*Cal. Inq. P.M. Hen. VII*, 1:143), which does not accord with a birthdate of 1476. The inheritance of the son was at least £1000 (*CPMR*, 6:111; *CLBL*, 156, 173, 179). The senior John Crosby is well known for having built Crosby Hall, a magnificent town house, in Bishopsgate Street; it was deemed palatial enough to serve as Richard of Gloucester's residence as Lord Protector in 1483. Now located in Chelsea, it is the only surviving merchant house from medieval London. Thomas and Thornley,

Great Chronicle of London, 230; John Schofield, *Medieval London Houses* (New Haven, Conn.: Yale University Press, 1994), 39, 41; Barron, *London in the Later Middle Ages*, 250; Nightingale, *Medieval Mercantile Community*, 537; Nightingale, "Crosby, Sir John." On the age of majority for London orphans, see Charles Carlton, *The Court of Orphans* (Leicester: Leicester University Press, 1974), 14, 21; and the will of John Stocton, 1473, TNA, PRO, PCC Prob. 11/6, 74r.

110. "Accessit ad cameram dicte Agnetis et ibidem familiariter communicauerunt inter se." GL, 9065, fol. 201v.

111. GL, 9065, fol. 201v.

112. GL, 9065, fol. 201v.

113. GL, 9065, fols. 201v–202r, 207r–208r.

114. Will of John Crosby, gent., of London, TNA, PRO, PCC Prob. 11/12, fol. 166v.

115. GL, 9065, fols. 230v, 233v–234v.

Chapter 3. By the Father's Will

1. GL, 9065B, fols. 11v–12v, 13r–15r.

2. TNA, PRO, PCC Prob. 11/13, fols. 152r–153v.

3. TNA, PRO, PCC Prob. 11/18, fols. 85v–86v.

4. Named as Richard Heed in Henry Heed's will. TNA, PRO, PCC Prob. 11/13, 152r–153v. He does not appear on the incomplete list of priors of Hertford in William Page, ed., *The Victoria History of the County of Hertford*, 4 vols. (London: Constable, 1902–14), 4:421, nor in *BRUO* or *BRUC*.

5. TNA, PRO, PCC Prob. 11/13, fols. 152r–153v.

6. GL, 9065, fols. 190v–191v (1494).

7. Apart from Diana O'Hara's book, there has been little discussion of the role of intermediaries in the making of premodern marriage. See O'Hara, *Courtship and Constraint*, 99–121; Poos, *Rural Society*, 137; John Bossy, "Blood and Baptism: Kinship, Community and Christianity in Western Europe from the Fourteenth to the Seventeenth Centuries," *Studies in Church History* 10 (1973): 131–32. P. P. A. Biller notes the assumption of the existence of mediators in Italian *pastoralia* but not in English. Biller, "Marriage Patterns and Women's Lives: A Sketch of a Pastoral Geography," in *Woman Is a Worthy Wight*, ed. Goldberg, 66. Alan Macfarlane, in his discussion of courtship, insists that individuals married without any outside help ("courtship was a game that, on the whole, people played for themselves," 295). Alan Macfarlane, *Marriage and Love in England: Modes of Reproduction, 1300–1840* (Oxford: Blackwell, 1986), 292–95.

8. Carol Lansing's observations on the rather different marital regime of thirteenth-century Bologna—where only women with a relatively considerable dowry could, in practice, contract a formal marriage—are nonetheless relevant for fifteenth-century England: understandings of sexual and other social relationships were quite different when they were divorced from the transmission of property and power. Carol Lansing, "Concubines, Lovers, Prostitutes: Infamy and Female

Identity in Medieval Bologna," in *Beyond Florence: The Contours of Medieval and Early Modern Italy*, ed. Paula Findlen, Michelle M. Fontaine, and Duane J. Osheim (Stanford, Calif.: Stanford University Press, 2003), 87–88, 91–94.

9. "How the Good Wijf tau3te hir Dou3tir," in Frederick James Furnivall, ed., *The Babees Book*, EETS, Original Series 32 (London: Trübner, 1868), 37. See Felicity Riddy, "Mother Knows Best: Reading Social Change in a Courtesy Text," *Speculum: A Journal of Medieval Studies* 71 (1996): 66–86.

10. William Langland, *Piers the Plowman*, ed. Walter W. Skeat (Oxford: Oxford University Press, 1886), B Text, Passus ix, ll. 116–19.

11. Diana O'Hara has termed those "friends" who were not blood relatives "fictive kin": " 'Ruled by my friends': Aspects of Marriage in the Diocese of Canterbury, c. 1540–1570," *Continuity and Change* 6 (1991): 10–11.

12. E.g., TNA, PRO, PCC Prob. 11/5, fol. 138v.

13. TNA, PRO, PCC Prob. 11/7, fol. 140r. About 10 percent of fifteenth-century London testators whose wills were proved at the Prerogative Court of Canterbury made bequests of marriage portions for poor women: J. A. F. Thomson, "Piety and Charity in Late Medieval London," *Journal of Ecclesiastical History* 16 (1965): 185–86.

14. "Dicit quod fuit mediator inter eosdem et laborauit ad inducendum eos ut contraherent matrimonium adinuicem, rogatus ad huc per utramque partem." LMA, DL/C/205, fol. 33v, cf. fols. 63v, 66v, 108v–110v, 123r–124r. Love may have died soon after his deposition: he was named among the deaths recorded on the bede roll of the parish clerks' fraternity in 1470. James and James, *Bede Roll*, 90.

15. He had known them for only four and two years respectively. LMA, DL/C/205, fol. 33r.

16. LMA, DL/C/205, fols. 34rv, cf. fol. 36v.

17. GL, 9065B, fol. 8r.

18. John may have refused to accept the token: Beatrice (who was a hostile witness to Alice's case) said that John, when learning the ring was from Alice, said "Haue it agayn" (the manuscript is somewhat damaged at this point, and he may have said more). There were also some cases where the tokens were traded back and forth between the couple (e.g., GL, 9065, fols. 108v–109r), so it is also possible John may have been offering it back as a token rather than refusing it. GL, 9065B, fol. 8r.

19. Robert Billingham may have been the man by the same name who was a tailor. Davies, *Merchant Taylors' Company*, 65, 94.

20. GL, 9065B, fols. 10v–11r.

21. GL, 9065B, fol. 10v, also 10r.

22. GL, 9065B, fol. 11r.

23. The MS has Thomas Wellis.

24. GL, 9065B, fols. 7rv.

25. GL, 9065B, fols. 7v–9r, 15v.

26. GL, 9065B, fols. 10r, 11r. The William Mariner cited in this case may be the same man as William Maryner, salter, and his wife (possibly the Agnes whom he mentions in his will). This William Maryner was a man active in the civic life of west London (ward of Faringdon Within): he appears in Letter Book L as, among

other things, one of the citizens of London elected by the common council to attend upon the chief butler of England in a banquet for the newly crowned King Richard III, July 1483 (*CLBL*, 208; see also 59, 148, 176, 279). This man left a will (TNA, PRO, PCC Prob. 11/17, fols. 56r–57v), dated 1512, showing that he held properties in London and Tottenham, Haringay, Staines, and Ashford.

27. GL, 9065B, fols. 3v–4r, 5v–6v; for Brond, see *CLBL*, 172.

28. "Credit in consciencia sua quod si amici dicte Johanne Blacman essent presentes ibidem, ipsa sic contraxisset cum eodem Johanne Yonge." LMA, DL/C/205, fols. 3r–4r, 4v–6r (quotation at 6r).

29. *CLBL*, 65–66. The will of her father, William Blakeman, citizen and tailor, is registered in GL, 9171/5, fol. 385r (1466), where he names her along with her brother as his heirs, both underage.

30. LMA, DL/C/205, fol. 29v.

31. LMA, DL/C/205, fols. 32r–33r.

32. It is unclear whether Joan Blacman or John Yonge won the case, but when John Yonge died in 1481, his wife was named Cicely. GL, 9171/6, fol. 312v.

33. TNA, PRO, C 1/22/122. On Olney, see Thrupp, *Merchant Class*, 358; *CPMR*, vol. 5 passim; *CLBK*, passim.

34. GL, 9065, fols. 10r–12r.

35. LMA, DL/C/205, fols. 19r–19v, 29r. Chapman claimed the contract was conditional.

36. LMA, DL/C/205, fol. 23r.

37. TNA, PRO, C 1/154/60 (datable to between 1504 and 1515). The plaintiff, Antony Pontisbury, appears as Marlond's apprentice in 1508 in Laetitia Lyell and Frank D. Watney, eds., *Acts of the Court of the Mercers' Company 1453–1527* (Cambridge: Cambridge University Press, 1936), 314. Cf. TNA, PRO, C 1/75/83, C 1/22/122.

38. William Gerardson may not himself have been "of virtuous condition"; he was cited as an adulterer before the Commissary court in 1471. GL, 9064/1, fol. 89v.

39. TNA, PRO, C 1/67/199.

40. Sir William, however, refused to reimburse Lady Joan, for which she sued him in Chancery. TNA, PRO, C 1/48/416 (1473–75). Joan Kirby, ed., *The Plumpton Letters and Papers*, Camden, 5th ser., 8 (Cambridge: Cambridge University Press for the Royal Historical Society, 1996), 32, 36–37, 320–21.

41. Stourbridge Fair was one of the major fairs of fifteenth-century England, held from 14 September each year. Cornelius Walford, *Fairs, Past and Present: A Chapter in the History of Commerce* (London: Elliot Stock, 1883; reprint New York: Augustus M. Kelley Publishers, 1968), 54–67. Margaret Hawkyn said that Spenser made this promise about the feast of the Nativity of the Virgin (8 September).

42. LMA, DL/C/205, fols. 123r–124r.

43. LMA, DL/C/205, fols. 60v–68r.

44. Sheehan, *Marriage, Family, and Law*, esp. 38–176. For other literature on canon law and the consensual theory, see Brundage, *Law, Sex, and Christian Society*, 187, 235–238, 262–269, 334–35, 414, 588, 615.

45. As Beatrice Gottlieb points out, even in "love marriages" parental consent was often a necessary condition of marriage: "When parents disapproved, the usual result was that the match was broken off." Gottlieb, "Meaning of Clandestine Marriage,"69.

46. LMA, DL/C/205, fol. 48r. "Willelmus Heley tractauit et communicauit pluries cum ista iurata de matrimonio inter eos habendo, et ista iurata eidem respondebat quod si posset adquirere et habere voluntatem et consensum proaui sui, videlicet David Kenryk, libenter voluit consentire ipsum habere." Joan Kenryk lost her case, and she subsequently appealed it to the papal court: *Calendar of Papal Registers*, 12:802.

47. TNA, PRO, PCC Prob. 11/4, fols. 11r–12v (1454).

48. Miranda Chaytor, "Household and Kinship: Ryton in the Late 16th and Early 17th Centuries," *History Workshop Journal* 10 (1980): 42–44. See also O'Hara, "Ruled by my friends," 13–17; Peter Rushton, "Property, Power and Family Networks: The Problem of Disputed Marriage in Early Modern England," *Journal of Family History* 11 (1986): 205–19, esp. 207, 216.

49. Cf. Davis, "Boundaries and the Sense of Self," 55, 61–63; and Gowing, *Domestic Dangers*, 144–46, 151–54.

50. GL, 9065, fols. 3v–5r, quotations at fol. 4r.

51. LMA, DL/C/205, fols. 131v–132r.

52. LMA, DL/C/205, fols. 132rv, quotation at fol. 132v. "Ad hunc finem quod dicta Beatrix melius diligeret dictum Johannem, pro eo quod ipse accepit antedictam Elizabeth in eius uxorem. Et dicta Beatrix statim dedit ad requisacionem dicti Johannis voluntatem suam."

53. LMA, DL/C/205, fol. 277r. "Et ego volo habere vos in maritum meum si auunculus meus Thomas Roby et Anna eius uxor auuncula mea velu<erunt> ad hoc consentire, sin autem nunquam volo habere vos in maritum meum neque aliquem alium." This conversation had taken place in Coventry. For other examples, see the following notes and LMA, DL/C/205, fols. 11v–12r, 250v; GL, 9065, fols. 24v, 126r, 149v.

54. LMA, DL/C/205, fols. 4rv. The occasion of the suit in this case is unclear. Possibly Robert Forster sued Katherine Pekke in order to establish that a marriage had *not* taken place, as Katherine herself claimed that she had contracted with Robert and wished to have him as her husband. Or both parties desired the marriage, but some obstacle forced them to undertake the suit to prove the marriage definitively.

55. LMA, DL/C/205, fol. 7r. "Dixit dicta Katerina isti iurato et uxori sue quod voluit regi in hac re secundum eos in omnibus."

56. LMA, DL/C/205, fols. 4rv, 6v–7v, 10rv.

57. LMA, DL/C/205, fol. 36v.

58. LMA, DL/C/205, fol. 55v. "Non tamen illa dona dedit eidem Agneti ad intencionem habendi eam in uxorem suam, sed ad complacendum et continuandum sibi in peccata."

59. GL, 9065, fols. 24v, 26r. "Dixit quod voluit gubernari secundum parentes et amicos suos et aliter non."

60. GL, 9065, fols. 22r–24r.

61. GL, 9065, fols. 18r–20r, quotation at fol. 20r.

62. GL, 9065, fol. 52r.

63. LMA, DL/C/205, fols. 10v–12r.

64. GL, 9065, fols. 181v–182r, 188rv, quotation at fol. 182r. It is possible that Elizabeth was the unnamed posthumous child of Thomas Crofte, tailor, who along with his or her siblings became orphans of the city in 1470 following the death of their father. At that time, however, none of the guardians named was Banks. *CLBL*, 88. Thomas Crofte's will survives (TNA, PRO, PCC Prob. 11/5, fol. 155r, 1467), where one of the children is indicated as in the womb. Each of the children was to have 20 marks when he or she came to age twenty-two or married.

65. LMA, DL/C/205, fols. 166r–170r, 172v–177r, 182v.

66. GL, 9065, fol. 149r.

67. GL, 9065, fol. 199v. "Eo quod fuit cognata huic iurato."

68. LMA, DL/C/205, fol. 114v. "Iste iuratus obviabat dicte Agneti, ad tunc existenti in venella vocata Botulphe lane iuxta Bylyngesgate, quam alloquebatur iste iuratus sub ista forma: 'Agnes, dicitur michi quod vos estis uxor Johannis Holder et eidem affidata,' que incontinenti respondebat huic iurato et dixit, 'Ego miror multum quod vos cognoscitis istam materiam inter ipsum et me. Rogo vos ne referatis parentibus meis, quia si feceritis, culpabar ab eisdem; sed vobis dico plane quod ipse est maritus meus et eidem sum affidata.' "

69. GL, 9065, fol. 271v.

70. LMA, DL/C/205, fol. 53v.

71. GL, 9065, fols. 114v–115r.

72. LMA, DL/C/205, fols. 37r–41r; TNA, PRO, PCC Prob. 11/4, fols. 167r–169v, Will of John Roberd of Cranbrook, 1460.

73. LMA, DL/C/205, fol. 246r.

74. GL, 9065, fols. 10r–12r.

75. GL, 9065, fol. 64r.

76. "Dixit quod non erat dispositus ad maritandum nisi prius haberet consensus et voluntatem parentum suorum, et addidit quam plura alia fuisse ad domum necessaria quam iiii^{or} nudas tibias." GL, 9065B, fol. 15v.

77. Cf. Laura Gowing's observation that in later sixteenth-century London it was mothers who played the predominant role in their daughters' marriages. *Domestic Dangers*, 154–55.

78. LMA, DL/C/205, fols. 136v–137v. Margery's mother, Alice Forde, also objected but said that she did so at Margery's request, not on her own authority.

79. LMA, DL/C/205, fols. 209r–212r, 216r–218v, 224v–225r.

80. GL, 9065, fols. 81r–82r.

81. GL, 9065, fol. 39v. See also fols. 221v–222r and 223v–225r.

82. Davis, *Paston Letters*, 1:613.

83. Ibid., 1:614, 640.

84. For instance, the Pastons, a Norfolk gentry family, undertook much of their marital scouting and negotiations in London: e.g., Davis, *Paston Letters*, 1:599, 603, 613, 650–51.

85. Davis, *Paston Letters*; Kirby, *Plumpton Letters*; Christine Carpenter, ed., *Kingsford's Stonor Letters and Papers, 1290–1483* (Cambridge: Cambridge University

Press, 1996); Alison Hanham, ed., *The Cely Letters, 1472–1488*, EETS, Original Series 273 (London: Oxford University Press, 1974). Colin Richmond, "For Love or Money" in *The Paston Family in the Fifteenth Century: Endings* (Manchester: Manchester University Press, 2000) is the best account of the complexities of elite marriage in late medieval England. For other scholarship on the Plumptons, Pastons, and Stonors, see J. Taylor, "The Plumpton Letters, 1416–1552," *Northern History* 10 (1975): 72–87; Keith R. Dockray, "Why Did the Fifteenth-Century English Gentry Marry? The Pastons, Plumptons, and Stonors Reconsidered," in *Gentry and Lesser Nobility in Late Medieval England*, ed. Michael Jones (Gloucester: Alan Sutton, 1986), 61–80; Ann S. Haskell, "The Paston Women on Marriage in Fifteenth-Century England," *Viator* 4 (1973): 459–71; Colin Richmond, "The Pastons Revisited: Marriage and the Family in Fifteenth-Century England," *Bulletin of the Institute for Historical Research* 58 (1985): 25–36. On the Celys, see Alison Hanham's study, *The Celys and Their World: An English Merchant Family of the Fifteenth Century* (Cambridge: Cambridge University Press, 1985), esp. 309–16 on their marriages.

86. Davis, *Paston Letters*, 1:286–87.

87. Kirby, *Plumpton Letters*, 119.

88. Eric Acheson, *A Gentry Community: Leicestershire in the Fifteenth Century, c. 1422–c. 1485* (Cambridge: Cambridge University Press, 1992), 156–58. See also Anthony Molho, *Marriage Alliance in Late Medieval Florence* (Cambridge, Mass.: Harvard University Press, 1994), 15 and passim for endogamic marital practices of the Florentine elite in the same period.

89. Davis, *Paston Letters*, 2:32.

90. Ibid., 1:254. See also regarding other possible husbands for Elizabeth letters exchanged between Edmond Lord Grey, John Paston, and William Paston in 1454. Ibid., 2:96, 1:82, 1:155.

91. Hanham, *Cely Letters*, xii, 133.

92. Ibid., 150–53.

93. Ibid., 155.

94. Ibid., 281. See also *CLBL*, 247: on 18 January 1488, Bryan entered into a bond with three other merchants for £100, to be paid to the two youngest daughters of the now-deceased Rawson when they came of age to be married, indicating he was one of their guardians.

95. Hanham, *Cely Letters*, 123–24, 133, 143, 146–47.

96. They married sometime before February 1483. Ibid., xv.

97. Carpenter, *Kingsford's Stonor Letters*, 275.

98. Davis, *Paston Letters*, 2:105.

99. Norman Davis thinks Margery Paston was born sometime (shortly) before 1450; the only other sister of whom mention is specifically made in the letters, Agnes, was likely born around 1454 or 1455. Ibid., 1:lxii.

100. Margery, who may have been the subject of Fastolf's letter (ibid., 2:105), was certainly the subject of further soundings regarding possible marriages both before and after she reached adolescence (ibid., 1:157, 287; 2:393). Her eventual marriage is a fine illustration that daughters, sons, and wards were less pliable than their fathers and guardians had assumed or hoped: Margery, much to her

family's consternation, secretly made a love marriage with the family's head bailiff (a servant who acted as business manager for the family's estate), ending her utility to the family as the means by which political relationships could be forged. This was egregious indeed; after the family's attempts to have the marriage annulled failed, Margery was cut off from the family, at least temporarily, although her husband continued in his role as bailiff. Ibid., 1:341–44, 351, 408–10, 541–42.

101. Kirby, *Plumpton Letters*, 118.

102. Ibid., 118–21. Regarding Edward Plumpton, see also Joan W. Kirby, "A Fifteenth-Century Family, the Plumptons of Plumpton, and their Lawyers, 1461–1515," *Northern History* 25 (1989): 116. Edward's courtship of Agnes may have been successful—according to a Chancery petition of 1500–1502, he married a woman named Agnes (TNA, PRO, C 1/239/56)—but if the courtship was successful, the marriage was not (the Agnes who married him "without cause resonable unlefully departed"). Edward was apparently murdered. *Calendar of Patent Rolls Preserved in the Public Record Office: Henry VII* (London: Public Record Office, 1916), 2:233. The entry, dated 4 February 1501, reads: "Pardon to Robert Tykhull of the parish of St. Andrew Holborn, without the bars of the Old Temple, *alias* of Benyngton, co. Surrey, 'gentliman,' for the death of Edward Plompton, whereof he was appealed by Agnes, late the wife of the said Edward, as it appears by the record of the said appeal before the king that he killed him in self-defence; he having surrendered to the Marshalsea prison, as John Fyneux, knight, chief justice of pleas before the king, has certified in chancery."

103. For a selection of literature on this topic, see J. R. Lander, "Marriage and Politics in the Fifteenth Century: The Nevilles and the Wydevilles," *Bulletin of the Institute of Historical Research* 36 (1963): 119–52; Haskell, "Paston Women"; Joel T. Rosenthal, "Aristocratic Marriage and the English Peerage, 1350–1500: Social, Institutional, and Personal Bond," *Journal of Medieval History* 10 (1984): 181–94; Richmond, "Pastons Revisited"; Dockray, "Why Did the Fifteenth-Century English Gentry Marry?"; Jennifer C. Ward, *English Noblewomen in the Later Middle Ages* (London: Longman, 1992), 12–33; Acheson, *Gentry Community*, 135–73: Harris, *Aristocratic Women*, esp. 43–60.

104. For instance, Lady Elizabeth Brews, writing to her prospective son-in-law John (III) Paston, insisted that her daughter Margery would not let her rest until she (Lady Elizabeth) finalized the marriage negotiations with Sir John; she urged him to come to finish the matter on St. Valentine's Day, when "every bird chooseth him a mate." Davis, *Paston Letters*, 2:436, cf. 1:662–63.

105. Ibid., 1:500.

106. Kirby, *Plumpton Letters*, 118, 119.

107. Ibid., 120.

108. Davis, *Paston Letters*, 1:287.

109. Harris, *Aristocratic Women*, 165–66.

110. Carpenter, *Kingsford's Stonor Letters*, 211–16.

111. Ibid., 49–50.

112. On Boleyn, whose great-granddaughter Anne would become queen, see Thrupp, *Merchant Class*, 325.

113. Davis, *Paston Letters*, 1:397.

114. Lyell and Watney, *Acts of the Court of the Mercers' Company*, 299.

115. See Rosemary Horrox, "Service," in *Fifteenth-Century Attitudes: Perceptions of Society in Late Medieval England*, ed. Rosemary Horrox (Cambridge: Cambridge University Press, 1994), 61–78.

116. TNA, PRO, C 1/26/286. Bruyn alleged in the petition that Whetenale refused to pay the agreed-upon fee, and after Whetenale died his executors likewise refused. For Whetenale, see *CLBK*, 183–333; Kingdon, *Facsimile . . . Grocers*, 2:256–60, 289; TNA, PRO, PCC Prob. 11/4, fols. 119rv.

117. TNA, PRO, C 1/66/387.

118. TNA, PRO, C 1/20/137.

119. TNA, PRO, C 1/43/65, dated either 1432–43 or 1467–72.

120. TNA, PRO, C 1/64/271. For William Philip, see *CPMR*, 6:82; *CLBL*, 123, 133, 144, 151, 157, 166; T. F. Reddaway and Lorna E. M. Walker, *The Early History of the Goldsmiths' Company, 1327–1509* (London: Arnold, 1975), 335–337.

121. TNA, PRO, C 1/20/13.

122. By London custom, at least one-third of a deceased person's property went to the children, divided equally among them, male or female. Sharpe, "Introduction," *Cal. Husting*, 1:xxxiii.

123. The City required that guardians post a bond to the City's chamberlain for the children's share of the deceased citizen's estate, and the City's letter books have many references to both the posting of bonds and the delivery of inheritances to the orphans or their husbands when they came of age or married. On orphans, see Carlton, *Court of Orphans*, 13–22; Elaine Clark, "City Orphans and Custody Laws in Medieval England," *American Journal of Legal History* 34 (1990): 168–87; Hanawalt, *Growing Up*, 88–107; Barron, *London in the Later Middle Ages*, 268–73.

124. "Isto die licenciatum est Thome Kelet grocer desponsare Petronillam filiam Roberti Stokker pannarii, orphanam civitatis, etc." CLRO, Journal 7, fol. 20r; such licenses are common throughout the journals.

125. CLRO, Journal 4, fols. 224r, 227v. (In using Journals 1 through 6, I was greatly aided by Caroline Barron's card index to those volumes, situated at the CLRO.) When Goldwell died in 1466, he left a will (with a widow named Elizabeth), which indicated that he was a fairly wealthy man with property in Kent and Surrey as well as in London. TNA, PRO, PCC Prob. 11/5, fols. 114rv.

126. CLRO, Repertory of the Court of Aldermen, vol. 1, fol. 66r.

127. CLRO, Journal 8, fol. 227r; *CLBL*, 87, 88, 145–46, 172.

128. Thomas and Thornley, *Great Chronicle of London*, 227; "MS Vitellius A XVI," in *Chronicles of London*, ed. Lethbridge, 188; Fabyan, *The New Chronicles*, 666. The texts of these chronicles are closely related to one another. Mary-Rose McLaren, *The London Chronicles of the Fifteenth Century: A Revolution in English Writing, with an Annotated Edition of Bradford, West Yorkshire Archives Ms 32d86/42* (Cambridge: D. S. Brewer, 2002), 100–103, 265–66.

129. CLRO, Journal 9, fol. 27r.

130. CLRO, Journal 10, fol. 54r; *CLBL*, 282.

131. CLRO, Journal 5, fol. 181v. William Coumbes or Combes, stockfishmonger, was a longtime alderman who also served as M.P. and sheriff of London. *CLBK*, 219–341 passim; Wedgwood, *History of Parliament*, 2:210–11. His will

(TNA, PRO, PCC Prob. 11/1, fols. 132v–134r, dated 25 May 1452 and probated soon after) stated that George was to come into his considerable inheritance when he was twenty-four years old; the city journal records that he came of age on 16 May 1455 (CLRO, Journal 5, fol. 243r), suggesting that he was twenty-three when he was examined regarding his marriage. Hugh Dene, on the other hand, left few traces in the civic records, although he was evidently not a pauper as he sold a ship in 1439. *CPMR*, 5:22; see also *CLBK*, 196.

132. Technically any contract made by a ten-year-old girl was conditional, as it could be repudiated when she turned twelve. Helmholz, *Marriage Litigation*, 98–99.

133. CLRO, Journal 7, fol. 162r.

134. Two entries in Letter Book L in 1464 note that Alice was one of five children of William Luke, brewer, who became orphans of the city after his death; Alice's share was about £27. Edward Luke was among the children's guardians. *CLBL*, 49–50.

135. CLRO, Journal 7, fols. 9v, 13r; *CLBL*, 8. Hayman Voet (Heyman Voecht) was active as a physician already by 1452 (ten years before the marriage to Agnes Heydon), suggesting that he was at least in his later thirties when they married. Stuart Jenks, "Medizinische Fachkräfte in England zur Zeit Heinrichs VI (1428/29–1460/61)," *Sudhoffs Archiv* 69 (1985): 217–18.

136. Carpenter, *Kingsford's Stonor Letters*, 275.

Chapter 4. Gender, Power, and Logistics

1. *BRUC*, 667.

2. In 169 marriage suits in LMA, DL/C/205 and GL, 9065 and 9065B where the plaintiff was clear, about 56 percent had male plaintiffs, 44 percent female plaintiffs (the proportions were similar in each of the books; all figures regarding numbers of cases or deponents are approximate because it is sometimes difficult to identify to which case a particular deposition belongs or the basis of a suit; countersuits are here counted together with the original suit rather than separately). More interestingly, perhaps, there was a tendency for those cases that were sued to enforce a marriage to be sued by a man, and for those that were sued to dissolve a marriage, especially divorce *a mensa et thoro*, to be sued by women. For instance, in cases where the plaintiff sued to enforce a contract, roughly two-thirds were sued by men, one-third by women. The difference is particularly marked in three-cornered suits (where two plaintiffs sue the same person, each plaintiff claiming the defendant as spouse, here counted as a single suit): there were twenty-five cases where two men claimed a contract with the same woman, but only nine cases where two women claimed a contract with the same man. At the same time, while nine separation cases (divorce *a mensa et thoro*) were sued by women—seven for cruelty, one for adultery, and one on unclear grounds—only one case of divorce *a mensa et thoro* was sued by a man, the grounds of which were apparently either adultery or cruelty or both.

3. Ingram, *Church Courts, Sex and Marriage in England*, 194; Carlson, *Marriage and the English Reformation*, 112–13; Gowing, *Domestic Dangers*, 142. Gowing notes that the London Consistory court saw women suing marriage cases more frequently in the seventeenth century; she links this with the general "feminization" of the church courts in the seventeenth century, particularly in defamation cases, which had become by that point the most frequent basis of Consistory court cases.

4. Donahue, "Female Plaintiffs." See also Frederik Pedersen, "Did the Medieval Laity Know the Canon Law Rules on Marriage? Some Evidence from Fourteenth-Century York Cause Papers," *Mediaeval Studies* 56 (1994): 111–52.

5. See TNA, PRO, C 1/46/64, or C 1/117/6 (an eleven-year-old female plaintiff).

6. See Powell, "Arbitration and the Law"; Musson, *Medieval Law in Context*, 16–17.

7. See, e.g., LMA, DL/C/205, fols. 56r, 296v–297r; GL, 9065, fols. 124v–125r, 161r, 166v, 175v–176r, 190v–191r, 232rv.

8. GL, 9065, fols. 24v–25r, 37v.

9. GL, 9065, fols. 25v–26r.

10. LMA, DL/C/205, fols. 241v–242v, 246v–247r.

11. Cooke, *Act Book of the Ecclesiastical Court of Whalley*, 93.

12. LMA, DL/C/205, fols. 191r–193r (see some of the depositions from this case translated in McSheffrey, *Love and Marriage*, 84–85).

13. A good example, albeit not from London, is a three-cornered case from St. Albans, *John Lorymer* c. *Christian Bate* and *William Twygge* c. *Christian Bate*, sued in 1474. LMA, DL/C/205, fols. 209r–212r, 216r–218v, 224v–225r, 248r–249v. As all the witnesses to the case, and presumably the parties themselves, were from St. Albans, which (as they themselves say) was in the diocese of Lincoln, it is unclear why this case was heard in the London Consistory. See also Chancery petitions in TNA, PRO, C 1/6/318–21; C 1/60/177; C 1/46/204.

14. *Calendar of Papal Registers*, 12:468.

15. GL, 9065, fols. 201r–202r, 207r–208r. On Dawbeney, see *BRUC*, 173; *Calendar of Papal Registers*, 12:593 and 13:688, 692; LMA, DL/C/205, fols. 258r, 321v; CLRO, Journal 5, 246v–247r; *CPMR*, 6:179; TNA, PRO, C 1/66/252.

16. LMA, DL/C/205, fols. 166r–168r, 172v–175r; McSheffrey, *Love and Marriage*, 59–65.

17. LMA, DL/C/205, fol. 182v.

18. TNA, PRO, C 1/61/486. The involvement of the archdeacon of Westminster—known for being willing to grant licenses to marry in questionable circumstances (see Chapter 1)—suggests even more strongly that there was something fishy about the marriage in the first place.

19. TNA, PRO, C 1/61/486; *Calendar of Papal Registers*, 13:734.

20. The entry in the papal register suggests that it was Croke who sued Baxster for divorce; *Calendar of Papal Registers*, 13:734.

21. See his will, probated 1485: TNA, PRO, PCC Prob. 11/7, fol. 159v.

22. *Calendar of Papal Registers*, 13:734; TNA, PRO, C 1/61/486.

23. On Gregory, see Thrupp, *Merchant Class*, 347. The attribution to William Gregory of the authorship of one of fifteenth-century London's most famous chronicles (published as James Gairdner, ed., *The Historical Collections of a Citizen of London*, Camden Society, New Series 17 [London: Camden Society, 1876]) is no longer accepted. McLaren, *London Chronicles*, 29–33.

24. Wills of John Croke Sr., TNA, PRO, PCC Prob. 11/6, fols. 252rv and 11/7, fols. 26r–28r; and of Margaret Croke, TNA, PRO, PCC 11/9, fols. 44rv; Carpenter, *Kingsford's Stonor Letters*, 54–56, 281–82; Kay Lacey, "Margaret Croke (d. 1491)," in *Medieval London Widows 1300–1500*, ed. Caroline M. Barron and Anne F. Sutton (London: Hambledon, 1994), 143–64.

25. TNA, PRO, PCC Prob. 11/7, fol. 159v. John Croke was the author of one of the Stonor letters: about 1477, he wrote to his brother-in-law William Stonor, in which he reports, among other things, that he has been considering marriage to the daughter of local gentleman Geoffrey Poole. Carpenter, *Kingsford's Stonor Letters*, 281–82.

26. GL, 9065, fols. 13r, 251v.

27. It is not clear how the case was resolved, although the abbreviated examination of Agnes Hill herself (GL, MS 9065, fol. 251v) suggests that the case was settled before it proceeded any further in 1487. It may have been that the couple's marriage came about in another way, however: there was almost a four-year time lag between the launch of the suit in late January 1487 and the point at which they married. In 1488 Agnes was apparently underage and still unmarried (*CLBL*, 237–38, 249), while in October 1490 the marriage between Agnes and John had still not been celebrated, although this was apparently imminent, and John Croke was disputing with Agnes's mother and Thomas Hill, Agnes's brother, about the dowry. CLRO, Journal 9, fols. 262r, 263r; my thanks to Evan May for spotting this. The marriage must have been solemnized soon thereafter, as in November 1490 Croke was described as Agnes's husband, and he acknowledged receipt of his wife's inheritance. CLRO, Journal 9, fols. 265v, 266r–266v; *CLBL*, 249 n. 1. The evidence for the hostility of Agnes Hill's family is inferred both from the dispute over the marriage settlement (Thomas Hill, for instance, was warned severely about breaking the king's peace against Croke; CLRO, Journal 9, fol. 262r), and from the examination in the Consistory court of John Dawes, likely one of Agnes's cousins (see the will of her father, Sir Thomas Hill, TNA, PRO, PCC Prob. 11/7, fol. 131v, where he names Alice Dawes as his sister): Dawes repeatedly called John Croke a knave when the citation was delivered to Agnes Hill asking her to appear in the Consistory to answer Croke's case. GL, 9065, fol. 13r. Lacey, "Margaret Croke," states that at the time that Agnes Hill married John Croke the younger she was the widow of William Chester, who had died in 1476 (151–52 and 151 n. 23); as Agnes was still underage twelve years later in 1488 (*CLBL*, 249) this must be an error. I have found no evidence that she had been married before.

28. TNA, PRO, C 1/125/14, *c.* 1486–93 or 1504–15 (he referred to the cost of obtaining a dispensation for marrying within forbidden degrees of consanguinity); see also C 1/106/29, C 1/199/64.

29. Helmholz, *Marriage Litigation*, 161.

30. LMA, DL/C/205, fol. 128r. "Ego volo expendere xx^ta nobilia pocius quam dictus Johannes Holder habebit dictam Agnetem in uxorem contra ius."

31. LMA, DL/C/205, fol. 129v.

32. LMA, DL/C/205, fols. 29v, 32v–33r.

33. LMA, DL/C/205, fols. 242r, 246v–247r.

34. *The Book of Margery Kempe*, trans. B. A. Windeatt (Harmondsworth: Penguin Books, 1985), ch. 25, pp. 94–95; in the original, *The Book of Margery Kempe*, ed. Lynn Staley, TEAMS Middle English Texts Series (Kalamazoo, Mich.: Medieval Institute Publications, 1996), ch. 25, pp. 67–68.

35. E.g., *John Brake c. Margery Prowde*, LMA, DL/C/205, fols. 266v–268r, 271r–272r, 274r; *Richard Tymond c. Margery Shepherd*, GL, 9065, fols. 18r–20r; *John Brocher c. Joan Cardif alias Peryn*, GL, 9065, fols. 22r–24r. In *John Bedeman c. Agnes Nicholas*, the parents of Agnes Nicholas appear to be testifying on plaintiff John Bedeman's behalf, although the grounds of the suit are not clear. LMA, DL/C/205, fols. 56v–58r.

Chapter 5. Place, Space, and Respectability

1. Considerations of the social construction of space go back at least as far as Emile Durkheim, *The Elementary Forms of the Religious Life*, trans. Joseph Ward Swain (London: G. Allen and Unwin, 1915; repr. New York: Free Press, 1968), 11–12. I have found particularly useful Henri LeFebvre, *The Production of Space* (Oxford: Blackwell, 1991), esp. 26–67; Bill Hiller and Julienne Hanson, *The Social Logic of Space* (Cambridge: Cambridge University Press, 1984), esp. 1–51, 184; Doreen Massey, *Space, Place, and Gender* (Minneapolis: University of Minnesota Press, 1994), esp. 1–11; Daphne Spain, *Gendered Spaces* (Chapel Hill: University of North Carolina Press, 1992), esp. 3–29.

2. For recent literature on medieval conceptions of space, see Barbara Hanawalt and Michal Kobialka, eds., *Medieval Practices of Space* (Minneapolis: University of Minnesota Press, 2000), and references there; see especially in that volume Charles Burroughs's essay, "Spaces of Arbitration and the Organization of Space in Late Medieval Italian Cities," 64–100. For England, see the many influential works of John Schofield, especially "Social Perceptions of Space in Medieval and Tudor London Houses," in *Meaningful Architecture: Social Interpretations of Buildings*, ed. Martin Locock (Aldershot: Avebury, 1994), 188–206; *Medieval London Houses*; "Urban Housing in England, 1400–1600," in *The Age of Transition: The Archaeology of English Culture, 1400–1600*, ed. David Gaimster and Paul Stamper (Oxford: Oxbow Books, 1997). Also important for issues of spatiality in medieval England are Jane Grenville, *Medieval Housing* (London: University of Leicester Press, 1997); Paul Strohm, *Theory and the Premodern Text* (Minneapolis: University of Minnesota Press, 2000), 3–19; Sarah Rees Jones, "Women's Influence in the Design of Urban Homes," in *Gendering the Master Narrative: Medieval Women and Power in the Middle Ages*, ed. Mary C. Erler and Maryanne Kowaleski (Ithaca, N.Y.: Cornell University Press, 2003), 190–211;

Felicity Riddy, "Looking Closely: Authority and Intimacy in the Late Medieval Urban Home," in *Gendering the Master Narrative*, ed. Erler and Kowaleski, 212–28; Anna Dronzek, "No Separate Spheres: The Household as Masculine and Feminine Space in Late Medieval England," Paper presented at the North American Conference on British Studies Annual Meeting, Baltimore, Maryland, 2002. On early modern London, see the subtle discussion of gender and space in Laura Gowing's "'The Freedom of the Streets': Women and Social Space, 1560–1640," in *Londinopolis: Essays in the Cultural and Social History of Early Modern London*, ed. Paul Griffiths and Mark S. R. Jenner, Politics, Culture and Society in Early Modern Britain (Manchester: Manchester University Press, 2000), 130–51.

3. As posited, for instance, by Martine Segalen, *Love and Power in the Peasant Family: Rural France in the Nineteenth Century* (Chicago: Chicago University Press, 1983), esp. 78–111. For similar interpretations in relation to medieval England, see Barbara Hanawalt, *The Ties That Bound: Peasant Families in Medieval England* (New York: Oxford University Press, 1986), 141–55, esp. 145; cf. P. J. P. Goldberg, "The Public and the Private: Women in the Pre-Plague Economy," in *Thirteenth-Century England III*, ed. Peter R. Coss and S. D. Lloyd (Woodbridge: Boydell and Brewer, 1991), 75–89. Hanawalt's more recent discussions of gender and space tend to follow the same directions, with some discussion of the additional complexities posed by the urban environment: Hanawalt, "Medieval English Women in Rural and Domestic Space," *Dumbarton Oaks Papers* 52 (1998): 19–26; *"Of Good and Ill Repute": Gender and Social Control in Medieval England* (New York: Oxford University Press, 1998), 70–87, esp. 73, 76–78.

4. Dronzek, "No Separate Spheres."

5. See, on the interpenetration of medieval perceptions of sacred and profane space, Susan Signe Morrison, *Women Pilgrims in Medieval England: Private Piety as Public Performance* (London: Routledge, 2000), 92–100.

6. As Charles Burroughs has commented, the impact of a legal transaction derives partly "from the setting of its enactment, which might confer, for example, prestige or charisma, or offer a symbolic testimonial function." Burroughs, "Spaces of Arbitration," 65.

7. "Et tunc ibidem post diuersas communicaciones habitas inter dictos Stephanum et Annam ac alios amicos eorundem ibidem presentes de matrimonio contahendo inter eosdem Stephanum et Annam, dictus Stephanus cepit eandem Annam per manum dexteram et dixit eidem Anne, 'Ego Stephanus Robert accipio te Annam Clyfford in uxorem meam, et ad hoc do tibi fidem meam,' et retraxuerunt manus. Et tunc dicta Anna cepit eundem Stephanum per manum et <ad informacionem Ricardi Culpeper *deleted*> dixit eidem, 'Et ego Anna accipio te Stephanum Robert in maritum meum et ad hoc do tibi fidem meam.'" LMA, DL/C/205, fols. 37rv.

8. E.g., LMA, DL/C/205, fols. 19r–20r, 42r–43r, 49v, 57v, 96v–97r, 131v–132v, 134r, 168r; GL, 9065, fols. 10r, 55r–56v, 270r, 277v–279v.

9. Almost a third of domestic contracts were reported to have taken place in the home of the woman (e.g., *in domo Margarete*); deponents may not always have meant to indicate that the woman was the householder but rather simply

that she lived in the house. Nonetheless most of these took place in houses where the woman was evidently the householder.

10. Sarah Rees Jones has noted recently that urban testators fairly commonly left houses to single women in order to provide them with a place to live. "Women's Influence," 201. In none of the cases in the London deposition books is a woman householder clearly a never-married woman.

11. E.g., GL, 9065, fols. 22r–24r; 181v–182r; GL, 9065B, fols. 2v–3r.

12. GL, 9065, fols. 113v–114r.

13. E.g., LMA, DL/C/205, fol. 183r.

14. See, e.g., LMA, DL/C/205, 9rv, 257v–258r; GL, 9065, 85rv; GL, 9065B, 11v–15r.

15. Thomas Torald was styled gentleman not only by Maude, but also in civic records, where he was given a life grant of a gown of ray and a sum of 6s. 8d. to be delivered yearly out of the Chamber for life for unnamed services to the city. *CLBL*, 82, and CLRO, Journal 7, 185v, 20 January 1469. Robert Grene at least had "generosi amatores" testifying on his behalf and may possibly be the man of the same name, citizen and future warden of the mercers' company with ties, and perhaps origins, in Norfolk, who died in 1505, leaving a will that indicates that he died wealthy. TNA, PRO, PCC Prob. 11/14, fols. 278rv; Lyell and Watney, *Acts of the Court of the Mercers' Company*, 192, 252, 631–33, 642, 648–50.

16. "Ecce notifico vobis quod iste generosus Thomas Torald hic sedens est maritus meus quia nos duo contraximus insimul matrimoniam." LMA, DL/C/205, 63v–64v; see also, for another deposition in the case, McSheffrey, *Love and Marriage*, 70–71.

17. See depositions in LMA, DL/C/205, fols. 62v–64v, 65v–68v.

18. LMA, DL/C/205, fols. 117rv.

19. LMA, DL/C/205, fols. 20rv; for other examples see ibid., fols. 206v–207r; GL, 9065, 10v–11r.

20. Schofield, "Social Perceptions," 202.

21. LMA, DL/C/205, fols. 43v–44r; other examples include ibid., fols. 19r–20r, 38r–41r, 42v–43r, 104r–105r; GL, 9065, fols. 77rv, 273v–275r; GL, 9065B, fols. 3v–4r, 5v–6r. Isabel Palgrave may have died soon after the case was heard; an Isabel Palgrave is recorded among names of the dead on the bede roll for 1470 for the fraternity of St. Nicholas. James and James, *Bede Roll*, 90.

22. LMA, DL/C/205, fols. 37rv; for examples, see GL, 9065, fols. 39v–40r; Davis, *Paston Letters*, 1:448. Schofield, "Social Perceptions," 199, and *Medieval London Houses*, 66–67.

23. Schofield, "Social Perceptions," 202.

24. LMA, DL/C/205, fols. 56v–57r.

25. See, for instance, LMA, DL/C/205, fols. 253r, 276r.

26. GL, 9065B, fols. 3rv. Apart from this example, there were no contracts made in kitchens or other menial rooms in the records examined.

27. See above, p. 70.

28. Chaucer, *The Clerk's Tale*, ll. 323–29, in *Riverside Chaucer*, 141; Kathryn Jacobs, *Marriage Contracts from Chaucer to the Renaissance Stage* (Gainesville: University Press of Florida, 2001), 34, 123.

29. LMA, DL/C/205, fols. 166r–168r; McSheffrey, *Love and Marriage*, 60–61.

30. GL, 9065, fols. 35r–37r.

31. GL, 9065, fols. 80rv, 82rv.

32. LMA, DL/C/205, fols. 38r–40r.

33. LMA, DL/C/205, fols. 33r–34r, 35r. See also *Parker c. Tenwinter* discussed earlier, in which a conversation in a bedchamber was overheard from the hall.

34. LMA, DL/C/205, fols. 60v–62v; McSheffrey, *Love and Marriage*, 68–69.

35. Gowing, "Freedom of the Streets," discusses thresholds and defamation suits in the later sixteenth and early seventeenth centuries; many defamation suits of the fifteenth century also featured defamers or the defamed standing in a doorway or just outside a house when the defamatory words were spoken. Gowing notes that we need not make recourse to anthropological theories of liminality to explain this phenomenon: "doorsteps were a primary workplace, where [women] sewed, made lace, knitted, or nursed babies" (137).

36. GL, 9065, fols. 268v–270r, 275v. See also LMA, DL/C/205, fol. 246r.

37. This differs from the evidence for rural courtships in the later sixteenth century: Diana O'Hara has found that fairs and markets were "a favourite venue" for social activity and for courting in particular in sixteenth-century Kent. O'Hara, *Courtship*, 138.

38. Hanawalt, *Of Good and Ill Repute*, 74–76, 81.

39. Legrand and Caxton, *Good Maners*, sig. N1r.

40. Goldberg, "Household," 60–61.

41. TNA, PRO, C 1/214/91 (1493–1500).

42. E.g., LMA, DL/C/205, fol. 114r; GL, 9065, fols. 11v–12r.

43. Hanawalt, *Of Good and Ill Repute*, 105, 109–10; Ruth Mazo Karras, *Common Women: Prostitution and Sexuality in Medieval England* (New York: Oxford University Press, 1996), 15, 72. See also Judith M. Bennett, *Ale, Beer, and Brewsters in England: Women's Work in a Changing World, 1300–1600* (New York: Oxford University Press, 1996), esp. 123–44.

44. See, for instance, complaints made about the area behind the Pye in Queenhithe, a resort of thieves, pimps, and prostitutes: CLRO, P&MR, roll A5, m.7b (*CPMR*, 4:138), or the 1393 London civic ordinance that claimed that "many and divers affrays, broils, and dissensions, have arisen in times past, and many men have been slain and murdered, by reason of the frequent resort of, and consorting with, common harlots, at taverns, brewhouses of *huksters*, and other places of ill-fame, within the said city." H. T. Riley, ed. and trans., *Memorials of London and London Life in the Thirteenth, Fourteenth, and Fifteenth Centuries* (London: Longman, 1868), 535 (italics in original), a translation of the French in CLRO, Letter Book H, fol. 287r (strictly calendared in *CLBH*, 402).

45. Peter Clark suggests in relation to early modern alehouses that there were occasions on which women could visit alehouses without damage to their reputations, including courting. Clark, *The English Alehouse: A Social History, 1200–1830* (London: Longman, 1983), 131–32.

46. Although there are no accurate data on numbers of drinking establishments, we can generally extrapolate from Peter Clark's report that in 1309 there were 354 taverns and more than 1,300 places in which ale was sold in London and that the number of alehouses seems to have expanded considerably in the fifteenth century. Clark, *English Alehouse*, 21.

47. On the larger inns, see Caroline Barron, "Centres of Conspicuous Consumption: The Aristocratic Town House in London, 1200–1550," *London Journal* 20 (1995): 12–13; for other types of drinking establishments, see Clark, *English Alehouse*, 5–6, 14, 20–38; Schofield, *Medieval London Houses*, 53–55, 150. For those just outside London, see Gervase Rosser, *Medieval Westminster* (Oxford: Clarendon Press, 1989), 122–33; Martha Carlin, *Medieval Southwark* (London: Hambledon, 1996), 191–208.

48. Schofield, *Medieval London Houses*, 53–54; Clark, *English Alehouse*, 5–6, 20–38.

49. Schofield, *Medieval London Houses*, 150.

50. Residential tenements, like taverns, were known by names and marked by signs (Schofield, *Medieval London Houses*, 54, 150), and sometimes it is not clear if an episode being described by a witness occurs in an alehouse or in someone's home. There is no word used in the Latin depositions for "alehouse" (as opposed to *taberna* for "tavern"); a person drinking "at the house at the sign of the . . ." could have been a guest in a friend's home or in an alehouse. Here I have tried to confine myself to examples where it is clear that a drinking establishment is meant. On signs in the late medieval city, see Michael Camille, "Signs of the City: Place, Power, and Public Fantasy in Medieval Paris," in *Medieval Practices of Space*, ed. Hanawalt and Kobialka, 1–36.

51. See, e.g., LMA, DL/C/205, fols. 35v–36r, 54v–55r; GL, 9065, fols. 176v–177r.

52. LMA, DL/C/205, fols. 312v–313r.

53. LMA, DL/C/205, fols. 149v–150r.

54. LMA, DL/C/205, fol. 4r.

55. LMA, DL/C/205, fols. 165rv (parts of this case are translated in McSheffrey, *Love and Marriage*, 45–46). Many similar stories are told in the depositions; apart from others cited here, see LMA, DL/C/205, fols. 106v–107r, 110v, 179rv, 182r, 213r–214r, 281rv, 283rv; GL, 9065, fols. 1r–2r, 47rv, 53v–55r, 69v, 71rv, 74v, 98r, 273v–274r.

56. LMA, DL/C/205, fols. 69v–70r.

57. GL, 9065, fols. 60rv; a woman who worked at the tavern also gave testimony in the case, fol. 64r.

58. "Et incontinenter accepit eandem Aliciam per manum dexteram et dixit eidem, 'I John take the Alice to my weddid wif, and therto I pliȝt the my trouth.' Et retractis et iterum iunctis eorum manibus, ipsa Alicia dixit eidem Johanni, 'I Alice take the John to my weddid husbond, and therto I pliȝt the my trouth.'" GL, 9065, fols. 60r–61r.

59. LMA, DL/C/205, fols. 53v–54v.

60. LMA, DL/C/205, fols. 54v–55r, 58v.

61. LMA, DL/C/205, fols. 17r–19v.

62. GL, 9065B, fol. 14v. The chief justice was Sir Thomas Bryan, who served in this capacity at the court of common pleas from 1471 until his death in 1500, surviving the vicissitudes of dynastic change. He was knighted by Edward IV in 1475. See Edward Foss, *The Judges of England*, 9 vols. (London: Longman, Brown, Green, Longmans, and Roberts, 1848–64), 5:40–41; J. H. Baker, "Bryan, Sir Thomas (*d.* 1500)," *ODNB*, available from http://www.oxforddnb.com/view/article/49667, accessed 26 May 2005. Bryan's will (TNA, PRO, PCC Prob. 11/12, fols. 105v–106r, dated 1495, probated 1500), names Henry Heed as one of the witnesses, indicating a close relationship with him. On this case, see Chapter 3 in this volume.

63. GL, 9065B, fols. 11v–12v, 13r–15r.

64. GL, 9065, fol. 98r. The rejection of the tavern as an appropriate site for a contract evinced in one thirteenth-century synodal statute (Sheehan, *Marriage, Family, and Law*, 137) appears not to have been influential in fifteenth-century London, as there is no evidence that the contracts that took place there were regarded by the ecclesiastical courts as illegitimate because of their location.

65. See Chapter 3.

66. Clark, *English Alehouse*, 131–32.

67. Ibid.

68. In the London deposition books, reported male witnesses to marriage contracts outnumbered female witnesses by a ratio of about 4:1. This favoring of male witnesses was also characteristic of litigation in the York Consistory. Goldberg, *Women, Work, and Life Cycle*, 221.

Chapter 6. Governance

1. CLRO, Journal 5, fol. 72r; Journal 10, fol. 10v; Letter Book K, fol. 11v (*CLBK*, 17). Similar phrases are found throughout the journals, the letter books, and the Commissary court act books (e.g., GL, 9064/2, fol. 206v; 9064/3, fol. 189r; 9064/4, fol. 275v; 9064/8, fol. 162r). For secondary literature, see McIntosh, *Controlling Misbehavior*, 11–14, 70–71, 127–28, 131–32, 162–64, 175; Marjorie McIntosh, "Finding Language for Misconduct: Jurors in Fifteenth-Century Local Courts," in *Bodies and Disciplines: Intersections of Literature and History in Fifteenth-Century England*, ed. Barbara A. Hanawalt and David Wallace (Minneapolis: University of Minnesota Press, 1996), 87–122, esp. 90–97, 112–13; Ben R. McRee, "Religious Gilds and Regulation of Behavior in Late Medieval Towns," in *People, Politics and Community in the Later Middle Ages,* ed. Joel Rosenthal and Colin Richmond (Gloucester: Alan Sutton, 1987), 108–22; Barbara Hanawalt, " 'Good Governance' in the Medieval and Early Modern Context," *Journal of British Studies* 37 (1998): 246–57.

2. Sarah Rees Jones, "The Household and English Urban Government in the Later Middle Ages," in *The Household in Late Medieval Cities: Italy and Northwestern Europe Compared*, ed. Myriam Carlier and Tim Soens (Leuven-Apeldoorn: Garant, 2001), 73, 83–86.

3. Thrupp, *Merchant Class*, 16–17; Riddy, "Looking Closely," 212–14.

4. "How the Good Wijf Tau3te Hir Dou3tir," in Furnivall, *Babees Book*, 41.

5. GL, 9064/2, fol. 210v.

6. Thomas and Thornley, *Great Chronicle of London*, 249.

7. Lyell and Watney, *Acts of the Court of the Mercers' Company*, 221.

8. Ibid., 589.

9. "Edwardus Newton notatur officio quod est vir male disposicionis, malum regimen in domo sua fouenda, eo quod permittit male fame viros intrare in domum suam in tempore illicito." GL, 9064/8, fol. 162r. See R. H. Helmholz, "Harboring Sexual Offenders: Ecclesiastical Courts and Controlling Misbehavior," *Journal of British Studies* 37 (1998): 258–68.

10. *Missale*, sig. E1v; see Chapter 1 in this volume. Elizabeth Isaak, according to her brother, contracted marriage with John Bold in words that recalled some of this language: "And I will have you as my husband and be governed by you [Et ego volo habere vos in maritum meum et gubernari secundum vos]." LMA, DL/C/205, fol. 132r.

11. "Voluit gubernari secundum parentes et amicos suos." GL, 9065, fol. 24v; see also, for virtually identical language, LMA, DL/C/205, fols. 7r, 54v.

12. "How the Wise Man Tau3t his Sonne," in Furnivall, *Babees Book*, 50.

13. D'Evelyn, *Peter Idley's Instructions to His Son*, 101.

14. TNA, PRO, C 1/67/174.

15. "Maritum suum et magistrum." LMA, DL/C/205, fol. 63r.

16. TNA, PRO, C 1/64/223.

17. 25 Edward III, c. 2., *Statutes of the Realm*, 10 vols. (London: Eyre and Strahan, 1810–28; reprint London: Dawson of Pall Mall, 1963), 1:320.

18. William Blackstone, *Commentaries on the Laws of England*, 4 vols. (Oxford: Clarendon Press, 1765–69), 4:75.

19. On physical abuse within late medieval marriages, see Sara M. Butler, "The Language of Abuse: Marital Violence in Later Medieval England" (Ph.D. thesis, Dalhousie University, 2001).

20. TNA, PRO, C 1/82/87.

21. LMA, DL/C/205, fols. 58r, 92v–93r, 288r–289r, 292v–293r, 312v–314r; GL, 9065, fols. 57rv, 61v–62r; *Calendar of Papal Registers*, 11:319. The City could also become involved: in 1459, Joan Heron came before the mayor to seek a peace bond against her husband William, although she later withdrew the request as the couple had been reconciled. CLRO, Journal 6, Photo 242 (fol. 154r).

22. "Dicit quod quodam die contingenti in estate ultima preterita ad septem annos elapsos, iste iuratus veniens cum quadam toga reparata ad domum cuiusdam nuncupati Burgoyn, situatam infra dictum hospitale sancti Bartholomei, vidit prefatum Alexandrum currentem post dictam Alianorum ad tunc existentem in tunica sua et currentem capite nudam crinibus extensis, cum armicudio nudo in manu dicti Alexandri et pre timore eadem Alianora sic currens intrabat prefatam domum nuncupati Burgoyn ubi erat dicte Alianore soror, que susceperit existentes in dicta domo et ostium claudebant, quod videns prefatus Alexander dixit alta voce et iurauit quod voluit ipsam Alianoram interficere cum proxime obuiaret

eidem nisi existentes in dicta domo ipsam sibi ad tunc deliberarent. Quod cum facere nollent idem Alexander recessit. Et dicit iste iuratus quod credit in consciencia sua quod dicta Alianora ad tunc fuisset interfecta seu saltem mutulata nisi sic fuisse infra dictam domum suscepta. Et dicit ultra quod infra quinque annos ultimos elapsos quodam die de quo modo non recolit, prefatus Alexander intrabat tabernam ad signum Solis in Lumbardstrete ciuitatis London, ubi et quando idem Alexander in presencia istius iurati tenuit armicudium nudum in manu sua, et terrebat prefatam Alianoram cum eodum, pretextu cuius terroris eadem Alianora saltabat in quandam vacuam aream distantem a saltu eiusdem per longitudinem quatuor hominum ad minus, que deposit iste iuratus de visu suis propriis ut dicit. Et dicit ultra quod deposita superius per eum sunt vera et infra precinctum dicti Hospitalis laborauerunt et laborant publica vox et fama ut dicit." LMA, DL/C/205, fols. 203v–204r.

23. Morris S. Arnold, ed., *Select Cases of Trespass from the King's Courts, 1307–1399*, 2 vols. Selden Society, 100 and 103 (London: Selden Society, 1985, 1987), 1:xlv–xlviii.

24. TNA, PRO, C 1/82/87

25. See, e.g., TNA, PRO, C 1/46/47, C 1/46/115, C 1/66/224.

26. TNA, PRO, C 1/67/104

27. GL, 9065, fols. 95v–97v, 112rv; see also GL, 9064/2, fols. 208v, 290r. It is not clear whether William Newport sought his divorce on the grounds of cruelty or adultery, as both were alleged. Although rare (as indeed are cruelty suits brought at the wife's instance), there are other examples in the late fifteenth and early sixteenth centuries of divorces sought by husbands on grounds of the wife's cruelty. Cooke, *Act Book of Whalley*, 181; Elvey, *Courts of Archdeaconry of Buckingham*, 144.

28. "Credit iste juratus in consciencia sua periculosum esse dicto Willelmo cohabitare cum eadem quam regere et gubernare non potest." GL, 9065, fol. 96r.

29. E.g., GL, 9064/5, fol. 32r; 9064/6, fol. 163r.

30. GL, 9065, fol. 41v; *OED*, s.v. "wittol."

31. GL, 9064/1, fol. 33v.

32. GL, 9064/1, fol. 57v.

33. GL, 9064/5, fol. 11r.

34. GL, 9064/2, fol 123v.

35. E.g., La Tour Landry and Caxton, *The Booke which the knyght of the toure made*, sigs. E5v–E8r, L5v; La Tour Landry, *The book of the knight of La Tour-Landry*, 71–78, 174.

36. La Tour Landry and Caxton, *The Booke which the knyght of the toure made*, sigs. F1r–F3v (quotation at F2v). The same story appears in a different translation in La Tour Landry, *The Book of the Knight of La Tour-Landry*, 79–83. Wright (who edited the latter book) suggests in a note that the story appears also in the French *fabliaux* (ibid., 214).

37. La Tour Landry and Caxton, *The Booke which the knyght of the toure made*, sigs K6v–K7r; cf. La Tour Landry, *The book of the knight of La Tour-Landry*, 162.

38. *CBLK*, 385–90 (quotations at 386 and 387).

39. J. L. Bolton, "The City and the Crown, 1456–61," *London Journal* 12 (1986): 11–24 (quotation at 15); Nightingale, *Medieval Mercantile Community*, 505; Barron, *London in the Later Middle Ages*, 113–14.

40. E.g., CLRO, Letter Book I, fol. 286v (*CLBI*, 276); Letter Book K, fol. 179r (*CLBK*, 230); Journal 5, fol. 214r; Journal 8, fols. 47r–49r; GL, 9064/1, fols. 24v, 27v, 35v, 65v; GL, 9064/2, fols. 158v, 210r, 236v; GL, 9064/3, fols. 11r, 169r; GL, 9064/4, fol. 7v; GL, 9064/7, fols. 7v, 20v; GL, 9064/8, fol. 119v.

41. CLRO, Letter Book I, fol. 288r (*CLBI*, 281).

42. The servant Martyn was also accused of being a "vile mediator" between Elizabeth and another man, none other than the merchant stranger Galiot Scot, whose adulterous adventures contributed to his death the following year. CLRO, Journal 5, fols. 214v–215r, 216v: Journal 6, Photo 10 (26v).

43. CLRO, Journal 5, fols. 214v–215r, 216v; Journal 6, Photo 10 (26v).

44. CLRO, Journal 2, fol. 68v; Journal 6, photos 124, 126, 127.

45. GL, 9064/6, fol. 30v. For other examples, see GL, 9064/2, fol. 76r; GL, 9064/4, fols. 23r, 30r, 167v 235v; GL, 9064/5, fol. 15r.

46. GL, 9064/3, fol. 6v.

47. GL, 9064/4, fol. 167v.

48. GL, 9064/1–8 passim.

49. GL, 9064/2, fol. 221v; *CLBL*, 126, 189; TNA, PRO, PCC Prob. 11/12, fol. 3r.

50. E.g TNA, PRO, CC Prob. 11/7, fol. 140r. See Thomson, "Piety and Charity," 185–86; P. H. Cullum, "'And Hir Name Was Charite': Charitable Giving by and for Women in Late Medieval Yorkshire," in Goldberg, *Woman Is a Worthy Wight*, 198–99.

51. See Lyell and Watney, *Acts of the Court of the Mercers' Company*, 60–61, 85–86; he was also allegedly the victim of a strange murder plot: see below, p. 162.

52. See below p. 222, note 97.

53. GL, 9064/1, fol. 64r; one of his male servants had also been implicated in a fornication charge in 1470 (ibid., fol. 4v). On Bassett, see Wedgwood, *History of Parliament*, 2:49; *CLBL*, 8–210 passim.

54. Colin Richmond, "Fauconberg's Kentish Rising of May 1471," *English Historical Review* 85 (1970): 673–92, at 680.

55. Thomas and Thornley, *Great Chronicle of London*, 219–20; Richmond, "Fauconberg." Despite his service to the Yorkists, he was apparently not knighted by Edward IV in the aftermath of the attack on the city as a number of other aldermen were. CLRO, Letter Book L, fol. 79r (*CLBL*, 98–99).

56. *CLBL*, 134–44. See *OED*, s.v. "closh" and "cailes."

57. In a sample of about 840 citations recorded in the surviving Commissary court act books between 1470 and 1500 (GL, 9064/1–8) that relate to sexual misbehavior of some kind, about 90 involved the citation of an employer for a sexual relationship with a servant; of these, two-thirds involved the citation of a male employer, one-third the citation of a female employer.

58. TNA, PRO, C 1/94/14.

59. Quoted in Thrupp, *Merchant Class*, 231.

60. "How the Wise Man Tauȝt his Sonne," in Furnivall, *Babees Book*, 50.

61. See, for instance, TNA, PRO, C 1/61/382, C 1/61/574, C 1/63/176, C 1/66/259, C 1/150/54, C 1/158/35, C 1/214/91, C 1/229/18, C 1/234/71; CLRO, Journal 4, fol. 113v. The placing of primary responsibility for a wife's or daughter's misbehavior on another, especially a man, is partly because of the structure of English law (wives and daughters could not be sued by husbands or fathers, but their seducers could be). Nonetheless, assumptions about women's culpability in the Chancery petitions reflect widespread notions of women's lack of agency.

62. TNA, PRO, C 1/158/47.

63. GL, 9064/4, fols. 38r, 83r, 227v, 239v, 263v.

64. TNA, PRO, C 1/29/400.

65. On the rarity of accusations of sodomy in late medieval England, see David Lorenzo Boyd and Ruth Mazo Karras, "'Ut cum muliere': A Male Transvestite Prostitute in Fourteenth-Century London," in *Premodern Sexualities*, ed. Louise Fradenburg and Carla Freccero (New York: Routledge, 1996), 99–116, esp. 102, 105; and Derek Neal, "Meanings of Masculinity in Late Medieval England: Self, Body, and Society" (Ph.D. thesis, McGill University, 2004), 291–92.

66. See Warren Johansson and William A. Percy, "Homosexuality," and Jacqueline Murray, "Twice Marginal and Twice Invisible: Lesbians in the Middle Ages," in *Handbook of Medieval Sexuality*, ed. Vern L. Bullough and James Brundage (New York: Garland, 1999), 155–90 and 191–222; Michael Rocke, *Forbidden Friendships: Homosexuality and Male Culture in Renaissance Florence* (New York: Oxford University Press, 1996); Helmut Puff, *Sodomy in Reformation Germany and Switzerland, 1400–1600* (Chicago: University of Chicago Press, 2003).

67. In 1470, William Smyth boasted that he had committed sodomy with Master Thomas Tunley, the rector of St. Margaret Lothbury; Tunley was dismissed of the accusation by the Commissary after he underwent compurgation. He was also accused (and purged himself) of having raped or attempted to rape a seven-year-old girl. GL, 9064/1, fols. 4r, 53r. Suspiciously, less than two months after his compurgation, Tunley was transferred from St. Margaret to the remote rectory of St. Phillack in western Cornwall, which living he held until his death in 1476. *BRUC to 1500*, 596–97. In 1483, Giles Johnson was accused of defaming Derek Deher by saying that he had been a heretic and had committed sodomy with several men. Johnson admitted the defamation. GL, 9064/3, fol. 185r.

68. Several men were named as "harlots of their bodies" in the Portsoken and Tower ward wardmote presentments; it is possible that they were trading sex for money (with men? with women?), but more probable that heterosexual promiscuity rather than commercial prostitution was at issue given the relatively mild reaction. CLRO, Journal 8, fol. 48r (1473); Portsoken ward presentments, mm. 12, 14, 1480 and 1482.

69. Neal discusses the particular association in literature with friars: Neal, "Meanings of Masculinity," 236, 237–39.

70. Helmut Puff, "Localizing Sodomy: The 'Priest and Sodomite' in Pre-Reformation Germany and Switzerland," *Journal of the History of Sexuality* 8 (1997): 165–95.

71. Two priests were denounced for having been caught together in bed with a woman in 1476. CLRO, Letter Book L, fol. 123r (*CLBL*, 145); same case also recorded in CLRO, Journal 8, fol. 142r.

72. Most notably Jonathan Ned Katz, *The Invention of Heterosexuality* (New York: Dutton, 1995). While Katz's insights have been crucial for denaturalizing heterosexuality, his conclusions about premodern sexual identities are sometimes too crude.

73. David Lorenzo Boyd and Ruth Mazo Karras, "The Interrogation of a Male Transvestite Prostitute in Fourteenth Century London," *GLQ: A Journal of Lesbian and Gay Studies* 1 (1995): 459–65; Boyd and Karras, "Ut cum muliere."

74. Boyd and Karras, "Interrogation."

75. Craig A. Williams, *Roman Homosexuality: Ideologies of Masculinity in Classical Antiquity* (New York: Oxford University Press, 1999), 3–14.

76. GL, 9065, fol. 54r.

77. GL, 9065, fols. 48v–49v, 53v–55r (Calton's testimony and quotations are on fols. 49rv). Note that Margaret Isot denied that she had ever exchanged vows with Thomas (fol. 48v). Thomas's father (named in the entry also as Thomas) and his mother were called before the Commissary court in early 1472 to answer to the charge of impeding the solemnization of the marriage between their son and Margaret "Isaac," a charge that they denied. GL, 9064/1, fol. 134r.

78. GL, 9065, fols. 49rv.

79. Clive Burgess, "Shaping the Parish: St. Mary at Hill, London, in the Fifteenth Century," in *The Cloister and the World: Essays in Medieval History in Honour of Barbara Harvey*, ed. John Blair and Brian Golding (Oxford: Oxford University Press, 1996), 254–69. For intersections between presenters in local lay and church courts in the well-documented courts of Hartlebury, Worcs., see Christopher Dyer, *Lords and Peasants in a Changing Society: The Estates of the Bishopric of Worcester, 680–1540* (Cambridge: Cambridge University Press, 1980), 363.

80. William Wylde was rector of St. Mary at Hill from 1467 until his death in 1504 (*BRUC*, 656–57; Littlehales, *Medieval Records of St. Mary at Hill*, 246, 255), commissary of the bishop of London, 1467–83 (GL, 9171/6 passim), and bishop's official (presiding over the Consistory court of the bishop of London, the same court that heard Stevenes's case) from 1468 to 1470 (LMA, DL/C/205, 13v–64v passim). It is possible that John Palmer was the man by the same name who served as churchwarden for the parish of St. Mary at Hill in 1477–79 (Burgess, "Shaping the Parish," 285).

81. As a result of his loss of reputation, William Stevenes sued John Palmer for defamation. LMA, DL/C/205, fols. 146v–148r; see also McSheffrey, *Love and Marriage*, 87–88. In 1377, Matilda Bakere had also sued for defamation in a church court after wardmote jurors presented her as a "woman of bad character." *CPMR*, 2:244.

82. "Ubi et quando iste iuratus, pro eo quod in dicta parrochia publice dicebatur quod prefatus Richardus nimis suspiciose frequentabat domum eiusdem Agnetis, iste iuratus dixit eidem quod non haberet tales frequentes secursus ad eam nisi sciret utrum vellet habere eam in uxorem vel non." GL, 9065, fol. 12v.

83. An ex officio or office case was undertaken at the initiative of the court. See Helmholz, *Marriage Litigation*, 70–71, for office cases, noting that in Consistory courts they usually arose from consanguinity problems; see also L. R. Poos, "Sex, Lies, and the Church Courts of Pre-Reformation England," *Journal of Interdisciplinary History* 25 (1995): 585–607.

84. "Maior pars vicinie ibidem opinatur et sentit premissa fuisse et esse vera et male loquitur de eisdem ut dicit." LMA, DL/C/205, fol. 211. See also a case where a putative bigamist in London was urged by one of the witnesses to his first marriage to put aside his second wife and return to his original marriage bed: William Malton, a London ironmonger, told the court that he had "made many entreaties to William Hathewey to take Petronilla as his wife and dismiss the said Margaret Spyndeler, whom he held in adultery [fecit instancias diuersas Willelmo Hathewey ut acciperet dictam Petronillam in uxorem et dimitteret dictam Margaretam Spyndeler quam tenuit in adulterio ut dixit]." LMA, DL/C/205, fols. 9rv, quotation at 9v.

85. LMA, DL/C/205, fols. 312v–313v.

86. Barron, *London in the Later Middle Ages*, 4–5; Clive Burgess, "London Parishioners in Times of Change: St. Andrew Hubbard, Eastcheap, c. 1450–1570," *Journal of Ecclesiastical History* 53 (2002): 38

87. Clive Burgess, "Pre-Reformation Churchwardens' Accounts and Parish Government: Lessons from London and Bristol," *English Historical Review* 117 (2002): 316–23; Burgess, "Shaping the Parish," 254–60.

88. Burgess, "Shaping the Parish," 254–60.

89. For some of the recent work on the parish based on the churchwardens' accounts, see Beat A. Kümin, *The Shaping of a Community: The Rise and Reformation of the English Parish, c. 1400–1560* (Aldershot: Scolar Press, 1996); French, *People of the Parish*; Burgess, "London Parishioners"; Burgess, "Shaping the Parish"; Burgess, "Pre-Reformation Churchwardens' Accounts."

90. French, *People of the Parish*, 31–36, 72; Kümin, *Shaping of a Community*, 226–28; Dyer, *Lords and Peasants*, 363.

91. Wunderli, *London Church Courts*, 36–37.

92. Ibid., 81.

93. Ibid., 38.

94. "A slyer boye nas noon in engelond; / For subtilly he hadde his espiaille, / That taughte hym wel wher that hym myghte availle. / He koude spare of lecchours oon or two, To techen hym to foure and twenty mo." Chaucer, *The Friar's Tale*, ll. 22–26, in *Riverside Chaucer*, 123. The importance of the summoner in the making of presentments in the courts of the diocese of Canterbury is argued, for instance, by Brian L. Woodcock in *Medieval Ecclesiastical Courts of the Diocese of Canterbury* (London: Oxford University Press, 1953), 49, 69.

95. Wunderli, *London Church Courts*, 37–38.

96. Ibid., 35–37; Poos, *Lower Ecclesiastical Jurisdiction*, lx–lxii; Poos, "Sex, Lies." Accusations also came directly to the commissary through an interested party, in a process that was similar to litigation; indeed some of these cases were sent up to the Consistory court when they proved too complicated to be handled in the lower court. Wunderli, *London Church Courts*, 31–33.

97. GL, 9064/1, fol. 65r.

98. See below p. 245, notes 80 and 81.

99. Caroline M. Barron, "The Parish Fraternities of Medieval London," in *The Church in Pre-Reformation Society: Essays in Honour of F. R. H. Du Boulay*, ed. Caroline M. Barron and Christopher Harper-Bill (Woodbridge: Boydell, 1985), 13–37; C. David Benson, *Public Piers Plowman: Modern Scholarship and Late Medieval English Culture* (University Park: Pennsylvania State University Press, 2004), 214–22; Barbara A. Hanawalt and Ben R. McRee, "The Guilds of *homo prudens* in Late Medieval England," *Continuity and Change* 7 (1992): 163–79; McRee, "Religious Guilds"; Rosser, "Going to the Fraternity Feast."

100. Rosser, "Going to the Fraternity Feast," 438–44 (quotation at 438).

101. As quoted (my modernization) in Benson, *Public Piers Plowman*, 219.

102. E.g., CLRO, Letter Book H, fol. 238r (*CLBH*, 339); Letter Book I, fols. 287r–290r (*CLBI*, 277–87); CLRO, Journal 6, photo 360 (fol. 217v); Journal 8, fol. 92v. There may have been considerable tension about sexual misbehavior among city clerics and civic authorities' perceptions that ecclesiastical authorities did not treat the problem seriously. I am preparing an article on this subject.

103. E.g., GL, 9064/1, fols. 3v, 6r, 7v, 8v, 13v, 15v, 16r, 18v, etc. Cf. Wunderli, *London Church Courts*, 35.

104. An exception to this was a certain amount of tension regarding fornicating priests.

105. See Caroline Barron, "Lay Solidarities: The Wards of Medieval London," in *Law, Laity and Solidarities: Essays in Honour of Susan Reynolds*, ed. Pauline Stafford, Janet L. Nelson, and Jane Martindale (Manchester: Manchester University Press, 2001), 218–33; Barron, *London in the Later Middle Ages*, 121–27. My description of the workings of the wardmote courts, drawn from sources Barron did not use, differs slightly from hers.

106. "Ulterius interrogatus, dicit se tantum scire quod quodam die profesto contingente infra duodecim dies immediate contingentes post festum natalis domini ultimum preteritum, quem diem aliter specificare nescit, dictus Johannes Palmer venit ad quemdam locum vulgariter nuncupatum Hewlyns Place, ubi et quando post meridiem eiusdem diei idem Johannes Palmer presentauit se coram xiii personis nominatis, assumptis, et electis per dominum Georgium Irlond, Aldermannum Warde vocate Cordwere Strete, ad inquirendum <et> inuestigandum de et super criminibus in dicta Warda perpetratis et de et super personis criminosis de dicta Warda expellendis propter suum malum regiminem et crimina perpetrata per eosdem et usitata." LMA, DL/C/205, fols. 146v–147r.

107. McIntosh, *Controlling Misbehavior*, 34–45; R. B. Goheen, "Peasant Politics? Village Community and the Crown in Fifteenth-Century England," *American Historical Review* 96 (1991): 42–62; Neal, "Meanings of Masculinity," 95–99; Ian Blanchard, "Social Structure and Social Organization in an English Village at the Close of the Middle Ages: Chewton, 1526," in *The Salt of Common Life: Individuality and Choice in the Medieval Town, Countryside, and Church*, ed. Edwin Brezette DeWindt (Kalamazoo, Michigan: Medieval Institute Publications, 1995), 318–24, 327–28.

108. *Munimenta Gildhallae Londoniensis*, pt. 1, *Liber Albus*, ed. Henry Thomas Riley, Rolls Series 12/1 (London: Longman, Brown, Green, Longmans, and Roberts, 1859), 275, 283, 332, 337–38, 456–60.

109. CLRO, Journal 8, fol. 49v.

110. Riley, *Liber Albus*, 457–60; CLRO, Letter Book K, fol. 179r; *CLBK*, 230–31.

111. See Barron, *London in the Later Middle Ages*, 124–25, on these ward officials.

112. For examples of such presentments, ranging from the 1440s to the 1490s: CLRO, Journal 4, fols. 60r, 135r, 137r–138v, 141v, 221r; Journal 5, fols. 214r, 234r; Journal 6, photo 110 (fol. 122v); Journal 8, fols. 92r, 230v; Journal 10, fols. 78v, 109r.

113. CLRO, Journal 9, fol. 129r (1486).

114. Riley, *Liber Albus*, 275, 283, 332, 337–38, 456–60; *CLBG*, 149; CLRO, Letter Book H, fol. 238r (*CLBH*, 339); Letter Book I, fols. 286r–290r (*CLBI*, 273–87); Letter Book K, fols. 11rv, 168r, 179r (*CLBK*, 17, 215, 230–31); Letter Book L, fols. 83r, 275v–276r, 282rv (*CLBL*, 103, 269, 276). See also evidence cited later from LMA, DL/C/205 and GL, 9065.

115. One set of fifteenth-century ward presentments survives in original written form: CLRO, Portsoken ward presentments, 1465–1482 and 1507. Other wards probably also recorded their presentments, at least according to a reference to "rotulo Wardemote" of Billingsgate ward in 1456 (CLRO, Journal 6, photo 6 [fol. 30v]); see also references to "indentures and veredictis" of the inquests (CLRO, Journal 9, fol. 129r). Other evidence from the civic records for wardmote presentments and activities of ward officials can be found in: CLRO, Journal 4, fols. 13r, 16v; Journal 5, fols. 54r, 214v–215r, 216v; Journal 6, photos 512–13, 519 (fols. 20rv, 7v); Journal 8, 47r–50v, 87v–88r; Journal 10, fols. 10v, 39v; *Calendar of Early Mayor's Court Rolls Preserved among the Archives of the Corporation of the City of London at the Guildhall, AD 1298–1307*, ed. A. H. Thomas (Cambridge: Cambridge University Press, 1924), 23–24, 211, 218–19; *CPMR*, 1:108–9, 116, 124–26, 156, 167, 173, 187–89, 212; 2:7, 139, 151, 156–57, 244; 3:148; CLRO, P&MR, roll A50, mm. 5a–7b; roll A51, mm. 2a–4b; roll A71, m. 4b; roll A72, m. 3b (*CPMR*, 4:115–41, 150–59; 5:72, 88).

116. Karras has argued for the blurred nature of the categories, promiscuity being a more important marker of the whore than her acceptance of money in return for sex: *Common Women*, passim, esp. 16–17, 27–28, 131.

117. The Journals, for instance, frequently record that a couple was caught ("capti fuerunt") by the beadles or constables of the ward, but nothing more. See CLRO, Journal 4, fols. 75v, 92v, 211v; Journal 5, fols. 52v, 61v, 116v, 161r, 195v, 217v, 251r, 268v; Journal 6, photo 98 (fol. 116v), photo 360 (fol. 217v); Journal 7, fols. 59v, 102r.

118. See below, p. 245, note 77.

119. E.g., CLRO, Letter Book I, fols. 288r–289r (*CLBI*, 282–85).

120. GL, 9065, fol. 197v.

121. GL, 9064/4, fol. 42r.

122. GL, 9064/1, fol. 96v; GL, 9064/4, fol. 134v.

123. LMA, DL/C/205, fols. 263r–264r.

124. In other examples the constables were also assisted by neighbors: CLRO, Journal 5, fol. 268v; Journal 6, photo 360 (fol. 217v).

125. TNA, PRO, C 1/65/226; see also GL, 9064/1, fol. 53v; CLRO, Journal 7, fol. 52v.

126. LMA, DL/C/205, fols. 191r–192v; see also McSheffrey, *Love and Marriage*, 84–85. Ecclesiastical courts also sometimes directed fornicating couples to exchange marriage vows in court. See Poos, "The Heavy-Handed Marriage Counsellor," 297; and Helmholz, *Marriage Litigation*, 172–81.

127. "Tam timore corporis sui <quam> pudore comparacionis coram maiore et Aldermannis iste iuratus contraxit ibidem matrimonium cum prefata Agnete." LMA, DL/C/205, fols. 266rv; the rest of the case appears in fols. 252v–256r, 258v, 265v, 275r–276v. See also McSheffrey, *Love and Marriage*, 81–82.

128. E.g., LMA, DL/C/205, fols. 86r, 147v–148r, 158v, 244r–246r, 248v, 249r, 268v; Thrupp, *Merchant Class*, 15–16.

129. See Thrupp, *Merchant Class*, esp. 100–102; Burgess, "Shaping the Parish," 259, 273.

130. *CLBK*, 215. This is the wording used in 1437 and again in 1461. See also Gwyn Williams, *Medieval London: From Commune to Capital* (London: Athlone Press, 1963), 42–43, 80.

131. See Thrupp, *Merchant Class*, 80–81; Wunderli, *London Church Courts*, 34; and CLRO, Portsoken ward presentments.

132. Rees Jones, "Household and English Urban Government," 85; Davies, *Merchant Taylors' Company*, 25.

133. Davies, *Merchant Taylors' Company*, 25, 237. Members of the merchant taylors' company commonly submitted themselves to internal arbitration over quarrels that might in other circumstances have made their way to a defamation complaint in a church court. Ibid., 96, 131, 137, 152, 207–10, 217–18, 266–67.

134. W. P. Baildon, ed., *The Records of the Honorable Society of Lincoln's Inn: The Black Books*, 4 vols. (London: Lincoln's Inn, 1897), 1:71. Elys had been in trouble before with the same woman. Ibid., 1:66, 68. Others were also expelled (and readmitted after paying a fine) for having women in their chambers between 1482 and 1486 (1:74, 76–77, 79, 86), and in 1489, the Society ordained that any member of the Society who should henceforth commit fornication with a woman on the grounds of the inn would be fined 100s., and if he was caught with a woman near the inn (including Chancery Lane) he would be fined 20s. (1:89–90).

135. Kingdon, *Facsimile . . . Grocers*, 2:299; Nightingale, *Medieval Mercantile Community*, 472.

136. Lyell and Watney, *Acts of the Court of the Mercers' Company*, 130–31.

137. Ibid., 60–61, 85–86; on the rape accusation, see above, p. 145.

138. The result of the arbitration, undertaken by the six aldermen who were mercers and two other members of the company, is described in Lyell and Watney, *Acts of the Court of the Mercers' Company*, 132–34.

139. There were some women churchwardens in England in the 1540s (likely a product of male "flight from office" in the troublesome period of religious upheaval), but none have been found for London. See French, *People of the Parish*,

87–88. The Maryn Gerens or Garet, warden of St. Andrew Hubbard a number of times in the first decades of the sixteenth century, whom Kümin suggested may have been a woman (*Shaping of a Community*, 40), was called "Master" in the accounts at one point. Clive Burgess, ed., *The Church Records of St. Andrew Hubbard Eastcheap, c. 1450–c. 1570*, London Record Society, 34 (London: London Record Society, 1999), 120.

140. See McSheffrey, "Jurors, Respectable Masculinity."

Chapter 7. Gender, Sex, and Reputation

1. TNA, PRO, C 1/32/337. The parties were also involved in another legal dispute, undoubtedly related in some way to the matter in the petition: Humphrey Bawde and his wife were cited before the London Commissary court in 1480 for having defamed Matilda Olyff (Olyve), calling her a prostitute and a bawd, especially for a certain John Travase. GL, 9064/3, fol. 30v.

2. See Karras, *Common Women*, 58, for an example of a young girl being rescued from a descent into a life of prostitution "for Our Lady's sake."

3. Humphrey, according to the petition, was living with his employer, Thomas Hart, baker, in Smithfield, while Joan remained in their house in the parish of St. Giles without Cripplegate. TNA, PRO, C 1/32/337. The farthest boundaries of the large parish of St. Giles was no more than a mile from Smithfield; although it may seem odd that they found it necessary to live separately, this was common for bakers' servants. In 1441 the "servant Bakeres" of London complained to the mayor and aldermen that they were fined 10d. if any of them "goo hoome to his wif" any day but Sunday. *CLBK*, 266.

4. On Hobbys, see C. H. Talbot and E. A. Hammond, *The Medical Practitioners in Medieval England: A Biographical Register* (London: Wellcome Historical Medical Library, 1965), 401–2; *BRUO*, 2:xix, 938; *BRUC*, 307; Sidney Young, ed., *Annals of the Barber Surgeons* (London: Blades, East and Blades, 1890), 3, 18; C. H. Talbot, *Medicine in Medieval England* (London: Oldbourne, 1967), 70–71; Carole Rawcliffe, *Medicine and Society in Later Medieval England* (Gloucester: Alan Sutton, 1995), 125–26. He left wills both in the Court of Husting (roll 219, m. 15; calendared in *Cal. Husting*, 2:590–91) and in the Prerogative Court of Canterbury (TNA, PRO, PCC Prob. 11/8, fol. 133v–134r); see p. 187 below. Hobbys is also referred to in CLRO, Journal 6, Photo 551 (fol. 15v), 9 February 1462, being bound over for 100s. to the chamberlain of the City to obey an arbitration.

5. LMA, DL/C/205, fols. 315r–320r.

6. Talbot and Hammond, *Medical Practitioners*, 187, 276, 401–2. Staveley is called Stanley in Talbot and Hammond, but it seems likely that the same man is referred to.

7. Not surprisingly, it may have been common for those associated with England's armies to avail themselves both of prostitutes and of military metaphors while overseas: John Pympe, in a letter to Sir John Paston, then at Calais, made

jocular references to the women of Bruges, who "with their high caps have given some of you great claps, and that the feet of their arms doing is such that they smite all at the mouth and at the great end of the thigh; but in faith we care not for you, for we know well that you be good enough at defence." Davis, *Paston Letters*, 2:414.

8. Halyday appears in Talbot and Hammond, *Medical Practitioners*, 296. He would become warden of the Surgeons' Company of London in 1489.

9. The recording of the sentence (and a number of other administrative matters related to the case) in the deposition book is very unusual, perhaps because of the exceptional nature of the case (it is the only divorce case clearly sought on the grounds of adultery among the roughly 250 cases recorded in LMA, DL/C/205 and GL, 9065); another case that may be a suit for divorce on the grounds of adultery (neither the goal of the suit nor the grounds are clear from the testimony) is *William Newport c. Isabel Newport*, 1491–92, GL, 9065, fols. 79v, 95r, 112rv.

10. On the contradictions inherent in premodern masculine identity, see Jacqueline Murray, "Hiding Behind the Universal Man: Male Sexuality in the Middle Ages," in *Handbook of Medieval Sexuality*, ed. Vern L. Bullough and James A. Brundage (New York: Garland, 1996), 129–39; Lyndal Roper, *Oedipus and the Devil: Witchcraft, Sexuality and Religion in Early Modern Europe* (London and New York: Routledge, 1994), 108–9, 119–20; Jacqueline Murray, ed., *Conflicting Identities and Multiple Masculinities: Men in the Medieval West* (New York: Garland, 1999); Ruth Mazo Karras, *From Boys to Men: Formations of Masculinity in Late Medieval Europe* (Philadelphia: University of Pennsylvania Press, 2003); Neal, "Meanings of Masculinity"; Alexandra Shepard, "Manhood, Credit and Patriarchy in Early Modern England, c. 1580–1640," *Past & Present* 167 (2000): 75–106, esp. 77–79, 102–6; Capp, "Double Standard Revisited," 97–98.

11. For divorces on grounds of cruelty, see *Elizabeth Machon c. Yon Machon*, LMA, DL/C/205, fol. 58r; *Joan Baron alias Howton alias Palmer c. Robert Howton alias Palmer*, ibid., fols. 92v–93v; *Eleanor Brownynge c. Alexander Brownynge*, ibid., fols. 203r–204r; *Joan Hyndeley c. William Hyndeley*, ibid., fols. 288r–289r, 292v–293r; *Elizabeth Redy c. Richard Redy*, ibid., fol. 298v; *Katherine Burwell alias Bachelere c. William Bachelere*, ibid., fols. 312v–313v, 314r; *Ann Styward c. Richard Styward*, GL, 9065B, 16v; GL, 9065, 57rv, 61v–62r. *Elizabeth Benet c. Richard Benet* (LMA, DL/C/205, fol. 313v) is apparently a suit for divorce, but the grounds are unclear. The grounds for *William Newport c. Isabel Newport* (GL, 9065, fols. 79v, 95r, 112rv), the only divorce suit undertaken by the husband, may have been both adultery and cruelty: witnesses detailed both Isabel's adultery and her violence toward him, but focused on the latter.

12. I have found two other divorces on grounds of adultery sought by women in medieval England: Mabel Smith of Ware sued her husband, Robert, for divorce on the grounds of both cruelty and adultery, probably in the London Consistory, in the 1450s; she was granted her separation, a sentence that was confirmed in the papal court. *Calendar of Papal Registers*, 11:188–89. Another wife in Norwich diocese sought a divorce for adultery in 1508. *Norwich Consistory Court Depositions*, no. 87. Goldberg noted that there were six causes for divorce *a mensa*

et thoro among the York cause papers, but he does not distinguish the suits by the grounds on which they were sought. Goldberg, *Women, Work, and Life Cycle*, 251–52. On such divorces generally, see Helmholz, *Marriage Litigation*, 101; Brundage, *Law, Sex, and Christian Society*, 453–55, 513–14.

13. Helmholz, *Marriage Litigation*, 100–101; Brundage concurs, *Law, Sex, and Christian Society*, 453–54, 514.

14. GL, 9168/1, fol. 4v, 1496–97. The entry reads: "Alicia Hobbys decessit intestata vii decembris [1496?]. Comparuit Thomas Neele et peciit administracionem sibi committi et exhibuit quoddam testamentum et allegans quod prefata decedens revocauit idem ante eius mortem. Tunc dominus assignauit sibi ad probandum die veneris, quo die comparuit et traduxit Johanni Deysy idem(?) testamentum. Postea vii Januarii comparuit et introduxit dominum Henricum Meld quem dominus iurauit super reuocacione testamenti." In margin: "Notatur pro falso inventario qui defuit murrazeuis [i.e. mazers?] et iiii s. in pecunia." Thomas Neele is not otherwise known to have had connections with either Alice or William Hobbys.

15. See note 4 in this chapter.

16. Young, *Annals of the Barber Surgeons*, 2, 3.

17. Talbot and Hammond, *Medical Practitioners*, 401–2; *BRUC*, 307; Rawcliffe, *Medicine and Society*, 110, 112, 125–26.

18. C. H. Talbot notes, without giving a source, that despite William Hobbys's M.D., he "made surgery his sole occupation." Talbot, *Medicine in Medieval England*, 206. Hobbys was called physician and surgeon in contemporary documents, including his tombstone. See Talbot and Hammond, *Medical Practitioners*, 401–2; *Cal. Husting*, 2:591.

19. Rosemary Horrox, ed., "Edward IV: Parliament of 1472, Text and Translation," item 11, in *PROME* (*RP*, 6:83); Rawcliffe, *Medicine and Society*, 109–11; Talbot and Hammond, *Medical Practitioners*, 401–2.

20. "Hic iacet Willelmus Hobbys quondam medicus et cirurgicus illustrissimi domini ducis Eborici ac filiorum suorum regum illustrissimorum Edwardi quarti et Ricardi tercii quorum anime et animabus propicietur Deus amen." TNA, PRO, PCC Prob. 11/8, fol. 134r; this part of his will was also enrolled in the court of Husting in London and is transcribed in *Cal. Husting*, 2:590–91.

21. Of the four witnesses who testified against William Hobbys, further information about their careers as surgeons can be found about three. On Robert Halyday, a prominent London surgeon, see p. 188. The two who witnessed William's dalliance with prostitutes in France, Richard Chambyr and John Staveley, are known to have been among the medical staff of the English army for Edward IV's expedition to France in 1475 along with William Hobbys. Both Chambyr and Staveley noted in their depositions that they had known both William and Alice Hobbys since their mid teens, suggesting that they might have been William's apprentices in the craft of surgery. Richard Chambyr was to go on to some prominence in the London guild of barber-surgeons, acting as its warden for three separate stints in the later 1470s and the 1480s. John Staveley may have subsequently married one of William's and Alice's daughters—see below, p. 187. LMA, DL/C/205, fols. 316v–319r; Young, *Annals of the Barber Surgeons*, 3; Talbot and Hammond, *Medical Practitioners*, 276, 296, 187 (Staveley called Stanley).

22. CLRO, Letter Book L, fol. 106v; the entry is briefly calendared in *CLBL*, 125–26. I have not been able to locate the original Chancery bill.

23. "Willelmus Keynys adulterauit cum Elizabeth famula sua et imprignauit eandem." GL, 9064/4, fol. 134v (1490).

24. "Magister Lodowicus Kaerleon in maximum obprobrium Christianorum imprignauit Margaretam seruientem suam et misit eam ad patriam ibi expectando quousque edidit partum et post reuersa est ad domum suam. Et iterum eam imprignauit et similiter misit eam extra Ciuitatem et ad huc est prignans. Nec curat de deo nec de domino rege cui seruit nec de lege nec de ministris legis et habet uxorem iuuenem que certa est de istis et omnes vicinos suos." GL, 9064/4, fol. 228v.

25. Pearl Kibre, "Lewis of Caerleon, Doctor of Medicine, Astronomer, and Mathematician (d. 1494?)," *Isis* 43 (1952): 100–108; *BRUC*, 116–17; Talbot and Hammond, *Medical Practitioners*, 203; Damian Riehl Leader, *A History of the University of Cambridge*, vol. 1, *The University to 1546* (Cambridge: Cambridge University Press, 1988), 153–54; Rawcliffe, *Medicine and Society*, 118–19; Keith Snedegar, "Caerleon, Lewis (*d.* in or after 1495)," *ODNB*, available from http://www.oxforddnb.com/view/article/4324, accessed 26 May 2005. From the late 1470s (when the records begin) to 1492, the name of Lewis, "ffisician," appears in rentals of properties belonging to the parish of St. Mary at Hill for a tenement in Foster Lane (for which he paid 40s. yearly). Littlehales, *Medieval Records of St. Mary at Hill*, 76, 87, 107, 114, 119, 120, 123, 125, 138, 152, 166, 177; Burgess, "Shaping the Parish," 283.

26. Leader, *History of the University of Cambridge*, 154; Rawcliffe, *Medicine and Society*, 118–19.

27. Polydore Vergil, *Three Books of Polydore Vergil's English History*, ed. Henry Ellis, Camden Society, 1st Ser., 29 (London: J. B. Nichols, 1844; rept., New York: Johnson Reprint Company, 1968), 195–97.

28. Kibre, "Lewis of Caerleon," 100–103. No will for him has been found.

29. For the rarity of married physicians in the fifteenth century, see Rawcliffe, *Medicine and Society*, 110–12. None of the previous scholarship on Lewis of Caerleon, cited earlier in note 25, mentions a marriage.

30. See Chapter 6 and later in this chapter.

31. GL, 9064/1–8 (1470–1500). See also Wunderli, *London Church Courts*, 84–88, 144.

32. E.g., CLRO, P&MR, roll 71, m. 4b (*CPMR*, 5:72); roll A72, m. 3b (*CPMR*, 5:88); roll A90, mm. 1–2b (*CPMR*, 6:57–64); CLRO, Journal 4, fols. 62r, 75v, 106v, 122r; Journal 5, fols. 217rv; Journal 7, fol. 193r; Journal 8, fol. 47r; Journal 10, fol. 3v, CLRO, Letter Book I, fols. 286r–287r, 288v–289r. (This list includes only laypeople; clerics were also frequently charged.) These records include only those cases that were referred to the mayor and aldermen; it seems likely that the lower-level courts, the wardmote inquests, were more likely to be concerned with adultery (which was probably seen as a lesser problem than the prostitution and bawdry that was more commonly seen at the higher levels). In 1473, wardmote inquest juries were instructed to "present the names of all persones within your said Wardes which late hath commytted or doon any aduoutry, and the names also of

all suche persones with whom such aduoutry is doon, wheþere thei be common Aduouterers or not." Journal 8, fol. 49v (see also Letter Book K, fol. 179r, *c.* 1439 [*CLBK*, 230–31]). The Commissary court act books indicate that people were commonly charged with adultery before the ecclesiastical court after (and because of) their indictment for adultery in their wards: see some cases from the early 1470s, e.g., GL, 9064/1, fols. 7v, 15v, 16r, 20v, 45v, 58r, 63r, 65v, 66r, 84v. For discussion of the prosecution of sexual offenses in the leet courts of market towns in the fifteenth century, see McIntosh, *Controlling Misbehavior*, 69–74.

      33. GL, 9064/3, fol. 220r; GL, 9064/4, fol. 212v; GL, 9064/6, fols. 43r, 141r.

      34. GL, 9064/1, fol. 56v; GL, 9064/6, fol. 179r; see also GL, 9064/6, fol. 133r.

      35. These arguments challenge the strict double standard—for women sexual reputation was everything, for men it was irrelevant—that some have posited for late medieval society (see, for instance, Karras, *Common Women*, 31, 42–43, 52–53, 76, 134; see also Keith Thomas, "The Double Standard," *Journal of the History of Ideas* 20 [1959]: 195–216; Susan Dwyer Amussen, *An Ordered Society: Gender and Class in Early Modern England* [Oxford: Blackwell, 1988], 102–4; Laura Gowing, "Gender and the Language of Insult in Early Modern London," *History Workshop Journal* 35 [1993]: 1–21; Gowing, *Domestic Dangers*, 1–5, 30–110). Others have also disputed the double standard: see McIntosh, *Controlling Misbehavior*, 73–74, arguing (as I am) that sexual reputation was important for both men and women; and Goldberg, *Women, Work, and Life Cycle*, 153–57, 232, 330, and Hanawalt, *Growing Up in Medieval London*, 121, 186–88, who contend that chastity was *not* particularly important for late medieval women (or men) below the elite, Goldberg referring particularly to the early fifteenth century. For the early modern period, Capp, "Double Standard Revisited," has challenged the double-standard model in much the same terms as I have here for the fifteenth century. On gender and sexual reputation generally, see also Poos, "Sex, Lies"; Guido Ruggiero, " 'More Dear to Me Than Life Itself ': Marriage, Honor, and a Woman's Reputation in the Renaissance," in *Binding Passions: Tales of Magic, Marriage, and Power at the End of the Renaissance* (New York: Oxford University Press, 1993), 57–87; Lyndal Roper, " 'The Common Man,' 'The Common Good,' 'Common Women': Gender and Meaning in the German Reformation Commune," *Social History* 12 (1987): 1–21; Roper, *Oedipus and the Devil*, 40–41, 46, 65, 107, 119–20.

      36. See Roper, "Common Man"; Karras, *Common Women*, 10–11, 86, 138; Jacques Rossiaud, *Medieval Prostitution*, trans. Lydia G. Cochrane (Oxford: Blackwell, 1988), 32–37.

      37. Gowing, *Domestic Dangers*, 122–23.

      38. GL, 9065, fols. 182r–183v.

      39. I would, however, argue that it was not constructed *entirely* of their sexual reputation as some historians have alleged (see, e.g., Karras, *Common Women*, 31); it was possible for a woman to be defamed or slandered for misdeeds regarding her property or her occupation. See, for instance, TNA, PRO, C 1/31/493 (a woman accused of not being "true" after allegedly stealing her master's property);

LMA, DL/C/205, fols. 162r–164v (a woman defamed as a leper, which harmed her trade as an ale-brewster).

40. D'Evelyn, *Peter Idley's Instructions to His Son*, 83.

41. CLRO, Journals 5–8 and 10, passim (e.g., Journal 5, fols. 39v, 71r, 72r, 107r, 244r; Journal 6, Photo 136 [fol. 174r], Photo 297 [fol. 169v], Photo 445 [fol. 3v]; Journal 7, fols. 12r, 25v, 29r, 34v, 50r, 51r, 153v, 177r, 200r; Journal 8, fols. 20r, 89r, 120r, 178v; Journal 10, fols. 3v–4v, 12r, 16v, 25v, 43v, 47r, 60v, 70r, 97v, 98v, 101v, 104r, 147v).

42. LMA, DL/C/205, fols. 283v–290v.

43. "Prefatus Willelmus Boteler dixit huic iurato circiter idem tempus quod quidam Johannes Stampe carnaliter cognouit quamdam Johannam Folke, quorum pretextu status et bona fama prefate Johanne Folke quam prefati Johannis Stampe multum ledebantur et grauabantur." LMA, DL/C/205, fol. 305r.

44. TNA, PRO, C 1/45/46. See also TNA, PRO, C 1/32/34.

45. Karras, *Common Women*, 11.

46. CLRO, Journal 8, fol. 48r.

47. CLRO, Letter Book H, fol. 146v; Riley, *Liber Albus*, 1:457

48. See CLRO, Journal 5, fols. 7v, 54r; Journal 8, fols. 49rv; Journal 10, fol. 31v; P&MR, roll A50, m. 7b; *CPMR*, 4:138. Although the word, deriving grammatically from a male form, is almost always applied to men, in one case a woman was labeled "a comon puterer and an harlotte of her body." CLRO, Portsoken ward presentments, m. 2. The 1494 entry in a London chronicle (MS Vitellius A XVI) uses the word *putry* as the correlative of *bawdry* in its account of a man who was convicted in a civic court of being "a comon putrer of his body" (Lethbridge, *Chronicles of London*, 200; CLRO, Journal 10, fol. 31v).

49. CLRO, P&MR, roll A50, m. 6; *CPMR*, 4:127.

50. This word was not frequently used (*bawd* or the Latin *pronuba* were far more common), but it occurs, in relation to men only, in wardmote presentments recorded in CLRO, Journal 5, fol. 53r (1451) and Journal 8, fols. 47r–49r (1473), and in defamations recorded in GL, 9064/2, fols. 55r, 193r; GL, 9065, fol. 116v.

51. GL, 9065, fols. 70rv, 85r, 86v, 184r, 267r; TNA, PRO, C 1/45/24, C 1/70/126.

52. See especially Goldberg, *Women, Work, and Life Cycle*, 7, 155–57, 261–63, 276–78.

53. GL, 9065, fols. 2rv.

54. As the *OED* (s.v. "knight") notes—although assigning the earliest instances to the late sixteenth century—this term denoted "one who got his living by giving false evidence."

55. GL, 9065, fols. 1r–2v, 90r–93r.

56. For other examples, see LMA, DL/C/205, fols. 79v–80v, 83v–84r, 221r–225v, 234v–240v, 257v–258v, 262v, 263r, 304v–306r; TNA, PRO, C 1/27/417; CLRO, P&MR, roll A50, m. 6 (*CPMR*, 4:124); roll A51, m. 2b (*CPMR*, 4:152); roll A51, m. 3 (*CPMR*, 4:154).

57. Legrand, *Good Maners*, sigs. D6r, E1r–E5v (quotation at sig. E2v); see also La Tour Landry, *The book of the knight of La Tour-Landry*, 170 .

58. LMA, DL/C/205, fols. 304v–305v (his original testimony at fols. 270rv). For such punishments, see Riley, *Liber Albus,* 456–60; CLRO, Letter Book I, fol. 290r (*CLBI,* 286–87); Letter Book K, fols. 11rv (*CLBK,* 16–17); Letter Book L, fols. 275v, 282rv (*CLBL,* 269, 276).

59. La Tour Landry and Caxton, *The booke which the knyght of the toure made,* sig. D2r.

60. See the London Commissary court act books for 1470–1501 (GL, 9064/1–8), which record many prosecutions before that ecclesiastical court for fornication, adultery, bawdry, and defamation for sexual offenses, men and women being cited in roughly equal numbers (see Wunderli, *London Church Courts,* 86). For examples of prosecutions of men for sexual misbehavior by London civic officials, see CLRO, Letter Book H, fol. 238r (*CLBH,* 339); Letter Book I, fols. 286r–290r (*CLBI,* 273–87); Letter Book L, fols. 83r, 106rv, 123r, 275v (*CLBL,* 103, 125–26, 145, 269); CLRO, Portsoken ward presentments, mm. 12, 14; CLRO, Journal 2, fol. 107v; Journal 4, fols. 37v, 52r, 62rv, 65v, 75v, 82r, 84v, 92v, 106v–107v, 122r, 134v, 141v, 149v, 208v; Journal 5, fols. 52v, 53r, 54r, 60v, 61v, 116v, 135v, 161r, 173r, 182rv, 188v–189r, 195v, 214r, 214v, 217rv, 248v, 251r, 252r; Journal 6, Photo 184 (fol. 241v), Photo 360 (fol. 217v), Photo 512 (fol. 20r), Photo 519 (fol. 7v); Journal 7, fols. 18r, 57v, 59v, 92v, 148v, 167rv, 173r, 188v–189r, 193r, 206r; Journal 8, fols. 14r, 15v, 18r, 47r–48r, 49r, 87v–88r, 92r, 92v, 142r, 153v, 177r; Journal 9, fols. 230v, 264rv, 294r, 295rv, 296v, 297r; Journal 10, fols. 1v, 3v, 31v, 78v; CLRO, P&MR, roll A50, mm. 5ab, 6ab (*CPMR,* 4:122, 124, 127, 131, 134); roll A51, m. 3a (*CPMR,* 4:154); roll A71, m. 4b (*CPMR,* 5:72); roll A72, m. 3v (*CPMR,* 5:88); roll A90, mm. 1a–2b (*CPMR,* 6:57–64). Marjorie McIntosh has similarly found that juries in local courts outside London presented both men and women for sexual offenses. McIntosh, *Controlling Misbehavior,* 71–74.

61. McIntosh, *Controlling Misbehavior,* 167–68.

62. Thomas and Thornley, *Great Chronicle of London,* 222; CLRO, Journal 8, fols. 47r–60r.

63. Stephanie Tarbin, "Tropes of Behaviour: The Prosecution of Sexual Misconduct in Fifteenth-Century London," unpublished paper.

64. E.g., LMA, DL/C/205, fols. 86r, 147v–148r, 158v, 244r–246r, 248v, 249r, 268v; Thrupp, *Merchant Class,* 15–16. McIntosh has found that those marginal to the local community were more likely to be presented by juries than those who were at the center. McIntosh, *Controlling Misbehavior,* 12–13, 96–97, 191.

65. On the pillory and public punishments more generally in late medieval London, see Benson, *Public Piers Plowman,* 228–45.

66. Lansing suggests this for female sexual identities in thirteenth-century Bologna. Lansing, "Concubines, Lovers, Prostitutes," 85–86.

67. CLRO, P&MR, roll A71, m. 4b (*CPMR,* 5:72). Margaret Kirby, formerly one of Fynse's servants, claimed in 1446 that Fynse's wife "lette the said Marget to ferme [i.e. rented her out]" to a friar, for the price of a piece of cloth and 40s. in money. CLRO, Journal 4, fol. 66v.

68. CLRO, P&MR, roll A90, mm. 1–2b (*CPMR,* 6:57–64).

69. CLRO, P&MR, roll A90, mm. 1–2b (*CPMR,* 6:57–64). I have not found Robert Marchall's will, although Thrupp makes a cryptic reference to it (*Mer-*

chant Class, 283 n. 102) and says that he died in 1446. Robert Marchall was sheriff of London in 1439–40 (*CLBK*, 229, 231, 241, 244).

70. Horrox, "Shore, Elizabeth."

71. Hanham, *Cely Letters*, 50, 81–82, 92–94, 107, 128–30, 156, 167, 173.

72. CLRO, P&MR, roll A72, m. 3b (*CPMR*, 5:88).

73. Harris, *Aristocratic Women*, 82–84. Illegitimate children fathered by gentle or aristocratic men, especially in their youth before marriage, were common and often accepted by their families, sometimes brought up in the households of their legitimate relatives. Among the Pastons, for instance, John (III) Paston, then about twenty-four, wrote to his mother Margaret to make sure that she was caring for his "little Jack" properly and seeing to his education. Davis, *Paston Letters*, 1:540; see also 579, 597. Sir John (II) Paston writes to his brother John (III) at another point of "my little Tom," another possible reference to a bastard son. Ibid., 1:415. This apparently open acknowledgment of bastards (and family responsibility for them) may have caused some pursed lips on Margaret's part, given that she apparently disapproved strongly enough of fornication to have a male servant dismissed for having sex with a "quene" or whore. Ibid., 1:635.

The story of a troubled gentry marriage in mid-fifteenth-century Norfolk suggests both that a gentlewoman's adultery was a serious matter and that even male adultery, or at least the putting aside of a wife, could be a cause for grave concern. John Heydon, a Norfolk lawyer of humble stock, who had risen to the rank of gentleman and political player in the tumultuous world of mid-fifteenth-century politics, had an uneasy marriage with Eleanor, daughter of another local Norfolk gentleman (Anthony Smith, "Heydon, John [*d.* 1479]," *ODNB*, http://www.oxforddnb.com/view/article/52787, accessed 26 May 2005). In Norfolk politics he aligned opposite to the Pastons, and his marital problems were a subject of gleeful gossip in the Paston letters: in 1444, Margaret reported to her husband that Eleanor had recently had a child, but that her husband would have nothing to do with it or her, as he believed that the child was not his; as Margaret wrote to John, "I heard say that he said if she came in his presence to make her excuse, that he should cut off her nose to make her known [for] what she is, and if her child come in his presence, he said he would kill [it]. He will not be entreated to have her again in no wise, as I heard say." Davis, *Paston Letters*, 1:220. By 1450, things were apparently no better between the couple: a family functionary reported to John Paston another piece of gossip regarding the Heydons, that Chief Justice Markham had chided Heydon "that he lived ungoodly in putting away his wife and kept another," whereupon Heydon "turned pale color" and replied that "he lived not but as God was pleased with." Ibid., 2:51.

74. See Mary Dormer Harris, ed., *Coventry Leet Book, 1420–1555*, 4 parts (continuously paginated), EETS, Original Series 134–35, 138, 146 (London: K. Paul, Trench, Trübner, 1907–13): 544–45, 568.

75. CLRO, Journal 4, fol. 82r (1445); Journal 5, fol. 16r (1449); Journal 7, fol. 92v (1465); Journal 8, fol. 32r (1472).

76. See McIntosh, *Controlling Misbehavior*, 13–14, 128, 158–64, 175–77; McIntosh, "Finding Language for Misconduct"; Goldberg, *Women, Work, and Life Cycle*, 7, 155–57, 261–63, 276–78. Margaret Spufford, "Puritanism and Social

Control?" in *Order and Disorder in Early Modern England*, ed. Anthony Fletcher and John Stevenson (Cambridge: Cambridge University Press, 1985), 41–57, suggests that the so-called Puritan attempts to control behavior from the 1580s onward were paralleled by similar efforts in the early fourteenth century; she connects in both cases anxiety about misbehavior to difficult economic conditions.

77. Vergil, *Three Books*, 117, 172. See also Philippe de Comines, *The History of Comines, Englished by Thomas Danett Anno 1596*, 2 vols. (New York: AMS Press, 1967), 2:120.

78. TNA, PRO, C 1/45/139.

79. Gairdner, *Historical Collections of a Citizen*, 207.

80. GL, 9064/3, fol. 179v. Another case mentioning "Master Paston" is at GL, 9064/2, fol. iv. William Paston II (1436–96) lived in London from 1474, while William III (1459 to after 1503) is known to have visited London in the early 1480s. Davis, *Paston Letters*, 1:lvii, lxiii.

81. Caroline Barron, "Chivalry, Pageantry and Merchant Culture in Medieval London," in *Heraldry, Pageantry and Social Display in Medieval England*, ed. Peter Coss and Maurice Keen (Woodbridge: Sutton, 2002), 219–41, esp. 239–41; Thrupp, *Merchant Class*, 265–69.

82. GL, 9064/5, fol. 26r; see also GL, 9064/4, fols. 101v, 128v, 228v, 269r; GL, 9064/8, fol. 217v; CLRO, Journal 10, fols. 109r; 148r.

83. GL, 9064/1, fols. 8v, 41r, 43r, 50r; GL, 9064/3, fol. 6v; GL, 9064/4, fols. 10r, 13r; CLRO, Journal 10, fol. 78v.

84. TNA, PRO, C 1/214/91.

85. Another case that probably involves a foreigner was the citation of Janus Justinian before the Commissary court, accused of secretly abducting and violently carrying off Parnell Payne from her father's house. GL, 9064/4, fol. 18v.

86. See Karras, *Common Women*, passim.

87. Roper, *Oedipus and the Devil*, 108–9, 119–20.

88. Cited in Karras, *Common Women*, 96; Larry Poos first brought the case to my attention.

89. GL, 9064/4A, fol. 7v, and GL, 9064/3, fol. 214r; see also GL, 9064/3, fol. 100v; GL, 9064/4, fol. 37r; GL, 9064/5, fol. 18v; GL, 9064/6, fols. 76v, 89r, 127r, 159r. For early modern sexual boasting, see Capp, "Double Standard Revisited," 71.

90. See, on this, Neal, "Meanings of Masculinity," 290–91.

91. *CLBK*, 230–31; see also Riley, *Liber Albus*, 456. McIntosh, *Controlling Misbehavior* and "Finding Language for Misconduct," describes attempts by local jurors—perhaps more concerned with not encroaching on ecclesiastical jurisdiction than were Londoners?—to find secular rather than religious language that justified prosecution of sexual offenses.

92. On processions, see Mervyn James, "Ritual, Drama and Social Body in the Late Medieval English Town," *Past & Present* 98 (1983): 3–29. On interdependence of religious guilds and civic hierarchy, see the case of Coventry, in Charles Phythian-Adams, *Desolation of a City: Coventry and the Urban Crisis of*

the Late Middle Ages (Cambridge: Cambridge University Press, 1979), 102, 112, 118–25, 137–39; Mary Dormer Harris and G. Templeman, eds., *Register of the Guild of the Holy Trinity, St. Mary, St. John the Baptist and St. Katherine of Coventry*, 2 vols., Dugdale Society, 13, 19 (Oxford: Oxford University Press, 1935, 1944), 1:xviii. Hanawalt and McRee, "Guilds of *homo prudens*," 171, discuss the importance of religious guilds in reinforcing wealth and status.

93. This interpretation differs from that of Caroline Barron: she argues that London civic culture was becoming increasingly secular. Barron, *London in the Later Middle Ages*, 2, 267. Instead I see growing laicization rather than secularization.

94. Eamon Duffy, *The Stripping of the Altars: Traditional Religion in England, 1400–1580* (New Haven, Conn.: Yale University Press, 1992), describes similar ideas, although Duffy ascribes this style of Catholicism to a much wider proportion of the population than I do. Hanawalt and McRee, "Guilds of *homo prudens*," note the strict moral codes established by late medieval religious guilds.

95. See especially Keith Wrightson and David Levine, *Poverty and Piety in an English Village: Terling, 1525–1700* (New York: Academic Press, 1979), esp. 125–41, 155–85.

96. Personal e-mail correspondence, 8, 18 June 2004.

97. See, e.g., Charles Ross, "Rumour, Propaganda and Popular Opinion during the Wars of the Roses," in *Patronage, the Crown and the Provinces in Late Medieval England*, ed. Ralph A. Griffiths (Gloucester: Alan Sutton, 1981), 27–28.

98. Thomas Rymer, ed., *Foedera, conventiones, literae, et cujuscunque generis acta publica*, 20 vols. (London: J. Tonson, 1726–35) 12:204, available at *Gallica: La bibliothèque numérique de la Bibliothèque de France*, 1995, http://visualisateur.bnf.fr/Visualiseur?Destination=Gallica&O=NUMM-93491, retrieved 19 January 2005.

99. Ibid.

100. Rosemary Horrox, ed., "Richard III: Parliament of 1484, Text and Translation," item 1, in *PROME* (*RP*, 6:240).

101. TNA, PRO, PCC Prob. 11/8, fol. 133v, "Testamentum Magistri Willelmi Hobbys. In dei nomine Amen, cui ego Willelmus Hobbys lego animam meam, quia sibi pertinet ex oracione, et supplico Beatissime Marie matri Jhesu et omnibus sanctis ut me adiuuent in exitu spiritus anime mee, et sic spero contra omnes catenas diabolorum et eciam quia verum lumen expellit omnem tenebrositatem et omnes sancti sunt in lumine vero quia sunt in deo et deus in eis, quapropter inuoco adiutorium precitum et tunc sum certus quod nullus diabolorum erit ausus appropinquare talem presentie quia sunt omnes tenebrosi ubi nulla est comparacio adhuc potestas est eius, racione cuius omnia possunt existere et agere et deus est potens et omnes creatura habent potestatem ab ipse tunc sequitur quod potencia sanctorum semper et continue precessit potenciam demonum quare confortatur cor meum per spem quam habeo in vulneribus Christi et in Maria matre eius et in omnibus sanctis."

102. Young, *Annals of the Barber-Surgeons*, 3; Talbot and Hammond, *Medical Practitioners*, 296.

Conclusion

1. Philippe Ariès and Georges Duby, eds., *Histoire de la vie privée*, 5 vols. (Paris: Seuil, 1985–87), published in English as *A History of Private Life*, 5 vols. (Cambridge, Mass.: Harvard University Press, 1987–91). Subsequent references are to the English translation. On its scholarly success, see, for instance, the reviews of the medieval volume by John W. Baldwin (*The American Historical Review* 94 [1989]: 1355–56) and James Brundage (*Speculum* 64 [1989]: 939–41).

2. Baldwin, "Review," 1355.

3. Georges Duby, ed., *Revelations of the Medieval World*, trans. Arthur Goldhammer, vol. 2, *A History of Private Life*, ix (italics mine).

4. Recent critiques of *A History of Private Life* include Felicity Riddy's acute observations on the medieval volume in "Looking Closely," 214–15, and Carolyn Dean's essay on the twentieth-century volume "Speculations on Privacy, Identity, and the History of Sexuality in France," *Working Paper Series in European Studies* 4, no. 1 (2001), available at http://uw-madisonces.org/papers/dean .pdf, accessed 14 June 2003.

5. Duby, *Revelations*, ix.

6. Ibid., 157, see also x, xi, 8.

7. Ibid., xi.

8. LMA, DL/C/205, fols. 262v–264r.

9. See earlier discussion in Chapter 6.

10. Arnold, *Select Cases of Trespass*, 1:170–71; this entry came to my attention through a reference in Diane Shaw, "The Construction of the Private in Medieval London," *Journal of Medieval and Early Modern Studies* 26 (1996): 461.

11. Brief of Petitioners, *Lawrence v. Texas*, 2002 U.S. Briefs 02–102 (16 January 2003), 2–3.

12. Ibid., i, 3. As the petitioners' brief to the Supreme Court put it, "the charges rested solely on consensual, adult sexual relations with a partner of the same sex in the privacy of Lawrence's home." In oral argument on 26 March 2003, the petitioners' advocate, Paul M. Smith, said, "So you really have a tradition of respect for the privacy of couples in their home, going back to the founding [of the United States]." Quoted in Linda Greenhouse, "Court Appears Ready to Reverse Sodomy Law," *The New York Times*, 27 March 2003, A18.

13. *Lawrence v. Texas*, 539 U.S. 558 (2003), available at http://www .supremecourtus.gov/opinions/02pdf/02-102.pdf (dated 26 June 2003; last accessed 14 March 2004), 6.

14. Quoted in Geoffrey Stevens, "Bill Overhauls Criminal Code," *The Globe and Mail*, 22 December 1967, 1.

15. Repeat offenders might be banished from the city. See Riley, *Liber Albus*, 275, 283, 332, 337–38, 456–60; CLRO, Letter Book L, fols. 83r, 275v–276r, 282rv (*CLBL*, 103, 269, 276).

16. See, for instance, GL, 9065, fols. 48v–49v, 53v–55r, 197v.

17. Other similar complaints dating from 1302 to 1427—all using the word *secreta*—can be found in CLRO, misc. roll DD, mm. 3, 14d, 54, 54d, 55d, 57, 60,

61d, 63, 63d, 66, 66d, 72; misc. roll FF, mm. 11, 12, 12d, 15, 16, 21d, 24d, 37; misc. roll II, mm. 1d, 2, 3, 5, 5d, 7, 7d, 9, 10, 11. I used as my guide through the rolls Helena M. Chew and William Kellaway, eds., *London Assize of Nuisance 1301–1431: A Calendar*, London Record Society 10 (London: London Record Society, 1973), although my translation of the rolls here differs.

18. "habent in eodem tenemento suo duas magnas fenestras versus huiusmodi gardinum predictum apertas per quas tenentes et alii seruientes eorundum tenencium secreta dicti Roberti, seruiencium, et tenencium suorum vident ad graue nocumentum ipsius Roberti et contra consuetudinem ipsius Roberti et contra consuetudinem supradictam, etc." CLRO, misc. roll II, m. 9.

19. See, e.g., CLRO, misc. roll DD, mm. 49d, 54. In other situations, *secreta* could refer to insider knowledge both about skills and about domestic life: an apprentice's oath commonly required him, for instance, to keep his master's counsels or secrets. See, e.g., "Indenture of Apprenticeship, Temp. Ric. II," *The Archaeological Journal* 29 (1872): 184–85; Charles M. Clode, *Early History of the Merchant Taylors* (London: Harrison and Sons, 1888–[89]), 344.

20. Shaw, "Construction," 447–66 (quotation at 459).

21. Ibid., esp. 450, 459.

22. Feminist discussion of the liberal paradigm helped me formulate my argument here: Catherine A. MacKinnon, "Privacy v. Equality: Beyond Roe v. Wade," in *Feminism Unmodified: Discourses on Life and Law* (Cambridge, Mass.: Harvard University Press, 1987), 93–102; Jennifer Nedelsky, "Law, Boundaries, and the Bounded Self," *Representations* 30 (1990): 162–89; Linda C. McClain, "Inviolability and Privacy: The Castle, the Sanctuary, and the Body," *Yale Journal of Law and the Humanities* 7 (1995): 195–241; Anita L. Allen, "The Jurispolitics of Privacy," in *Reconstructing Political Theory: Feminist Perspectives*, ed. Mary Lyndon Shanley and Uma Narayan (University Park: Pennsylvania State University Press, 1997), 68–83. A convenient compendium of objections to the liberal paradigm coming from the political right can be found in Justice Scalia's dissent in *Lawrence v. Texas* (see note 13 above).

23. Fredric L. Cheyette, *Ermengard of Narbonne and the World of the Troubadours* (Ithaca, N.Y.: Cornell University Press, 2001), 234.

24. Hartman, *Household*.

Appendix

1. See, on marital litigation, Sheehan, *Marriage, Family, and Law*; Helmholz, *Marriage Litigation*; Donahue, "Canon Law"; Poos, "Heavy-Handed Marriage Counsellor"; Pedersen, *Marriage Disputes*; Goldberg, *Women, Work, and Life Cycle*, 203–79; Ingram, "Spousals Litigation"; Ralph Houlbrooke, *Church Courts and the People during the English Reformation* (Oxford: Oxford University Press, 1979), 56–67, 83–85. On Consistory courts, see Wunderli, *London Church Courts*, 7–9; Woodcock, *Medieval Ecclesiastical Courts*; Colin Morris, "A Consistory Court in the Middle Ages," *Journal of Ecclesiastical History* 14 (1963):

150–59; Sandra Lee Parker and L. R. Poos, "A Consistory Court from the Diocese of Rochester, 1363–4," *English Historical Review* 106 (1991): 652–65; R. W. Dunning, "The Wells Consistory Court in the Fifteenth Century," *Proceedings of the Somersetshire Archaeological and Natural History Society* 106 (1962): 46–61; James A. Brundage, "The Bar of the Ely Consistory Court in the Fourteenth Century: Advocates, Proctors, and Others," *Journal of Ecclesiastical History* 43 (1992): 541–60, esp. 551–54. A useful guide to the English medieval ecclesiastical courts is Charles Donahue Jr., *The Records of the Medieval Ecclesiastical Courts*, vol. 2, *England* (Berlin: Duncker and Humbolt, 1994).

2. From LMA, DL/C/205, and GL, 9065 and GL, 9065B. These comprise all the surviving depositions for the London Consistory court before 1500.

3. *Calendar of papal registers.*

4. GL, 9064/1 through 9064/8. On the London Commissary court, see Wunderli, *London Church Courts*, esp. 10–15; on lower-level church courts more generally, see Poos, *Lower Ecclesiastical Jurisdiction.*

5. See Wunderli, *London Church Courts*, 15–19.

6. GL, MSS 9171/5 through 9171/8; TNA, PRO, PCC Prob. 11.

7. A useful commentary on the records in the Corporation of London Record Office, and the bodies that produced them, is Barron, *London in the Later Middle Ages*, 121–46.

8. On Early Chancery, see Margaret Avery, "The History of the Equitable Jurisdiction of Chancery before 1460," *Bulletin of the Institute of Historical Research* 42 (1969): 129–44; Timothy S. Haskett, "The Medieval English Court of Chancery," *Law and History Review* 14 (1996): 245–311; Haskett, "Conscience, Justice and Authority in the Late-Medieval English Court of Chancery," in *Expectations of the Law in the Middle Ages*, ed. A. J. Musson (Woodbridge: Boydell Press, 2001), 151–63.

Bibliography

PRIMARY SOURCES: MANUSCRIPT

Kew, National Archives (Public Record Office)
    C 1 (Early Chancery Proceedings)
    KB 29 (Court of King's Bench: Crown Side: Controlment Rolls)
    Prerogative Court of Canterbury, Prob. 11 (Will Registers)
London, British Library
    Additional MS 18,629
London, Corporation of London Record Office
    Card Index to Journals 1 through 6, compiled by Caroline Barron
    Journals of the Court of Common Council, Journals 2 through 10
    Letter Books H through L
    Miscellaneous Rolls
    Plea and Memoranda Rolls
    Portsoken Ward Presentments, 1465–82 and 1507
    Repertory Book of the Court of Aldermen, vol. 1
London, Guildhall Library
    MSS 9064/1 through 9064/8, Act Books of the Commissary Court of the
        Diocese of London, 1470–1500
    MSS 9065 and 9065B, Consistory Court of the Diocese of London Deposition
        Book, 1487–97
    MS 9168/1, Commissary Court of London Probate Act Book
    MSS 9171/5 to 9171/8, Commissary Court of London Will Registers
London Metropolitan Archives
    MS DL/C/205, Consistory Court of the Diocese of London Deposition Book,
        1467–76.

PRIMARY SOURCES: PRINTED

*Acts of Chapter of the Collegiate Church of SS. Peter and Wilfrid, Ripon, A.D. 1452
    to A.D. 1506.* Surtees Society 64. Durham: Andrews, 1874.
Amt, Emilie, ed. *Women's Lives in Medieval Europe: A Sourcebook.* New York:
    Routledge, 1993.
Arnold, Morris S., ed. *Select Cases of Trespass from the King's Courts, 1307–1399.* 2
    vols. Selden Society, 100, 103. London: Selden Society, 1985, 1987.

Baildon, W. P., ed. *The Records of the Honorable Society of Lincoln's Inn: The Black Books.* 4 vols. London: Lincoln's Inn, 1897.

Burgess, Clive, ed. *The Church Records of St. Andrew Hubbard Eastcheap, c. 1450–c. 1570.* London Record Society, 34. London: London Record Society, 1999.

Calendar of Entries in the Papal Registers Relating to Great Britain and Ireland: Papal Letters. Edited by William Henry Bliss, Charles Johnson, and Jesse Alfred Twemlow. 18 vols. London: HMSO/Irish Manuscripts Commission, 1893–1955.

Calendar of Inquisitions Post Mortem . . . . Henry VII. 3 vols. London: Public Record Office, 1898–1955.

Calendar of Patent Rolls Preserved in the Public Record Office: Henry VII. 2 vols. London: Public Record Office, 1914–16.

Carpenter, Christine, ed. *Kingsford's Stonor Letters and Papers, 1290–1483.* Cambridge: Cambridge University Press, 1996.

Chaucer, Geoffrey. *The Riverside Chaucer.* 3rd ed. General editor Larry Benson. Boston: Houghton Mifflin, 1987.

Chew, Helena M., and William Kellaway, eds. *London Assize of Nuisance, 1301–1431: A Calendar.* London Record Society, 10. London: London Record Society, 1973.

Comines, Philippe de. *The History of Comines, Englished by Thomas Danett Anno 1596.* 2 vols. New York: AMS Press, 1967.

Cooke, Alice M., ed. *Act Book of the Ecclesiastical Court of Whalley, 1510–1538.* Chetham Society, New Series 44. Manchester: Chetham Society, 1901.

Davies, Matthew P., ed. *The Merchant Taylors' Company of London: Court Minutes, 1486–1493.* Stamford, U.K.: Richard III and Yorkist History Trust in association with Paul Watkins, 2000.

Davis, Norman, ed. *The Paston Letters and Papers of the Fifteenth Century.* 2 vols. Oxford: Clarendon Press, 1971, 1976.

D'Evelyn, Charlotte, ed. *Peter Idley's Instructions to His Son.* Boston: D. C. Heath, 1935.

Du Boulay, F. R. H., ed. *Registrum Thome Bourgchier Cantuariensis Archiepiscopi.* Canterbury and York Society, 54. Oxford: Oxford University Press, 1957.

Elvey, E. M., ed. *The Courts of the Archdeaconry of Buckingham, 1483–1523.* Buckinghamshire Record Society, 19. Aylesbury: Buckinghamshire Record Society, 1975.

Evans, Joan, and Mary S. Serjeantson, eds. *English Mediaeval Lapidaries.* EETS, Original Series 190. London: Oxford University Press, 1933.

Fabyan, Robert. *The New Chronicles of England and France, In Two Parts.* London: F. C. and J. Rivington, 1811.

Furnivall, Frederick James, ed. *The Babees Book.* EETS, Original Series 32. London: Trübner, 1868.

Gairdner, James, ed. *The Historical Collections of a Citizen of London.* Camden New Series 17. London: Camden Society, 1876.

Given-Wilson, Chris, gen. ed. *The Parliament Rolls of Medieval England.* CD-ROM. Leicester: Scholarly Digital Editions, 2005.

Greene, Richard Leighton, ed. *Early English Carols*. Oxford: Clarendon Press, 1935.

Hanham, Alison, ed. *The Cely Letters, 1472–1488*. EETS, Original Series 273. London: Oxford University Press, 1974.

Harris, Mary Dormer, ed. *Coventry Leet Book, 1420–1555*. 4 vols. EETS, Original Series 134–35, 138, 146. London: K. Paul, Trench, Trübner, 1907–13.

Harris, Mary Dormer, and G. Templeman, eds. *Register of the Guild of the Holy Trinity, St. Mary, St. John the Baptist and St. Katherine of Coventry*. 2 vols. Dugdale Society, 13, 19. Oxford: Oxford University Press, 1935, 1944.

"Indenture of Apprenticeship, Temp. Ric. II." *The Archaeological Journal* 29 (1872): 182–85.

James, N. W., and A. V. James. *The Bede Roll of the Fraternity of St. Nicholas*. 2 vols. London Record Society, 39. London: London Record Society, 2004.

Kingdon, John Abernethy, ed. *Facsimile of First Volume of MS. Archives of the Worshipful Company of Grocers of the City of London, A.D. 1345–1463*. 2 vols. London: Richard Clay and Sons, 1886.

Kingsford, Charles Lethbridge, ed. *Chronicles of London*. Oxford: Oxford University Press, 1905. Reprint, Gloucester: Alan Sutton, 1977.

Kirby, Joan, ed. *The Plumpton Letters and Papers*. Camden 5th ser., 8. Cambridge: Cambridge University Press for the Royal Historical Society, 1996.

La Tour Landry, Geoffroy de. *The Book of the Knight of La Tour-Landry, Compiled for the Instruction of His Daughters*. Rev. ed. Edited by Thomas Wright. New York: Greenwood Press, 1969.

La Tour Landry, Geoffroy de, and William Caxton. *Here begynneth the booke which the knyght of the toure made and speketh of many fayre ensamples and thensygnementys and techyng of his doughters*. Westminster: William Caxton, 1484; STC 15296.

Langland, William. *Piers the Plowman*. Edited by Walter W. Skeat. Oxford: Oxford University Press, 1886.

Lawrence v. Texas, 539 U.S. 558 (2003).

Lawrence v. Texas, Brief of Petitioners, 2002 U.S. Briefs 02–102 (16 January 2003).

Legrand, Jacques, and William Caxton. *Here begynneth a lytell boke called Good Maners*. Westminster: Wynkyn de Worde, 1498.

Littlehales, Henry, ed. *The Medieval Records of a London City Church, St. Mary at Hill, 1420–1559*. Early English Text Society, O.S., 125 and 128. London: Kegan Paul, Trench, Trübner & Co., 1904–5.

Lyell, Laetitia, and Frank D. Watney, eds. *Acts of the Court of the Mercers' Company, 1453–1527*. Cambridge: Cambridge University Press, 1936.

Lyndwood, William. *Provinciale; seu Constitutiones Angliae*. Farnborough, Hants.: Gregg International, 1968.

Magnus, Albertus. *Book of Minerals*. Translated by Dorothy Wyckoff. Oxford: Oxford University Press, 1967.

McSheffrey, Shannon, ed. *Love and Marriage in Late Medieval London*. Kalamazoo, Mich.: Medieval Institute Publications, 1995.

Missale secundum vsum Insignis Ecclesie Sarum. Westminster and Paris: Wynkyn de Worde and Michel Morin, 1497; STC 16169.

Page, William, ed. *The Victoria History of the County of Hertford.* 4 vols. London: Constable, 1902–14.

Poos, L. R. *Lower Ecclesiastical Jurisdiction in Late-Medieval England: The Courts of the Dean and Chapter of Lincoln, 1336–1349, and the Deanery of Wisbech, 1458–1484.* British Academy Records of Social Economic History, New Series 32. Oxford: Oxford University Press for the British Academy, 2001.

Riley, Henry Thomas, ed. *Memorials of London and London Life in the Thirteenth, Fourteenth, and Fifteenth Centuries.* London: Longman, 1868.

———, ed. *Munimenta Gildhallae Londoniensis.* 2 vols. Vol. 1, *Liber Albus.* Rolls Series 12. London: Longman, Brown, Green, Longmans, and Roberts, 1859.

Sharpe, Reginald R., ed. *Calendar of Letter-Books Preserved among the Archives of the Corporation of the City of London at the Guildhall.* 11 vols. (A through L). London: J. E. Francis, 1899–1912.

———, ed. *Calendar of Wills Proved and Enrolled in the Court of Husting, London, A.D. 1258–A.D. 1688.* 2 vols. London: Corporation of the City of London, 1890.

Staley, Lynn, ed. *The Book of Margery Kempe.* TEAMS Middle English Text Series. Kalamazoo, Mich.: Medieval Institute Publications, 1996.

Statutes of the Realm. 10 vols. London: Eyre and Strahan, 1810–28. Reprint, London: Dawson of Pall Mall, 1963.

Stone, E. D., and B. Cozens-Hardy, eds. *Norwich Consistory Court Depositions, 1499–1512 and 1518–30.* Norfolk Record Society 10. London: Wyman & Sons, 1938.

Strachey, J., ed. *Rotuli Parliamentorum; ut et petitiones et placita in Parliamento . . . 1278–1503.* 6 vols. London: n.p., 1783.

Thomas, A. H., ed. *Calendar of Early Mayor's Court Rolls Preserved among the Archives of the City of London at the Guildhall, AD 1298–1307.* Cambridge: Cambridge University Press, 1924.

Thomas, A. H., and Philip E. Jones, eds. *Calendar of Plea and Memoranda Rolls Preserved among the Archives of the Corporation of the City of London at the Guildhall, 1323–1482.* 6 vols. Cambridge: Cambridge University Press, 1926–61.

Thomas, A. H., and I. D. Thornley, eds. *The Great Chronicle of London.* London: George W. Jones, 1938.

Vergil, Polydore. *Three Books of Polydore Vergil's English History.* Edited by Henry Ellis. Camden 1st Ser., 29. London: J. B. Nichols, 1844. Reprint, New York: Johnson Reprint Company, 1968.

Windeatt, B. A., ed. *The Book of Margery Kempe.* Harmondsworth: Penguin Books, 1985.

Young, Sidney, ed. *Annals of the Barber Surgeons.* London: Blades, East and Blades, 1890.

SECONDARY SOURCES

Acheson, Eric. *A Gentry Community: Leicestershire in the Fifteenth Century, c. 1422–c. 1485.* Cambridge: Cambridge University Press, 1992.

Allen, Anita L. "The Jurispolitics of Privacy." In *Reconstructing Political Theory: Feminist Perspectives*, edited by Mary Lyndon Shanley and Uma Narayan, 68–83. University Park: Pennsylvania State University Press, 1997.

Amussen, Susan Dwyer. *An Ordered Society: Gender and Class in Early Modern England*. Oxford: Blackwell, 1988.

Ariès, Philippe, and Georges Duby, eds. *A History of Private Life*. 5 vols. Cambridge, Mass.: Belknap Press, 1987–91.

Austin, J. L. *How to Do Things with Words*. Edited by J. O. Urmson and Marina Sbisà. 2nd ed. Cambridge, Mass.: Harvard University Press, 1975.

Avery, Margaret. "The History of Equitable Jurisdiction of Chancery before 1460." *Bulletin of the Institute of Historical Research* 42 (1969): 129–44.

Baker, J. H. "Bryan, Sir Thomas (*d.* 1500)." *Oxford Dictionary of National Biography*. Oxford: Oxford University Press, 2004. Available from http://www.oxforddnb.com/view/article/49667, accessed 26 May 2005.

Baldwin, John W. "Review of Georges Duby, ed., *A History of Private Life*, vol. 2." *American Historical Review* 94 (1989): 1355–56.

Barron, Caroline M. "Centres of Conspicuous Consumption: The Aristocratic Town House in London, 1200–1550." *London Journal* 20 (1995): 1–16.

———. "Chivalry, Pageantry and Merchant Culture in Medieval London." In *Heraldry, Pageantry and Social Display in Medieval England*, edited by Peter Coss and Maurice Keen, 219–41. Woodbridge: Sutton, 2002.

———. "Lay Solidarities: The Wards of Medieval London." In *Law, Laity and Solidarities: Essays in Honour of Susan Reynolds*, edited by Pauline Stafford, Janet L. Nelson, and Jane Martindale, 218–33. Manchester: Manchester University Press, 2001.

———. "London 1300–1540." In *Cambridge Urban History of Britain*, vol. 1, *600–1540*, edited by David Palliser, 395–440. Cambridge: Cambridge University Press, 2000.

———. *London in the Later Middle Ages: Government and People, 1200–1500*. Oxford: Oxford University Press, 2004.

———. "The Parish Fraternities of Medieval London." In *The Church in Pre-Reformation Society: Essays in Honour of F. R. H. Du Boulay*, edited by Caroline M. Barron and Christopher Harper-Bill, 13–37. Woodbridge: Boydell, 1985.

Barron, Caroline M., and Anne F. Sutton, eds. *Medieval London Widows, 1300–1500*. London: Hambledon, 1994.

Beattie, Cordelia. "Single Women, Work, and Family: The Chancery Dispute of Jane Wynde and Margaret Clerk." In *Voices from the Bench: The Narratives of Lesser Folk in Medieval Trials*, edited by Michael Goodich. Houndmills, Hampshire: Palgrave Macmillan, forthcoming.

Bennett, Judith M. *Ale, Beer, and Brewsters in England: Women's Work in a Changing World, 1300–1600*. New York: Oxford University Press, 1996.

———. "Ventriloquisms: When Maidens Speak in English Songs, c. 1300–1550." In *Medieval Woman's Song: Cross-Cultural Approaches*, edited by Anne L. Klinck and Ann Marie Rasmussen, 187–204. Philadelphia: University of Pennsylvania Press, 2001.

Benson, C. David. *Public Piers Plowman: Modern Scholarship and Late Medieval English Culture*. University Park: Pennsylvania State University Press, 2004.

Biller, P. P. A. "Marriage Patterns and Women's Lives: A Sketch of a Pastoral Geography." In *Woman Is a Worthy Wight: Women in English Society, c. 1200–1500*, edited by P. J. P. Goldberg, 60–107. Gloucester: Alan Sutton, 1992.

Blackstone, William. *Commentaries on the Laws of England*. 4 vols. Oxford: Clarendon Press, 1765–69.

Blanchard, Ian. "Social Structure and Social Organization in an English Village at the Close of the Middle Ages: Chewton, 1526." In *The Salt of Common Life: Individuality and Choice in the Medieval Town, Countryside, and Church*, edited by Edwin Brezette DeWindt, 307–39. Kalamazoo, Mich.: Medieval Institute Publications, 1995.

Bolton, J. L. "The City and the Crown, 1456–61." *London Journal* 12 (1986): 11–24.

Bossy, John. "Blood and Baptism: Kinship, Community and Christianity in Western Europe from the Fourteenth to the Seventeenth Centuries." *Studies in Church History* 10 (1973): 129–43.

Boyd, David Lorenzo, and Ruth Mazo Karras. "The Interrogation of a Male Transvestite Prostitute in Fourteenth Century London." *GLQ: A Journal of Lesbian and Gay Studies* 1 (1995): 459–65.

———. " 'Ut cum muliere': A Male Transvestite Prostitute in Fourteenth Century London." In *Premodern Sexualities*, edited by Louise Fradenburg and Louise Freccero, 99–116. London: Routledge, 1996.

Brooke, Christopher. *The Medieval Idea of Marriage*. Oxford: Oxford University Press, 1989.

Brundage, James A. "The Bar of the Ely Consistory Court in the Fourteenth Century: Advocates, Proctors, and Others." *Journal of Ecclesiastical History* 43 (1992): 541–60.

———. *Law, Sex, and Christian Society in Medieval Europe*. Chicago: University of Chicago Press, 1987.

———. "Review of Georges Duby, ed., *A History of Private Life*, vol. 2." *Speculum: A Journal of Medieval Studies* 64 (1989): 939–41.

Burgess, Clive. "London Parishioners in Times of Change: St. Andrew Hubbard, Eastcheap, c. 1450–1570." *Journal of Ecclesiastical History* 53 (2002): 38–63.

———. "Pre-Reformation Churchwardens' Accounts and Parish Government: Lessons from London and Bristol." *English Historical Review* 117 (2002): 306–32.

———. "Shaping the Parish: St. Mary at Hill, London, in the Fifteenth Century." In *The Cloister and the World: Essays in Medieval History in Honour of Barbara Harvey*, edited by John Blair and Brian Golding, 246–86. Oxford: Oxford University Press, 1996.

———, and Beat A. Kümin. "Penitential Bequests and Parish Regimes in Late Medieval England." *Journal of Ecclesiastical History* 44 (1993): 610–30.

Burroughs, Charles. "Spaces of Arbitration and the Organization of Space in Late Medieval Italian Cities." In *Medieval Practices of Space*, edited by Barbara

Hanawalt and Michal Kobialka, 64–100. Minneapolis: University of Minnesota Press, 2000.

Butler, Sara M. "The Language of Abuse: Marital Violence in Later Medieval England." Ph.D. thesis, Dalhousie University, 2001.

Camille, Michael. "Signs of the City: Place, Power, and Public Fantasy in Medieval Paris." In *Medieval Practices of Space*, edited by Barbara Hanawalt and Michal Kobialka, 1–36. Minneapolis: University of Minnesota Press, 2000.

Capp, Bernard. "The Double Standard Revisited: Plebeian Women and Male Sexual Reputation in Early Modern England." *Past & Present* 162 (1999): 70–100.

Carlin, Martha. *Medieval Southwark*. London: Hambledon, 1996.

Carlson, Eric Josef. *Marriage and the English Reformation*. Oxford: Blackwell, 1994.

Carlton, Charles. *The Court of Orphans*. Leicester: Leicester University Press, 1974.

Chaytor, Miranda. "Household and Kinship: Ryton in the Late 16th and Early 17th Centuries." *History Workshop Journal* 10 (1980): 25–60.

Cheney, C. R. "William Lyndwood's *Provinciale*." In *Medieval Texts and Studies*, 158–84. Oxford: Clarendon Press, 1973.

Cheyette, Fredric L. *Ermengard of Narbonne and the World of the Troubadours*. Ithaca, N.Y.: Cornell University Press, 2001.

Clark, Elaine. "City Orphans and Custody Laws in Medieval England." *American Journal of Legal History* 34 (1990): 168–87.

Clark, Peter. *The English Alehouse: A Social History*. London: Longman, 1983.

Clode, Charles M. *Early History of the Merchant Taylors*. London: Harrison and Sons, 1888–89.

Cressy, David. *Birth, Marriage, and Death: Ritual, Religion, and the Life-Cycle in Tudor and Stuart England*. Oxford: Oxford University Press, 1997.

Cullum, P. H. "'And Hir Name was Charite': Charitable Giving by and for Women in Late Medieval Yorkshire." In *Woman is a Worthy Wight: Women in English Medieval Society c. 1200–1500*, edited by P. J. P. Goldberg, 182–211. Gloucester: Alan Sutton, 1992.

Davis, Natalie Zemon. "Boundaries and the Sense of Self in Sixteenth-Century France." In *Reconstructing Individualism: Autonomy, Individuality, and the Self in Western Thought*, edited by Thomas C. Heller, Morton Sosna, and David E. Wellbery, 53–63. Stanford, Calif.: Stanford University Press, 1986.

———. *Fiction in the Archives: Pardon Tales and Their Tellers in Sixteenth-Century France*. Stanford, Calif.: Stanford University Press, 1987.

Davis, Virginia. *Clergy in London in the Late Middle Ages: A Register of Clergy Ordained in the Diocese of London Based on Episcopal Ordination Lists, 1361–1539*. London: Centre for Metropolitan History, Institute of Historical Research, 2000.

Dean, Carolyn. "Speculations on Privacy, Identity, and the History of Sexuality in France." *Working Paper Series in European Studies* 4, no. 1 (2001). Available from http://uw-madison-ces.org/papers/dean.pdf (accessed 14 June 2003).

Dockray, Keith. "Why Did the Fifteenth-Century English Gentry Marry? The Pastons, Plumptons, and Stonors Reconsidered." In *Gentry and Lesser Nobility in Late Medieval England*, edited by Michael Jones, 61–80. Gloucester: Alan Sutton, 1986.

Donahue Jr., Charles. "The Canon Law on the Formation of Marriage and Social Practice in the Later Middle Ages." *Journal of Family History* 8 (1983): 144–58.

———. "Female Plaintiffs in Marriage Cases in the Court of York in the Later Middle Ages: What Can We Learn from the Numbers?" In *Wife and Widow in Medieval England*, edited by Sue Sheridan Walker, 183–213. Ann Arbor: University of Michigan Press, 1993.

———. *The Records of the Medieval Ecclesiastical Courts.* 2 vols. Berlin: Duncker and Humbolt, 1989, 1994.

Dronzek, Anna. "No Separate Spheres: The Household as Masculine and Feminine Space in Late Medieval England." Paper presented at the North American Conference on British Studies, Baltimore, Maryland, 2002.

Duby, Georges, ed. *Revelations of the Medieval World.* Vol. 2. of *A History of Private Life*. General editors Philippe Ariès and Georges Duby. Cambridge: Belknap Press, 1988.

Duffy, Eamon. *The Stripping of the Altars: Traditional Religion in England, 1400–1580.* New Haven: Yale University Press, 1992.

Dunning, R. W. "The Wells Consistory Court in the Fifteenth Century." *Proceedings of the Somersetshire Archaeology and Natural History Society* 106 (1962): 46–61.

Durkheim, Emile. *The Elementary Forms of the Religious Life.* London: G. Allen and Unwin, 1915. Reprint, New York: Free Press, 1968.

Dyer, Christopher. *Everyday Life in Medieval England.* London: Hambledon and London, 2000.

———. *Lords and Peasants in a Changing Society: The Estates of the Bishopric of Worcester, 680–1540.* Cambridge: Cambridge University Press, 1980.

Emden, A. B. *A Biographical Register of the University of Cambridge to 1500.* Cambridge: Cambridge University Press, 1963.

———. *A Biographical Register of the University of Oxford to A.D. 1500.* 3 vols. Oxford: Clarendon Press, 1957–59.

Ferrante, Lucia. "Marriage and Women's Subjectivity in a Patrilineal System: The Case of Early Modern Bologna." In *Gender, Kinship, Power: A Comparative and Interdisciplinary History*, edited by Mary Jo Maynes, Ann Waltner, Birgitte Soland, and Ulrike Strasser, 115–29. New York: Routledge, 1996.

Fitch, Marc, ed. *Index to Testamentary Records in the Commissary Court of London.* 2 vols. Historical Manuscripts Commission, Joint Publication 13. London: HMSO, 1974.

Fleming, Peter. *Family and Household in Medieval England.* New York: Palgrave, 2001.

Fletcher, Anthony. *Gender, Sex and Subordination in England, 1500–1800.* New Haven, Conn.: Yale University Press, 1995.

Foss, Edward. *The Judges of England.* 9 vols. London: Longman, Brown, Green, Longmans, and Roberts, 1848–64.

French, Katherine L. *The People of the Parish: Community Life in a Late Medieval English Diocese.* Philadelphia: University of Pennsylvania Press, 2001.

———. "'To Free Them from Binding': Women in the Late Medieval English Parish." *Journal of Interdisciplinary History* 27 (1997): 387–412.

Goheen, R. B. "Peasant Politics? Village Community and the Crown in Fifteenth-Century England." *American Historical Review* 96 (1991): 42–62.

Goldberg, P. J. P. "Household and the Organisation of Labour in Late Medieval Towns: Some English Evidence." In *The Household in Late Medieval Cities: Italy and Northwestern Europe Compared: Proceedings of the International Conference, Ghent, 21st–22nd January 2000*, edited by Myriam Carlier and Tim Soens, 59–70. Leuven-Apeldoorn: Garant, 2001.

———. "The Public and the Private: Women in the Pre-Plague Economy." In *Thirteenth-Century England III*, edited by Peter R. Coss and S. D. Lloyd, 75–89. Woodbridge: Boydell and Brewer, 1991.

———. *Women, Work, and Life Cycle in a Medieval Economy: Women in York and Yorkshire, c. 1300–1520.* Oxford: Clarendon Press, 1992.

Gottlieb, Beatrice. "The Meaning of Clandestine Marriage." In *Family and Sexuality in French History*, edited by Robert Wheaton and Tamara K. Hareven, 49–83. Philadelphia: University of Pennsylvania Press, 1980.

Gowing, Laura. *Domestic Dangers: Women, Words, and Sex in Early Modern London.* Oxford: Clarendon Press, 1996.

———. "'The Freedom of the Streets': Women and Social Space, 1560–1640." In *Londinopolis: Essays in the Cultural and Social History of Early Modern London*, edited by Paul Griffiths and Mark S. R. Jenner, 130–51. Manchester: Manchester University Press, 2000.

———. "Gender and the Language of Insult in Early Modern London." *History Workshop Journal* 35 (1993): 1–21.

Greenhouse, Linda. "Court Appears Ready to Reverse Sodomy Law." *The New York Times*, 27 March 2003, A18.

Grenville, Jane. *Medieval Housing.* London: University of Leicester Press, 1997.

Groebner, Valentin. *Liquid Assets, Dangerous Gifts: Presents and Politics at the End of the Middle Ages.* Translated by Pamela E. Selwyn. Philadelphia: University of Pennsylvania Press, 2002.

Hajnal, John. "European Marriage Patterns in Perspective." In *Population in History: Essays in Historical Demography*, edited by D. V. Glass and D. E. C. Eversley, 101–43. London: Edward Arnold, 1965.

Hanawalt, Barbara. "'Good Governance' in the Medieval and Early Modern Context." *Journal of British Studies* 37 (1998): 246–57.

———. *Growing Up in Medieval London: The Experience of Childhood in History.* New York: Oxford University Press, 1993.

———. "Medieval English Women in Rural and Domestic Space." *Dumbarton Oaks Papers* 52 (1998): 19–26.

———. *"Of Good and Ill Repute": Gender and Social Control in Medieval England.* New York: Oxford University Press, 1998.

———. *The Ties That Bound: Peasant Families in Medieval England.* New York: Oxford University Press, 1986.

Hanawalt, Barbara, and Michal Kobialka, eds. *Medieval Practices of Space*. Minneapolis: University of Minnesota Press, 2000.

Hanawalt, Barbara, and Ben R. McRee. "The Guilds of *homo prudens* in Late Medieval England." *Continuity and Change* 7 (1992): 163–79.

Hanham, Alison. *The Celys and Their World: An English Merchant Family of the Fifteenth Century*. Cambridge: Cambridge University Press, 1985.

Harris, Barbara J. *English Aristocratic Women, 1450–1550: Marriage and Family, Property and Careers*. Oxford: Oxford University Press, 2002.

Hartman, Mary S. *The Household and the Making of History: A Subversive View of the Western Past*. Cambridge: Cambridge University Press, 2004.

Haskell, Ann S. "The Paston Women on Marriage in Fifteenth-Century England." *Viator* 4 (1973): 459–71.

Haskett, Timothy S. "Conscience, Justice and Authority in the Late-Medieval English Court of Chancery." In *Expectations of the Law in the Middle Ages*, edited by A. J. Musson, 151–63. Woodbridge: Boydell Press, 2001.

———. "The Medieval English Court of Chancery." *Law and History Review* 14 (1996): 245–311.

Heath, Peter. *The English Parish Clergy on the Eve of the Reformation*. London: Routledge & Kegan Paul, 1969.

Helmholz, R. H. "Harboring Sexual Offenders: Ecclesiastical Courts and Controlling Misbehavior." *Journal of British Studies* 37 (1998): 258–68.

———. *Marriage Litigation in Medieval England*. London: Cambridge University Press, 1974.

Hiller, Bill, and Julienne Hanson. *The Social Logic of Space*. Cambridge: Cambridge University Press, 1984.

Horrox, Rosemary. "Service." In *Fifteenth-Century Attitudes: Perceptions of Society in Late Medieval England*, edited by Rosemary Horrox, 61–74. Cambridge: Cambridge University Press, 1994.

———. "Shore , Elizabeth [Jane] (*d.* 1526/7?)." *Oxford Dictionary of National Biography*. Oxford: Oxford University Press, 2004. Available from http://www.oxforddnb.com/view/article/25451, accessed 26 May 2005.

Houlbrooke, Ralph. *Church Courts and the People during the English Reformation*. Oxford: Oxford University Press, 1979.

Howell, Martha C. *The Marriage Exchange: Property, Social Place, and Gender in Cities of the Low Countries, 1300–1550*. Chicago: University of Chicago Press, 1998.

Hutton, Ronald. *The Rise and Fall of Merry England: The Ritual Year, 1400–1700*. Oxford: Oxford University Press, 1994.

Ibbetson, David. *A Historical Introduction to the Law of Obligations*. Oxford: Oxford University Press, 1999.

Ingram, Martin. *Church Courts, Sex and Marriage in England, 1570–1640*. Cambridge: Cambridge University Press, 1987.

———. "Spousals Litigation in the English Ecclesiastical Courts, c. 1350–1640." In *Marriage and Society: Studies in the Social History of Marriage*, edited by R. B. Outhwaite, 35–57. New York: St. Martin's Press, 1981.

Jacobs, Kathryn. *Marriage Contracts from Chaucer to the Renaissance Stage.* Gainesville: University Press of Florida, 2001.

James, Mervyn. "Ritual, Drama and Social Body in the Late Medieval English Town." *Past & Present* 98 (1983): 3–29.

Jenks, Stuart. "Medizinische Fachkräfte in England zur Zeit Heinrichs VI (1428/29–1460/61)." *Sudhoffs Archiv* 69 (1985): 214–27.

Johansson, Warren and William A. Percy. "Homosexuality." In *Handbook of Medieval Sexuality,* edited by Vern L. Bullough and James A. Brundage, 155–90. New York: Garland, 1999.

Kandiyoti, Deniz. "Bargaining with Patriarchy." *Gender and Society* 2 (1988): 274–90.

Karras, Ruth Mazo. *Common Women: Prostitution and Sexuality in Medieval England.* New York: Oxford University Press, 1996.

———. *From Boys to Men: Formations of Masculinity in Late Medieval Europe.* Philadelphia: University of Pennsylvania Press, 2003.

Kibre, Pearl. "Lewis of Caerleon, Doctor of Medicine, Astronomer, and Mathematician (d. 1494?)." *Isis* 43 (1952): 100–108.

Kirby, Joan W. "A Fifteenth-Century Family, the Plumptons of Plumpton, and Their Lawyers, 1461–1515." *Northern History* 25 (1989): 106–19.

Kowaleski, Maryanne. "Singlewomen in Medieval and Early Modern Europe: The Demographic Perspective." In *Singlewomen in the European Past, 1250–1800,* edited by Judith M. Bennett and Amy M. Froide, 38–81. Philadelphia: University of Pennsylvania Press, 1999.

Kümin, Beat A. *The Shaping of a Community: The Rise and Reformation of the English Parish, c. 1400–1560.* Aldershot: Scolar Press, 1996.

Lacey, Kay. "Margaret Croke (d. 1491)." In *Medieval London Widows, 1300–1500,* edited by Caroline M. Barron and Anne F. Sutton, 143–64. London: Hambledon, 1994.

Lander, J. R. "Marriage and Politics in the Fifteenth Century: The Nevilles and the Wydevilles." *Bulletin of the Institute of Historical Research* 36 (1963): 119–52.

Lansing, Carol. "Concubines, Lovers, Prostitutes: Infamy and Female Identity in Medieval Bologna." In *Beyond Florence: Contours and Medieval and Early Modern Italy,* edited by Paula Findlen, Michelle M. Fontaine and Duane J. Osheim, 85–100. Stanford, Calif.: Stanford University Press, 2003.

Latham, R. E. *Revised Medieval Latin Word-List.* London: Oxford University Press for the British Academy, 1965.

Leader, Damian Riehl. *A History of the University of Cambridge.* Vol. 1, *The University to 1546.* Cambridge: Cambridge University Press, 1988.

Lee, Becky R. "Men's Recollections of a Women's Rite: Medieval English Men's Recollections Regarding the Rite of Purification of Women after Childbirth." *Gender and History* 14 (2002): 224–41.

LeFebvre, Henri. *The Production of Space.* Oxford: Blackwell, 1991.

Macfarlane, Alan. *Marriage and Love in England: Modes of Reproduction, 1300–1840.* Oxford: Blackwell, 1986.

MacKinnon, Catherine A. *Feminism Unmodified: Discourses on Life and Law.* Cambridge, Mass.: Harvard University Press, 1987.

Massey, Doreen. *Space, Place, and Gender.* Minneapolis: University of Minnesota Press, 1994.

McClain, Linda C. "Inviolability and Privacy: The Castle, the Sanctuary, and the Body." *Yale Journal of Law and the Humanities* 7 (1995): 195–241.

McIntosh, Marjorie Keniston. *Controlling Misbehavior in England, 1370–1600.* Cambridge: Cambridge University Press, 1998.

———. "Finding Language for Misconduct: Jurors in Fifteenth-Century Local Courts." In *Bodies and Disciplines: The Intersection of Literature and History in Fifteenth-Century England,* edited by Barbara Hanawalt and David Wallace, 87–122. Minneapolis: University of Minnesota Press, 1996.

McLaren, Mary-Rose. *The London Chronicles of the Fifteenth Century: A Revolution in English Writing, with an Annotated Edition of Bradford, West Yorkshire Archives MS 32D86/42.* Cambridge: D. S. Brewer, 2002.

McRee, Ben R. "Religious Gilds and Regulation of Behavior in Late Medieval Towns." In *People, Politics and Community in the Later Middle Ages,* edited by Joel T. Rosenthal and Colin Richmond, 108–22. Gloucester: Alan Sutton, 1987.

McSheffrey, Shannon. "Jurors, Respectable Masculinity, and Christian Morality." *Journal of British Studies* 37 (1998): 269–78.

Molho, Anthony. *Marriage Alliance in Late Medieval Florence.* Cambridge, Mass.: Harvard University Press, 1994.

Morris, Colin. "A Consistory Court in the Middle Ages." *Journal of Ecclesiastical History* 14 (1963): 150–59.

Morrison, Susan Signe. *Women Pilgrims in Medieval England: Private Piety as Public Performance.* London: Routledge, 2000.

Murray, Jacqueline, ed. *Conflicted Identities and Multiple Masculinities: Men in the Medieval West.* New York: Garland, 1999.

———. "Hiding behind the Universal Man: Male Sexuality in the Middle Ages" and "Twice Marginal and Twice Invisible: Lesbians in the Middle Ages." In *Handbook of Medieval Sexuality,* edited by Vern L. Bullough and James A. Brundage, 129–39, 191–222. New York: Garland, 1996.

Musson, Anthony. *Medieval Law in Context: The Growth of Legal Consciousness from Magna Carta to the Peasants' Revolt.* Manchester: Manchester University Press, 2001.

Neal, Derek. "Meanings of Masculinity in Late Medieval England: Self, Body and Society." Ph.D. thesis, McGill University, 2004.

Nedelsky, Jennifer. "Law, Boundaries, and the Bounded Self." *Representations* 30 (1990): 162–89.

Nightingale, Pamela. "Crosby, Sir John (d. 1476)." *Oxford Dictionary of National Biography.* Oxford: Oxford University Press, 2004. http://www.oxforddnb .com/view/article/6785, accessed 8 June 2005.

———. *A Medieval Mercantile Community: The Grocers' Company and the Politics and Trade of London, 1000–1485.* New Haven, Conn.: Yale University Press, 1995.

O'Hara, Diana. *Courtship and Constraint: Rethinking the Making of Marriage in Tudor England.* Manchester: Manchester University Press, 2000.

———. "'Ruled by my friends': Aspects of Marriage in the Diocese of Canterbury, c. 1540–1570." *Continuity and Change* 6 (1991): 9–41.

Outhwaite, R. B. *Clandestine Marriage in England, 1500–1850.* London: Hambledon Press, 1995.

The Oxford English Dictionary Online. Oxford: Oxford University Press, 2005. Available from http://dictionary.oed.com.

Parker, Sandra Lee, and L. R. Poos. "A Consistory Court from the Diocese of Rochester, 1363–4." *English Historical Review* 106 (1991): 652–65.

Pearce, E. H. *The Monks of Westminster.* Cambridge: Cambridge University Press, 1916.

Pedersen, Frederik. "Did the Medieval Laity Know the Canon Law Rules on Marriage? Some Evidence from Fourteenth-Century York Cause Papers." *Mediaeval Studies* 56 (1994): 111–52.

———. *Marriage Disputes in Medieval England.* London: Hambledon, 2000.

Phythian-Adams, Charles. *Desolation of a City: Coventry and the Urban Crisis of the Late Middle Ages.* Cambridge: Cambridge University Press, 1979.

Pollock, Frederick, and Frederick William Maitland. *The History of English Law before the Time of Edward I.* 2nd ed. 2 vols. Cambridge: Cambridge University Press, 1968.

Poos, L. R. *A Rural Society after the Black Death: Essex, 1350–1525.* Cambridge: Cambridge University Press, 1991.

———. "The Heavy-Handed Marriage Counsellor: Regulating Marriage in Some Later-Medieval English Local Ecclesiastical-Court Jurisdictions." *American Journal of Legal History* 39 (1995): 291–309.

———. "Sex, Lies, and the Church Courts of Pre-Reformation England." *Journal of Interdisciplinary History* 25 (1995): 585–607.

Powell, Edward. "Arbitration and the Law in the Later Middle Ages." *Transactions of the Royal Historical Society,* 5th ser., 33 (1983): 49–67.

Power, Eileen. "The Position of Women." In *The Legacy of the Middle Ages,* edited by C. G. Crump and E. F. Jacob, 401–33. Oxford: Clarendon Press, 1926.

Puff, Helmut. "Localizing Sodomy: The 'Priest and Sodomite' in Pre-Reformation Germany and Switzerland." *Journal of the History of Sexuality* 8 (1997): 165–95.

———. *Sodomy in Reformation Germany and Switzerland, 1400–1600.* Chicago: University of Chicago Press, 2003.

Rawcliffe, Carole. *Medicine and Society in Later Medieval England.* Gloucester: Alan Sutton, 1995.

Reddaway, T. F., and Lorna E. M. Walker. *The Early History of the Goldsmiths' Company, 1327–1509.* London: Arnold, 1975.

Rees Jones, Sarah. "The Household and English Urban Government in the Later Middle Ages." In *The Household in Late Medieval Cities: Italy and Northwestern Europe Compared: Proceedings of the International Conference, Ghent, 21st–22nd January 2000,* edited by Myriam Carlier and Tim Soens, 71–87. Leuven-Apeldoorn: Garant, 2001.

———. "Women's Influence in the Design of Urban Homes." In *Gendering the Master Narrative: Medieval Women and Power*, edited by Mary Erler and Maryanne Kowaleski, 190–211. Ithaca, N.Y.: Cornell University Press, 2003.

Richmond, Colin. "Fauconberg's Kentish Rising of May 1471." *English Historical Review* 85 (1970): 673–92.

———. *The Paston Family in the Fifteenth Century: Endings*. Manchester: Manchester University Press, 2000.

———. "The Pastons Revisited: Marriage and the Family in Fifteenth-Century England." *Bulletin of the Institute of Historical Research* 58 (1985): 25–36.

Riddy, Felicity. "Looking Closely: Authority and Intimacy in the Late Medieval Urban Home." In *Gendering the Master Narrative: Women and Power in the Middle Ages*, edited by Mary C. Erler and Maryanne Kowaleski, 212–28. Ithaca, N.Y.: Cornell University Press, 2003.

———. "Mother Knows Best: Reading Social Change in a Courtesy Text." *Speculum: A Journal of Medieval Studies* 71 (1996): 66–86.

Rocke, Michael. *Forbidden Friendships: Homosexuality and Male Culture in Renaissance Florence*. New York: Oxford University Press, 1996.

Roper, Lyndal. "'The Common Man,' 'The Common Good,' 'Common Women': Gender and Meaning in the German Reformation Commune." *Social History* 12 (1987): 1–21.

———. "'Going to Church and Street': Weddings in Reformation Augsburg." *Past & Present* 106 (1985): 62–101.

———. *Oedipus and the Devil: Witchcraft, Sexuality and Religion in Early Modern Europe*. London: Routledge, 1994.

Rosenthal, Joel T. "Aristocratic Marriage and the English Peerage, 1350–1500: Social, Institutional, and Personal Bond." *Journal of Medieval History* 10 (1984): 181–94.

———. *Telling Tales: Sources and Narration in Late Medieval England*. University Park: Pennsylvania State University Press, 2003.

Ross, Charles. *Edward IV*. New Haven, Conn.: Yale University Press, 1974.

———. "Rumour, Propaganda and Popular Opinion during the Wars of the Roses." In *Patronage, the Crown and the Provinces in Late Medieval England*, edited by Ralph A. Griffiths, 15–32. Gloucester: Alan Sutton, 1981.

Rosser, Gervase. "Going to the Fraternity Feast: Commensality and Social Relations in Late Medieval England." *Journal of British Studies* 33 (1994): 430–46.

———. *Medieval Westminster, 1200–1540*. Oxford: Clarendon Press, 1989.

Rossiaud, Jacques. *Medieval Prostitution*. Translated by Lydia G. Cochrane. New York: Blackwell, 1988.

Ruggiero, Guido. *Binding Passions: Tales of Magic, Marriage, and Power at the End of the Renaissance*. New York: Oxford University Press, 1993.

Rushton, Peter. "Property, Power and Family Networks: The Problem of Disputed Marriage in Early Modern England." *Journal of Family History* 11 (1986): 205–19.

Schofield, John. *Medieval London Houses.* New Haven, Conn.: Yale University Press, 1994.

———. "Social Perceptions of Space in Medieval and Tudor London Houses." In *Meaningful Architecture: Social Interpretations of Buildings,* edited by Martin Locock, 188–206. Aldershot: Avebury, 1994.

———. "Urban Housing in England, 1400–1600." In *The Age of Transition: The Archaeology of English Culture, 1400–1600,* edited by David Gaimster and Paul Stamper, 127–44. Oxford: Oxbow Books, 1997.

Segalen, Martine. *Love and Power in the Peasant Family: Rural France in the Nineteenth Century.* Chicago: University of Chicago Press, 1983.

Shaw, Diane. "The Construction of the Private in Medieval London." *The Journal of Medieval and Early Modern Studies* 26 (1996): 447–67.

Sheehan, Michael M. *Marriage, Family, and Law in Medieval Europe: Collected Studies.* Edited by James K. Farge. Toronto: University of Toronto Press, 1996.

Shepard, Alexandra. "Manhood, Credit and Patriarchy in Early Modern England, c. 1580–1640." *Past & Present* 167 (2000): 75–106.

Smith, Anthony. "Heydon, John (*d.* 1479)." *Oxford Dictionary of National Biography.* Oxford: Oxford University Press, 2004. http://www.oxforddnb.com/view/article/52787, accessed 26 May 2005.

Smith, Richard M. "Geographical Diversity in the Resort to Marriage in Late Medieval Europe: Work, Reputation, and Unmarried Females in the Household Formation Systems of Northern and Southern Europe." In *Woman Is a Worthy Wight: Women in English Society, c. 1200–1500,* edited by P. J. P. Goldberg, 16–59. Gloucester: Alan Sutton, 1992.

———. "Marriage Processes in the English Past: Some Continuities." In *The World We Have Gained: Histories of Population and Social Structure,* edited by Lloyd Bonfield, Richard M. Smith, and Keith Wrightson, 43–99. Oxford: Basil Blackwell, 1986.

Snedegar, Keith. "Caerleon, Lewis (*d.* in or after 1495)." *Oxford Dictionary of National Biography.* Oxford: Oxford University Press, 2004. Available from http://www.oxforddnb.com/view/article/4324, accessed 26 May 2005.

Spain, Daphne. *Gendered Spaces.* Chapel Hill: University of North Carolina Press, 1992.

Spufford, Margaret. "Puritanism and Social Control?" In *Order and Disorder in Early Modern England,* edited by Anthony Fletcher and John Stevenson. Cambridge: Cambridge University Press, 1985.

Stevens, Geoffrey. "Bill Overhauls Criminal Code." *The Globe and Mail,* 22 December 1967, 1.

Strohm, Paul. *Hochon's Arrow: The Social Imagination of Fourteenth-Century Texts.* Princeton, N.J.: Princeton University Press, 1992.

———. *Theory and the Premodern Text.* Minneapolis: University of Minnesota Press, 2000.

Swanson, R. N. *Church and Society in Late Medieval England.* Oxford: Blackwell, 1989.

Talbot, C. H. *Medicine in Medieval England.* London: Oldbourne, 1967.

Talbot, C. H., and E. A. Hammond. *The Medical Practitioners in Medieval England: A Biographical Register.* London: Wellcome Historical Medical Library, 1965.

Tarbin, Stephanie. "Tropes of Behaviour: The Prosecution of Sexual Misconduct in Fifteenth-Century London." Unpublished paper, 1997.

Taylor, J. "The Plumpton Letters, 1416–1552." *Northern History* 10 (1975): 72–87.

Thomas, Keith. "The Double Standard." *Journal of the History of Ideas* 20 (1959): 195–216.

Thomson, J. A. F. "Piety and Charity in Late Medieval London." *Journal of Ecclesiastical History* 16 (1965): 178–95.

Thrupp, Sylvia L. *The Merchant Class of Medieval London, 1300–1500.* Ann Arbor: University of Michigan Press, 1962.

Walford, Cornelius. *Fairs, Past and Present: A Chapter in the History of Commerce.* London: Elliot Stock, 1883. Reprint, New York: Augustus M. Kelley, 1968.

Walker, Garthine. "Rereading Rape and Sexual Violence in Early Modern England." *Gender and History* 10 (1998): 1–25.

Ward, Jennifer C. *English Noblewomen in the Later Middle Ages.* London: Longman, 1992.

Watson, Alan. *Roman Law and Comparative Law.* Athens: University of Georgia Press, 1991.

Wedgwood, Josiah C. *History of Parliament, 1439–1509.* 2 vols. London: HMSO, 1936–38.

Williams, Craig A. *Roman Homosexuality: Ideologies of Masculinity in Classical Antiquity.* New York: Oxford University Press, 1999.

Williams, Gwyn. *Medieval London: From Commune to Capital.* London: Athlone Press, 1963.

Woodcock, Brian L. *Medieval Ecclesiastical Courts of the Diocese of Canterbury.* London: Oxford University Press, 1953.

Wrightson, Keith, and David Levine. *Poverty and Piety in an English Village: Terling, 1525–1700.* New York: Academic Press, 1979.

Wunderli, Richard M. *London Church Courts and Society on the Eve of the Reformation.* Cambridge, Mass.: Medieval Academy of America, 1981.

Index

Acknowledgments

This book has taken a long and circuitous route to reach this final form. The seed from which it grew was first planted by my doctoral supervisor, the late Michael Sheehan, in a class he taught at the University of Toronto in 1987–88 on marriage and the family in the Middle Ages. Although my doctoral dissertation was on another subject altogether, after I finished that project I picked up on what was, for me, the most fascinating part of that seminar: the reading of testimony offered in a fourteenth-century marriage suit. I remain grateful to Fr. Sheehan both for awakening my interest in medieval marriage and for his generous and humane scholarship.

Along the road through the last thirteen years when I have worked, in fits and starts, on this project, I have accumulated many debts from those who have helped me in various ways, sometimes just by chance comments that nonetheless influenced my approach, sometimes in more significant ways. I am deeply grateful to the following for their help and encouragement: Sandy Bardsley, Judith Bennett, Sara Butler, Martha Carlin, Anna Dronzek, Kit French, Jeremy Goldberg, Laura Gowing, Andrew Hall, Barbara Hanawalt, Richard Helmholz, Frank Henderson, Maryanne Kowaleski, Connie Morgenstern, Jacqueline Murray, Derek Neal, Alexandra Guerson de Oliveira, Larry Poos, Sarah Rees Jones, Ron Rudin, David Santiuste, Stephanie Tarbin, Bob Tittler, and Geneviève Vallerand. Students in my classes at Concordia through the years (some of whom are named individually above) have helped me think through historical problems from the perspective of the "real world" and have made me think differently about the audience I write for. The staff in various libraries and archives in Canada and the United Kingdom were also extremely helpful; I would especially like to single out the Interlibrary Loan department of the Webster Library at Concordia, without whose labors I would not have seen many of the printed sources that I have used for this book. Ruth Mazo Karras and Jerry Singerman at the University of Pennsylvania Press have been unfailingly helpful and enthusiastic about the project. Caroline Barron offered advice and encouragement at an early stage of my work on the London materials and then much more recently offered a thorough assessment of the manuscript for the Press; her suggestions have significantly improved the book. An anonymous second reader also made a number of helpful comments.

Without the generous financial assistance of the Social Sciences and Humanities Research Council of Canada and Québec's Fonds pour la formation de chercheurs et l'aide à la recherche, I could not have written this book; those funds allowed me to travel overseas to archives and libraries and to hire several generations of student research assistants. I thank for their invaluable help Nick Kluge, Sandy Ramos, Celeste Chamberland, Dominique McCaughey, Mark Moody, Jason McLinton, Denise Jones, Melanie Fishbane, and Evan May, who helped me compile databases, sat in front of microfilm readers for hours of boring scanning or photocopying, and, in Evan's case, did manuscript research.

Some of the sections of this book are revised versions of articles and book chapters I have published previously, and I am grateful to the editors and publishers who have granted permission to reprint that material. Parts of Chapters 1 and 5 and the Conclusion appeared as "Place, Space, and Situation: Public and Private in the Making of Marriage in Late-Medieval London," in *Speculum: A Journal of Medieval Studies*, 79 (2004). My thanks to *Speculum*'s editors and to the Medieval Academy of America for their permission. Part of Chapter 3 is derived from " 'I Will Never Have None Against My Father's Will: Consent and Making of Marriage in the Late Medieval Diocese of London," which appeared in *Women, Marriage, and Family in Medieval Christendom: Essays in Memory of Michael M. Sheehan, C.S.B.*, edited by Joel T. Rosenthal and Constance M. Rousseau (1998). It is reprinted with the permission of Medieval Institute Publications at the University of Western Michigan in Kalamazoo. Parts of Chapters 6 and 7 appeared as "Men and Masculinity in Late Medieval London Civic Culture: Governance, Patriarchy, and Reputation," in *Conflicting Identities and Multiple Masculinities: Men in the Middle Ages*, edited by Jacqueline Murray (New York: Garland Press, 1999), and appears by Jacqueline Murray's kind permission.

One of the reasons this book has taken me so long to write is that I undertook a number of other projects after I started work on it in 1992. Three of these projects have resulted in other books, now finished and sitting on shelves, but two projects are ongoing. Alice and Anna each, at different points, played happily in their playpen, at least for a few minutes at a time, while I worked on this book through maternity leaves. Alice is now old enough to read these acknowledgments and even write her own books, and Anna is not far behind. They have helped distract me when I needed to be distracted and are a never-ending source of wonderment to me. Their father, Eric Reiter, remains my best reader and best friend and in all kinds of ways I couldn't have done it without him.